Bess W. Truman

D0405009

ALSO BY MARGARET TRUMAN:

The picture of Bess that Harry Truman carried with him as a soldier in World War I. (*Courtesy of the Truman Family*)

Bess W. Truman

MARGARET TRUMAN

MACMILLAN PUBLISHING COMPANY

NEW YORK

Macmillan Publishing Company
866 Third Avenue, New York, N.Y. 10022
Collier Macmillan Canada, Inc.

Library of Congress Cataloging-in-Publication Data
Truman, Margaret, 1924–
Bess. W. Truman.
Includes index.
1. Truman, Bess Wallace.   2. Truman, Harry S.,
1884–1972—Family.   3. Presidents—United States—
Wives—Biography.   4. Presidents—United States—
Biography.   I. Title.
E814.1.T68T68   1986   973.918'092'4   [B]   85-30030

ISBN 0-915992-69-8

Printed in the United States of America
1994 Paperback Edition Printed By
Eastern National Park & Monument Association

10   9   8   7   6   5   4   3

Printed in the United States of America

For Clifton Daniel, my husband
and my sons,
Clifton Truman Daniel
William Wallace Daniel
Harrison Gates Daniel
Thomas Washington Daniel

A WORD TO THE READER

This is the most difficult book I have ever written. It is about a woman I thought I knew better than any other person in my life. But I discovered as I wrote it that it was about a woman who kept her deepest feelings, her most profound sorrows, sealed from my view— from almost everyone's view.

I suspect this is true of most mothers and daughters, perhaps equally true of most fathers and sons. Being a parent, a daughter, a son is a mysterious experience at best. Concealment, secrecy, are not produced by malice. On the contrary, they are invariably acts of love.

If there is one thing I know, it is the intensity of my mother's love for me, of mine for her. That is another reason why this is a difficult book to write. I am trying to step out of that circle of love, that private spotlight in which I have lived all my life, sometimes almost resenting the intensity. It is necessary, in order to help others see my mother. It has been necessary, in order for me to see her.

That is why, in this book, I am calling her by a name I never used once while she was alive: Bess.

That was the name my father used, along with a host of teasing alternatives: "The Boss," "Mrs. T," "Lizzie." Bess is also the name that other people—the amazing number of other people who loved my mother and were loved by her—used. Much of this book will be about those loves. My father will remain at the center, of course, where he always was for sixty-nine years. But there were others who loved Bess Wallace Truman, and were loved by her. They are an important part of this story, which is about a woman who loved in spite of starting with the worst possible odds against this fundamental experience, a woman who might have become a creature with a heart of stone.

ACKNOWLEDGMENTS

This book would never have been completed without the assistance of the staff of the Truman Library, who helped me organize Bess Wallace Truman's voluminous papers. In particular I would like to thank the library's director, Benedict K. Zobrist, archivist Harry Clark and Elizabeth Safly, the research librarian, whose skill at discovering (or confirming) facts both large and small on all aspects of the Trumans is phenomenal. I would also like to thank various friends and relatives who shared with me their memories of Mother, especially Drucie Snyder Horton and her father, former Secretary of the Treasury John Snyder, Reathel Odum, and Mary Shaw Branton. At least as important was my aunt, May Southern Wallace, whose recollections reach back to the early years of the century, Rufus Burrus, whose memories are almost as extensive, and Sue Gentry, who covered the Trumans in Independence for the Independence *Examiner*. Teresa F. Matchette of the National Archives made some very important discoveries on my behalf. Also helpful were Peter Calhoun, son of Mother's old friend Arry Calhoun, Michael S. Churchman, headmaster of the Barstow School, Richard S. Brownlee and Debra Duffen of the State Historical Society of Missouri, and Ron Cockrell, Research Historian of the U.S. Department of the Interior. Finally, I must thank Thomas Fleming, who assisted me in my biography of my father, *Harry S. Truman*. Mr. Fleming's research skills and literary advice have again proven invaluable.

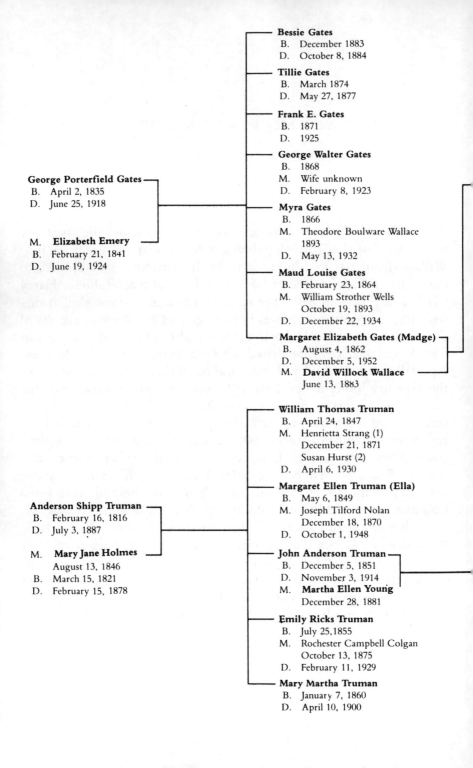

Bessie Gates
B. December 1883
D. October 8, 1884

Tillie Gates
B. March 1874
D. May 27, 1877

Frank E. Gates
B. 1871
D. 1925

George Walter Gates
B. 1868
M. Wife unknown
D. February 8, 1923

George Porterfield Gates
B. April 2, 1835
D. June 25, 1918

M. **Elizabeth Emery**
B. February 21, 1841
D. June 19, 1924

Myra Gates
B. 1866
M. Theodore Boulware Wallace
1893
D. May 13, 1932

Maud Louise Gates
B. February 23, 1864
M. William Strother Wells
October 19, 1893
D. December 22, 1934

Margaret Elizabeth Gates (Madge)
B. August 4, 1862
D. December 5, 1952
M. **David Willock Wallace**
June 13, 1883

William Thomas Truman
B. April 24, 1847
M. Henrietta Strang (1)
December 21, 1871
Susan Hurst (2)
D. April 6, 1930

Margaret Ellen Truman (Ella)
B. May 6, 1849
M. Joseph Tilford Nolan
December 18, 1870
D. October 1, 1948

Anderson Shipp Truman
B. February 16, 1816
D. July 3, 1887

M. **Mary Jane Holmes**
August 13, 1846
B. March 15, 1821
D. February 15, 1878

John Anderson Truman
B. December 5, 1851
D. November 3, 1914
M. **Martha Ellen Young**
December 28, 1881

Emily Ricks Truman
B. July 25, 1855
M. Rochester Campbell Colgan
October 13, 1875
D. February 11, 1929

Mary Martha Truman
B. January 7, 1860
D. April 10, 1900

David Frederick Wallace
B. January 7, 1900
M. Christine M. Meyer
  July 27, 1933
D. September 30, 1957

Infant Daughter
B. May 2, 1898
D. May 4, 1898

George Porterfield Wallace
B. May 1, 1892
M. Mary Frances Southern (May)
  October 24, 1916
D. May 24, 1963

Frank Gates Wallace
B. March 4, 1887
M. Natalie Ott
  April 6, 1915
D. August 12, 1960

Elizabeth Virginia Wallace (Bess)
B. February 13, 1885
M. Harry S. Truman
  June 28, 1919
D. October 20, 1982

Mary Margaret Truman
B. February 17, 1924

M. **Elbert Clifton Daniel**
  April 21, 1956

Harry S. Truman
B. May 8, 1884
M. Elizabeth Virginia Wallace
  June 28, 1919
D. December 26, 1972

John Vivian Truman
B. April 25, 1886
M. Luella Campbell
  October 1911
D. July 8, 1965

Mary Jane Truman
B. August 12, 1889
D. November 8, 1978

Infant Son
Stillborn October 28, 1882

Clifton Truman Daniel
B. June 5, 1957

William Wallace Daniel
B. May 19, 1959

Harrison Gates Daniel
B. March 3, 1963

Thomas Washington Daniel
B. May 28, 1966

Bess W. Truman

Chapter One

Elizabeth Virginia Wallace was born on February 13, 1885 in a comfortable house on Ruby Street in Independence, Missouri. She grew up in a world that seemed, at first glance, as stable, as full of love, as any child could wish. Her father, David Willock Wallace, was a tall, handsome man with a curling blond mustache and golden sideburns. Her mother, Margaret Gates Wallace, whom everyone called Madge, was a dark, petite beauty. She called the baby "Bessie" after her closest friend, New Yorker Bessie Madge Andrews, whom she had met while attending the Cincinnati Conservatory of Music.

In 1885, Independence was a peaceful country town of about 3,500 people. A St. Louis reporter visiting it in the 1870s called it "an orchard city," because the trees were so numerous and leafy it was difficult to see the houses. Almost everyone was on a first-name basis, and a great many families had become intricately connected in the fifty-eight years that had passed since the first settlers arrived. Some wit remarked that if a Woodson married a McCoy, everyone in Independence would be related to everyone else.

When Bess was two years old, her father sold the house on Ruby Street and moved to a larger house at 608 North Delaware Street, one of the most fashionable addresses in Independence. There is not much doubt that Bess's mother had a lot to say about their choice of a new home. She was now living only two blocks away from an imposing two-and-one-half-story mansion that Bess's grandfather, George Porterfield Gates, had built on the corner of North Delaware Street and Blue Avenue (since renamed Van Horne Road) in the year of her birth.

That house became almost a second home for Bess. Her mother's pretty sisters, Maud and Myra, fussed over her, and two younger uncles, Walter and Frank Gates, did their best to spoil her, an avuncular habit that I would rediscover to my delight in my own childhood. A frequent visitor was granduncle Edward P. Gates, a prominent attorney, soon to be a judge. But the central person in the house was tall (six feet four inches), bearded George Porterfield Gates, who bounced her on his knee and talked amusing nonsense to her. She was his first grandchild—a guarantee of special affection from him and his deeply religious wife, Elizabeth. Little Bess gave them special nicknames, "Nana" and "Mama"—names she used when she was learning to talk.

Her younger uncle, Frank Gates, was so fond of Bess, he corresponded regularly with her when he went off to college in 1889. Three of his letters to "my dear little Bessie" have survived the years. He wrote in the third person, cheerfully describing how "Uncle Frank" was the laughingstock of his boardinghouse because his eyes were swollen "about the size of a watermelon," telling her that "Uncle Frank" was going to stay in Chicago for his spring vacation and expected to have a good time "but not as good as he would if he could come home and see you."

It was virtually impossible for anyone not to love little Bess. She had her father's golden hair and the brightest blue eyes the family had ever seen. She was amazingly goodhumored and outgoing, traits she inherited from her father.

The Wallaces were not entirely absent from Bess's life. Her middle name, Virginia, came from her Wallace grandmother. As Bess grew past the toddling stage, Virginia Willock Wallace gave her a stream of beautiful silk dresses. She was a gifted amateur seamstress. There were numerous Wallace cousins living in Independence. The Wallaces were among the first settlers of the town, arriving from Kentucky in 1833. But her father's immediate family were far outnumbered by the Gates tribe. Her Wallace grandfather had died eight years before she was born, and "Dommie," as Bess called Virginia Willock Wallace, lived a considerable distance from North Delaware Street.

In Bess's own home, there were new arrivals that competed for the attention of her grandparents and uncles and aunts. Frank Gates Wallace was born on March 4, 1887 and George Porterfield Wallace arrived on May 1, 1892. The reader will notice the prevalence of the Gates family in the names. By the time her brother George was born, seven-year-old Bess was undoubtedly aware that the Gates side of her family tree was more important than the Wallace side. Dominating the town's skyline was the twelve-story grain elevator of the Waggoner-Gates Milling Company, where Queen of the Pantry flour was manufactured by the millions of pounds for housewives throughout the Midwest. It was undoubtedly pointed out to Bess as "Nana's mill." At Christmas and on her birthdays, except for a silk dress from Dommie, all the best presents came from Nana and Mama. Gradually, the growing Bess perceived that her handsome, genial father did not have much money.

When twenty-one-year-old Madge Gates fell in love with twenty-three-year-old David Wallace, George Gates had taken a very dim view of the match. Like most American fathers, he could not quite bring himself to forbid it. But he made ominous noises and did everything in his power to delay it, until the young couple threatened to elope. George Gates capitulated, and the wedding took place in the First Presbyterian Church on June 13, 1883. It was front-page news in the local paper.

George Gates did not think that David Wallace could support his oldest daughter in the style to which she was accustomed. The young husband had no training or interest in business. He was going to rely for an income on the perilous path of politics. David's father, Benjamin Wallace, had been elected mayor of Independence in 1869. Thereafter, he had represented a Jackson County district in the state legislature. With his political pull, he had David appointed to a clerkship in the state senate when he was fourteen. At the age of eighteen, the year after his father died, David was appointed Deputy Recorder of Marriage Licenses in Independence.

I doubt that David ever did a day's work at either job. The newspapers regularly inveighed against the political bosses for their habit of appointing assistants and deputies whose only task was to get out the vote on election day. But these youthful appointments probably gave David Wallace the illusion that politics was an easy way to make a living. That might have been true if he had remained a bachelor. But few political jobs paid enough to support a wife with Madge Gates's expensive tastes.

In the very first year of their marriage, there was an ominous sign of financial strain. The bridegroom had to mortgage their Ruby Street house to secure a $700 loan. Two years later, David Willock Wallace wrote to President Grover Cleveland, the first Democrat to get into the White House in twenty-five years. Addressing him as "Dear Sir and Friend," he reminded the President that he had supported him at the Democratic Convention and had once met him in Buffalo. Whereupon he asked him for a job in the customs house in

Kansas City. Although David Wallace said the appointment was of "vast importance" to him (another sign of financial strain), Cleveland turned him down in a brief note from his secretary, who claimed the President "declined all requests of this character."

Fortunately, in 1887, David Wallace was able to sell the house on Ruby Street for much more than he had paid for it and move to North Delaware Street. Independence was enjoying a real estate boom. The year of Bess Wallace's birth, 1885, was the last year of Independence's long career as a sleepy little country town.

In the first half of the 1880s, the twelve miles that separated Kansas City and Independence might as well have been twelve-hundred, for most people. The only connecting link was a dirt road full of ruts and impossible grades. In 1885, the big city came closer when the road was smoothed into a boulevard and, in 1887, the march of progress brought it practically next door when the Independence, Kansas City and Park Railway opened for business. Suddenly you could live in Independence and shop or work in Kansas City. Independence became a suburb of Kansas City.

Real estate values soared and over the next ten years the population doubled to about 6,000. To some old established families in Independence, this was disconcerting, even a little threatening. Independence had been a thriving town—"the Queen City of the Trails"—when Kansas City was a gaggle of riverboatmen and outlaws huddled along the Missouri's banks. For almost three decades before the Civil War, Independence had been the point of departure for the wagon trains that trekked west.

After the war the Missouri Pacific and half a dozen other railroads made Kansas City their headquarters. Its population had leaped tenfold, leaving Independence far behind in size, wealth, and political power. But Independence continued to look down its genteel nose at raucous Kansas City, with its loose women, its gambling parlors, its corrupt politics. The metropolis retained a fascination, nevertheless, particularly at its Board of Trade, where men bet fortunes on the future price of wheat.

Independence saw itself as more interested in books, ideas, culture. In the 1890s, the girlhood of Bess Wallace, the town abounded in study clubs, where women reported on the latest novels by their fellow Missourian, Mark Twain, or the notions of that wild man from Minnesota, Ignatius Donnelly, who violently attacked the American tendency to worship money.

For women, life in Independence revolved around culture, the family, and the church. By and large, the churches reflected the social scale. The so-called best people were Presbyterians. Next in quality were the Campbellites, now known as the Christian Church, who boasted one of the most famous preachers in the country at the time, Alexander Proctor. Farther down the scale were the Baptists, the Mormons and the Catholics. The Episcopalians were so few in number they were scarcely noticed.

Outside Independence was the country—a very different place. There, mostly Baptist farmers tilled some of the richest soil in America. Many of them were far wealthier than the genteel citizens of Independence, but they were regarded as largely uneducated, uncultured bumpkins. To be from town was a mark of distinction, from the country an invitation to mild disdain.

The people at the top of Independence's social scale built houses that no farmer ever dreamt of inhabiting. In 1881, Colonel E. T. Vaile, who had made a fortune operating western mail routes for the federal government, put up a stupendous red-brick Second Empire mansion, with a four-story tower and miles of gingerbread. Still standing on North Liberty Street, the Vaile mansion is the equal of any pile thrown up by the money barons of Chicago or San Francisco. The Swopes, who made their fortune in Kansas City real estate, built an equally imposing house with a full ballroom on the third floor. As other wealthy newcomers from Kansas City imitated these examples, Independence became known as "the Royal Suburb."

Social life in Independence tended to be as elegant, if not as opulent, as it was in Chicago and other large cities where wealth had accumulated. No one tried to equal Mrs. Vanderbilt's 1883 ball in her New York mansion, where women showed up wearing skirts quilted with diamonds. But dancing schools did a brisk business, and the newspapers constantly reported balls and receptions and dinners. Independence ladies kept dressmakers busy turning out the latest styles, which in 1885 featured a return to the bustle in its final, most outrageous form. For everything from fine furniture to furs, there was Bullene's in Kansas City, the biggest department store west of Chicago.

Independence men tended to be more interested in politics, national, state, and local. That was another reason to look askance at Kansas City. They tended to vote Republican in that vulgar city, while old Independence, the city that David Willock Wallace knew as a boy, was unswervingly, wholeheartedly, passionately Democratic. As Democratic as Virginia and South Carolina and Mississippi. On some streets in Independence—North Delaware was one of them—a visitor without a map would find it hard to tell that he was not in the Deep South.

The Civil War was still a bitter memory in old Independence. One of the most savage battles for control of Missouri, a border state that never seceded, was fought in and around the town. To snuff out the guerrilla war that raged after the rebels lost that battle, the Union general issued the infamous Order No. 11, which required everyone to abandon farms and crops in a three-county tier, thirty miles deep and a hundred miles long, on the Kansas border. Everything within that zone was forthwith burned, leaving 20,000 people homeless and destitute. It broke the back of rebel resistance in Missouri, but it left a legacy of political bitterness that old Independence never forgot.

It also spawned a legacy of lawlessness in the Jackson County countryside. Former Confederate guerrillas such as Jesse and Frank James and the Younger brothers could not adjust to peace. As late as 1879, only six years before Bess Wallace was born, they were still robbing Yankee banks and trains, to the embarrassment of many people in Independence who were related to them.

In new Independence, the royal suburb, with its steady influx of newcomers from Kansas City, this heritage of violence and hatred became more and more irrelevant. So did the wing of the Democratic Party to which David Willock Wallace belonged. The passions of the Civil War, the endless waving of "the bloody shirt" by the Republicans, the invoking of Order No. 11 by the Democrats, were fading fast.

David Wallace ran for Jackson County treasurer in 1888 and 1890, winning both times. But when his second term expired in 1892, the feuding, factionalized Democrats of Jackson County did not offer him another office. For almost a full year he was unemployed. Late in 1893, after Grover Cleveland became president for a second time—the only man the Democrats were able to get into the White House between 1856 and 1912—David Wallace finally wangled an appointment as Deputy United States Surveyor of Customs for the port of Kansas City, and abandoned elective politics.

This sounds like an important job. But the full title was "Deputy Surveyor and Clerk." The salary was $1,200 a year. That was pretty good pay in 1894, when the average worker was lucky to get a dollar a day. But it was not the sort of salary a man needed to support three children and a wife with expensive tastes.

Meanwhile, Elizabeth Virginia Wallace was growing up. Surviving letters from her mother indicate that by the time she reached high school, Bess was already assuming a surprising amount of responsibility for the care of her two younger brothers. For a while there was a fourth child in the house, a little sister named Madeline, born in the mid-1890s. She died when she was about three years old. Giving birth to four children in ten years—and losing one—strained Madge Wallace's health and nerves. She had always been considered "delicate" a word that suggested both physical and emotional fragility in this era. Madge took vacations at nearby Platte City, where her sister Maud had married a wealthy banker, William Strother Wells, and left her fourteen-year-old daughter in charge of the house.

One letter, somewhat incongruously addressed to "my dear little daughter," told Bess not to let her brother Frank out of the house after dark because he had a cold and to make sure Frank took citrate of magnesia every night and did not forget his Listerine. She was also told to "order what you need and want at the grocery and meat shop."

If this responsibility troubled Bess Wallace, there is no evidence of it in the serene gaze she gave the world in her youthful photographs. She looks as contented and self-confident as it was possible for a young woman to be, so far as I can see. And why not? The years of her girlhood were a good time to be a woman in America.

The current spokespersons for the women's movement tend to make us think that women were timid, trapped houseslaves until Betty Friedan wrote *The Feminine Mystique*. Actually, the movement toward a more independent woman began in 1848, and by 1890 there was a distinct whiff of liberation in the air. The bustle had finally been banished and women were asking and getting the right to play sports and join clubs and launch careers and speak their minds on an astonishing number of things from temperance to the vote. In 1901, the year sixteen-year-old Bess Wallace graduated from high school, a woman lawyer, Carey May Carroll, was named attorney to the Jackson County collector.

For Bess, participation in sports was her first stride toward self-confidence. By the time she was in high school, she was the best tennis player in Independence. She was also a demon ice skater and expert rider. In her younger days, she played third base on her brothers' sandlot baseball team and was their champion slugger. There is a story in the family of Bess happening by when the boys were losing to a team from a nearby neighborhood by three runs in the last of the ninth. Bess was on her way home from a tennis match. Her brother Frank begged her to get into the game as a pinch hitter. She agreed and they promptly put three men on base. Frank sent Bess up to bat, and she belted a home run over the centerfielder's head, winning the game.

Next door to Bess Wallace at 614 North Delaware Street lived her closest friend, Mary Paxton. She was the daughter of a successful attorney and, like Bess Wallace had a number of obstreperous brothers, who frequently got into fights with the Wallace boys. Both older sisters never hesitated to wade into these brawls, grabbing male arms and legs, swatting ears and backsides. Bess, taller and a year older than Mary, was the acknowledged peacemaker, although I gather it was the kind of peace imposed by gunslinging lawmen such as Bat Masterson and Wyatt Earp. The rascals were told to behave, or else. "They were all afraid of her," recalled Henry Chiles, a high school classmate who was probably one of the miscreants.

Bess also kept the peace and issued commands with her whistle. It was a piercing sound that carried for blocks. Moreover, she did it without putting her fingers near her mouth. "She was the only girl in Independence who could whistle through her teeth," Henry Chiles recalled. The whistle summoned wandering brothers and struck terror into their malicious male hearts when they were about to do something forbidden, such as smoke some of their father's cigarettes in the woodshed. For her girlfriends, Bess had a more pleasing, melodious whistle. On summer evenings they waited eagerly for it to sound from the Wallace back porch. It was a signal to come over for ice cream.

The Paxtons and the Wallaces had a good time together. On summer nights it was so good some of the neighbors—in particular Colonel William Southern, editor of the local paper—complained of not being able to get any sleep. In retaliation they called Southern "Sneaky Bill." A lot of the noise was probably generated by Frank Wallace and his big black dog. Visitors to Delaware Street would ask him what he called the mongrel, and Frank would say, deadpan, "U-Know."

The disconcerted visitor would say: "I don't know. I just asked you."

"U-Know," Frank would say.

And so on, while the visitor got madder and madder and everyone else collapsed with laughter.

U-Know became such an object of affection he thought he could get away with anything. Matthew Paxton, one of Mary's brothers, had stolen a handful of sugar lumps from his mother's kitchen and was enjoying them one day. U-Know watched, licking his chops. George Wallace jarred Matthew's elbow and the sugar flew up in the air and down U-Know's gullet. Matthew was so furious he bit U-Know! "Matthew spit black hair for a week," Mary Paxton recalled. No one seems to remember whether he inflicted any serious damage on U-Know.

While she hung around with these rowdy males, Bess was not allowed to forget that she was Madge Gates Wallace's daughter. She was expected to be a lady, most of the time. This idea of the lady who concerned herself only with the genteel aspects of life, with art and culture and spiritual values, was still very much alive in the 1880s and 1890s. Madge Gates Wallace was a lady from the top of her well-coifed head to the tips of her elegant fingers. Although she tolerated her daughter's athletic prowess, Madge insisted that Bess acquire the social graces.

In high school, Bess went to Miss Dunlap's dancing class on Jackson Square in the center of Independence. Scarcely a Saturday night went by without a hop at that particular ballroom. There were other dances and receptions at the Swope mansion, where Bess was welcomed by Margaret Swope, the daughter closest to her in age. Often Margaret asked Bess to join her in the receiving line, a sign of their close friendship as well as Bess's social status.

"We all learned the polka and the schottische and the Virginia reel," her friend Mary Paxton recalled. "But we mostly danced the waltz and two-step. We had much the same kind of party dresses, mull with silk sashes, colored or striped. But Bess always looked more stylish than anyone else in the crowd." In the summer they sometimes strung Japanese lanterns on the lawn and had outdoor parties. For refreshments in summer, there was ice cream and cake and mints; in the winter, chicken salad with beaten biscuits and fancy charlotte russe.

On summer nights after a dance, the party often piled into one or two old surreys for a ride through the moonlit town and countryside. They would sing songs and no doubt do a little surreptitious "spoon-

ing," although this adolescent sport—more or less synonymous with
the twentieth century's "necking"—was frowned upon if the girl
seemed too willing or too careless. One girl who spooned on a back
porch with a comparative stranger from Kansas City was never invited to another party.

By now you may be wondering about my omission of a name that
eventually became important in Bess Wallace's life—Harry S.
Truman. He was not a native of Independence. He was born on May
8, 1884 in Lamar, a tiny farm town some 120 miles to the south,
where his father, John Anderson Truman, was in business as a horse
and cattle trader. About nine months later, the Trumans moved to a
farm near Harrisonville, in Cass County, some thirty miles from
Independence, but part of Jackson County. There John Truman
helped his wife's family, the Youngs, run their 600-acre farm. In 1890,
when Harry was six years old, his mother, Martha Ellen Young
Truman, persuaded her husband to move to Independence, because
she wanted her children (a second son, Vivian, and a daughter, Mary,
had followed Harry) to get a better education than the rural schools
could give them.

Not long after they came to town, Martha Ellen Truman met the
local Presbyterian minister on the street. He invited her to send her
children to his Sunday school. Although she was a Baptist by birth,
she accepted the invitation. Thus, six-year-old Harry Truman
walked into the classroom of the First Presbyterian Church and saw
"a little blue-eyed golden-haired girl" named Bess Wallace. To the
end of his life, he insisted that he fell in love with five-year-old Bess
on the spot and never stopped loving her throughout his boyhood
years. "She sat behind me in the sixth, seventh and high school
grades," Harry Truman later recalled, "and I thought she was the
most beautiful and the sweetest person on earth."

Occasionally, Bess would allow Harry Truman to carry her books
home from school. He would be dazed with happiness for the rest of
the day. More moments of near ecstasy occurred when Bess joined
Harry and several other classmates at the home of his first cousin,
Ethel Noland, to be tutored in the intricacies of Latin verbs by her
older sister, Nellie. Both Nolands soon noted Harry's adoration of
Bess, and he did not try to conceal it from them.

One day he appeared at their house with a broad smile on his face
and announced that he wanted to play his first musical composition
for them. The Nolands seated themselves in their parlor, expecting

something very solemn and high-toned. Cousin Harry had been taking piano lessons for years and was playing Bach, Beethoven, Liszt, and other European masters. He reeled off a swarm of arpeggios and then played a series of lilting notes that they instantly recognized. "It's Bessie's ice cream whistle!" Ethel exclaimed.

Unfortunately, Bess Wallace did not have the slightest interest in Harry Truman, nor the least idea that he was in love with her. He was never part of the Delaware Street crowd. Never was he invited to a ball at the Swope mansion. Nor did he participate in those moonlit hayrides. The Trumans were far beneath the social world inhabited by the Wallaces and the Gates, the Waggoners and the Swopes. They were country folk and newcomers in the bargain. John Anderson Truman's profession, horse trading, was considered less than genteel by most people and his income was erratic. During high school, Harry had to work at odd jobs to improve the family's finances.

One story, told by Mary Paxton, sums up the gap between Harry Truman and Bess Wallace better than paragraphs of explanation. On one of those moonlit spooning expeditions, the Delaware Street crowd was riding around Jackson Square, singing merrily. As they paused for breath between songs, someone said: "Oh look, there's Harry Truman."

Harry was in the process of sweeping out Clinton's Drug Store, his last chore for the day. "What a shame he has to work so much," Bess Wallace said. The words were utterly casual, an observation with very little emotional content.

There was another reason, probably as important as social standing, why Bess Wallace found Harry Truman less than interesting. His bad eyes made him a hopeless athlete. His crueler schoolmates called him "Four Eyes" and also ridiculed him for taking piano lessons. A young man needed more than average athletic ability to win Bess Wallace's attention in those days. Bill Bostian, the postmaster's son, adored her and took up tennis to promote his standing. Alas, when they played doubles, he had a habit of yelling "I'll get it Bessie," and then not getting it. Bill's status plummeted.

Throughout these grammar and high school years, another man was the central figure in Bess's happiness: her father. She adored him as only an only daughter can. (How well I know that!) In her grade-school days, David Willock Wallace was always romping with her and the other children in the neighborhood. Every Fourth of July, he personally set up and fired off a magnificent display of fireworks for

Delaware Street. At patriotic parades on the Fourth and other days, he frequently was asked to be grand marshal, and he would lead the strutting show on a great black horse. It is not hard to imagine what effect this must have had on a girl whose imagination had been fed on southern ideals of masculine chivalry. David Wallace was Bess's Bayard, the knight without stain or reproach. As she grew older, her awareness of his comparative poverty added a heartwrenching pity to her love.

Behind his facade of good cheer, David Wallace was an unhappy man. A fifth child, David Frederick, born in 1900, added to his financial problems. He made a stab at starting an importing business in Kansas City, a natural connection to his customs job, but it went nowhere and probably left him even deeper in debt. Like most local politicians, he spent a great deal of time in the Independence courthouse. The hours of his customs job were not very demanding. Next door to the courthouse was a political saloon, where he spent even more time. As his debts increased, so did his drinking.

For Bess and her two older brothers, Frank and George, this must have been the beginning of a troubled time. They knew about their father's drinking and so did the neighbors—often he was carried home by friends and deposited on the front porch. Complicating the problem was Madge Gates Wallace's refusal to recognize it. She never reproached or lectured her husband for one of these lapses. That would have been ungenteel. She was polite and even sympathetic as he struggled through the following day's hangover and remorse. She acted as if Father had twisted his ankle or caught a bad cold.

Another shadow that descended on Bess around this time was the illness of Mary Paxton's mother, a brilliant woman who had been a college teacher and was the leader of one of the most intellectual study clubs in Independence. The doctors diagnosed tuberculosis. A three-year stay in Colorado's mountain air during Mary's grammar school years had done little but make the family miserable over the perpetual separation. Mary Gentry Paxton returned home, and the family and the neighbors could only watch helplessly as she slipped slowly away from them.

The illness of a mother, the failures of a father saddened but did not disrupt young lives. As far as anyone could see, Bess and Mary continued to enjoy themselves. They eluded the troubled adult world (and troublesome younger brothers) at deliciously clandestine meetings of the Cadiz Club. This all-female organization met in a barn behind Grandfather Gates's house. Soon they were staging plays there, written by Mary and performed under her direction. Bess was the manager. She collected admissions and saw that the profits went to charity.

In high school, Bess was an excellent student. She saved many of the essays she wrote in her senior year on writers such as James Russell Lowell. Her marks were never less than 90 and there were several 100s. But she was not a scholar. She left that title to Charlie Ross, a handsome young man who had a flair for writing, and Laura Kingsbury, the class's second-ranking student. Charlie was the editor of their class yearbook, *The Gleam*. His chief assistant was Harry Truman. The title, drawn from Tennyson's poem, "Merlin and the Gleam," blended idealism and ambition for these young men. They were looking forward to participating as leaders—achievers—in the America beyond the boundaries of Independence and even of Kansas City.

For Bess Wallace, the gleam did not carry such dramatic overtones. She listened to Mary Paxton's plans for college and a career with wistful longing. (Because of childhood illnesses and time lost with her mother in Colorado, Mary was three years behind Bess in school.) The presence of a new baby in the household made Madge Wallace even more dependent on her daughter. Still, there were several servants on the payroll. As someone who knew her well put it, "Mrs. Wallace never spent much time in the kitchen."

Her mother's health and bad nerves, exacerbated by her husband's drinking, were not the real reasons why Bess did not go away to college, as her mother had gone to the Cincinnati Conservatory and her friend Mary Paxton was eventually to depart for Hollins in Virginia, and their mutual friend, Charlie Ross, was to go to the University of Missouri at Columbia. The real explanation was the sad fact that Bess's father could not afford to send her.

This failure was the first public acknowledgment of David Wallace's financial straits. His money troubles were already well known within the family. In a box in the basement of 219 North Delaware Street I found a series of faded letters from him to George Porterfield Gates, thanking his father-in-law again and again for "your many kindnesses to me and my family." In the American world of the early 1900s—and in the 1980s—an inability to support one's wife and children was a failing that was extremely humiliating to most men. For David Wallace, it would have been even more painful, since he was being forced to ask for help from a man who had doubted his ability to support his daughter from the first.

By sad coincidence, Harry Truman's family was also painfully short of money. In 1901, John Truman lost his life savings and a small farm his wife had inherited speculating on grain futures at the Kansas City Board of Trade. Even their home on West Waldo Street, a few blocks from Delaware Street, had to be sold, and the family moved to modest quarters in Kansas City. Harry abandoned all thoughts of a college education and went to work as a timekeeper for a section gang on the Santa Fe Railroad.

The Trumans at least coped with their financial straits. This seemed beyond David Wallace's ability. Worse, as his debts piled up, his political future grew dismal. For Democrats in Missouri and elsewhere, the opening years of the new century were not promising ones. A new, enormously popular Republican president, Theodore Roosevelt, had replaced Ohioan William McKinley, who had been assassinated by an anarchist in 1901. A war hero as well as a bold, progressive politician, Teddy was certain to be reelected in 1904, which meant there was little hope of advancement for Democratic appointees. David Wallace's customs job had been placed under civil service protection during the Cleveland administration, but this was not much consolation to a man who desperately needed to make more money. Instead, he only spiraled deeper into alcoholism and debt.

Thanks to some dedicated researchers at the National Archives, I have obtained another painful glimpse of David Wallace's financial problems from letters that flowed between Kansas City and Washington, D.C.

In 1889, his sympathetic boss, Surveyor William L. Kessinger, wrote to the Secretary of the Treasury asking for "additional compensation" for David Wallace and another deputy surveyor for extra work performed by them. The request was stonily denied by the Republican Secretary.

In 1901, the Surveyor asked the Treasury Department to increase David Wallace's salary to $1,500 a year. The Treasury agreed to $1,400. The extra money did not do much good, because in the following year David Wallace was dunned by the Credit Clearing House for an unpaid debt of $3.50. The debt collection agency sent the complaint to Washington, D.C. and a brisk letter from an assistant secretary of the treasury ordered the Surveyor to look into the matter. More letters followed, in which the clearing house claimed "we have seen Mr. Wallace at least half a dozen times and on each occasion he has promised to settle the matter but when called upon for the money is ready with another excuse and now we do not believe he has any intention of carrying out his promises."

In 1902, $3.50 was the equivalent of about $75 in today's inflated currency. To be unable to pay this size debt, and go through the humiliation of being reported to his employers, must have been an excruciating experience for Madge Gates Wallace's husband. But all he could do was beg the reluctant government for more money. This time his boss decided to get some backing, and he persuaded two inspectors from the New Orleans District headquarters to issue a report stating that David Wallace "was the most efficient man in the office at this port [Kansas City], yet his salary, $1,400 per annum, is the smallest paid any clerk here." This endorsement persuaded the parsimonious Republicans in Washington to approve a $200 a year raise.

During these same years, David Wallace was borrowing money from his father-in-law to pay his taxes. In 1901, he was two years in arrears and was in a panic that his house was going to be advertised and sold by the county collector. That same year George Porterfield Gates paid for some badly needed shingling and painting, which cost several hundred dollars. When Grandfather Gates gave eleven-year-old George Wallace $5 for a Christmas present, his mother used it to help pay for an overcoat, which he "needed badly."

His double life as cheerful hail-fellow politician and debt-haunted failure became more and more unbearable to David Wallace. At home he received little consolation or support from his wife. Madge Gates Wallace had been raised as a lady, shielded from the harsh economic realities of American life. Like most women of her era, she believed there was a "woman's sphere" and a "man's sphere," and what happened in the man's sphere was none of a wife's business, especially if she was a lady. Her two sisters had married successful men. She could not understand—and probably could not love—a man who was a failure.

Complicating matters during these years was the illness of Madge Gates Wallace's brother Frank. He contracted tuberculosis and his parents took him to Colorado, to Texas, and finally to Mexico in a desperate attempt to cure him. Madge missed her mother and father acutely and became "homesick," David Wallace told George Gates, every time she got a letter from them. In several letters David Wallace remarked how "lonesome" 219 North Delaware looked, standing dark and empty.

David Wallace struck an even gloomier note when he discussed his finances. "To be frank with you, I get pretty *blue* [his italics] over matters. I do the very best that I can but it seems that little good results." In another letter he wrote: "I try to look on the bright side of things, but even then it is dark."

In the summer of 1902, Madge Wallace and her four children vacationed in Colorado Springs at the home of a Gates relative, possibly her uncle Walter Gates, leaving her husband alone in Independence. Mary Paxton, already a shrewd observer of people, wrote Bess a letter full of cheerful gossip about who was falling in and out of love with whom. Then she told how one night "I sat over in your yard with your father so he didn't have time to be lonely." There is more than a hint in those words that Bess had confided to Mary her fear that her father would gravitate to the courthouse saloon.

When his family returned from their vacation in Colorado, David Wallace seems to have made an attempt to control his drinking. He avoided his cronies at the courthouse saloon and even eschewed local meetings of the Masons, where he, like most Missouri politicians, had long been a popular figure. He divided his time between home and office. When Mary Paxton's mother died of tuberculosis on May 15, 1903, David was on hand to help his neighbors with the funeral arrangements. Mary long remembered his kindness and sympathy; she even recalled the way he had come over to the house on the morning of the funeral to set up chairs in their parlor for the mourners. But his good intentions, his innate good nature, did not prevent Bess Wallace's father from sinking deeper and deeper into debt—and depression.

Mary Gentry Paxton had, among her many gifts, a talent for poetry. On May 22, 1903, a week after her death, the Jackson *Examiner* prefaced her obituary with one of her poems.

> This morning I heard that one I loved is dead.
> The house is still, her friends in whispers speak
> Move here and there, sad faced, with tear stained cheek.
> I sat beside her watching there a space
> And thought, Is't death, this change from strife to rest?
> Would not her nearest friend say it is best
> Beholding her and so be comforted?

Is dying to cease struggling to be free
From pain and dread, from weakness, longings vain?
To feel himself restored, once more to be
Whole, rested, strong, without a sense of pain?
Then hasten Death, come thou to visit me,
Give me rest and immortality.

That was a lovely poem for a woman dying of tuberculosis to write. But some of those thoughts may have had sinister implications for David Wallace. He too had struggled with pain and dread and weakness and longings vain. He too yearned to be restored, whole, rested, strong.

On June 17, 1903, four days after his twentieth wedding anniversary, David Wallace went to bed early. But he did not sleep well. He awoke in the dawn, not uncommon for people suffering from depression. He lay there listening to the first twittering birds in the elms around his house. His wife slept soundly beside him. David Wallace got up and tiptoed to a writing desk in the bedroom. Slowly, carefully, he opened a drawer. In the semidarkness, his eyes found the blue-black gleam of a revolver.

It was not unusual for a man to have a gun in his house in those days. Missouri was a western state. Police forces were small and burglaries surprisingly frequent, even on fashionable Delaware Street. David Wallace picked up the revolver and walked softly, steadily down the hall to a bathroom in the rear of the house. Perhaps he paused there to stare at himself in the shadowy mirror, to tell himself one last time that it was all a bad dream, that somehow, somewhere, he could find a way to make his wife happy, his children proud of him. Then he placed the muzzle behind his left ear and pulled the trigger.

The gun crashed in the dawn. The harsh sound reverberated through the house. In her bedroom, eighteen-year-old Bess Wallace sat up, trembling. She heard her brother Frank running down the hall to the bathroom. There was a cry of anguish. "Papa! Papa's shot himself!"

Chapter Two

Next door, Mary Paxton was awakened by her father. "Mr. Wallace just shot himself," he said. "Go see what you can do for Bessie."

Mary flung on her clothes and rushed into the dawn. She found Bess walking back and forth behind the house, her head down, her hands clenched. Police, a doctor, other neighbors pounded up and down the stairs inside the house. For a half hour, there was a faint hope that David Wallace might live. Then Madge Gates Wallace began screaming and sobbing. The two young women, already best friends, and now united by a searing bond of sorrow, walked back and forth together, saying nothing. What was there to say?

Those first hours were only the beginning of the Wallaces' agony. Two days later, the Jackson *Examiner* published a graphic account of the suicide on the front page. It contained a moving tribute to the "sweetness" of David Wallace's nature, his "natural and spontaneous" attractiveness. It also included such grisly lines as: "The ball passed through his head and out at the right temple and fell into the bath tub." The story ended on an emotional note that could only have been heartwrenching for the family to read: "Why should such a man take his own life? It is a question we who loved him are unable to answer and one which has been asked many times from hearts torn in rebellion against the things that are."

Meanwhile, David Wallace's fellow Masons had taken charge of the funeral. He recently had been elected the presiding officer of the Knights Templars in the state of Missouri. They attempted to console the family by giving the dead man what some people have called the most elaborate funeral ever held in Independence. Hundreds of plumed and beribboned knights escorted the body from the First Presbyterian Church to the Wallace plot in Woodlawn Cemetery. A fellow Knight Templar from Kansas City gave a sonorous oration at the grave. He too paid tribute to David Wallace's gift for friendship and closed with the claim that his "genial smile and warm heart" would "shine with greater glory and refulgence in the beautiful but unexplored beyond."

No one among these well-intentioned people seemed to have realized that they were only worsening the family's agony with all this public attention. Even today, most families will try to persuade a newspaper not to publish that a loved one has committed suicide. In 1903, it was considered a far worse stigma. For Madge Gates Wallace it was mortifying beyond belief. It flung her from the top of Independence's social hierarchy to the bottom. She could not bear the disgrace. "She just went to pieces," was the way one member of the family described it, years later.

Complicating her collapse was the discovery that David Wallace was heavily in debt and had left no will. The ever sympathetic surveyor of the port of Kansas City, William Kessinger, wrote to Washington suggesting that his deputy's salary for the month of June be paid in full. The Republican scrooges at the Treasury informed him that there was "no authority of law" to pay a nickel beyond the day of David Wallace's death.

It is chilling to think about what might have happened to Bess and her three younger brothers if her grandparents were not alive and willing and able to rescue them. George Gates and his wife rushed back to Independence by the fastest available trains to comfort their shattered daughter and her children. Nana's tall, bearded presence not only guaranteed economic security; he was a crucial, steadying influence. His gentle wife Elizabeth played an equally vital role in offering their shattered daughter and grandchildren a loving refuge. Elizabeth Gates knew from firsthand experience the blows that fate could deliver. When she was a child of eight in England, her entire family had died of some epidemic disease and she had been sent to America to live with her sister.

The four young Wallaces and their mother were welcomed into the big house on North Delaware Street. But Madge Wallace's grief and shame could not be assuaged by this retreat. Her parents decided it might be better if they all retreated from Independence for a while. They had left their ailing son, Frank, in Colorado Springs, probably with the same Gates relative whom Madge and the children had visited during the previous summer. Telegraphs whizzed to this sympathetic man. In twenty-four hours the grief-stricken refugees were aboard the Missouri Pacific's crack flyer, The Santa Fe, which deposited them in Colorado Springs the following day.

They stayed a full year. A year that is a blank in young Bess

Wallace's life—a year from which not a single letter survives. But it is not an unimportant year. In those twelve months in Colorado Spring's clear air, with Pike's Peak and the other majestic crags of the Rockies towering above her, Bess struggled to understand her father's suicide. A terrible wound had been inflicted on her spirit. Never again could she regard the world with the serene self-confidence, the blithe optimism, of her girlhood. In sleepless nights and on lonely walks she had to cope with agonizing questions of guilt and responsibility.

When a woman loves someone as intensely as Bess had loved her father, and he turns his back on her and that love in such an absolute, devastating way, inevitably she questions her very ability to love. As an intelligent, observant young woman, she also had to question the nature of her mother's love. Something fundamental had failed. She could not bring herself to place all the blame on her father, on ideas such as moral weakness. He had been a loving man, a generous one. Why had his wife's love failed to sustain him? Was it the cruelty, the callousness of American politics that had destroyed him?

No one, above all not an eighteen-year-old girl, could answer these tormenting questions. They settled into Bess Wallace's mind and soul as doubts, voices that whispered to her in the night. But in this year in Colorado Bess was able to reach certain conclusions. She saw that her mother's way of loving her father, the passive, tender but more or less mindless love of the genteel lady, was a mistake. It failed to share the bruises, the fears, the defeats a man experienced in his world. It left him exposed to spiritual loneliness. If she ever found a man she could trust—and that must have seemed a dubious proposition during that first sorrowful year—Bess Wallace vowed she would share his whole life, no matter how much pain it cost her. She rejected absolutely and totally the idea of a woman's sphere and a man's sphere.

Bess did not blame her mother for her father's death. She loved Madge Wallace too. To love was added the pity she undoubtedly felt when she saw how shattered her mother was by the catastrophe. Blame was not a word Bess could ever use. But a kind of judgment, an emotional separation took place between mother and daughter during that year in Colorado, or soon after their return to Independence in 1904.

Bess saw that she had to become a very different woman from her mother. Her success as an athlete and her role as an older sister probably prepared her for this change. But the primary force was sheer necessity. Someone had to take charge of their family and Madge Wallace was incapable of it. At nineteen, Bess became the parent of her three brothers—and the semi-parent of her mother. Even then, it was obvious that Madge Wallace would never resume a normal life.

I am speaking here of leadership, of a person as a spiritual and psychological force in others' lives. Grandfather Gates's money paid for servants and food and clothing. Although he was sixty-nine and his wife was sixty-three, they should not be underestimated as forces in their own right. But they had four other children, all of whom had produced grandchildren. Their feelings for the Wallaces, however poignant, were inevitably diluted by these other descendants.

The Wallaces were acutely aware of these other relatives. Although there was very little overt hostility, there must have been some rumblings of discontent about the possibility that the Wallaces would devour all Grandfather Gates's money and leave nothing for the rest of the heirs. At any rate, soon after the return to Independence, Frank Wallace decided to quit high school and get a job because he did not want to take any more help from his grandfather. Only someone who knows the importance Bess Wallace attached to a college education can appreciate the pain this decision must have caused her.

In 1905, twenty-year-old Bess enrolled in the Barstow School in Kansas City. Founded by Wellesley graduate Mary Barstow in 1884, the school's chief purpose was the preparation of young women for admission to the leading eastern colleges, Vassar, Smith, Radcliffe, whose requirements were printed in the back of the Barstow catalog. Well-to-do people in Independence and Kansas City also sent their daughters to Barstow for the academic course, which offered a "broad and thorough" education to those who did not plan to attend college. Barstow was a finishing school, but a very tough one. Mary Barstow believed that "to educate women was to educate a nation."

A glimpse at Barstow's approach to things emerges from an account of their first basketball game with Kansas City's Manual Training High School. As the Manual team came out on the floor, its supporters shouted: "I yell, you yell, all yell, Manual!" To which Barstow replied: "Ho oi, yo ho! Ho oi, yo ho! Barstow!" an adaptation of the warrior maidens' cry in Wagner's *Die Walküre*. Adding injury to this elitist insult, Barstow won, 12–10.

Bess enjoyed her year at Barstow. As usual, her marks were excellent, an A in Rhetoric, an A+ in Literature, an A in French. She made new friends, in particular Agnes and Laura Salisbury, whose father owned a 600-acre stock farm outside Independence. She came in touch with the larger world of Kansas City. She used her athletic ability to become the star forward on the basketball team and in a spring track meet she won the shot put.

For Bess, one of the high points of the year was the challenge match with the Independence High School team. Barstow was used to playing basketball outdoors, and the game was their first under a roof. The girls had to become used to the "inconveniences of the ceiling," which suggests it was a rather low one. But they were soon playing, according to the reporter in the *Weathercock*, the Barstow paper, as though they always had practiced under a roof. Amid Valkyrian cheers, Bess and her fellow Barstow warrior maidens trounced poor Independence, 22–10.

During this same year, Bess resumed her social life in Independence. Her name appeared as a guest at various receptions, in particular at the Swope mansion. But there was no mention of Madge Gates Wallace's name in the social notices. That year was the beginning of a lifelong retreat from the world around her. Other Independence women busied themselves in charitable activities, such as The Needlework Guild, which made clothes for the poor, pursued culture in study clubs, and enjoyed themselves at weekly bridge club meetings. Sadly, Madge Wallace remained behind the substantial walls of her parents' house, a virtual recluse.

It is not hard to imagine the pain this caused her children, especially her daughter. At the end of her year at Barstow, Bess did not go east to college like many of her classmates. She went home and resumed her role as head of the Wallace family and her mother's companion. But she did not become a recluse. With that interesting blend of pity and objective judgment that colored her relationship with her mother, Bess continued to enjoy the world around her.

She helped organize a bridge club among friends from high school as well as from Barstow. She became active in The Needlework Guild, which in spite of its Dickensian name, was a very effective charity. She continued to enjoy sports, particularly tennis and horseback riding. Her Barstow friends, Agnes and Laura Salisbury, usually had enough horses on their farm to mount a cavalry troop, which was what the Delaware Street crowd looked like, sometimes, trotting down the narrow dirt roads in the spring and summer, throwing up clouds of dust.

Young men from Independence and from Kansas City began to call on twenty-one-year-old Bess Wallace. One of these callers was Chrisman Swope, the second son of that wealthy clan. It must have been more than a little exciting to be wooed by one of the richest young men in town. He was often at the door of 219 North Delaware Street to take Bess for rides in his buggy. But Chrisman's money seems to have been his only recommendation. He was, like other members of his family, a little odd. One evening as Bess climbed into the buggy, she heard a strange quacking sound. "I hope you won't mind a stop at the market, Bessie," Chrisman said. "I want to sell a few of my ducks."

Raising fowl was a hobby that many people practiced in Independence. But Bess took an exceedingly dim view of sharing Chrisman's buggy with a dozen noisy ducks. She was not inclined to tolerate that much eccentricity, even for a slice of the Swope fortune. Chrisman's buggy was seen no more on Delaware Street.

Around this time, Bess announced she did not want to be called Bessie, which she had never liked, although she had signed it on her high school papers. "Bess" was what her close friends such as Mary Paxton called her from now on.

Like her father, Bess had a remarkable capacity for friendship. "She set the styles; she was always the leader of our crowd," her friend, Mary Paxton recalled. When people married or moved away, they could not seem to let Bess go. They wrote her letter after letter, continuing to share their lives with her. But no friend was as close as Mary Paxton. Although most of their letters are lost, we can be sure that they continued to correspond throughout Mary's year at Hollins College in Virginia.

In the fall of 1907, Mary heard the news—perhaps from Bess—that the University of Missouri was about to open a school of journalism. In January 1908, Mary abandoned Hollins and headed for Columbia, although the journalism school was not scheduled to open until the following September. There was an extracurricular reason for this haste. During the preceding summer in Independence, Mary had fallen in love with Charles Ross, the scholar of the class of 1901. Charlie was going to be on the journalism school faculty.

After graduating from the University of Missouri in 1905, Charlie had worked for the local paper, the Columbia *Herald*, and then switched to the *St. Louis Post-Dispatch*. Next, in the manner of young reporters then and now, he switched to the St. Louis *Republic*, where he was rapidly promoted to the head of the copy desk. When the editor of the Columbia *Herald*, Walter Williams, was named head of the journalism school, Charlie was the first man he hired.

Always bright, Mary had by this time developed a wide-ranging almost omnivorous interest in books and ideas. Elmer Twyman, son of one of Independence's leading physicians and a member of the class of 1901, wooed her for a while by reading the English philosopher, Herbert Spencer, to her. Spencer was considered daring by most people in 1905 because he pooh-poohed religion and favored the theory of evolution. Mary had attracted Charlie and vice versa even before she went to Hollins, and they had corresponded in somewhat desultory fashion until the summer of 1907, when their feelings became serious. After a moonlit buggy ride, they stood beneath one of the huge whispering trees on the Paxton lawn and exchanged a kiss that said everything.

Bess's emotional life also grew more complicated around this time. A young man named Julian Harvey began coming out from Kansas City to call. Soon he was on the porch at 219 North Delaware Street two or three nights a week. A great many watching neighbors and friends began to think that Bess took his attentions seriously. There was no doubt that Mr. Harvey was serious about her.

But this romance could not compare in intensity with the flame that began to glow on the campus of the University of Missouri, as Charlie Ross and Mary Paxton saw each other night and day. She was his pupil while the sun was shining, his sweetheart when the stars came out. By the summer of 1909, when Mary returned to Independence, she and Charlie were exchanging two letters a day—and discussing marriage. But there were problems. Mary wanted to put her journalistic training—and herself—to the test.

Mary got a job on the Kansas City *Post*, a newspaper that imitated the sensational techniques of Joseph Pulitzer and William Randolph Hearst. This bold move put Charlie Ross in a terrible dilemma. He could not deny he was proud that his pupil had become the first woman reporter in Kansas City. But he did not want a fiancée who was working beside the rogues and lechers that he visualized in the Kansas City *Post*'s newsroom. Charlie's letters to Mary over the next year are a poignant study of a man in torment.

Mary lived at home and dated other men, notably one Pete Harris.

This enabled her to be a close observer of Bess Wallace's romance with Julian Harvey. One day Bess and Julian and Mary and Pete walked into the country to visit some friends. It turned out to be a six-mile stroll, and their hosts—when they finally got there—fed them nothing but thin cocoa and bread-and-butter sandwiches. They retreated three miles in the other direction to the Salisbury farm, where they were sure of a warmer welcome. There they dined on fried chicken and ham and chocolate cake and discussed their expedition. Bess offhandedly declared that she thought it was a minor jaunt, at best. Whereupon the men asked her what she considered a real walk.

"Oh, to Lee's Summit," she said.

To Lee's Summit and back was a good twenty-five mile hike.

"You're on," said Julian and Pete.

A few days later, Mary and Bess packed a lunch, to which Mary contributed deviled eggs. Everyone wore clothes that would not be ruined by prevailing dust and mud on the unpaved roads. Off they went to Lee's Summit, stopping to picnic along the way. An indication of what they were really up to is visible in their dining arrangements. At a bridge over a creek, they split up, and Bess and Julian ate on the upstream side; Mary and Pete enjoyed the downstream view.

Intimate conversation was interrupted by a strange sight: a flotilla of deviled eggs floating past. "What's the matter with my eggs?" Mary called.

"Taste them," Bess replied.

One of Mary's charming younger brothers had filled them with red pepper.

The point of this story is not culinary. Nor is it aimed at confirming the villainy of younger brothers. Anyone who goes on a twenty-five mile hike with a young man and makes a point of dining alone with him on the bank of a country creek must be enjoying his company quite a lot. Bess Wallace was obviously almost as serious about Julian Harvey as he was about her. In fact, as we shall soon see from a letter she wrote to another man, she was applying one of her own personally designed tests to Mr. Harvey on this jaunt. She had realized it was practically impossible to decide how she felt about a man under her mother's eternally vigilant eye at 219 North Delaware Street. Nor did dating him in a crowd of people her own age tell her much. But a picnic was a chance to study him at close quarters, in comparative solitude.

Mr. Harvey seems to have failed the picnic test. In later years he claimed to have liked Bess but, for some reason he could not specify, he never got around to asking the crucial question. Anyone with a little experience in matters of the heart knows that the probable reason for this failure was lack of encouragement. On the other hand, Mr. Harvey may have been intimidated by what he saw at 219 North Delaware Street. It was obvious that anyone who married Bess would have to be prepared to spend a great deal of time with Madge Gates Wallace. Those who got to know Bess well soon learned the deep and complex feelings that bound her to her mother. They also learned that Madge Wallace regarded a suitor as someone who was trying to steal her only daughter, the consolation of her tragic life, from her. It took more courage than the average man possessed to face this hostility—with the awareness that he would have to live with it for the rest of his life.

Meanwhile, at the University of Missouri, another romance was going sour. Charlie Ross was in a flap about the stories Mary Paxton was writing for the Kansas City *Post*. Mary was daring in all senses of the word. She took a stroll through the red-light district of Kansas City and wrote a vivid report on it. Then the U.S. Army announced it was testing a contraption that would enable observers to spot enemy troop movements and artillery positions from the air. They had tried balloons in the Spanish-American War, and the enemy had shot them down with dismaying rapidity. This new flying observation post consisted of a collection of giant kites. Mary volunteered to go up in it.

Before she had time to realize that she was risking life and limb, Mary was soaring several hundred feet above Kansas City, clutching a few ropes, with nothing between her and annihilation but steady nerves. Her story of the adventure created a sensation, but the reception it got from her father and Charlie Ross was very different.

Her father was furious. So was her older brother, Frank, who probably only echoed his father when he said: "You've disgraced the family." Charlie's disapproval was cooler, but no less severe. "I don't want to talk about any such thing as your hanging to the tail of a kite or anything of that sort," he wrote. Then he hastily added: "You are an angel—most of the time. If you were an angel all of the time, I guess I wouldn't love you so much."

As Mary got story after story on the front page of the Kansas City *Post*, Charlie's feelings about her became more and more confused.

He was encountering a new kind of woman and he did not know what to do about it. Then came a crisis that seemed to restore the balance Charlie wanted in their relationship. Mary collapsed with an attack of appendicitis on the streetcar while going to work. Charlie rushed to Independence and helped Mary decide that the operation—serious surgery in 1910—made an early return to the *Post's* hectic city room out of the question. Soon he was back in Columbia writing to her: "I certainly do hope we can be married in June."

Mary convalesced for six months, expecting Charlie to arrive in Independence with a diamond ring in June. She had had her year of success as a reporter and was ready to become the kind of wife Charlie wanted, one who would stay home, have children, and let him support her. But instead of a ring in June, Charlie arrived with a hangdog expression on his face. He told Mary that his mother violently objected to the wedding. She had lectured him on his responsibility to help send his five sisters to college. Charlie's father was working in Colorado as a miner but apparently sent home very little money.

It is pretty evident that Mrs. Ross's objections to the match were strongly influenced by Mary's career as a journalist. Why did Charlie succumb to this maternal edict? The reason is visible in one of Charlie's letters. "I love you," he wrote, "but I find it harder to tell you about it—a woman, than I did to you—a girl."

I am convinced that if Mary had burst into tears and told Charlie she could not live without him, he would have gone home and informed his mother that he was getting married the next day. But Mary was so stunned and hurt, she barely reacted. She was a very proud, independent young woman. She was not going to beg any man for his love.

Coolly, almost casually, without betraying a trace of her inner turmoil, Mary turned slightly away from Charlie and said: "That's too bad. I understand perfectly."

Charlie went back to Columbia convinced that all his fears and doubts were true: Mary had changed and no longer really loved him. Mary careened into an emotional and physical collapse that lasted for the next two years.

Mary's story is part of Bess's story not only because they remained friends for the rest of their lives. At a crucial moment in a then unforeseen and unimaginable future, Mary and Charlie would rejoin Bess in an entirely different dimension, when she stepped onto the stage of world and national history. Mary was so hurt, she was never able to reveal what Charlie had done to her for almost fifty years. But Bess undoubtedly knew that some male had deeply disappointed her best friend. Henceforth Mary's letters were full of wry, often bitter comments about men.

By this time Mary's father had married again, always a difficult experience for a daughter, and especially for an oldest child, who had been as close and even more worshipful of her father than Bess. Mary lost weight to the point of becoming a virtual skeleton. Everyone was convinced she was developing the tuberculosis that had killed her mother. Finally, her father persuaded her to go to Mississippi, where she lived for two years with cousins who owned a large plantation near Greenville.

During the same years that Charlie's romance with Mary flowered and faded, Bess Wallace had another kind of experience in Independence. It did not affect her deepest feelings as directly, but it was difficult, not to say disillusioning, in its own way. As a frequent guest in the Swope home, Bess knew a good deal about its emotional strains and stresses. The oldest daughter, Frances, had fallen in love with a doctor named Bennett Clark Hyde, whom her mother found objectionable. Frances and Dr. Hyde eventually eloped, and Mrs. Swope did not speak to her for a year. Then there was a tearful reconciliation and Dr. Hyde became a frequent guest at the Swope mansion.

The man who possessed the fortune was Tom Swope, a reclusive bachelor who had more or less adopted Mrs. Swope and her children when her husband, his brother, died. Tom Swope felt embarrassed by his riches, which he often said he did not deserve. He simply had been lucky enough to hold onto the right real estate in Kansas City until it was worth millions. A cousin, Moss Hunton, an amiable fellow, lived with Tom, and to assuage his guilt used to wander the streets of Independence almost every day, giving away Tom's money to anyone who asked for it. As for the Swope children, anything they wanted, from trips to Europe to expensive ball gowns, were instantly supplied by Uncle Tom.

Dr. Bennett Clark Hyde observed all this guilt and generosity with a jaundiced eye. From his point of view, the Swope fortune, a good chunk of which he had expected to inherit, was vanishing day by day. He decided to do something about it. His first step was to order a box of five-grain capsules of cyanide of potassium sent to his office.

He brushed aside the druggists' objections to putting this dangerous poison in capsules. It was never done because it could easily be mistaken for medicine.

One night, as a number of the children's friends gathered at the Swope dinner table for a pleasant meal, Cousin Moss Hunton proposed a toast. As he raised his glass, he toppled to the floor. Tom Swope was so upset, he took to his bed. Both men were put under the care of Dr. Hyde, who gave them medicine in capsule form. In three days, both were dead.

Next, on the pretext that he was performing some experiments on animals, Dr. Hyde obtained from a medical friend a number of cultures for typhoid fever. Soon, four of the younger members of the family were violently ill. Dr. Hyde diagnosed typhoid fever and told his wife, Frances, to stop drinking water from the house cistern. Henceforth they drank only bottled water. The sick younger Swopes were all put under Dr. Hyde's care. He gave Chrisman a medicinal capsule and within an hour he died in awful convulsions.

Lest the Swopes seem to have been naive beyond belief, it should be noted that the night after Chrisman died, Dr. Hyde was elected president of the Jackson County Medical Association. He was a highly respected physician. A few days later, Bess's friend Margaret Swope swallowed one of Dr. Hyde's medicinal capsules and had a seizure not unlike Chrisman's, but she did not die.

At this point in this bizarre tale, the nurses became very upset. They went to Dr. Elmer Twyman, father of Mary Paxton's beau, and told him what they suspected. Meanwhile, Dr. Hyde had decamped to New York, where he met Lucie Lee Swope, who had rushed back from Europe on hearing of the outbreak of disease and death in her family. On the train to Missouri, Lucie Lee became violently ill. Apparently Dr. Hyde had poisoned her, too. But his career as a mass murderer came to an abrupt end when they reached Independence. John Paxton, Mary Paxton's father, and the Swope family lawyer, had ordered the bodies of Moss Hunton and Tom Swope exhumed. They discovered cyanide in both corpses, as well as strychnine in Tom's.

On March 5, 1910, Dr. Hyde went on trial for multiple murder. It was the most sensational event to take place in Independence since Jesse James stopped robbing trains. After a month of wrangling over the evidence, the case went to the jury, which returned a verdict of guilty. But the Missouri Supreme Court reversed the verdict and ordered a new trial. To this day, no one knows why the Supreme

Court reversed; under Missouri law, such decisions can be made without stating a reason.

Two more trials, which dragged on through 1912, resulted in hung juries. Mrs. Swope, who had spent more than $250,000 hiring lawyers to prosecute her son-in-law, gave up. The Swopes' reign as the social leaders of Independence had long since collapsed. The family scattered, most of them moving to California.

For two years, Bess Wallace had watched people whom she considered her friends writhing in the grip of publicity. Day after day she saw the Swopes and their personal habits and wealth discussed by prying, vulgar strangers. She herself had experienced the anguish that public knowledge of private sorrows can cause. Her mother, the self-sentenced prisoner of shame at 219 North Delaware Street, was living proof of the damage, the pain. Then there was her friend Mary Paxton, once so brilliant, so promising, so full of self-confidence, now a wan wraith in Mississippi.

What else could these experiences do but give Bess added reasons to regard the world with wariness and doubt, to wonder again if any man could be trusted, to ask herself if marriage to a husband who piled up money was a promise of happiness any more than marriage to a man who failed? Frequently she was tempted to imitate her mother, to choose retirement from this raw, brutal, threatening American world, a retreat to a life of a quiet, dignified mourning.

One night in the summer of 1910, while the gossip and grisly jokes about the Swopes were still reverberating through Independence, the doorbell rang at 219 North Delaware Street. Bess opened it, and there stood someone whom she had not seen or heard from or even thought about in the nine years that had passed since her graduation from Independence High School: Harry Truman. In his hand was an empty cake plate.

Madge Gates Wallace often baked cakes and pies and sent samples to the neighbors. It was the only kind of cooking she enjoyed. Harry's cousins, the Nolands, now lived at 216 North Delaware, the house across the street. They had recently received one of these gifts and had asked Harry Truman if he would like to return the plate. He had accepted, they later recalled, "with something approaching the speed of light."

"Aunt Ella told me to thank your mother for the cake," Harry said. "I guess I ought to thank her too. I ate a big piece."

"Come in," Bess said.

Chapter Three

The twenty-six-year-old Harry Truman that twenty-five-year-old Bess Wallace saw in the porch lamplight on that summer night in 1910 had changed in interesting ways from the quiet, scholarly nonathlete she had known and pretty much ignored in school. This man had gained weight and muscle. There was a solidity to his shoulders, a physical self-confidence in his erect stance. His skin was tanned and windburned and glowing with the health that comes from constant exercise. How in the world had Four Eyes turned into this rugged looking specimen of vitality?

Bess Wallace may have heard that Harry had become a bank teller after the family had moved to Kansas City. A perfect job for him, she probably thought. But that windburned skin, those calloused hands were not acquired in a bank. Mere curiosity, aside from friendly feelings, no doubt impelled Bess Wallace to invite Harry Truman into the Gates parlor. There he was greeted by Mrs. Wallace and the Gateses, and perhaps by one or two of Bess's three brothers. After the ritual thanks for the cake, the older and younger folks probably let the ex-schoolmates go out on the porch and catch up with each other.

Harry soon satisfied Bess's curiosity. He was no longer working at the Union National Bank in Kansas City, although he had done very well there, winning a series of raises and promotions. He was a farmer, helping his father and his brother Vivian run the 600-acre Young farm in Grandview. Harry's mother and his uncle, Harrison Young, had inherited it from his grandmother, Harriet Louisa Young, when she died in 1909. It was hard work, but he enjoyed it—and it paid a lot better than a bank. In a good year the farm could clear $7,000, and his share of that would be about $4,000. There was also the prospect of inheriting the whole works, or a good hunk of it, when his Uncle Harrison and his mother died.

He was also a part-time soldier, which helped to explain his erect, square-shouldered stance. In 1905, he had joined Battery B of the Missouri National Guard and spent a few weeks each summer training with them. He had been promoted to corporal, which pleased him immensely. Bess was no doubt surprised to learn that Harry had hoped to become a professional soldier and had taken special tutoring for the entrance examination for West Point the year after they graduated from high school. One day it occurred to him that he ought to take a preliminary eye test at the Army Recruiting Station in Kansas City. They told him he did not have a chance to get into the U.S. Military Academy. So he decided to get a taste of military life, at least, in Battery B.

Harry may have amused Bess with the story of his grandmother's reaction when he came out to the farm in his blue national guard uniform one day. All Harriet Louisa Young could think about were the gloating Kansans who had burned and looted the farm in the course of executing Order No. 11 in 1863. She told Harry never to wear his uniform home again.

The passions of the Civil War had become quaint, almost amusing, to the younger generation. I don't know what else Harry and Bess talked about that night, but the visit lasted two hours. When Harry returned to the Noland home, his eyes were aglow. "Well, I saw her," he said.

There is a glimpse of the awe and longing with which Harry Truman already regarded Bess Wallace in those words. He told the Nolands that he had asked Bess if he could call on her again, and the answer had been an offhand yes. The Nolands were forthwith warned that they were going to see a good deal of Cousin Harry from now on.

But Independence was at least a four-hour trip one way from Grandview in a buggy, and the train connections were very bad. Harry had to walk a mile from the farm to Grandview and wait for a Kansas City and Southern train, which was invariably late and did not take him directly to Independence. He had to walk a mile and a half along the tracks to the Kansas City terminal of the Air Line streetcars. As an alternative he could drive the Truman family buggy into nearby Dodson, where he could catch an interurban streetcar which, alas, required a transfer to another streetcar in Kansas City to get to Independence. Either way, the trip seldom took less than two hours. Inevitably, therefore, to our great fortune, Harry and Bess began to communicate through the mails.

The first few letters have been lost, but by the end of December 1910, Bess had begun saving his letters, a good sign, although Harry did not know it. I doubt very much if he ever found out how many of his letters Bess saved over the years. Everyone, including their daughter, was astonished to discover some 1,600 letters from him, as well as hundreds more from Madge Gates Wallace, Mary Paxton, and other correspondents in the attic at 219 North Delaware Street after Bess Wallace Truman died. Included in this unique historical treasure trove, which is the foundation of this book, are hundreds of letters from Bess to these same correspondents.

Harry's first surviving letter revealed that they were exchanging favorite novels and that Bess had issued Harry an invitation to visit over the Christmas holidays. But he mournfully informed her that it was out of the question.

Nothing would please me better than to come to see you during the holidays or any other time for the matter of that, but Papa broke his leg the other day and I am chief nurse, next to my mother, besides being farm boss now. So you see I'll be somewhat closely confined for some time to come. I hope you'll let the invitation be a standing one though and I shall avail myself of it at the very first opportunity. . . .
We haven't quite got over the excitement yet. A horse pulled a big beam over on him in the barn. We were so glad he wasn't killed we didn't know what to do.
If you see fit to let me hear from you sometimes, I shall certainly appreciate it. Farm life as an everyday affair is not generally exciting. Wishing you and all of you the very happiest New Year, I am

Very Sincerely

Harry S. Truman

It is clear that Harry Truman was aware of the awesome challenge he faced in his pursuit of Bess Wallace's affection. In school, the distance between them had been social. Now the gap had been widened, not only geographically but psychologically. By going back to the farm, he had activated the classic conflict between town and country that was bred into every member of the Independence upper class.

Let there be no misunderstanding about Harry Truman's status. He was a farmer, as thoroughly and completely as any American who has ever dug a plow into the fertile soil of Missouri. On the Youngs' 600 acres—a square mile of land—he and his father and

brother Vivian were raising corn, wheat, and oats, as well as Black
Angus cattle and Hampshire hogs. As far as John Truman was concerned, it was a seven day a week job, 52 weeks a year. He demanded as
much work from his sons as he extracted from the hired hands, who
frequently quit in exasperation at his sharp tongue and minimal
wages. He expected his sons to be out on a gang plow wrestling a four-
horse team across the fields each day at 5 A.M. If the furrows Harry
plowed were not straight, "I heard about it from my father for the next
year," he said. "When it rained and we couldn't plow or harvest, we'd
take down the old scythe—and we had a dozen of them—and cut
weeds in the fence corners and along the fences bordering the roads."

    John Truman was a driven man. He had formed a company, J. A.
Truman & Son, which took on the responsibility for paying off some
$12,500 in debts he still owed from his financial collapse in 1901. By
becoming a partner in that company, Harry Truman made himself
equally liable for those debts. But he combined this loyalty to his
father with a quiet determination to preserve his psychological
independence. When the Trumans and the hired hands trooped
in from the fields to eat the lunch that Martha Ellen Truman had prepared for them, Harry amazed the hired hands by sitting down at the
piano and playing Chopin or Liszt while they waited for the food to
be served.

    He also continued to be an omnivorous reader, especially of his-
tory and biography. Beyond that habit, which went back to his
school days, when he read every book in the Independence Library,
his chief recreation was the Masonic Order. He founded a lodge in
Grandview and traveled miles at night when he should have been
resting or sleeping to administer degrees in other lodges. If he found
any other consolation in this rural life, it was his mother's company.
He always had been her favorite child, and he reciprocated her affection with wholehearted admiration and gratitude.

    It was she who had noticed his bad eyesight when he was five and
taken him in a farm wagon to Kansas City for an examination by a
specialist. She knew that the thick glasses he had to wear prevented
him from participating in sports like other boys his age and encouraged him to become a reader and a pianist. She selected many of the
books he read in his early years. She had graduated from the Baptist
Female College in Lexington, Missouri, where she majored in music
and art. Between Martha Ellen Truman and her oldest son there was
an intellectual as well as an emotional bond. He admired her caustic

opinions about everything from windy preachers to crooked politicians and the blunt way she stated them.

At first glance, this did not seem a good preparation to win the heart of Bess Wallace, a very different woman. In fact, there seemed to be very little in Harry Truman's world that Bess Wallace would want to hear about. For the first year, the opening words of every letter he wrote her emphasized the distance between them. He addressed her as "My dear Bessie." He did not know that Bess's intimate friends, such as Mary Paxton, had abandoned that unwanted name. But Harry Truman had resources that were not immediately apparent. He set out to make himself interesting to Bess Wallace.

From his earliest letters, he never missed a chance to portray himself as a rugged outdoor man. In one letter he told her that after sowing oats and hauling six tons of hay in a fierce wind, his face was so windburned "I look like raw beef or a confirmed booze fighter." He described his farmer's rags—"dirty and tattered and torn with hog snoot marks, splashed milk and other things too numerous to mention." He casually added: "Mamma ropes me in once in a while and makes me exchange for a clean set, but they don't feel right until I wear them a day or two." My favorite is his description of wrestling hogs to the ground to vaccinate them. "A 200 pound hog can almost jerk the ribs loose from your backbone when you get him by the hind leg. It is far and away the best exercise in the list. It beats Jack Johnson's [the heavyweight champion] whole training camp as a muscle toughener."

At the same time, Harry displayed his taste in literature, music, and art to Bess. During his years as a bank clerk in Kansas City, he had attended the opera for a season and decided he did not like it nearly so much as classical piano music. He also had seen the great tragedians of the day, such as E. H. Sothern and Richard Mansfield, when they came to Kansas City. In an offhand, unpretentious way, Harry made it clear that he was no country bumpkin. But he was also honest enough to admit that he agreed with his Uncle Harrison, who "says he'd rather go to the Orpheum [a vaudeville theater] and laugh all evening than sit and grate the enamel off his false teeth to see Mansfield or Sothern or any other big gun."

This confession was as shrewd as it was honest. Very early, Harry Truman noticed that Bess Wallace loved a good laugh. He was soon amusing her with vivid glimpses of the comic side of country life. Here are some wry observations on the party line telephone.

When you want to use it you have to take down the receiver and listen while some good sister tells some other good sister who is not so wise how to make butter or how to raise chickens or when it is the right time in the moon to plant onion sets or something else equally important. About the time you think the world is coming to an end or some other direful calamity will certainly overtake you if you don't get to express your feelings into that phone the good sister will quit and then if you are quick and have a good strong voice you can have your say, but you know confidently that everyone in the neighborhood has heard you.

His wit was even dryer when it came to farm manners.

They are endeavoring faithfully to better the farmers' condition . . . all the time. You know our friend Roosevelt [Theodore] appointed a country life commission to spend the extra cash in the U.S. Treasury. Some fellow with a good heart has also invented a soup spoon that won't rattle. I know he had farmers in mind when he did that. Some other good fellow has invented peas that are cubes instead of spheres so they won't roll off the knife when you eat them. If I can get the seed I will certainly raise them. . . . Now if someone would invent a fork with a spring, so you could press it and spear a biscuit at arm's length without having to reach over and incommode your neighbor—well he'd just simply be elected President, that's all.

During a visit to Delaware Street, Harry heard Bess and Nellie Noland discuss Ethel Noland's dislike of emotional excitement in religion. This inspired one of his best letters.

I think you and Nellie could probably get up some religious excitement on Ethel's part if you would do as a certain woman did Aunt Susan [his mother's sister] was telling me about.

You know they used to hold outdoor meetings when the weather was good and everyone for miles around attended and stayed sometimes for weeks. Along in the fifties they were holding a meeting not far from here and the preacher had exhorted and ranted and done everything else they usually do when they try to get something started, as they call it, but it was no use. He wasn't a quitter though. Finally down one of the aisles one of the good sisters jumped out and began screaming and dancing up and down as they usually do when they get religion. The preacher made a dive for her with his hand extended, saying, "Oh, Sister I am so glad to see you come out and say you have religion." Her answer between screams was, "I haven't got it. I haven't got it. There's a lizard on my dress," and she kept on dancing until Aunt Sue and someone else took her outside and one of those little lizards fell off her dress. Try it on Ethel. It will work I think.

Like Bess, who had become an Episcopalian, Harry had "strayed from the Presbyterian fold," although he still remembered his Sun-

day school days "very well." He had become a member of the Baptist
Church in Grandview, but he had very independent ideas about
religion.

I am by religion like everything else. I think there is more in acting than in
talking. . . . We had a neighbor out here who could pray louder and talk
more fervently in meetin' than anyone I ever heard. He'd say in every
prayer, "O Lord help this congregation to stop and think where they's a
going at." We finally found that he beat his wife and did everything else
that's "ornery."

I think religion is something one should have on Wednesday and Thursday as well as Sunday. Therefore I don't believe that these protracted meetings do any real good. They are mostly excitement and when the excitement
wears off people are as they always were.

I like to play cards and dance as far as I know how and go to shows and do
all the things they [the Baptists] said I shouldn't but I don't feel badly about
it. I go when I feel like it and the good church members are glad to hear
what it's like. You see I'm a member but not a strenuous one.

Another colorful aspect of farm life, horse trading (his father's
profession), inspired a lively letter and some significant thoughts
about men and morals.

A fellow traded me a horse yesterday. That is, he parted me from a
hundred dollars and I have a horse. You know horse trading is the cause of
the death of truth in America. When you go to buy they'll tell you anything
on earth to get your money. You simply have to use your own judgment if
you have any. I haven't much but I think I got my money's worth. Can't tell
though until I work him a few days.

A neighbor of ours once had a sale of his furniture and stock. He had a
great many horses and some that were no good. He had one that was
probably an octogenarian in the horse world. He was very aged anyway.
This horse he wanted to sell to a poor lame man who had tried to buy it
before the sale. So he took a quart of bad whiskey and soaked the poor lame
one and then told him he wasn't going to put the horse up. Well that fellow
begged so hard that the horse was sold to him for $170. Just about $100 more
than he was worth. The owner had a "buy bidder" to run him up. So that
between the booze and the bidder he was mulcted for $100. O he the honest
farmer. I have found that they sell gold bricks now. That is what rural
delivery and party-line phones have done for our uplift.

I am not a pessimist though. There are some honest ones and they are
always well thought of even by crooks. They are always the last ones you
get acquainted with too.

We have moved around quite a bit and always the best people are hardest
to know. I don't know why that is, either. . . . It's all a matter of viewpoint.
A man's mighty lucky if he has two.

In this letter, Bess Wallace encountered one of Harry Trumans' most remarkable gifts, the ability to look at himself and other people, including his father, and see their shortcomings with an amazingly clear and steady gaze without relapsing into cynicism. He remained an optimist about himself, his fellow Americans, the future. Her father's suicide had left Bess with a very different attitude toward life. She was much closer to being a pessimist. Psychologists say that people who fall in love instinctively reach out for qualities in the other person that they sense they lack in themselves. I think this may explain why Bess Wallace was attracted to Harry Truman. But it was an attraction that had to overcome deep doubts and hesitations.

In mid-April 1911, continuing the streak of bad luck that had been haunting the Trumans since his father went bankrupt in 1901, a calf broke Harry's leg. That too was used for Farmer Truman's pursuit of the athletic Miss Wallace. He joked about the injury, declaring it reminded him of the Irishwoman who mourned her husband after he drowned in the Big Blue River by howling: "To think that Mike should a crossed the great ocean and thin be drowned in a hole like the dirty Blue. Tis a disgrass indeed it is." Harry said that he felt the same way about having a sucking calf break his leg. In another letter, he casually mentioned that the calf weighed a mere 300 pounds.

Harry's broken leg soon healed, but it became apparent that 1911 was not going to be a good year for farmers. It simply refused to rain. Even the Trumans' vegetable garden failed. "We are living on bread and bacon with some canned goods thrown in," Harry wrote.

This did not prevent Harry from discussing with remarkable candor the probable state of mind of a mutual friend named Minnie Clements, who had just married. Bess remarked that she suspected Minnie wished she could turn back the clock. Harry replied that he thought it took several months for that kind of disillusion to set in.

They tell me that for the first few months she can burn the biscuits every morning if she chooses and it's all right, but after that she learns what a good cook her ma-in-law was. And . . . he can be as no-account and good-for-nothing as he wants to be but he soon learns how his pa-in-law made his money. Then it's ho for Reno or South Dakota [divorce mill capitals in 1911]. It's certainly awful what pessimists those two places have made of people. I am a Catholic when it comes to divorce. . . .

Marriage was clearly on Harry's mind. On June 22, 1911, less than a year after he appeared at the door of 219 Delaware Street with Mrs.

Wallace's cake plate, he proposed. He began obliquely, commenting that the drought was making water as much of a luxury as diamonds. Then he took the plunge.

Speaking of diamonds, would you wear a solitaire on your left hand should I get it? Now that is a rather personal or pointed question provided you take it for all it means. You know, were I an Italian or a poet I would commence and use all the luscious language of two continents. I am not either but only a kind of good-for-nothing American farmer. I've always had a sneakin' notion that some day maybe I'd amount to something. I doubt it now though like everything. It is a family failing of ours to be poor financiers. I am blest that way. Still that doesn't keep me from having always thought that you were all that a girl could be possibly and impossibly. You may not have guessed it but I've been crazy about you ever since we went to Sunday school together. But I never had the nerve to think you'd even look at me. I don't think so now but I can't keep from telling you what I think of you.

Bess's reply was a devastating silence. She obviously did not know what to make of this incredibly honest farmer, who was asking her to marry him and simultaneously admitting that he was probably going to be a financial failure. If Harry Truman had deliberately tried to wreck his chances with Bess Wallace, he could not have chosen a more ruinous remark. Here was a man asking her to repeat her mother's experience! Yet there was something about this man that stirred a response in Bess Wallace's bruised, wary heart. That amazing optimism in the face of experiences that would have discouraged or disillusioned most men. The energy, the vitality he exuded. She could not say yes but she did not want to say no.

After three weeks of agony, Harry wrote a wary letter. "I have just about come to the conclusion that I have offended you in some way. . . . Would you object to my coming down this Saturday evening?"

Although the phone service between Grandview and Independence was erratic at best, this letter must have been answered that way, because two days later Harry was writing Bess another letter, telling her how he felt about his visit and their talk. She had turned him down. But she had done it in the gentlest, most considerate way. She had said that she hoped they could continue to be friends.

You turned me down so easy that I am almost happy anyway. I never was fool enough to think that a girl like you could ever care for a fellow like me but I couldn't help telling you how I felt. . . . I have been so afraid you were not even going to let me be your good friend. To be even in that class is something.

I never had any desire to say such things to anyone else. All my girl friends think I am a cheerful idiot and a confirmed old bach. . . . I have never met a girl in my life that you were not the first to be compared with her, to see wherein she was lacking and she always was.

Please don't think I am talking nonsense or bosh, for if ever I told the truth I am telling it now and I'll never tell such things to anyone else or bother you with them again. I have always been more idealist than practical anyway, so I really never expected any reward for loving you. I shall always hope, though.

Here was candor that ought to have melted any woman's heart. But Bess only agreed to let Harry give her his picture. By the end of July he had delivered the "cat chaser," as he called it. Then he launched a campaign to lure the athletic Miss Wallace to Grandview. He undertook to build a tennis court on the family farm.

For the next month his letters were full of references to this project. He planned a grass court. "We have a heavy field roller and I can make it as hard as the road and mow the grass real short," he told her. "I am going to have it ready by Labor Day."

On the eve of Labor Day weekend, he sent Bess a map of the road to Grandview. All day Sunday, Harry toiled on the court. On Monday, instead of Bess and her friends in their tennis outfits, there was only a message that she had decided not to come because it was raining in Independence. Forlornly, Harry reported that the sun had been shining brightly in Grandview.

Refusing to allow the word discouraged into his vocabulary, Harry persuaded the elusive Miss Wallace to set another date for a visit to Grandview. She declined to do so—and then made an impromptu visit, with virtually no warning. The tennis court in the meantime had deteriorated from exposure to wind and weather and was pronounced unusable. It was not level enough. Harry was reduced to hoping he could persuade the road overseer to come in with his grader to flatten it out.

No more was said about the tennis court. Harry began finding an amazing number of excuses to go to Independence and Kansas City. By October 1, 1911, he was inviting Bess to a matinee of *H.M.S. Pinafore*, which was arriving shortly at the Shubert Theater in Kansas City. He added an invitation to the evening's vaudeville show at the

Orpheum and dinner in Kansas City, because "it will take so long to go to Independence and back so many times." Bess accepted, and Farmer Truman abandoned his rural ways to become Miss Wallace's escort to the metropolis.

A few weeks later, Harry traveled to Omaha, Nebraska, with several friends to file claims for mineral rights in the nearby hills. It was a kind of lottery, with about 400 claims available, worth from $16,000 to $40. Alas, he reported to Bess he did not even draw a $40 claim. "I never could draw anything though. Not even the lady I wanted," Harry wrote, adding that he was sure he was born under an unlucky star.

Ignoring this uncharacteristic outburst of pessimism, Miss Wallace replied by asking if "wanted" meant his interest in her had waned. Harry hastily replied that the past tense only meant his grammar was at fault. His feelings for her were "something that will never be past with me." He spent the rest of the letter bemoaning his lack of a "benzine buggy," as hoboes called an automobile. If he had one, he would "burn the pike from here to Independence" so often he would "make myself monotonous to you."

By the end of 1911, in the eighteenth month of their courtship, Harry had a standing invitation to visit 219 North Delaware Street every Sunday. But he was still far from getting Miss Wallace to consider marriage. On one of these Sundays, which happened to be rainy, Harry asked her if she was getting tired of him hanging around so much. Bess replied that she thought he was the one who would get tired of it.

"I'll never get tired," Harry said.

Bess looked out the window at the rain and said: "I wish I had some rubber boots!"

A day or two later, Harry wrote her a letter, recalling the scene. He told her she should not have been afraid "of my getting slushy or proposing until I can urge you to come to as good a home as you have already." Then, either with great shrewdness or great honesty or both, he added: "Still, if I thought you cared a little I'd double my efforts to amount to something and maybe would succeed."

Bess responded with some thoughts on husbands and money. Harry could not know, at this point, the painful memories this subject stirred in Bess's mind. She told him that she and her friend Mary Paxton had decided that a woman should never get seriously involved with a man who was unable to support her in decent style.

Mary, obviously reacting to her bitter experience with Charlie Ross, added that lately she was inclined to wait around for a millionaire.

Harry replied that he was surprised to find that he agreed with Mary Paxton for once. When they were kids, they were never able to agree on anything. But Mary was not the point here, although he wished her the best of luck in her hunt for a millionaire. "I am going to start in real earnest now to get some of the dirty pelf," Harry wrote. "For what you say sounds kind of encouraging, whether you meant it that way or not."

After that exchange, money became a frequent topic of discussion. When Bess invited Harry to dinner at the Salisbury farm and told him they would walk the three miles from Independence, he protested that he was more than willing to hire a buggy. He obviously was not acquainted with Miss Wallace's fondness for marathon walks, or that this invitation was another favorable sign.

On Bess's twenty-seventh birthday, February 13, 1912, Harry apologized for not giving her a birthday present or sending a valentine for the following day, because he did not have the money to buy anything "good enough." Bess replied by giving him a stickpin with her birthstone in it for Valentine's Day. Harry reported that he had found a fortune teller's prospectus in a cough-drop box and it said that people with February birthdays had a quieting effect on the insane. "I suppose that means those they have caused to become dippy. Don't you?" he asked.

Three weeks later, on March 4, 1912, ten months after she turned him down, Harry began calling her "Bess." He had been admitted to the inner circle. Even more encouraging was the way she took him into her confidence about her name. She told him she was not really happy with Bess and was considering several other variations on her baptismal name, Elizabeth. Harry offered some lively comments and observations on the subject.

My Dear Elizabeth:
How does that look to you? I just wrote it that way to see how it would look.

You know we have associations for every name. England's great Queen always goes to Elizabeth for me. When I was a very small kid I read a history of England and it had a facsimile signature of hers to Queen Mary's death warrant. I'll never forget how it looked if I live to be a hundred. But that didn't put me against her, for I always thought she was a great woman. I never think of you as Elizabeth. Bess or Bessie are you. Aren't you most awful glad they didn't call you the middle syllable? It is my pet aversion. There is an old woman out in this neck of the woods who is blest with enough curiosity for a whole suffragette meeting and a marvelous ability for gratifying it, to her own satisfaction. She has a wart on the end of her nose and a face like the Witch of Endor. Her first name is Liz. She is an ideal person to carry the name. I am sure it is not a nickname but her real one as no one of her caliber could possibly be called Elizabeth. I have a very belligerent (spelled right?) cousin whose name is Lizzie. Therefore I care not for Liz and Lizzie for those two very good reasons. . . . I don't know what got me started on this line of talk, but I hope you won't be offended because I don't like some of the nicknames of your good name. But please remember that I like yours muchly—anyway—as well as the real one.

Making some money became almost an obsession with Harry Truman. He dashed to New Mexico in search of prime farmland that he hoped he could buy or lease, with his Uncle Harrison's help. At the farm, he watched his brother Vivian depart to his own farm—he had married in the fall of 1911—and then let the hired men go too. He was going to work the entire farm on his own to try to raise the profits. His father was planning to run for road overseer for the town of Grandview, and that was going to take much of John Truman's time. "Work is the only way I see to arrive at conclusions," Harry wrote. "This thing of sitting down and waiting for plutocratic relatives to decease [he was referring to his Uncle Harrison] doesn't go with me."

Now began a terrific struggle to make the farm profitable and simultaneously keep Bess Wallace's interest in him alive. Everything seemed to conspire against him. Trains failed to run, and he would lose a whole night's sleep trying to get back to Grandview. His father became more and more surly about the time Harry spent in Independence. John Truman began going out of his way to make life difficult for his son.

In this letter, written in mid-August of 1912, Harry gives Bess (and us) a graphic picture of a particularly bad night and day. It began with the train sitting on the tracks halfway to Grandview until 6 A.M.

There was a bunch of hoodlums behind me [on the stalled train] . . . and every time we'd get to sleep they'd let out a roar and wake me up. Mr. Galt [a fellow passenger] seemed to sleep placidly on. We both called ourselves some bad names for not going into the Pullman. But I thought every minute would be the last and it would only take them thirty minutes to get to Grandview.

Well you could put all the sleep I got last night under a postage stamp. I got home at 7 A.M. which by the way is the latest yet for me, and changed my glad rags for my sorry ones and went to loading baled hay into a car. That is the hottest job there is, I think, except shoveling coal for His Majesty [his name for the Devil]. We finally managed to get 289 bales into the car at seven thirty this evening. I came home and put on my clean overalls and a white soft shirt, had supper and was just getting ready to come up and start this letter when Papa came in and said it was lightning around and that we should go over to a haystack some three quarters of a mile away where the baler had been at work and cover up the hay. I almost told him we'd let the hay go hang, for you can imagine how very much I'd feel like going three quarters of a mile across a stubble field with low shoes and silk stockings after being up all night and working all day—at 9 P.M. besides. I went though and handed up thirty two boards a foot wide and fourteen long while Papa placed them on the hay. I'll bet two dollars to two cents it doesn't rain now, but it sure would if I'd refused to go.

It might be helpful to note that Harry was twenty-eight years old at this point. He displayed an almost saintly forbearance with his father's tantrums. But he also stood up to him. "Papa says he's going to adopt a boy if I don't stay home on Sundays. I told him to go ahead," he wrote.

A few weeks later, he excused a disconnected letter, explaining: "I have to write this on the installment plan, as usual Papa keeps wanting something." Next came a report that his father was "on his ear" because he had come home with two loads of cows and Harry was not there to meet him. His father angrily telephoned Independence and was frustrated by an uncooperative operator. Harry was "glad." He said that there was "no harm done and I spent the evening where I wanted to."

His letters are full of references to his exhaustion. One day he fell asleep shelling corn. But he doggedly continued his visits to Independence. His devotion clearly began to make an impression on Bess Wallace. In the fall of 1912, they went for a walk in the country on which Farmer Truman proved he could more than match Bess's endurance. He wrote her the next day, cheerfully asking how she felt. "With the exception of a blister, I was as fit as could be this morning."

A new form of entertainment was sweeping the country, motion pictures. Harry used them to extend an ingenious invitation. He suggested going to lunch at some Kansas City restaurant and then seeing all the pictures that could be crowded in four hours. He ad-

mitted it was a "Twelfth Street stunt" [Twelfth Street was the Broadway of Kansas City] but "if a person don't have a good time doing
what everybody does, he'll lead a mighty bored life."

Along with this sophistication, Harry Truman continued to reveal
his feelings to Bess about the life he led on the farm. Now his
thoughts were often more serious than amusing.

Do you know that I did the orneriest thing this morning. I was cutting
oats right here close to the house and amputated the left foot of an old hen
with five chickens. I felt badly about it too. She was over in the oats where I
couldn't see her till I'd already done it. Mamma says she'll get all right. I
hope so. I'd rather do most anything than to hurt something that can't tell
me what it thinks of me.

Politics also became an excuse for escorting Miss Wallace. They
went to a political rally at which William Jennings Bryan spoke on
behalf of the Democratic candidate for president in 1912, Woodrow
Wilson. The nominee, a former president of Princeton University
who had turned politician and become governor of New Jersey in
1910, was unknown to Missourians. But Bryan was a famous name
to every western farmer. Almost to a man, they had worshipped him
ever since he electrified the Democratic Convention of 1896 with his
famous speech attacking the gold standard. His call for using silver to
back American currency was really a demand for cheaper money,
always popular with debt burdened farmers. Bryan turned it into a
crusade by proclaiming: "You shall not crucify mankind upon a cross
of gold" and denouncing as Antichrists the railroad barons and Wall
Street tycoons who favored the gold standard. Three times his fervid
oratory had won him the Democratic nomination for the presidency.

But in 1912, Bryan was persona non grata to many Missourians.
He had double-crossed Missouri's hero, Champ Clark, speaker of the
House of Representatives, who thought he deserved the Democratic
Party's nomination for the progressive legislation he had pushed
through Congress. Because Clark was supported by New York's
Tammany Hall bosses, Bryan decided he represented "the predatory
interests" and threw his support to the political newcomer, Wilson.

Jackson County Democrats were not that fond of Champ Clark,
who represented the dominant St. Louis bosses as far as they were
concerned. Bryan drew a huge crowd and Harry Truman enjoyed
him immensely. In spite of the way the Nebraskan had led the Democratic Party to disaster in three presidential elections since 1896,

Harry was one of his "staunchest admirers." He liked the idealism that Bryan tried, however ineptly, to inject into American politics.

I don't know what Bess thought of the aging "Boy Orator of the Platte," but she was undoubtedly pleased by Harry's remark that he would not have enjoyed the great man nearly so much if she had not been present. This sounds to me as if she had displayed a certain reluctance to attend this political jamboree. It is easy to see why politics would remain a subject Bess preferred to avoid.

But she could not stop Harry from following the tumultuous campaign of 1912 with passionate interest. Teddy Roosevelt, running as the candidate of the Progressive Party, split the Republican Party, and Woodrow Wilson became the first Democratic president in sixteen years. In the three-cornered melee, the incumbent, President William Howard Taft, suffered one of the worst political humiliations in our history, carrying only two states.

Another issue loose in this campaign was votes for women. The Jackson County *Examiner* carried an editorial in favor of it. It was close to the high tide of the suffragette movement. Emmeline Pankhurst and her followers were making headlines in England with their hunger strikes, and in New York brigades of militant women were marching up Fifth Avenue. But the movement had few supporters in Missouri, and Harry Truman and Bess Wallace were not among them. In one of his letters Harry offhandedly remarked that a young farm horse "kicked like a starving suffragette," and in another letter he compared Mrs. Pankhurst to one of the farm's guinea hens, who squalled all night and all day.

It may puzzle some people that Bess Wallace, so independent in many ways, with a best friend, Mary Paxton, who was even more independent, did not instinctively support the suffragettes. But votes for women was not a popular idea outside the media capital of New York. In Massachusetts, when it was submitted to the people in a referendum with women permitted to vote, it was defeated by almost 2 to 1, and the most shocking part of the story is the fact that only 23,000 women voted in favor of it. In Missouri, the question was put to a vote in 1914—and lost by 5 to 1, with only males voting.

The installation of a Democratic president in 1913 did little to improve the fortunes of Harry Truman. The country, at least the western half, promptly reeled into a slump that sent farm prices plummeting, and with them Harry's hopes of making a profit from his backbreaking labors. To worsen things for the Trumans, their right to the farm was menaced by a lawsuit brought by their Young relatives, who resented the way their mother Harriet Louisa Young had left her property to Harrison and Martha Ellen and cut the rest of the family off with $5 each.

The brief alleged that Mamma Truman was the villain who persuaded her weak-minded mother to write this will. The accusation made Harry so mad, "I could fight a boilermaker." Harriet Young was the best businesswoman he had ever seen and a woman of fierce integrity. "If we'd ever mentioned property to her, it would have finished us," he told Bess. But there was nothing to do except hire a lawyer and slug it out. The legal expenses devoured what little money the farm produced during these painful years.

In spite of his poverty, Harry was clearly gaining ground with Miss Wallace. Early in the summer of 1913, a little more than two years after Bess had turned down his proposal, she paid another of her rare visits to Grandview. Madge Wallace revealed her displeasure—disguised, of course, as concern—by taking it into her head that some sort of accident had happened on the trip out. She tried to call the Trumans, and the operator refused to connect her. This apparently convinced her that a major disaster had occurred, and she was frantic until Bess came home. Harry apologized for the awful phone service—he vowed not to pay the bill—and asked anxiously: "Do you suppose she'll ever let you come again?"

Bess's solution to her mother's hovering presence was longer and longer walks. Harry cheerfully accepted the opportunity to be alone with her. The expeditions undoubtedly involved picnics, and Harry apparently passed this crucial test, without realizing it. They also took up a sport for which Harry Truman had no enthusiasm whatsoever—fishing. Bess loved it, except for one detail—baiting the hook. She would let Harry handle the worms, and then he would read or talk while she pulled carp and catfish from the Little Blue River or some lesser stream.

On the eve of a fishing expedition in early August 1913, Harry showed how seriously he took his baiting job—while flavoring it with his wry wit.

It looks as if it might rain this morning. I hope it does. That's what we need . . . it'll make the fish bite better. They say that liver is the best bait. Perhaps you wouldn't object to baiting your hook with liver. It is necessary to bury it for three days. That might cause it to be as objectionable as worms. There's an old man by the name of Moore living at Hickman Mills

who is an expert in the fishing line and he says liver is the best bait on earth.
I don't know what effect the burying has on it but I suppose it adds to the
flavor. English are said to have buried their deer meat to make it good. I'd
prefer mine to stay on top of the ground.

We can come home by way of Missouri River and buy a few fish if we
don't catch any in the Blue. I think that is the usual mode of procedure
anyway. . . .

The walks, meanwhile, stretched into marathons. In the fall of
1913, Harry was asking Bess if she had recovered from their most
recent outing. "I am just now up to date," he admitted. A few weeks
later he was warning her: *Be ready to walk Sunday.*

So it went through the fall of 1913 until the first Sunday in November. On that day, three years and five months after they had renewed
their friendship on the porch of 219 Delaware Street, Bess confided to
Harry Truman news that he did not believe at first. She told him that
in the two and a half years since she had rejected his proposal, her
feelings for him had undergone a profound change. She had begun to
think that if she married anyone, he would be the man.

Harry was literally speechless. He could only sit and look at this
golden-haired young woman. Once more, Bess did not know what
to make of him. She found herself wondering again what there was
about this odd mixture of farmer and thinker and humorist and
roughneck who was tempting her to leave the sanctuary of 219 North
Delaware Street to risk disappointment and perhaps worse in an
uncaring world. "Harry Truman," she cried, "you're an enigma!"

Chapter Four

Back in Grandview, Harry got a letter from Bess, which reiterated her change of heart. His answer explained his silence on Sunday—and announced his almost delirious happiness.

Your letter has made a confirmed optimist out of me sure enough. I know now that everything is good and grand and this footstool is a fine place to be. I have been all up in the air, clear above earth ever since it came. I guess you thought I didn't have much sense Sunday, but I just couldn't say anything—only just sit and look. It doesn't seem real that you should care for me. I have always hoped you would but some way feared very much you wouldn't. You know, I've always thought that the best man in the world is hardly good enough for any woman. But when it comes to the best girl in all the universe caring for an ordinary gink like me—well, you'll have to let me get used to it.

Do you want to be a farmer? or shall I do some other business. When Mamma wins her suit and we get all the lawyers and things out of the way I will then have a chance for myself. We intend to raise a four hundred-acre wheat crop, which if it hits will put us out of the woods. If we lose, which I don't think about, it will mean starting all over for me. . . . I sure want to have a decent place to ask you to. I'm hoping it won't be long. I wish it was tomorrow. Let's get engaged anyway to see how it feels. No one need know it but you and me until we get ready to tell it anyway. If you see a man you think more of in the meantime, engagements are easy enough broken. I've always said I'd have you or no one and that's what I mean to do.

Harry's sense of disbelief at his good fortune persisted for the rest of the week and still pervaded his mind during their next date, for which he had tickets to a hit musical, *The Girl from Utah*. Sitting in the theatre, holding Bess's hand, he heard the show's leading man sing a ballad by an up-and-coming new songwriter, Jerome Kern. It's title was: "They'll Never Believe Me." It struck him as uncanny, as he listened to the stage lover tell the leading lady that he could not believe someone so wonderful had fallen in love with him. The words were a perfect summary of Harry's feelings. He would remember the song and the experience for the rest of his life.

Then he recalled Bess's baffled cry and began worrying whether his dream had really come true. "Bess, why am I an enigma?" he asked. "I try to be just what I am and tell the truth about as much as the average person. If there's anything you don't understand, I'll try and explain it or remedy it."

In another letter he tried to explain why he found it hard to express his feelings to her, face to face.

You really didn't know I had so much softness and sentimentality in me, did you? I'm full of it. But I'd die if I had to talk it. I can tell you on paper how much I love you and what one grand woman I think you, but to tell it to you I can't. I'm always afraid I'd do it clumsily and you'd laugh. Then I'd die really. When a person's airing his most sacred thoughts he's very easily distressed. No one ever knew I ever had any but you. You are the one girl I'd ever want to tell them to. I could die happy doing something for you. (Just imagine a guy with spectacles and a girl mouth doing the Sir Lancelot.) Since I can't rescue you from any monster or carry you from a burning building or save you from a sinking ship—simply because I'd be afraid of the monsters, couldn't carry you and can't swim—I'll have to go to work and make money enough to pay my debts and then get you to take me for what I am: just a common everyday man whose instincts are to be ornery, who's anxious to be right. You'll not have any trouble getting along with me for I'm awful good-natured, and I'm sure we'd live happy ever after sure enough. I'm writing this at 1 A.M. just because I can't help it and if you get tired of it . . . put it in the kitchen stove. . . . If you don't like mushy letters, just tell me so. I never had any desire to write them before or to preach my own good points so strongly.

Bess was not entirely pleased by Harry's assurance that if she decided to break their engagement and marry someone else, he would understand. A little tartly, she told him that if he met another girl he liked better, he had the same freedom. Harry insisted this was out of the question. He combined this reiteration of his love with some interesting comments on his ambitions.

You were most awful nice about the other girl but don't suppose they'll ever be one. If a fellow can pick his idol at ten and still be loyal to it at thirty, there's not much danger of his finding another. One or two of my aunties and good matron friends have sought to arrange things for me several times but could never understand why they never had any luck. Maybe they will before long. How does it feel being engaged to a clodhopper who has

ambitions to be Governor of Montana and Chief Executive of U.S. He'll do
well if he gets to be a retired farmer. That sure was a good dream though,
and I have them in the daytime . . . along the same line. It looks like an
uphill business sometimes though. But I intend to keep peggin' away and I
suppose I'll arrive at something. You'll never be sorry if you take me for
better or for worse because I'll always try to make it better.

Although he poured out all this emotion, Harry still signed his
letters "Most sincerely." A reason for this odd hesitation may have
been a worry that he aired at the end of one letter, a few weeks after
Bess told him of her change of heart. "Do you suppose your
mother'll care for me well enough to have me in her family?" By this
time he had been visiting the Wallaces and Gateses long enough to
grasp Madge Gates Wallace's formidable presence in Bess's life and
the lives of her other children. He had also detected Madge's polite,
subtle antagonism to him and his pursuit of her only daughter.

The desire to make some money in a hurry inclined Harry to cast
his eyes beyond Missouri's borders to Montana and Wyoming where
a lucky few got rich mining silver and other metals. Both politics and
business were more wide open there, and this was why he could
entertain thoughts about becoming Montana's governor. But he soon
became more realistic about Montana. "It's such a beautiful climate
up there. Only forty seven below last winter. The wind sometimes
blows sixty miles an hour straight from Alaska."

For a few months it looked like the Truman luck was going to
turn. Early in 1914, the lawsuit was settled in Mamma Truman's
favor, and for the first time in five years they could feel secure about
their farm. Harry promptly borrowed $600 from Mamma Truman
and invested in a 1911 Stafford, an open touring car made in Kansas
City. Detroit was not yet the auto capital of America. The Stafford
was a pretty spiffy car. New, it sold for over $2,000—a huge price in
1914. There were ads for lesser cars in the Jackson *Examiner* for as
little as $490, but Harry wanted a car that Bess Wallace would be
proud to ride in.

The Stafford made the trip to Independence a lot easier, although
for the first few weeks, until Harry mastered his machine, it did not
seem that way. Harry had stalls by the dozen and blowouts by the
half dozen. At one point he spent ten minutes cranking the motor
and then the handle flew off the crankshaft, spraining his wrist and
banging his head against the radiator. "When you have an auto, there
is nothing else to cuss about," Harry remarked.

But the car was worth the early pain and suffering. It gave Harry

and Bess a marvelous sense of freedom. Bouncing along the mostly
dirt roads at twenty miles an hour, they picnicked all over Jackson
County on Sundays, often taking Frank Wallace and his steady girl, a
dark, tiny beauty named Natalie Ott, with them. George Wallace
also was a frequent member of the group. He had become very
serious about a pretty, cheerful young lady named May Southern,
daughter of the publisher of the local newspaper.

The Stafford also gave Harry a sense of power. When Bess told
him that she was considering a visit to some Gates cousins in San
Francisco, he announced that if she stayed too long, he was going to
buy 150 gallons of gas and drive out to see her. He figured it would
take him two weeks, but he could afford it if he managed not to eat
en route. Bess decided not to go, so that crisis was averted.

At the wedding of a Truman relative, Virginia Kritely, Harry met
Bess's grandmother, Virginia Willock Wallace, and her cousin, the
town librarian, Carrie Wallace. Mrs. Wallace kissed Harry before the
houseful of guests and said she conferred such favors on all her
relatives. "I nearly shrank to nothing," he said. But he obviously
enjoyed telling Bess the story.

Then came an unexpected blow. John Truman strained himself
trying to move a huge boulder while working as road overseer. The
strain aggravated a hernia from which he had been suffering for
years, closing the lower part of his stomach. He was sixty-three, old
for an operation in 1914, but there was no other choice. He survived
the surgery but slowly slipped away in the fall of that year, dying on
November 3. Harry was devastated by the loss. He felt guilty about
the antagonism that had flared between him and his father when he
began spending so much time in Independence.

Bess was a vital presence in Harry's life during this difficult period.
She wrote him a letter that "helped out wonderfully." The letter has
been lost, alas, but I suspect she shared some of the pain she felt at her
father's death. Nothing could have been more helpful to Harry than
to learn that Bess too had complicated and even more heartbreaking
feelings about her father. She let him talk about how badly he missed
John Truman, to the point of belittling his own ability as a farmer.
"I've been in the habit of running the farm, but Papa always made it
go," he said. Harry praised his father's ability to drive a sharp bargain
when he was selling horses or cows, where before he had deplored it.
It was grief at work, and Bess helped Harry bear it.

During the three trying months of his father's illness, Harry had little time for Bess. She occasionally went out with other men in Independence, no doubt among the thinning ranks of bachelors from the old Delaware Street crowd. Bess felt compelled to tell Harry about these dates. She hoped he would not be jealous, because there was nothing for him to worry about. She may have told him about the exchange Mary Paxton once had with Elmer Twyman. Mary asked him why so few of them had married within the crowd. "Maybe we all liked each other too much," Elmer said.

Harry's reply made it clear that the essential Harry Truman was emerging from his grief, intact. "You needn't ever be afraid of my being jealous of your having a good time with some other fellow. . . . It's my opinion that when people come to the point where they are jealous of each other (which is nothing more nor less than distrust) it is time to quit. I never intend to arrive at that stage myself—i.e., I never intend to quit."

While Bess and Harry were struggling to achieve some happiness in their small private world, history was rumbling in the distance. Although they never mentioned it in their letters, a horrendous war had begun in Europe in August 1914, around the time that John Truman became ill. Germans and Frenchmen and Englishmen and Russians began slaughtering each other by the tens of thousands. It is amazing to read the Jackson *Examiner* for this period and see how little attention Missouri paid to World War I during these early days. It is barely mentioned at all, and never on the front page. For people living in the center of the immense continent of North America, it all seemed very far away.

Bess was much more interested in the travails of the Trumans— and the renewed adventures of Mary Paxton, who had recovered from her breakdown after two and a half years in Mississippi. On the advice of the dean of the University of Missouri School of Journalism, Mary decided to become a specialist. She took a masters in home economics at the University of Chicago and then discovered that there was more opportunity for someone with this degree in public education. She got a job with the U.S. Department of Agriculture as a district home demonstration agent. Operating from Roanoke, Virginia, she supervised a large staff of county agents who taught farm wives how to run their homes more economically and how to feed their families more nutritiously. It was very hard work. She traveled as much as 1,000 miles a week and seldom slept in the same bed more than one night.

During Mary's absence, Bess had become a good friend of Mary's younger sister, Libby. Both Paxton girls also had a tender, touching, relationship with Madge Gates Wallace. Apparently, they never stopped yearning for the mother they had lost in 1903, and Mrs. Wallace was a substitute with whom they corresponded and to whom they often sent Christmas presents.

Libby was as independent as and even more headstrong than her sister Mary. She too wanted a career, and when Mary offered to get her a job as a county agent in Virginia she leaped at the opportunity. Once there, she discovered she did not at all like working for her older sister. A violent conflict ensued, which Bess was asked to referee by mail. Bess firmly sided with her fellow older sister. She told Mary that she was "afraid [Libby] thinks she can do as she pleases under you. Yet it's a question whether anybody else would put up with her." Libby solved the problem by falling in love and getting married.

Other friends wrote to Bess from Illinois, Michigan, California, New York. The letters make it clear that she still had her father's gift for winning people's affection. She was particularly close to her first cousins, Louise Gates Wells, her Aunt Maud's daughter, and Helen Wallace, Aunt Myra's daughter. Myra had married a Kansas City lawyer named Boulware Wallace, who was not related to the Independence Wallaces. All these women were around the same age, and marriage was on all their minds. One letter, written from Lexington, Kentucky, by a bridge club member, Nelle Rugg, reported that a mutual friend had been asking when Bess and Harry were going to get married. "I told her *we* hadn't set the date yet but that *he* had given you a sparkler for Xmas."

I fear that Nelle was tippling some Kentucky moonshine when she wrote that one—or teasing the nosy friend. Harry Truman did not have the money to buy a diamond. But everyone was obviously watching and waiting for the sound of wedding bells on North Delaware Street. No one was more eager to hear them than Harry Truman. But first he had to get his hands on some "dirty pelf." For a while 1915 looked like a promising year. The war in Europe had created thousands of jobs in American factories, and farm prices rose with the booming economy.

But Harry's hopes were shadowed by the $12,500 debt that he had assumed when he became his father's partner in J. A. Truman & Son, the company they had formed to run the farm. When his father died, he became responsible for the full amount. Yet even this sum could be cleared if they "hit" with a bumper harvest. "Things look fine. . . . If the crops only turn out as well as they appear now, there won't be anything to worry about," he wrote to Bess in April 1915.

Alas, by July there was plenty to worry about. This time, instead of a drought there was its opposite, torrential rains. Ditches and furrows filled with water, making it difficult to cut the wheat. In the moisture, another enemy, the Hessian fly, a tiny parasite that had been ruining wheat since Revolutionary days, flourished. To worsen matters totally, Missouri's old rival, Kansas, had perfect weather and a stupendous wheat crop, which drove prices down everywhere. By November, a discouraged Harry Truman was again looking beyond Jackson County's borders for a rainbow with some gold at the end of it.

First he dashed to Texas, hoping to find cheaper land where he could expand his chances of making big money fast. He told Bess that he could clear $25,000 in three years and still have enough left over to own a farm worth $150 an acre, if he could only persuade his Uncle Harrison to put up the money to get him started. But Uncle Harrison seemed mainly interested in having a good time with his money. For several years, Harry had been dragging him out of half the saloons in Kansas City. Bess, who knew from cruel experience how little confidence anyone can put in an alcoholic's promises, must have begun to wonder if she would ever become Mrs. Harry Truman.

Making her unhappiness more acute was the marriage of her brother Frank to Natalie Ott, in March 1915. George Wallace was very close to repeating the performance with May Southern. Nothing could make an older sister more uneasy than the marriage of younger brothers. It gave Bess the distinct feeling that she was on her way to becoming an old maid. Then there was her mother, always there to solicit her companionship, to suggest, however subtly, that maybe it did not matter if Harry Truman failed. Without ever quite saying it, Madge Wallace hinted in her oblique elegiac way that it might be better for all concerned if Bess lived out her youth as her mother's companion, endlessly solacing her grief, wordlessly commemorating the tragedy they shared.

The power of Madge's influence in the family became visible when Frank and George Wallace married. Madge persuaded her father to divide the garden and give her sons two lots on which he built virtually identical bungalows. There they began their wedded lives,

under their mother's direct observation. They and their wives soon
learned that Madge Wallace never went to bed until all the lights in
these two houses were out. She never permitted either wife to walk
past 219 North Delaware Street without emerging to ask where she
was going. It was not done in a tyrannical way or with a nasty tone of
voice. Madge Wallace was still a lady. Words of endearment, a gentle
smile accompanied the question. But it was very clear to both
women that their husbands were never going to be permitted to leave
their mother's presence, as long as she lived.

If this was how Madge Wallace regarded her sons, it is not hard to
imagine how intense was her attachment to her only daughter. Nor is
it hard for me to imagine—because in this case I saw, in later years,
the persistence of the antagonism—her dislike of Harry Truman, the
farmer who was threatening to take her daughter away from her.
That Bess Wallace was able to resist this steady, subtle but oh-so-
powerful opposition to the man she had come to love after so much
hesitation is a tribute to her strength of character—and to the power
of Harry Truman's love.

Early in 1916, after he had been informally engaged to Bess for
two and a half years, Harry sent her a cry of the heart, if there ever
was one.

Nearly every time I see you I want to urge you to throw prudence to the
winds and take me anyway just as things are . . . and then I think of all the
debts I am saddled with and of my present inability even to buy you a decent
ring and I haven't the nerve to do it.

Then I see myself in an ideal country home with everything as it should
be and you to run it and me and it's almost unbearable to wait. Then I wake
up and see our old house going to wreck for want of painting and repairs
because I must pay interest on a debt I had no hand in making and my dream
has to keep waiting.

He could only beg her "to keep backing me to win through and I
will."

This plea was repeated with varying phrases throughout the rest of
1916. Abandoning Texas and Uncle Harrison, who was rapidly
drinking himself into his grave, Harry next tried to strike it rich in a
lead-and-zinc mine. His brother Vivian's father-in-law had made
over $100,000 in one of these ventures, and together they talked
Harry into investing $11,000 of borrowed money into a mine near
Commerce, Oklahoma.

The Truman luck stayed bad. Everything that could possibly go wrong with a mine proceeded to do so. The market price of metals sank, the machinery failed, the workers were unreliable. The men Harry had hired to run the farm in Grandview quit, and he had to rush back and harvest the crops. But Bess refused to lose faith in him. She sent him letters that made him "see rainbows in the darkest kind of sky." When the mine finally quit for good, he was able to write: "If you still have faith in my poor judgment I can still win."

Then he added one of those Trumanesque comments on life that had a lot to do with Bess Wallace keeping her faith in him. "You know a man's judgment is good or bad accordingly as he wins or loses on a proposition. It seems to me that it's one big guess and the fellow who guesses right is the man of good judgment."

Absorbed in Harry's struggle, they still ignored the war in Europe in their letters. By now it had been raging for almost two years. Even local papers such as the *Examiner* began carrying stories on it. One Independence resident was serving with the British army and sent letters to friends that were published in the paper. The Kansas City *Star* and the other papers of the metropolis covered it even more extensively. But most Missourians shared the opinion of the state's congressional delegation, that the United States should stay out of it. Missouri's senior senator, William J. Stone, had grown famous for denouncing Woodrow Wilson's flirtation with intervention on the allied side. Harry Truman's political hero, William Jennings Bryan, had resigned as Secretary of State to protest Wilson's policies.

Bess and Harry probably discussed the war when they were together. All his life, Harry had been fascinated by military history, and he followed the great battles being fought in France, Russia, and Turkey with intense interest. But they had no special enthusiasm for either side. A glimpse of their typically Missourian neutrality emerges from a letter he wrote Bess about her dog.

While he was mining lead and zinc in Oklahoma, he was also raising a greyhound that Bess had acquired somewhere. When he brought him home from the defunct mine, he was calling him Don Juan of Austria, after the hero of the battle of Lepanto. But he remarked that Bess could easily change his name. "If you are an English sympathizer, you could hardly call him anything Austrian. . . . You could call him Kitchen (short for Kitchener) [the English general]. You could even name him Willy [after William Jennings Bryan] and be Democratically right."

But the drumbeat of history refused to stay out of their lives, no matter what they thought and felt about it. The war dominated the presidential campaign of 1916 in which Woodrow Wilson ran for reelection against Chief Justice Charles Evans Hughes. Wilson won by carrying California by 3,773 squeaky votes. The embittered Republican regulars had refused to give the nomination to Theodore Roosevelt, because of his bolt from the party in 1912. Teddy had been calling the President everything from a coward to a hypocrite for what he considered Wilson's halfhearted support of the Allies. Roosevelt's abuse stirred a lukewarm sympathy for Wilson in Missouri. But as Harry Truman's letter casually demonstrated, it was a long way from enthusiastic support.

Meanwhile, Harry went from lead-and-zinc mining into the oil business. His finances had been improved by a sad but not unexpected event, the death of his Uncle Harrison. The old bachelor left his share of the Young farm to Harry, his mother, and sister. With the farm for collateral, Harry was able to raise enough money to go into business with Kansas City attorney Jerry Culbertson (who had been a partner in the zinc mine) and an oil speculator named David H. Morgan, who was sure there were millions to be made from oil beneath the farmlands of Kansas and Oklahoma.

They formed a company and began selling shares of stock. One of the first investors was Bess Wallace. I do not know how much she invested or where she got the money—she may have borrowed it from her grandfather. But it was another example of her faith in Harry Truman. There were plenty of other investors, thanks to the war-stimulated economy. In January 1917, Harry was excitedly reporting to Bess that "the money is coming in by the basketful."

They were taking in as much as $1,500 a day, and he proudly informed her that her shares now owned a refinery and leases on some 15,000 acres of promising oil land. "Hope to call you and say we're over the rocks soon," he wrote. "Here's wishing you all the happiness on earth and hoping to share it."

By March 1917, a few weeks after Bess's thirty-second birthday, things look sufficiently promising to discuss an engagement announcement in the spring and marriage in the fall. Bess excitedly informed her closest friends of the good news. Louise Gates Wells, who was living in New York, replied with a spritely letter to "Dearest Bess(ie)." She was "delighted to hear that you were thinking of matrimony in a most serious fashion." In her opinion, "Cousin

Harry . . . is about the luckiest chap alive, not because of his investment prospects but the other prospects." Another friend, Catherine
Woodson, sent her congratulations and remarked that if she were a
man, Harry would have had her as a rival. Mary Paxton was less
ebullient, but more intimate. "I was surprised," she wrote. "I don't
believe your mother will ever be used to doing without you."

Another comment in Mary's letter makes it even clearer that Bess
was planning to leave 219 North Delaware Street. "I know you will
love living on the farm," Mary wrote. "I expect to have a farm some
day but I don't know whether I will buy one or marry one." These
words clarify a passing comment that Harry Truman made around
this time. He said he yearned "to build me a bungalow." He was
obviously going to build a separate house on the Grandview farm
and commute to Kansas City to help run the Morgan Oil Company.
This made very good sense. A man was needed on the farm to make
sure the hired hands did their jobs.

But the drumbeat of history was booming louder in the lives of
Harry Truman and Bess Wallace as these joyous hopes were rising.
Although Woodrow Wilson had been reelected on the slogan, "He
kept us out of war," he took an increasingly confrontational position
against the Central Powers, Germany and Austria. He began expand-
ing the army and navy. Shortly before his second inauguration, he
made it clear that if Germany resumed unrestricted submarine warfare, and sank American merchant ships, the United States would
declare war. Germany promptly announced it was going to do exactly that and gamble on bringing the Allies to their knees before
America could organize an army large enough to make a difference.

Woodrow Wilson sent a declaration of war to Congress on April 2,
1917. One of Missouri's senators and four of her congressmen voted
against it. But that was irrelevant as far as Harry Truman and Bess
Wallace were concerned. Almost instantly, the value of the stock in
the Morgan Oil Company sank to zero. There was no manpower
available to sink wells on the land they had leased and the stream of
money from investors dried up. Harry Truman was enormously
discouraged.

I seem to have a grand and admirable ability for calling tails when heads
come up. My luck should surely change. Sometime I should win. I have
tried to stick. Worked, really did, like thunder for ten years to get that old
farm in line for some big production. Have it in shape and have a crop
failure every year. Thought I'd change my luck, got a mine, and see what I

did get. Tried again in the other long chance, oil. Still have high hopes on that, but then I'm naturally a hopeful happy person, one of the "Books in brooks, Tongues in trees and Good in everything" sort of guy. . . . I was very impressionable when I was a kid and I believed all the Sunday school books and idealist dope we were taught and it's taken me twenty odd years to find out that Mark [Twain] is right when he says that the boy who stole the jam and lied about it and killed the cat and sassed his ma, grew up and became a highly honored citizen. . . . The poor gink who stands around and waits for someone to find out his real worth just naturally continues to stand, but the gink who toots his horn and tells 'em how good he is makes 'em believe it when they know he's a bluff and would steal from his grandma.

I don't believe that. I'm just feeling that way now. If I can't win straight, I'll continue to lose. I'm the luckiest guy in the world to have you to love and to know that when I've arrived at a sensible solution to these direful financial difficulties I've gotten into, that I'll have the finest, best-looking, and all the other adjectives in the superlative girl in the world to make the happiest home in the world with. Now isn't that a real heaven on earth to contemplate? I think it is and I know I'll have just that in the not far off future, unless it is necessary for me to get myself shot in this war—and then I'll find you somewhere. I dreamt that you and I were living in Rome when togas were the fashion. I am always dreaming of you. I'm never anywhere in a dream or out of it that I don't imagine you there too. Last night I thought I was in an airplane in France. I fell about 17,000 feet and didn't get much hurt and I was idiot enough to weep because I couldn't see you in the hospital. It seemed that you were outside and they wouldn't let you in. Some dream, what? (I had a cheese omlet for supper.) I'm going to eat one every night.

Those comments about the war warned Bess Wallace that Harry Truman was finding it very difficult to ignore the appeals to patriotism and courage that President Woodrow Wilson was issuing in Washington. Years later, Harry recalled that he was "stirred heart and soul" by these war messages. Bess was soon dismayed to learn that Harry had rejoined the Missouri National Guard. (He had let his original enlistment lapse in 1911.) He threw himself into the local effort to expand Kansas City's Battery B and Independence's Battery C into a regiment. As a former member of the guard, he was ideally suited to this task. He recruited so many men that he was elected a first lieutenant of a new Battery, F.

Although Frank and George Wallace were both younger than thirty-three-year-old Harry Truman, neither enlisted. I am certain that their mother was the reason. A woman who would not permit married sons to move off her family's property could not bear the thought of them going to war in distant France. Bess struggled to support Harry's decision but it was very, very hard to accept. Madge Wallace undoubtedly used all her mournful guile to make him look uncaring and indifferent.

For a month Bess managed to control a dangerous mixture of anger and disappointment. She told herself that there were millions of other women in America going through the same experience. But she had waited so long and marriage had seemed so certain. In six months she would be thirty-three years old. Many people were predicting the war would last at least four years. She might be too old to have a child when Harry Truman came back—if he came back.

She tried to conceal her feelings from Harry. But they burst out one night in July. A week later he wrote to her, admitting that he had "felt like a dog" for the past seven days. "It seems I have caused you to be unhappy by my overenthusiastic action in getting myself sent to war." Another woman about whom he cared deeply had had a similar reaction.

Two big tears came in Mamma's eyes last night when I started off to Lodge in my soldier clothes. You are the two people in the world I would rather see smile and that I like to cause to smile and here I've gone done the opposite to both of you. Perhaps I can make you all happier for it. I'll try my best. Some way I seem to have an ability for getting myself into things by my overzealous conduct or anxiety to see them a success and do not see the consequences for myself or others until the conclusion comes.

For a while Harry tried to disguise the seriousness of his decision. He told Bess that it was not yet certain that all the national guard units would be incorporated in the new U.S. Army immediately. They might not have room for them and the hundreds of thousands of men the government was drafting. His bad eyes might keep him out of combat. The Russians, who had had a democratic revolution and kicked out the Czar, were launching a massive offensive that might win the war in a month or two.

Harry must have known he was trying to avoid the moment of truth. He was already in uniform, living in a tent city opposite the Kansas City Convention Hall. On August 11, 1917, he could no longer disguise his commitment. "I have some news for you that perhaps you won't consider good," he wrote. "The Federal Mustering Officer passed me into the service of the United States today. I

am accepted and have to go. I will have to confess that I am not very
sorry, because I have been crazy to be a military man almost since I
can remember."

It is a sad letter. I found my eyes filling with tears as I read it. I am
sure Bess wept far more copious tears. "I wish I was in your backyard," Lieutenant Truman blurts at one point. Then he writes a
whole paragraph full of pride about the way he has learned to drill
the battery. Although Harry Truman joked about letting her "run
him," Bess was discovering that she was in love with a man who
could insist on doing things his way.

In spite of her turmoil, Bess remained committed to Harry. Early
in that history-filled summer of 1917, she asked her mother to announce her engagement. A long subterranean struggle came to a
climax in this encounter. In many ways the situation, the nation at
war and Harry Truman, still far from a financial success, embroiled
in it against her deepest wishes, made Bess more vulnerable. But it
also made her decision more formidable, more final. She was not
doing this because Harry Truman had finally made some money or
had pleased her in some other extraordinary way. She was doing it
even though he had displeased her. She was doing it because she
loved him.

Bess handed her mother a piece of paper she had picked up when
she went to visit Harry in Kansas City. It was the instruction page for
a form women filled out to register for war service. On the back, the
following words were written in Harry Truman's bold scrawl: "Mrs.
David W. Wallace of Independence announces the engagement of her
daughter, Elizabeth Virginia, to Lieutenant Harry S. Truman of the
Second Missouri Field Artillery." Sixty-five years later I found that
piece of paper in the attic at 219 North Delaware Street. Bess knew
that it was one of the most important documents in her life.

Chapter Five

By this time, Harry Truman had decided that they could not be married in the fall of 1917. He explained his decision in one of the most emotional letters he ever wrote.

Bess, I'm dead crazy to ask you to marry me before I leave but I'm not going to because I don't think it would be right for me to ask you to tie yourself to a prospective cripple—or a sentiment. You, I know, would love me just as much, perhaps more, with one hand as with two, but I don't think I should cause you to do it. Besides, if the war ends happily and I can steal the Russian or German crown jewels, just think what a grand military wedding you can have, get a major general maybe.

If you don't marry me before I go, you may be sure that I'll be just as loyal to you as if you were my wife, and I'll not try to exact any promises from you either if you want to go with any other guy, why all right, but I'll be as jealous as the mischief although not begrudging you the good time.

Bess, this is a crazy letter but I'm crazy about you and I can't say all these nutty things to you without making you weep. When you weep, I want to. If you'd looked right closely the other night, you might have discovered it, and a weeping man is an abomination unto the Lord. All I ask is love me always and if I have to be shot I'll try and not have it in the back or before a stone wall because I'm afraid not to do you honor.

Other officers in the Battery were married—Captain Spencer Salisbury, for instance. He was the brother of Bess's good friend, Agnes Salisbury. Lieutenant Kenneth Bostian, brother of Bess's tennis partner, Bill Bostian, had just married Agnes's younger sister, Mary. Harry mentioned that these wives had come to a Battery picnic the preceding Saturday, but he had not invited Bess because "I was afraid you wouldn't come."

He added that he was sending Bess a picture of him. "It is in uniform, I am sorry to say, but I can't appear as a plain citizen any more until the war is over. If you don't like it you can tear it up or send it to Mamma."

Those words suggest just how serious Harry feared the rift between them might become. Wistfully, he asked her if she could drive by Convention Hall sometime and watch him drill the Battery. "Some of the other officers have an audience sometimes."

Bess did not tear up Harry's picture. At his request, she returned the favor by sending him her picture, a very special one on which she and the photographer lavished a great deal of care. It is my favorite picture of Bess. I have always considered it a remarkable study in character. The photographer had the instincts of an artist. He caught Bess Wallace's unique blend of strength and femininity, and he also captured the regret and doubt that were troubling her in that tumultuous year. There is no smile on her face. She looks straight at the camera, as she had forced herself to look at life—serious, determined but not uncaring. I also see, now, a vulnerability that I never saw before.

The inscription on the back of the picture was a kind of prayer. It also marked the beginning of Bess Wallace's decades of worrying about Harry Truman's fondness for living dangerously. "Dear Harry, May this photograph bring you safely home again from France—Bess."

The men of the 129th Field Artillery were soon on their way to Camp Doniphan, near Lawton, Oklahoma. Bess and Harry Truman were back to relying on the mails for communication. Just as he had throughout his travails as farmer, miner, and oil speculator, he kept her informed about the most minute details of his army experience, from branding horses to washing socks by hand. She was able to all but live his success as operator of the regimental canteen, which drew him into frequent conferences with his colonel. He and a friend named Eddie Jacobson teamed up to run the most profitable canteen in the camp, and possibly in the U.S. Army.

Although he was a soldier, he was still a tenderhearted man, who hated to hurt anyone and was deeply distressed when he was forced to do it, even for the best of reasons.

I caught one of my men stealing money out of the cash drawer [of the canteen] night before last and had him put in the guardhouse. It took me all afternoon yesterday to draw up the charges. I guess he'll get about two years. I backed him into a corner and made him admit that he took the money. He had ten dollars in one pocket and three dollars in another, and two in another, and three in another. Did it all in about an hour. I was at school [artillery school] when the canteen steward came up and called me out and told me about it. They say the poor fellow is a good soldier but so much money in sight all at once was too much for him.

Bess's picture did a lot to restore Harry's confidence in her affection. He stopped closing his letters with "Most Sincerely," and began to use "Lovingly," or "Yours always." He told her there was "Nothin' but Indians in Lawton, and ugly ones at that, so you have no reason for thinking that anyone else but you ever enters my thoughts. You wouldn't have anyway if all the Lillian Russells and Pauline Fredericks in this Republic were down here for I don't like but one style of beauty and that's yours.

"You should send me two letters the day you get this one for that last remark."

That page Bess brought home telling her how to register for war service was no accident. She volunteered to sell war bonds and was soon assigned to canvass the citizens of Blue Township, not far from Independence. She also joined the wives and fiancées of other members of the 129th regiment in a woman's auxiliary, which held regular meetings to entertain themselves and compare notes on what the men needed. In the following year—1918—she served on an Independence committee that welcomed and entertained visiting soldiers from Fort Leavenworth.

What really pleased Harry was the time and attention Bess gave to Mamma Truman and his sister, Mary. Bess arranged for Mary to be elected secretary of the Woman's Auxiliary, and visited Mamma Truman at the farm. When she sent Mamma Truman a picture, she got a delightful little note, which she enjoyed enough to save. Mamma thanked her for the gift and then chatted about how she got along while Mary was away for several nights, no doubt on a trip connected with her growing involvement in the Eastern Star, the woman's counterpart of the Masons. Mamma mentioned a cousin who had visited one night and then remarked: "I guess the Nolands are all dead. They have never spoken a word to Mary or me since Harry left." She ended the letter with: "Come out."

Along with selling Liberty bonds, Bess coped with wartime shortages of such commodities as sugar, flour, coal. She also had to cope with her mother's anxiety when her brother Frank Wallace was called in the draft. She shared this worry with Harry, who wrote: "Hope Frank will be blind the day of the exam." He knew that in many ways Frank was as essential to Madge Wallace's well-being as Bess. Every

day when he came home from work, Frank visited 219 North Delaware and spent a half hour with his mother.

Frank failed the eye test and stayed home for the time being. But
another of Bess's brothers, George, was also on the draft rolls and
was certain to pass when called. If the war lasted long enough,
Frank's eyes would not keep him out either. In the salty Missouri
slang of my Aunt May, George's widow, with whom I have spent
many hours discussing the early years of Bess's life, Madge Wallace
"went up in smoke" at the thought of her sons going to France. Bess
had to put aside her own more complicated anxiety about Harry
Truman and spend hours calming and reassuring her mother.

Bess continued to correspond with Mary Paxton, and as usual, the
letters were lively. Toward the end of 1917, Mary remarked: "I can
sympathize with you about Harry because I sent the nicest man in the
world to France about two days ago." A few months later, another
letter brought really startling news: "I am a pretty happy person. I am
accepted for canteen work YMCA overseas. . . . If they have a service flag in the church tell them to put a star in it for me and tell Mr.
Plunkett [the Episcopal minister] to please say some prayers for me
when I am on the ocean.

"I am trying to make it as easy as I can for one man who loves me
too much and trying to make it as hard as I can for one man who
does not love me enough."

Mary obviously had mastered the art of multiple romances. She
was determined not to risk all her feelings with one man again.
Although Bess had chosen a different route to happiness, she never
uttered a word of reproach or criticism to Mary. Perhaps she knew
that Mary was too headstrong to take advice, even from her.

Harry Truman too was moving inexorably toward France. There
were several false starts. At one point the Battery had everything
packed and the canteen closed down, and their departure was canceled. Everyone was discouraged, and Harry moaned that they
might yet get "benzined" [dismissed from the army] and sent home.
He did not really believe it and was soon trying to keep up Bess's
spirits by describing the war as a moral crusade as well as a rare
opportunity to participate in the history of their times.

We heard a lecture by an English colonel from the Western Front last night
and it sure put the pep into us. He made us all want to brace up and go to it
with renewed energy. He made us feel like we were fighting for you and
mother earth and I am of the same belief. I wouldn't be left out of the

greatest history making epoch the world has ever seen for all there is to live for because there'd be nothing to live for under German control. When we come home a victorious army we can hold our heads up in the greatest old country on earth and make up for lost time by really living. Don't you think that would be better than to miss out entirely? I am crazy to get it over with though because I wouldn't cause you a heartache for all there is in the world.

Another time, Harry and a small group of other officers and men were supposed to rush to the East Coast to catch a ship to France for a special assignment. The orders were canceled at the last minute and they learned a few weeks later that the ship had been torpedoed off the coast of Ireland. Harry tried to make light of it.

Don't you worry about what's going to happen to me because there's not a bullet molded for me nor has Neptune any use for me. Had I been on the boat that went down, I'd have been in Dublin by this time with some Irish woman at a dance (if she looked like you) or taking a look for the man who invented corks and corkscrews. Ireland's a great country so they say. . . .

She also participated through Harry's letters in his struggle to win promotion to captain. He told her about his appearance before an examining board headed by a terrible-tempered general named Berry and his narrow escape from the medical officer, who thought his eyes were so bad he wanted to send him to division headquarters. Lieutenant Truman talked him out of it. In another letter he gave her a fascinating inside glimpse of army life, along with some good news about his promotion.

I got an underground intimation that I passed my captain's examination all right. I don't believe it though until I see the evidence from Washington. I am telling you only because I thought maybe it would be nice to share good news with you if it is only a rumor, and I know you won't kid me about it if it's false. To tell you the honest truth I'd rather be a first lieutenant than anything else in the army except a buck private in the rear rank. He's the guy that has no responsibility and he's the guy that does the real work. I heard a good one the other day which said that a lieutenant knows nothing and does everything, a captain knows everything and does nothing, a major knows nothing and does nothing. Very true except that a captain has to know everything from sealing wax to sewing machines and has to run them. He also is responsible for about $750,000 worth of materiel and 193 men, their lives, their morals, their clothes, and their horses, which isn't much for $200 a month and pay your own expenses. I shall probably get the swell head just as all captains do if I get it, and it will be lots better for me if I don't. . . .

Then came a telegram that must have made Bess wonder about her resolution to share all aspects of the life of the man she loved.

WE ARE MOVING TODAY. YOUR PACKAGE CAME ALL RIGHT AND WAS VERY FINE. WILL WRITE YOU FROM TRAIN. HARRY S. TRUMAN

At 5 A.M. on March 21, 1918, the telephone rang at 219 North Delaware Street. It was Lieutenant Harry Truman calling from a railroad phone in Kansas City, where the troop train had stopped to change engines. The switchman who let him use the phone said: "If she doesn't break the engagement at five o'clock in the morning, she really loves you." The engagement stayed unbroken.

When Harry reached New York, he got a telegram from Bess, asking him for a picture. She even told him where to go—White's, one of the best photographers in the city. Harry sensed what she was thinking, or, to put it more exactly, fearing. "Don't you worry about me not taking care of myself. . . . I'm going to use my brains, if I have any, for Uncle Sam's best advantage and I'm going to aim to keep them in good working order, which can't be done by stopping bullets."

Harry tried to cheer her up with a lively letter from his room at the Hotel McAlpin in New York.

Would you believe it? I am here at this joint along with four other Missouri guys. We are having the time of our innocent young lives lookin' out the window up Broadway. . . . Got up this morning [at Camp Merritt, New Jersey] had breakfast of ham and eggs at a cafeteria in the camp, and then got permission to come to the city. Got a taxi, five of us did, and drove thirteen miles to 130th Street, rode the ferry across, and then began hunting for the subway downtown. They told us it was only a block from the ferry. We walked around and hunted and finally decided to take the elevated, which was nearby about four stories up. Well the elevated turned out to be the subway! The devilish thing runs out of the ground about 120th Street and runs over a low place on stilts. We couldn't recognize it as the subway. We have all had shines, shaves, baths, and are now in here to go to church somewhere this afternoon. We haven't decided whether it will be Al Jolson or George Cohan.

In France, letter by letter, Bess followed Harry through the exhausting ordeal of another, tougher artillery school, where he got to be so good at "trig and logs," as he called it (that's trigonometry and logarithms), that he was made an instructor. Then came even better news. On June 14, 1918, he wrote: "I am back with the regiment and a sure enough captain." It had taken six weeks for his promotion to catch up with him so he had "about a bushel and a half of francs back pay coming next payday."

Even better news followed exactly a month later. "I have attained my one ambition, to be a Battery commander. If I can only make good at it, I can hold my head up anyway for the rest of my days."

Subsequent letters revealed that this promotion was a mixed blessing. Battery D was composed mostly of Irish-Catholics from Kansas City. Contrary to earlier versions of their background, they were not all lower class mugs by any means. Many of them were college men but they all shared a fondness for breaking any and every army regulation on the books. They had already ruined three captains before Harry Truman got them. Nevertheless, in a week he was reporting more good news to Bess.

They gave me a Battery that was always in trouble and in bad, but we carried off all the credits this week. I hope to make a reputation for myself if the cards fall right and I don't get wounded or something. It is the Irish Battery I have and the adjutant has decided to put an O in front of my name to make me right. They seem to want to soldier for me and if I can get them to do it, I shall consider that I have made the greatest success there is to make. If I fail, it'll be a great failure too. That's always the case though. The men are as fine a bunch as were ever gotten together but they have been lax in discipline. Can you imagine me being a hard-boiled captain of a tough Irish Battery? I started things in a rough-cookie fashion. The very first man that was up before me for a lack of discipline got everything I was capable of giving. I took the Battery out to fire the next day and they were so anxious to please me and fire good that one of my gunners got the ague and simply blew up. I had to take him out. When I talked to him about it he almost wept and I felt so sorry for him I didn't even call him down. Tell George [Wallace] that little Higginbotham is one of my shootin' men. He pulls the hammer on No. 1 gun and he sure rides it. The other day it nearly bucked him off.

Bess matched Harry letter for letter. One day he got four—and a box of candy from Paris on which was written: "Sent by order of Miss Bess Wallace, Independence, Kansas City, Mo." Along with worrying her man through France, she had to cope with a family crisis at 219 North Delaware Street. Her grandfather was dying. Her mother all but collapsed at the thought of losing the one man who had sustained her. George P. Gates had been ill since early in 1918, suffering largely from the complications of old age. (He was eighty-two.) On June 26, 1918, he died. For Bess, too, it was a wrenching loss. A strong, genial, loving presence vanished from her life.

The loss also triggered considerable anxiety. Her grandfather left his wife Elizabeth an annuity, so she was financially secure. But the rest of his modest estate was divided between his five children. Madge Wallace received $23,247.39—not enough to support her and Bess and her youngest son, Fred, whom Madge had resolved to send to the University of Missouri, for more than a few years. If Harry Truman was killed in action, Bess's future would be bleak.

We know, now, that he was not killed. But the coming months and years of Bess Wallace's future were as opaque and threatening to her, in 1918, as they were to the women who sent men to all the other wars of our century. She threw herself into her war bond sales work and put a star in the flag of the Episcopal Church for Harry, even though he was a Baptist who seldom went to church. In her letters she shared some of her deepest feelings with him. She revealed how awful she had felt when he came to a Fourth of July party in his uniform in the summer of 1917. It is interesting that it took her an entire year to tell him this. As he neared combat, she seemed to want to let him know that her pain at the thought of losing him had been acute from the start.

Letters from another friend with a strange (but in my opinion lovely) name reveal that Bess was afraid that she might have a nervous breakdown in 1918. Arry Ellen Mayer had grown fond of Bess and vice versa when her family moved to North Delaware Street from Kansas City. When they moved again, this time to Toronto, Canada, the two young women began a heavy correspondence. Bess saved dozens of Arry's letters, almost as many as those of Mary Paxton. Where Mary was intense and dramatic, Arry was cheerful and high-spirited. She obviously gave Bess an emotional lift. But she was also close enough to let her write frankly.

"Don't for heaven's sake get nerves," Arry wrote in response to Bess's fear that she might have a breakdown. "They are the meanest things on earth and the only cure is a complete rest. And I know how you'd hate that. So do get rid of them quick, please." Arry cheered her by reporting that Canadian friends wrote from France that the Germans could not hold out much longer. "Take care of yourself," Arry wrote, "for you know . . . you want to be ready for a glorious time when Harry comes home. It's so splendid of him to be going—"

This was a sentiment Bess was not hearing at 219 North Delaware. Other letters reveal Bess's interest in Arry's romantic experiences. When she hinted that she was falling in love with a Canadian major, Bess wondered how she could possibly marry a foreigner. "It's a shame to have made you so excited about my thoughts of embracing matrimony," Arry wrote. "I will confess I am mightily tempted but I haven't the courage. You're quite right, I simply couldn't marry anyone but an American."

Bess sent Arry a copy of the photograph she had sent to Captain Truman and received an ecstatic reply. "It's the one picture I've always wanted and most given up hopes of ever having," Arry wrote. "My but I am glad the 'General' had to have it. That's surely one of the good things out of this war."

Then came the letter from France that Bess had been dreading. Captain Truman was in combat. "I . . . have accomplished my greatest wish. Have fired five hundred rounds at the Germans . . . been shelled, didn't run away thank the Lord, and never lost a man." With that uncanny instinct for fulfilling her deepest wish, to know, to share everything with him, Harry added: "Probably shouldn't have told you but you'll not worry any more if you know I'm in it than if you think I am."

At the same time, the letter revealed his caution about telling every detail, especially those that would worry her. Not until the war was over did Captain Truman report just how hairy that first encounter with the enemy had been. "The first sergeant failed to get the horses up in time and The Hun gave me a good shelling. The sergeant ran away and I had one high old time getting out of that place. I finally did with two guns and went back to my former position. . . . The boys called that engagement the Battle of Who Run because some of them ran when the first sergeant did and some of them didn't. I made some corporals and first class privates out of those who stayed with me and busted the sergeant."

From this first brush with the Germans in the Vosges Mountains, the Battery soon moved into one of the major battles of the war, St.-Mihiel. Bess got a stream of vivid letters from Harry describing his experiences. He told her about bringing the Battery forward under fire, with shells falling on all sides of them, and never losing a man. "I am as sure as I am sitting here that the Lord was and is with me," he wrote.

Peace rumors began sweeping Europe, as the German armies

reeled back under the American assault. Captain Truman read them and promptly turned his mind from shellfire to something much more pleasant. "Would you meet me in New York and go to the Little Church Around the Corner if I get sent home?"

But the peace rumors faded and the fighting resumed. This time the 129th fired the opening rounds in one of the most stupendous battles in history, the American drive into the Argonne. "I have just finished putting 1,800 shells over on the Germans in the last five hours," Captain Truman told Bess on November 1. He also reported he had gotten a commendation for having the best-conditioned guns in the U.S. Army. He gave the credit to his chief mechanic and put a copy of the letter in the files. But he said he was going to save the original. "It will be nice to have someday if some low-browed north-end politician tries to remark that I wasn't in the war when I'm running for eastern judge or something."

This must have been startling news for Bess. Eastern judge was an administrative job in Jackson County. There were three judges—actually commissioners—who supervised the county government, in particular the roads. For a few months after his father died, Harry had served as road overseer in Grandview. He had proposed an ambitious road-building program and been fired for his trouble. The judgeship was one of the most fiercely contested jobs in Missouri, because so much patronage power was connected with it. Bess could hardly have been thrilled to discover that Harry Truman was thinking about plunging into the cutthroat political world that had destroyed her father.

Within minutes of floating that future, Captain Truman was telling her that he would be just as happy "to follow a mule down a corn row the balance of my days—that is, always providing such an arrangement is also a pleasure to you."

The next day, in another letter, he was telling her how proud he was to learn that she had been made manager of her district for the latest Liberty Loan bond drive. "Should we decide to promote some of my numerous oil leases when I return, I shall know whom to elect secretary and money getter." He confessed somewhat ruefully that he had yet to buy a bond because each payday he lent most of his centimes and francs "to worthless birds in this regiment." He had no real hope of collecting these loans. "Maybe I can make them collect votes for me when I go to run for Congress on my war record—when I get tired of chasing that mule up that corn row."

Captain Truman obviously did not have a clearcut plan for his postwar life, except for marrying Bess Wallace as soon as possible. It is interesting that there is not a hint in any of these letters that Bess tried to take advantage of this uncertainty and tell him what she thought he should do. Instead, she concentrated on praying and worrying him through that rain of shellfire through which he rode so confidently in France.

Suddenly, incredibly, it was over. At 219 North Delaware, everyone was awakened about 4 A.M. on November 11 by the sound of clanging church bells. As dawn broke, people took to the streets for the wildest celebration in the history of Independence. Bells rang, fire engines sounded their sirens, factories blew whistles, automobiles blared horns continually for the next twelve hours. Bess and her friends joined the exultant crowds in Jackson Square. It was all marvelously joyous and goodnatured. Not a single person was injured, and the only reported property damage occurred when some celebrator fired off a gun and the bullet went through a window.

In France, on November 11, Captain Truman gave Bess a blow by blow [or boom by boom] account of how the war ended for him and Battery D.

We are all wondering what the Hun is going to do about Marshal Foch's proposition to him. We don't care what he does. He's licked either way he goes. . . . Their time for acceptance will be up in thirty minutes. There is a great big 155 battery right behind me across the road that seems to want to get rid of all its ammunition before the time is up. It has been banging away almost as fast as a 75 Battery for the last two hours. Every time one of the guns goes off it shakes my house like an earthquake.

I just got official notice that hostilities would cease at eleven o'clock. Everyone is about to have a fit. I fired 164 rounds at him before he quit this morning anyway. It seems everyone was just about to blow up wondering if Heinie would come in. I knew that Germany could not stand the gaff. For all their preparedness and swashbuckling talk they cannot stand adversity. France was whipped for four years and never gave up and one good licking suffices for Germany. What pleases me most is the fact that I was lucky enough to take a Battery through the last drive. The Battery has shot something over ten thousand rounds at the Hun and I am sure they had a slight effect.

Even before this long letter ended, he was thinking of Bess and marriage. He included a nice compliment for her war work.

It is pleasant also to hear that Mrs. Wells [Bess's Aunt Maud] has adopted me as a real nephew and I shall certainly be more than pleased to call her Auntie Maud and I hope it won't be long before I can do it.

You evidently did some excellent work as a Liberty bond saleswoman because I saw in *The Stars and Stripes* where some twenty-two million people bought them and that they were oversubscribed by $1 billion, which is some stunt for you to have helped pull off. I know that it had as much to do with breaking the German morale as our cannon shots and we owe you as much for an early homecoming as we do the fighters.

Bess was proud of the part she played in this tremendous fund-raising achievement. In those attic files at 219 North Delaware Street I found carefully preserved her commission as a "Liberty Soldier" on the "ladies committee" that sold $1,780,000 in bonds in Blue Township.

That Thanksgiving, Maud Gates Wells invited the Wallaces and Grandmother Gates to Platte City. The invitation was gratefully accepted. No one wanted to spend the day at 219 North Delaware without Grandfather Gates to carve the turkey. Everyone had a lovely time in the Wells's spacious mansion. There was a good deal of joking about whether Captain Truman might go AWOL and swim the Atlantic to get home and marry Bess. The well-fed guests returned home by interurban streetcar, which required a change in Kansas City. As they waited for the Independence car, May Wallace noted that Bess and her brother George (now May's husband) were both shivering violently. There was a chilly wind blowing, but it was not that cold. The next morning, they were still shivering. Both had the flu.

In 1918, that was not good news. That year's flu was not the ordinary bug that gave its victims twenty-four or thirty-six hours of chills and went its way. It was a killer that had already wiped out whole families and villages in Europe and other parts of the world. George was lucky. He recovered fairly soon. So did Mary Truman who caught it in Grandview. But Bess sank into a nightmare world of fever and delirium that lasted for weeks. More than once, the family was sure she was dying.

The rest of Independence was not doing much better. As the number of dead and dying mounted, the authorities closed schools and theaters and factories to try to isolate people and break the momentum of the epidemic. At 219 North Delaware, as Bess slowly recovered, she found that she could hear practically nothing in her left ear. The doctor informed her that it was a not uncommon legacy of this killer flu. But at least she was alive. Everyone knew that Bess was herself again when she announced, early in January, that she was going to take a walk.

Separated by 5,000 miles of water and land, Captain Truman blithely wrote Bess letters about a fabulous leave he was enjoying in Paris and Nice and Monte Carlo. He was horrified when he found out, weeks later, that she had the disease that was killing so many people.

I am so glad you are out of danger from that awful flu. You've no idea how uneasy I've been since hearing you and Mary had it. We over here can realize somewhat how you must have felt when we were under fire a little. Every day nearly someone of my outfit will hear that his mother, sister or sweetheart is dead. It is heartbreaking almost to think that we are so safe and so well over here and that the ones we'd like to protect more than all the world have been more exposed to death than we.

While she was recuperating from the flu, Bess received a letter from Mary Paxton that probably did her more good than any of the pills the doctor had in his materia medica. Mary was at a YMCA post trying to give 2,500 homesick soldiers an American Christmas on a very limited budget. She had met an Independence man who told her that the 129th Field Artillery had come through the battles with very light casualties, and Captain Truman was not among the killed or wounded. When "the boys" come home, she told Bess, "No one can do enough to appreciate what they have been up against— and the trenches are only part. It is impossible for anyone not here to understand the temptations they have. We don't preach to them but just talk it straight out to them. Don't worry about Harry though for he is a rock you can build on."

Now that Bess could consider the future without dread, she told Captain Truman that she did not think getting married in New York was a very good idea. She wanted to have the ceremony in Trinity Episcopal Church in Independence, where her family and friends could join in the celebration. The Captain said he was "perfectly willing" to accept that arrangement. "I just couldn't see how I was going to wait until I could get to Independence," he explained. But he had now learned that the army planned to discharge units en masse, which meant he would have to wait until the regiment got to Missouri anyway. "*But don't make any delay*," he warned.

The wedding and Captain Truman's growing dissatisfaction with army life mingled in other letters from France.

I have a nice boy in my Battery whose name is Bobby . . . and once in a while he brings me a letter that he doesn't want any second lieutenant [an army censor] nosing into, and it's always addressed to just Dearest and I feel like an ornery, low-down person when I read them—sometimes I don't, I just sign 'em up and let 'em go. But if that girl doesn't wait for that kid I know she's got a screw loose. He doesn't write a thing silly but he's all there and I hope she is too.

What I started out to say is that I'd like to write you a really silly, mushy letter that would honestly express just exactly what I feel tonight but I have command of neither the words nor the diction to do it right. Anyway I had the most pleasant dream last night and my oh how I did hate to wake up. Of course I was in U.S.A. parading down some big town's main street and I met you and there was a church handy and just as casually as you please we walked inside and the priest did the rest and then I thought we were in Paris and I woke up in a Godforsaken camp just outside of old ruined Verdun. . . .

We just live from one inspection to the next. You know these regular army colonels and lieutenant colonels who've had their feet on the desk ever since the argument started are hellbent for inspections. Some of 'em haven't been over here but a month or two but they can come around and tell us who went through it exactly and how we did not win the war. Some of 'em are nuts on horse feed and some are dippy on how to take care of harness and some think they know exactly how many ounces of axle grease will run a gun wheel to kingdom come and back. One important little major who had evidently read somebody's nonsensical book on how to feed a horse came along the other day and wanted us to feed the horses oatmeal, cooked!

Captain Truman particularly disliked the harsh West Point style discipline of the regulars. He was distressed to find himself being forced to imitate them, to maintain discipline in his bored soldiers.

If we stay in this place much longer, I'll either have a disposition like a hyena or be the dippy one. If there's one thing I've always hated in a man it is to see him take his spite out on someone who couldn't talk back to him. I've done my very best not to jump on someone under me when someone higher up jumps on me, because I hate the higher-up when he does it and I'm sure the next fellow will hate me if I treat him the same way. . . . Justice is an awful tyrant. Just to show how she works I took all the privileges away from a fellow for a small offense and gave him a terrific calling down and I had to do it four times more when I found out that four more were offenders in the same way. One of 'em was a man I particularly like too and I know he thinks I'm as mean as Kaiser Bill. . . .

Harry Truman was saying goodbye to his boyhood dream of becoming a soldier. In this letter he revealed to Bess the part she played in it.

You know when I was a kid, say about thirteen or fourteen, I was a tremendous reader of heavy literature like Homer, Abbott's Lives, Leviticus,

Isaiah and the memoirs of Napoleon. Then it was my ambition to make Napoleon look like a sucker and I thirsted for a West Point education so I could be one of the oppressors, as the kid said when asked why he wanted to go there. You'd never guess why I had such a wild desire and you'll laugh when I tell you. It was only so you could be the leading lady of the palace or empire or whatever it was I wanted to build. You may not believe it but my notion as to who is the best girl in the world has never changed and my military ambition has ended by having arrived at the post of centurion. That's a long way from Caesar, isn't it? Now I want to be a farmer. Can you beat it? I'm hoping you'll like the rube just as well as you would have the Napoleon. I'm sure the farmer will be happier.

Yet he remained proud of his military accomplishments.

Personally I'd rather be a Battery commander than a brigadier general. I am virtually the dictator of the actions of 194 men and if I succeed in making them work as one, keep them healthy morally and physically and make 'em write to the mammas and sweethearts, and bring 'em all home, I shall be as nearly pleased with myself as I ever expect to be—until the one great event of my life is pulled off, which I am fondly hoping will take place immediately on my having delivered that 194 men in U.S.A. You'll have to take a leading part in that event you know and then for one great future.

When the Thirty-fifth Division, to which the artillery regiment was attached, staged a review for General Pershing and the Prince of Wales, Battery D led the parade. Harry told Bess about it, but he was far more excited by what General Pershing said to him when he shook hands: the division would soon be on its way home. "Please get ready to march down the aisle with me as soon as you decently can," he implored. "I haven't any place to go but home [he meant Grandview] and I'm busted financially but I love you as madly as a man can and I'll find the other things. We'll be married anywhere you say at anytime you mention and if you want only one person or the whole town I don't care. . . . I have some army friends I'd like to ask and my own family and that's all I care about." He added that he had enough money to buy a Ford "and we can set sail in that and arrive in Happyland."

In her answering letter, the earliest that has survived, Bess made it clear that she was just as impatient as Harry, and was not fussing about the details. "You may invite the entire 35th Division to your wedding if you want to," she wrote. "I guess it's going to be yours as well as mine. I guess we might as well have the church full while we are at it. I rather think it will be anyway whether we invite them or not, judging from a few remarks I've heard."

Her mother was obviously exercising her prerogatives in regard to the wedding.

Bess's pride in her soldier is visible in the next paragraph. "What an experience the review etc must have been. I'll bet the Bty looked grand and no wonder they led the Div. . . . Were you overcome at greeting the Prince of Wales? He doesn't mean any more to me than the *orneriest* doughboy but I know I'd choke if I had to address him. It was splendid that you got to shake hands with Pershing."

Then she went back to the most important thing on both their minds. "We'll be about ready alrighty when you come and then we can settle the last details. Mary said Mr. Morgan [the oil speculator] had a job waiting for you and if you should decide to put in part of your time there, you'll have another home waiting for you in Indep. for nothing would please mother any better. She said we could have either floor we wanted. . . .

"Hold onto the money for the car—we'll surely need one. Most anything that will run on four wheels. I've been looking at used car bargains today. I'll frankly confess I'm scared to death of Fords. I've seen and heard of so many turning turtle this winter. But we can worry about that later. Just get yourself home and we won't worry about anything."

She closed with a comment that compared her picnic test to Harry's criticisms of some of his fellow officers. "It's strange that such widely different things as war and picnics will so surely show a man up. I've liked lots of people 'til I went on a picnic jaunt with them and you can say the same thing about several (?) men 'til you went on a war jaunt with them, eh?"

Then the letters from France were replaced by telegrams.

ARRIVED IN CAMP MILLS EASTER AFTERNOON . . .
NEW YORK GAVE US A GRAND WELCOME.
GOD'S COUNTRY SURE LOOKS GOOD. HARRY.

The next day, Captain Truman headed for Tiffany and Company, on the southeast corner of Thirty-seventh Street and Fifth Avenue, where he bought a beautiful gold wedding ring. Then he strolled down Broadway with two fellow officers and stopped in an ice-cream store for a snack. There, a pretty girl walked up to him and asked if he was with the Thirty-fifth Division. Captain Truman said his artillery regiment was attached to this mostly Missouri and Kansas division, and in response to another question, admitted that many of his batterymates were from Independence.

"Do you know Bess Wallace?" the girl asked.

"Yes—I do," said the astonished Captain.

"Tell her Stella Swope was asking for her."

The former heiress—she was the youngest daughter—strolled out onto Broadway on the arm of a sailor. What memories that encounter stirred, when Harry told Bess the story in a letter from New York. It evoked receptions and dances in the Swope mansion before tragedy devastated that family, a world of rustling silk dresses and casual sophistication and presumed wealth. Now Bess was about to marry a man who had never been part of that elegant world. A man who was not certain what he wanted to do with the rest of his life, except marry her. An ex-soldier who had a remarkably daring spirit concealed behind his modest, smiling demeanor. Who could guess in what unexpected direction he might take her?

For someone who regarded life with wary distrust, these were unsettling thoughts. But Bess had long since learned to put such thoughts aside, to live a normal life in spite of them. More than most people, she had already experienced the power of fate or destiny in her life. Everything, from her own deep feelings to the fortunes of war, had favored her union with Harry Truman. So, in obedience to the orders from the front lines, there was no delay.

At 4 P.M. on June 28, 1919, seven weeks after thirty-five-year-old Captain Truman was discharged at Camp Funston, almost nine full years since he began his courtship of Bess Wallace and six years since she accepted him, he waited at the altar in tiny Trinity Episcopal Church, a few blocks from 219 North Delaware Street. He was wearing a gray tailor-made suit, with small black-and-white checks in the cloth. It had been made by his best man, Ted Marks, who had been a fellow captain in the 129th Field Artillery. Before the war and after it, Ted ran the best gentleman's tailor shop in Kansas City.

It was a very hot day, but Harry Truman was oblivious to the weather. "Never did we see such a radiant groom," one friend wrote Bess after the ceremony, and added an interesting comment on some feelings that Bess had obviously shared with her. "Methot you did quite nobly, Bessie, now twastn't such a dreadful ordeal, was it."

Bess wore a gown of white georgette and a widebrimmed picture hat of white faille, and carried an armful of Aaron Ward roses. Her bridesmaids were her two favorite cousins, Helen Wallace and Louise Wells. Helen wore blue organdy and carried Sunset roses, Louise wore yellow organdy and carried Sweetheart roses. Tall, handsome Frank Wallace escorted Bess up the aisle and gave her away.

The church was beautifully decorated with garden flowers in pastel shades. The altar was a mass of daisies, pink hollyhock, and pale blue larkspur. Tall cathedral candles cast a golden glow on this array of color. "Elizabeth Virginia Wallace," the Reverend John V. Plunkett, rector of Trinity, asked the thirty-four-year-old bride, "Wilt thou have this man for thy wedded husband, to live together after God's ordinance in the holy estate of matrimony? Wilt thou love him, comfort him, honor, and keep him in sickness and in health; and forsaking all others, keep thee only unto him so long as ye both shall live?"

"I will," Bess Wallace said.

Chapter Six

In a roadster whose brand name I haven't been able to identify, the newlyweds headed for Chicago. Ex-Captain Truman cheerfully declined to set a time limit on this long-awaited honeymoon. He announced they would make up their schedule as they went along. This did not sit well with his mother-in-law, who wanted to know the day and hour when her daughter would return to her. In Chicago, Bess and Harry stayed at the Hotel Blackstone and enjoyed the Windy City so much they forgot to phone or write anybody.

On July 5, Bess's brother Fred wrote to her, reporting that there was a brisk traffic in wedding presents at 219 North Delaware. "You seem to be having some time in Chicago and must like it pretty well by the way you are sticking around," Fred observed. Then he revealed the instigator of his letter. "Mom says if she doesn't hear from you, she's going to telegraph the hotel."

Bess's friends pursued her with more amusing letters. One friend told her to see all the sights in Chicago but "don't get lost in the big city and don't you dare learn the 'Shimmie' [A forerunner of the Charleston, this dance was the rage in 1919]. Methinks you should have taken a chaperone. Cause when little girls leave the quiet little town and have anticipations of life on a tear they're apt to do anything."

From Chicago the honeymooners motored to Detroit and Port Huron, Michigan. North of that city there were (and still are) miles of golden beaches on vast Lake Huron. The air was marvelously free of summertime Missouri's awful humidity and scorching heat. For the rest of his life, whenever Harry Truman wanted to regain the radiance of those first days with Bess, he simply wrote: "Port Huron." For him it was a code word for happiness.

Bess had a wonderful time too, but it was she who decided that their honeymoon had to end because she could not stop worrying about her mother. So they rumbled home in their roadster and took up residence at 219 North Delaware. It was the logical place for them to stay, for emotional reasons—Madge Wallace's dependence on her daughter—as well as financial and geographical ones.

In the seven weeks between his discharge and his wedding, ex-Captain Truman had discovered that the job offered to him by the Morgan Oil Company no longer existed. The company was in financial disarray. Most of their leases had lapsed, and most of the money Harry and Bess had invested in 1917 had vanished. As part of a settlement, David Morgan gave the Trumans title to a large house at 3404 Karnes Boulevard in Kansas City. To sharpen the disappointment, while the Trumans were on their honeymoon, another oil company, drilling on land the Morgan Oil Company had leased and abandoned in Greenwood County, Kansas, reported a gusher. The newcomers had discovered the Teter Pool, one of the largest oil deposits in the United States. In 1918, Morgan had run out of money when he was 1,500 feet down in a well on the same land. It was more than a little painful for the Trumans to discover how close they had come to making millions.

That disappointment undoubtedly had a lot to do with ex-Captain Truman's decision not to follow a mule up a corn row and build a bungalow in Grandview. In a hurry to make some real money, he sold his equity in the farm to his mother and sister Mary and went into the haberdashery business.

His partner was Eddie Jacobson, the man with whom he had run the canteen at Camp Doniphan in Oklahoma before they sailed to France. They launched a very spiffy store opposite the Muehlebach Hotel on Twelfth Street, which I have already identified as Kansas City's Broadway.

Truman and Jacobson opened their doors in November 1919. The national economy was still booming along at a war pace. Wheat was selling at a ten-year high. The pockets of the average man were overflowing with cash, and many saw no reason why they should not invest in some of the expensive shirts and silk socks being sold by Truman and Jacobson.

Both men worked very hard. The store was open twelve hours a day, six days a week. They divided the back room chores between them, Eddie handling the buying and Harry keeping the books. Often he brought the books home with him, and Bess helped him with the laborious double entries, both of them toiling until long

Mother's grandfather, George Porter-field Gates, was one of the wealthiest men in Independence. He was born in Vermont and came to Missouri after the Civil War. (*Courtesy of the Truman Family*)

Deeply religious Elizabeth Emery Gates, Mother's grandmother, was born in England. She came to the United States at the age of eight, after her entire family died in an epidemic. (*Courtesy of the Truman Family*)

This picture of my grandmother, Madge Gates, was taken around 1883, the year she married David Willock Wallace. She was twenty-one, he was twenty-three. (*Courtesy of the Truman Family*)

My mother's father, David Willock Wallace, was known as the handsomest man in Independence. (*Courtesy of the Truman Family*)

This is one of my favorite pictures of Mother. It was taken when she was four and a half. (*Courtesy of the Truman Family*)

Bess Wallace (left) at sixteen with her lifelong friend, Mary Paxton. In 1909, Mary became the first woman to work on a newspaper in Kansas City. In later years she liked to say, "I was born liberated." (*Courtesy of the Truman Family*)

Bess Wallace is fourth from the left in this crowd of tennis players. On her left is her brother George. Second from the right is her brother Frank. Mother was the best woman tennis player in Independence. (*Courtesy of the Truman Family*)

The man in Bess Wallace's life, Harry Truman, became an even more constant caller after he bought this 1911 Stafford touring car. Here, with his sister Mary and his cousin Nellie Noland in the back seat, they pause on a country road near the Truman farm. (*Courtesy of the Truman Family*)

On June 28, 1919, ex–Captain Harry S. Truman married Bess Wallace, ending a nine-year courtship. Here the wedding party poses in the yard of 219 North Delaware Street. The bridesmaids on the left and right are Bess's first cousins, Louise Wells and Helen Wallace. In the back row are the best man, ex-Captain Ted Marks, and Bess's brother Frank, who gave her away. (*Courtesy of the Truman Family*)

after midnight in the dining room. But neither complained because all the ink they used was gloriously blue. Business was fantastic. The money poured in the way it had arrived during the heyday of the Morgan Oil Company—by the basketful.

Bess somehow found time to maintain a heavy correspondence with Mary Paxton and Arry Ellen Mayer, her two closest friends. Mary was enormously distressed to find herself in France when Bess was married. On June 9, 1919, she wrote her an emotion filled letter.

"I suppose by now you are married," she began. "Father wrote me that he was going to send you a wedding present for us both. I will bring you something too. I wanted it to be linen but that is out of reason here since the war." She discussed other possible presents, including china, and then confessed she had no money to buy anything. YMCA workers were not lavishly paid. "I only tell you this because I want you to know how much I am thinking of you and trying to find something for you. I surely do regret not being there. It is just a matter of weeks now till I come. I count not being there for your wedding one of the greatest sacrifices of the war for me.

"I must go now and entertain some soldiers at 2 A.M."

She closed with: "Dearest love and all the best wishes of every kind—"

Then, as if words could not express her feelings, she added, on separate lines, "Till we meet— Dearest love—"

Not long after Bess received this letter, Mary's father John Paxton, who still lived a few blocks away on Delaware Street, told her astonishing news. Mary had gotten married. It was apparently a very sudden decision. The man's name was Edmund Burke Keeley. He and Mary had worked together in Virginia before she went to France. (He was apparently the man who loved her too much.) He had met her at the ship in New York, and they had been married in the Little Church Around the Corner. They were now living on a farm he was managing near Richmond. You can imagine Bess's consternation. Mary's next letter was read, you can be sure, with lightning speed.

"I surely have a lot to tell you," she began. [I] "hardly know where to start. My husband is an Irishman but a genius on farming lines." Then comes a sentence that she inserted after she finished the letter. "He is perfectly dear to me." She went on to tell Bess that Edmund Burke Keeley (nicknamed Mike) "has a wonderful opportunity for he has this huge place to make into a model farming community with unlimited capital behind this place. (Oh no it is not our capital.) He did not want to wait for me to come home to be married. The wheat was half thrashed. So we came back here for our honeymoon.

"We have a house that looks like a small summer hotel. . . . I have the job of making it into a home. It surely will be fun." She hoped to visit Independence in December, and apropos of that, remarked: "This farm is so lovely I never want to leave it except coming to see you all."

Bess was more than a little hurt by Mary's casual tone and a little bewildered by her headlong marriage. She wrote to her, asking how she could have gotten married to a man none of her family or friends had ever heard of, much less met. In particular, she asked how Mary could have done this without sharing it with her.

In her next letter, which was written on stationery topped by "Curles Neck Farm," Mary tried to explain. "The honest truth is I could not tell anyone in advance I was going to be married because I only knew it twenty-four hours in advance myself. I was too tired to have any fuss over getting married."

Mary assured Bess that she had "everything anyone needs to make them happy, a good husband, a farm house, a dog, gold fish, a canary, and will have some chickens next week." She described some of the lavish wedding presents they had received from the owners of the farm and from the people who worked on it. Mary wished Bess lived closer to Curles Neck Farm, which was on the James River near Richmond. "I am going to bring Mike home in November but I can't bring the place to show you."

On January 8, 1920, Arry Ellen Mayer married a Canadian, Charles Calhoun, in Toronto. I am strictly an amateur in psychology, but I don't think one has to have taken a course in Sigmund Freud to see a connection in this rush to matrimony with Bess's marriage to Captain Truman.

Although the first year of Bess's marriage was brightened by Harry's success as a businessman, there was a sharp disappointment at the end of it. She had a miscarriage. It upset her a great deal. She and Harry were both anxious to have a child, and this unhappy accident at the age of thirty-five made her fear she had waited too long. Other events in 1920 were also inauspicious. The Republicans kicked the Democrats out of the White House and elected Warren G. Harding in a landslide. Almost immediately, a sharp deflation in the economy began, much of it caused, Harry Truman maintained, by

Republican tight money policies. The price of wheat began to slide and the pockets of those who frequented Twelfth Street were no longer full. Sales at the Truman and Jacobson Haberdashery dwindled. Red ink began to appear in the books on which Bess and Harry labored.

This was a dismaying shock to Bess. In early 1920, when business was good, she had begun to assume her natural role as one of the social leaders of Independence. She invited the Good Samaritan Class of the First Christian Church, to which her sister-in-law, May Wallace, belonged, to 219 North Delaware for a "musical tea." The house was decorated with spring flowers, and the singers and musicians performed twice, once in the afternoon for young people and again in the evening for adults. Everyone was charmed, and the social pages of the Jackson *Examiner* credited the occasion to "the courtesy of Mr. and Mrs. Harry Truman."

Throughout 1921, Truman and Jacobson slid slowly, inevitably toward collapse. It was a bitter disappointment for Harry Truman, too. It wiped out money he had received for his share of the Truman farm—the financial reserve on which he had planned to start married life. But he was not the sort of man who sat still in face of disaster— or took to drink. He had an alternative plan ready—one that stirred considerable anxiety in Bess. Reviving the idea he had mentioned in his letter from France, he was planning to run for eastern judge of Jackson County. He was plunging into the same political milieu that had destroyed her father. I have no recorded evidence of what Madge Wallace thought of this idea—but I do not need any. She undoubtedly expressed profound horror—especially when she was alone with Bess.

Frank Wallace had loaned Harry some money when the store began running short of cash. But Madge Wallace, who had the cash she had inherited from her father, never offered her son-in-law a cent, as far as I know. On the contrary, while Truman and Jacobson were closing their doors for the last time in April, Madge, as oblivious as ever to financial realities, was planning a trip to the East Coast with her son Fred when he finished the school year at the University of Missouri.

Fred always had been Madge's pet, but since Bess's marriage, she could not bear to let him out of her sight. She moved to Columbia and kept house for him during his first year away from home. Fred never objected in the least to being spoiled this way. In the opinion of some of the older members of the family, the trip east was probably his idea. "If there was any money around, Freddy could never resist spending it," one of my aunts once remarked.

Perhaps this egotism—I can't bring myself to call it selfishness because I don't think Madge Wallace was aware of what she was doing—enabled Bess to ignore her mother and back her husband's decision to become a politician. The best proof of her approval is not in writing, but in the actions of the Wallace men on behalf of Harry Truman. At this time, Frank Wallace was the leader of the Fourth Ward in Independence. He began taking Harry around the ward, introducing him to people. One can be certain that he never would have done such a thing if his sister had opposed the candidacy. George Wallace, too, although he professed a disdain for politics and politicians, talked up his brother-in-law's candidacy.

But not opposing this plunge into politics and warmly, enthusiastically approving it are two very different things. As Bess already had done at many other times in her life, she managed to suppress her negative feelings and support her husband's decision. But she paid a price in sleeplessness and tension that soon led to an even heavier price.

Another source of emotional stress was her awareness that Mary Paxton Keeley was pregnant and was having no difficulty carrying the baby to term. Much as Bess and Mary loved each other, there was a subtle element of competition in their relationship. They had chosen such different paths through life, I suppose it was inevitable. It must have been a bit exasperating for Bess to see Mary achieving what she yearned for, after making such an impulsive marriage. When you have waited and planned and hoped for so long and life disappoints you, it is doubly difficult to bear.

At the end of October 1921, just as her husband was launching his campaign for eastern judge, Bess received a triumphant letter from Mary. It is also, as are so many of their letters, very touching.

Dear Bess:
    I thought by this time you know I have a precious little son. I never believed I could think anything as sweet. He is tiny but started gaining today. He has brown hair, gray eyes, quite a nose, flat ears, a *good* head. I believe he is going to be like Father. . . .
    Bess, it was the hardest thing I was ever up against. But such a small price to pay for a treasure. He came a little soon and Mike was away and I entirely among strangers. Mike is so proud of him and proud of himself for being the father of such a fine baby. . . .

It does not seem right that you and your mother cannot come and tell me what a nice son I have. . . .

In Independence, the year 1922, the third year of the Truman marriage, began with very little joy and a lot of apprehension. Truman and Jacobson collapsed. They had a lease on the store that ran for several more years but no money to pay the rent. Harry Truman refused to declare bankruptcy. He persuaded Eddie Jacobson to join him, and together they went to their creditors and arranged to begin paying off the debt on the installment plan. To prove his good faith, Dad sold the Karnes Boulevard house and deeded to the bank a 160-acre Kansas farm he had bought as an investment.

Meanwhile, he plunged into the melee for eastern judge. Jackson County politics had not changed very much since the days of David Willock Wallace. The Democrats were still divided into feuding factions. In 1922, the two factions were known as the Goats and the Rabbits. They supposedly got their name from the Democrats' habit of herding everything living (and occasionally, a few of the dead) to the polls, including the goats and rabbits that their Irish constituents used to maintain around their shanties. The Goats were loyal to the Democratic boss in Kansas City, Tom Pendergast. The Rabbits were led by another Irishman, Joseph Shannon. According to legend, this was the election in which Boss Tom Pendergast and Harry Truman joined forces. In the army, Dad had been friendly with Jim Pendergast, Tom's nephew, and when the campaign began, Jim had introduced him to Boss Tom, who offered to support him.

Harry Truman said he was looking for support anywhere he could find it but it would have to come with no strings attached. Pendergast assured him that this was the case and then coolly executed a backroom deal with Joe Shannon that would give Shannon the eastern judgeship in return for letting Boss Tom get his man into the western job. But Harry Truman had some backers in the campaign that Boss Tom could not control. One of the most significant was William Southern, editor of the Jackson *Examiner*, the most widely read paper in the county outside Kansas City, and the father of Bess's sister-in-law, May Wallace.

It is fascinating—and I think virtually unnoticed heretofore—just how important Bess Wallace Truman's family connections were in launching her husband's political career. I suspect Bess also had a hand in an appeal to a new force in Jackson County's politics—the woman's vote. After failing to win referendums in Missouri and other states, the suffragettes had concentrated their efforts on Washington, D.C., and persuaded Congress to pass the Nineteenth Amendment in 1919. In the 1922 election, a very effective campaign to persuade women to vote for Harry Truman was conducted by Mary Paxton's stepmother and Mrs. W.L.C. Palmer, one of the favorite teachers of the class of 1901. They canvassed Independence door to door, the way the Liberty Loan soldiers had sold bonds during the war.

Not to be discounted, of course, was the candidate's superb war record and the tremendous energy he threw into the campaign. He drove his aging roadster over almost every mile of Jackson County's atrocious roads. He also terrified his wife by flying to several rallies in an airplane that looked like it had been put together with paper and string. The campaign reached its climax in the blazing heat of the summer of 1922. Between June 1 and August 5, the date of the primary, Harry Truman visited every township and precinct in the county.

Bess did not go with him. She stayed home for a supremely important reason: she was pregnant again. Not many women in Jackson County went to political rallies anyway, even though they had gotten the vote. But the tension and turmoil of the campaign swirled through Bess's mind and spirit, nevertheless. In late June or early July, she had another miscarriage.

As an amateur psychologist, I will only speculate on whether the political uproar had anything to do with this second disappointment at the even more discouraging age of thirty-seven. We only know that it left Bess tremendously upset. This time she thought sure that she was going to have a breakdown. She poured out her woes to the correspondent she favored when she was unhappy, Arry Ellen Mayer Calhoun, who was still living in Toronto, and, coincidentally, pregnant at this time.

"Dear Bess," Arry replied on the 12th of July. "Words simply can't tell you how distressed I am to know all you have been through. . . . I am so thankful you are all right yourself. Do please get well and strong and don't raise your finger next time."

While Bess was going through this ordeal, her mother was touring the East Coast with her son Fred. They stayed at the Copley Plaza in Boston and visited some Gates cousins in Newburyport. They sashayed on to the Belmont in New York, where they did the town from "Fifth Avenue to the slums." They went on to the Bellevue-

Stratford in Philadelphia and from there to the New Willard in Washington, and finally to Richmond, where Mary Paxton Keeley met them and took them out to Curles Neck Farm.

Throughout this three week expedition, Madge Wallace wrote numerous letters to Bess, one of which began: "My dear little girl"—the same salutation she had used when Bess was fourteen. Madge frequently told Bess she hoped that she was "feeling fine" or "well"—but not once did Bess mention the miscarriage or her nerves to her. It is equally significant, I suppose, that in the nine or ten letters and postcards from the travelers, there is not one mention of Harry Truman or his political struggle. Madge Wallace seldom expressed her disapproval directly. That was not a lady's style.

On August 5, 1922, candidate Truman won his first election, becoming the eastern judge of Jackson County by 500 votes. Most of the voters in that end of the county were Democrats, so the primary was the only election that mattered. Bess's nerves took a distinct turn for the better, and Arry Ellen was soon writing to her with her usual cheer. "It is surely good to know you are feeling something like yourself again. But do be careful and take good care of yourself until you get your strength back and cease to have any nerves. . . . Congratulate Harry on winning the nomination."

Arry added that she was "still making doll clothes. I only hope I finish them in time for the arrival." She assured Bess, in another letter, that she would wire her "when the eventful day arrives."

Alas, when it finally arrived a few months later, it was Arry's turn to suffer a bitter disappointment. The baby was born dead. Bess could hardly have been encouraged by that piece of bad news. Nevertheless, with that courageous determination that was the essence of her character, she resolved to try again.

Meanwhile, she had become the wife of a politician. A Jackson County judge was really a commissioner of public works, with over a thousand jobs to dispense to the political faithful. Judge Truman began getting phone calls and visitors at all hours of the day and night. To his mother-in-law's considerable distaste, he decided to see some of them at 219 North Delaware Street. With her determination to share her husband's life, Bess backed him in this decision. He in turn shared with her the acrimonious disputes on the three-judge court.

Although Harry Truman owed Pendergast very little, he voted with the presiding judge, an all-out Pendergast man named Henry F.

McElroy, most of the time, because he at least had a businesslike approach to the county's problems. Previous courts had spent Jackson County into near ruinous debt. Judge Truman went to St. Louis and Chicago and found bankers willing to loan them money at far better rates than local bankers were offering. In two years he and McElroy reduced the county's debt by $600,000.

Judge Truman also tried to arrange a truce between the Goats and the Rabbits, but neither side was interested. His armistice did not last more than a day. McElroy insisted on appointing only Goats to county jobs. The Rabbits remained furiously convinced that Pendergast had double-crossed them and elected Truman.

A cauldron of political bickering boiled around them, while unwashed jobseekers turned up on the front porch every night. None of this would seem to be ingredients for happiness, as the Truman marriage entered its fourth year. One might logically assume that aristocratic Bess Wallace's feelings for Harry Truman would decline in intensity under such unpleasant stress. Your logic would be perfect, but the facts, which so often ignore logic, would be wrong. In the summer of 1923, Harry Truman went off to Fort Leavenworth for two weeks of active duty with the Missouri National Guard. He had stayed in the reserve when he left the army and had been promoted to major. Bess wrote to him every day while he was away, and these letters, the first connected sequence that has survived, give us a revealing look at her state of mind and heart.

"Dear Pettie," she began the first letter, invoking a private nickname I never heard before. "It is now 10:20 and I am in bed. There was a big black bug on my bed when I turned the sheet down and I had to kill it myself—but that wasn't the first time I had wished for you." She teased him about a lady to whom he and another part-time soldier had given a ride to a town on the road to Leavenworth and closed with: "Lots and lots of good night kisses. Yours, Bess."

The next letter began: "Dear old Sweetness" and told him how glad she was to get his letter, which described the enormous amounts of food the army was feeding him. "You'll have to be pretty strenuous to keep that *front* down," she warned. She told him that two of his army friends, Eddie McKim and Ted Marks (the best man at their wedding) were thinking of going up to Leavenworth to see him. "I'd give my head to go," she remarked. Then she penned an amusing word picture of some neighbors who loaded their car and departed for Colorado that morning at 5 A.M. She sat at the window and watched them, because, she said, "I wouldn't have missed seeing Mrs. Swift in knickers for a hundred dollars."

Finally, she returned to how "awfully darned lonesome" it was without him, "But I know you are going to get lots of good out of the trip. And I'm glad too you are taking it by yourself for I am sure you needed to get away from everything and everybody."

Another letter began "Sweetie— [Then came a parenthesis] (Burn this in the kitchen stove)." She told him that she had been sitting at the front window for hours, waiting for his letter. She reported with delight that Eddie Jacobson and his wife and Eddie McKim had invited her to drive up to Leavenworth for a visit. They planned to have dinner in the town of Leavenworth and urged him to join them. "I think we'll want to visit a hotel by that time and that will solve the question, eh?"

When she came home for the visit, she told "Dear Harry" that "yesterday seems just a happy dream." She recalled how she "sure did hate to leave last night. . . . I looked and looked to see you drive off—"

Bess wrote "Friend Husband" (another salutation) every day and on one day wrote twice. When she did not get a letter from him she was "sick." Toward the end of the two-week separation, she was telling him how "homesick for you" she was and added "last night was the worst night yet."

As Major Truman's tour of duty ended, she could not help chiding him a little for his infatuation with army life. "I know you are *almost* sorry your two weeks are up. But I can't say that I am." Then she added: "The *Examiner* last night said you would be home Sat. so I guess there will be a million calls tomorrow."

Even in her love letters, Bess interwove a keen appreciation of her husband's political responsibilities. While Harry was away, she dealt with callers who wanted to have their roads oiled to keep down the summer dust. She astutely noted that a lot of calls had come from women around Bristol and Maywood, two small townships in the country. "They must have a league [against Truman] out there."

She finished the letter with "Lots of love."

After reading this chapter, you may not be completely surprised to learn that when Bess visited her husband at Fort Leavenworth, she was already two months pregnant.

Chapter Seven

Throughout the fall of 1923, Bess struggled with a tangle of hope and fear. After two disappointments, she had become so superstitious about expecting a happy ending to her pregnancy that she presumed the opposite. She refused to buy a single item of baby clothes or even a bassinet. Christmas that year was, nevertheless, a time of hope. By then, Bess was almost in her eighth month and was feeling fine.

But she remembered Arry and her dead baby, and still feared the worst. She also fretted about whether the baby would be a boy. She maintained that Harry wanted a boy—although he vowed a hundred times that he did not care, as long as she and the new arrival survived. I suspect that Mary Paxton Keeley's proud possession of a son had more influence on Bess's feelings than she was ready to admit.

As her time neared, there was a debate about hospital versus home. Mary Paxton Keeley had gone to a hospital. I am not sure what Arry Calhoun did. But Bess decided to have her baby at 219 North Delaware Street. Maybe she was influenced by her mother, who had had all her children at home. Or by her grandmother, who had had three children in that comfortable old house.

Home turned out to be a good decision. On February 17, when Bess went into labor, one of the worst blizzards in memory was burying Independence and most of the Midwest. It would have been a nightmare to try to get to a hospital. The doctor had enough trouble getting to the house, and he was a professional at dealing with the weather.

After twelve hours of labor, the writer of this book was born, four days after Bess's thirty-ninth birthday. Bess cried when she learned the baby was a girl, and only extravagant reassurances from the ecstatic father calmed her down. Meanwhile, everyone was scurrying around in search of something in which to clothe me. They finally found a few garments and parked me in an open bureau drawer, by way of a bassinet, until the snowstorm abated and Judge Truman could plow through the drifts to buy a long shopping list of baby things.

Letters poured in from Bess's friends as the good news was spread by newspaper and letter and telephone. Mary Paxton Keeley was one of the first to write. "To say I am glad is putting it mildly," Mary declared. "Well, you have the time of your life before you the next two years as I know. There is nothing like a baby except maybe two. I wish I could see this precious thing of yours."

Then Mary added some dismaying news. "I did not write you about our troubles because I did not desire to have you worry about us. . . . Mike is at Battle Creek but will come back here. What we have is invested in two farms which we don't want to sacrifice so I will get a job in Richmond or in Kansas City after I have rested. . . . Life is pretty difficult but the only thing you can do with trouble is take it standing. What ever comes I have this sweet lamb to work for. He complicates things in getting a job and a place to live but he is the best reason I know for making a success."

Even when she wrote this, Mary half knew that Mike Keeley had an incurable kidney disease. But she wanted her letter to Bess to "be about you and the little dear whose name I don't know." Alas, it was some time before Bess was able to tell Mary the little dear's name. What to name her (me) became a major bone of contention. Bess wanted to name me Margaret Wallace Truman after her mother. Dad absolutely refused to agree. He insisted that the Trumans have equal representation in this matter.

The argument continued for the better part of four years, which gives you some idea of how stubborn both Harry and Bess could be on things they cared about. They finally compromised on Mary (after his sister) Margaret Truman. By that time, the argument was irrelevant to everyone but my two godmothers, Mary Paxton Keeley and Arry Calhoun, and the Episcopal priest who performed my much delayed christening. To everyone else, I was Margaret.

Although I was now on the scene, I was not exactly functioning as a biographer. I must still rely on research and family memories for what happened in this first year of my life, the fifth of Bess's marriage. It would seem that I have no claim whatsoever to being a good luck charm. No sooner was I installed in a bassinet and given enough clothes to let me pose decently for a picture or two than Bess and her husband found themselves in the ugliest political brawl of their lives.

Judge Truman's term as eastern judge lasted only two years, and he was up for reelection in 1924. The Shannon Rabbits were still convinced that he personified the Pendergast double cross, and they made him their target for the primary election. Turning things even uglier, if possible, was the presence of the Ku Klux Klan, which offered to support Judge Truman if he promised not to appoint any Catholic or Jew to a county job.

Without telling Bess or anyone else what he had in mind, Harry Truman drove out to a Klan political rally in Lee's Summit, alone. He got up on the platform and told them exactly how despicable he thought their ideas were. He praised the fighting spirit of the Irish Catholics he had commanded in Battery D and scornfully implied that most of the Klansmen had been so busy hating their fellow Americans, they had stayed home. "If any Catholic or Jew who's a good Democrat needs help, I'm going to give him a job," he said. He walked off the platform and strode through the glaring crowd to his car. There he discovered a half dozen of his friends, armed with loaded shotguns. They had heard about his daring act of defiance and had driven out to protect him. Dad always said that he was glad they had not arrived until he finished speaking. The Klansmen had shotguns too, and gunfire might well have punctuated his blazing speech.

The national Democratic Party, meanwhile, was committing political suicide in New York. They had convened presuming they were choosing the next president. The Republicans had been caught up to their eyeballs in games with oil leases on the Teapot Dome Naval Reserve field in Wyoming, and their candidate was the colorless vice president Calvin Coolidge. He had succeeded Warren Harding, who had died in 1923, humiliated by the malfeasance of his friends. The Democrats proceeded to quarrel over whether to nominate Al Smith, the Irish Catholic governor of New York, or William Gibbs McAdoo, Woodrow Wilson's son-in-law. After some 103 ballots, they chose a candidate nobody wanted, a corporate attorney from Ohio named John W. Davis, who was even more colorless than Coolidge. Worse, the convention came within a quarter of a vote of accepting a resolution to condemn the Ku Klux Klan, leaving both halves of the party infuriated, disgusted, or both.

As far as Missouri, and Jackson County, was concerned, this display of national disunity was fatal. In the November election, the Klan and the Shannon Democrats teamed up to destroy the local Democratic Party. Judge Truman lost and so did almost every other Democrat in sight.

At the age of forty, Harry Truman was out of a job again.

Once more, he declined to panic or even to grow discouraged. Almost as if he wanted to prove how steady his nerves were, he took offices in the Board of Trade Building in Kansas City, where his father had lost everything the Trumans owned twenty-two years before gambling on wheat futures. He had been in the road building business as a judge, and it was logical for him to switch to doing business with the people who were driving on the roads. Detroit was setting records selling automobiles, and people needed advice on how and where to use them. He began selling memberships in the Kansas City Automobile Club, directing a staff of salesmen and pitching in to sell 1,500 personally. He cleared $5,000 or $6,000 in his first year.

Next, he toyed with going back into another business he knew well, banking. Bess's brother, Frank, and his father-in-law, Albert Ott were both bankers. So there were plenty of good advice givers in the family. Harry and several friends, including Spencer Salisbury, brother of Bess's good friend, Agnes, and a fellow captain in the 129th Field Artillery, organized the Community Savings and Loan Association in Independence. People were building houses almost as fast as they were buying cars and needed mortgages, so this too seemed a logical move. Harry Truman sold stock in the bank and everyone prospered nicely.

Meanwhile, Bess was learning motherhood. She got lots of help from friends near and distant. Mary Paxton shipped her instructions on breast feeding, bathing, oiling, and burping me. Pictures were dispatched to her and other friends, and appropriate comments were made about my beauty. There is not a hint of financial or any other kind of anxiety in Bess's letters to her husband in the summer of 1925, when Major Truman again went off for two weeks of reserve training, this time at Fort Riley, Kansas. Once more, Bess missed him acutely ("like the mischief," she wrote in one letter). Now she could add: "Your daughter kept asking all day for 'da-da'—then 'bye?' "

I was eighteen months old at this point, so don't expect any brilliant dialogue.

In this series of letters, the big issue rapidly became whether Mrs. Truman should bob her hair. Women all over America had been going through agonies and quarrels with husbands and boyfriends over this question for several years. The men seemed, in general, to resist it. To them, bobbed hair apparently suggested flappers, free love, and all sorts of other terrible things, such as bathtub gin. Major Truman was among the resisters, mainly, it would seem, because he wanted Bess to go on looking exactly like the woman he had taken to Port Huron.

Bess launched a propaganda campaign to change his mind. She told him that Ethel and Nellie Noland, old maid school teachers now, had done it and "looked perfectly fine." Bess said she was "crazier than ever to get mine off" and wanted to know why her husband would not agree "*enthusiastically*." She maintained that her hair grew so fast, she could soon put it up again if it looked "*very badly*."

"Please!" she cried. "I'm much more conspicuous having long hair than I will be with it short."

Major Truman stood his ground. Apparently, distance not only makes the heart grow fonder, it also encourages husbands to be stubborn. In the next letter Bess returned to the assault. "When may I do it? I never wanted to do anything as badly in my life. Come on, be a sport. Ask all the married men in camp about their wives' heads & I'll bet anything I have there isn't one under sixty who has long hair."

I was dismayed to see I was a mere footnote to this raging debate. "Your daughter seems well but is powerfully cross."

In the next letter, the strategy shifted. There was a variety of family news, a bit more data on my dotty eighteen-month-old antics, and then a postscript. "What about the hair cut?"

Major Truman capitulated. "If you want your hair bobbed so badly, go on and get it done. I want you to be happy regardless of what I think about it. I am very sure you'll be just as beautiful with it off and I'll not say anything to make you sorry for doing it. I can still see you as the finest on earth so go and have it done."

"That was a dear letter you wrote me about bobbing my hair," Bess replied. "It almost put a crimp in my wanting to do it. But if you knew the utter discomfort of all this pile on top of my head and the time I waste every day getting it there, you would insist on me cutting it.

"I most sincerely hope you'll never feel otherwise than you said you do in that letter—for life would be a dreary outlook if you ever ceased to feel just that way."

Still Bess hesitated. The hair stayed on until Major Truman returned from Fort Riley and personally reassured Bess of his approval of the shearing. On the night before he came home, Bess wrote:

"Lots and lots of love and please keep on loving me as hard as ever. You know I just feel as if a large part of me has been gone for the last few days."

Back in Independence, Harry Truman resumed his whirlwind schedule as combined automobile club manager and banker. He piled these two careers on top of going to law school at night in Kansas City. This was a move which Bess had suggested in 1923, when he was eastern judge. Her Aunt Myra's husband, Boulware Wallace, was one of the more successful lawyers in Missouri, and Bess saw no reason why her husband could not do as well. But in 1925, after two years of combining school and a grueling work schedule, he gave it up. He told Bess that his boys from Battery D would not let him study. They invaded the law school library to ask for advice and help on getting jobs. Some of them probably did, but this was an oblique way of telling her that he had had a taste of being a political man and he liked it.

The Battery D boys were not the only ones who turned to Harry Truman as a leader. He was in constant demand as a speaker at local political meetings. With an office in Kansas City, he was in close contact with major political changes taking place there. In the spring of 1926, a good-government group proposed a new city charter, providing for a city manager and a city council of nine aldermen. They thought they were going to get rid of Tom Pendergast and Joe Shannon, but the amateurs were stunned to discover that Boss Tom emerged with even more political power. He elected a majority of the aldermen and appointed his own city manager.

The new charter ended the warfare between the Goats and the Rabbits. Joe Shannon and his followers accepted Tom Pendergast as the leader of Kansas City and Jackson County. Harry Truman went to see Tom's brother, Mike, who was the leader of the eastern half of the county and told him he wanted to run for county collector. This was the best job in the county. The collector got a percentage of the taxes he collected, and his annual income was around $25,000. It was a good example of how big Harry Truman was thinking in those days.

Unfortunately, a Democrat with more seniority had laid claim to the collector's job. But the Pendergasts offered to back Harry Truman for presiding judge of the county court. The salary was modest—$6,000 a year—but there was a real chance to build a political reputation in this controversial job. After a conference with Bess, they jointly decided he should accept the offer. It was a very important decision and they both knew it. Harry Truman was now forty-two years old. He was getting past the time when a man can switch careers.

There was no opposition in the Democratic primary—proof of Pendergast hegemony—and Harry Truman felt free to go off to reserve officers' training camp in the summer of 1926. Again, he and Bess exchanged daily letters, giving us a good look at what she was thinking and feeling about him and her daughter and other matters.

She alternated salutations in these letters between "My dear—" and "Honey—" and "Dear Husband—." Again and again she closed with "All my love" or "Loads of love." She missed him acutely. "Today didn't seem to have any beginning or any end," she wrote, early in the first week. "That letter helped a *lot*." On the other hand, when a letter failed to come, the tone could be acerbic. "I came mighty near not writing this—as I didn't get a letter today," she wrote, later in the first week. "Thought I'd give you a dose of your own medicine."

In these letters I am a year older and have mastered the art of making a lovable nuisance of myself. My dialogue is still not very scintillating, except to my parents and relatives. I kept asking where my Daddy had gone, and Bess finally gave me an elaborate explanation of the role of the army reserve in the nation's defense. A graduate of West Point might have had trouble digesting it. Only one fact stuck in my small brain: at lunch I mournfully announced: "My Daddy gone two weeks." The next morning even this intelligence had vanished. I awoke and asked, "Where *is* Daddy?" In her letter reporting this exchange, Bess added: "She is chattering just as hard as she can right now. She didn't wake up [from my nap] until 5:15 so I guess I'm in for a long session."

She also reported that she gave me "a small paddling for taking her nighty off." This was my first—but not my last—encounter with Mother as a disciplinarian. As an older sister who had spent a lot of time making unruly brothers obey orders, her first instinct was to reach for the hairbrush when I misbehaved.

These letters also reveal Bess's sharp eye for human foibles (besides mine), and how well she knew the men with whom her husband was serving. "I am greatly relieved about your morals," she wrote in another letter. "I am very sure if they are in Mr. Lee's keeping, [J. M. Lee was a fellow politician and major in the reserve.] they are safe. He couldn't lead you into temptation if it were staring him straight in his face. Has marriage made him any different? Any more human and like other people?"

In another letter, she told Harry that "Arthur's stenog called up this morning and wanted your address so I guess you'll find out soon what it was he had on his mind (?)" All by itself, that question mark demolished Arthur.

Bess remained keenly aware of her husband's political role. She forwarded him a letter from a Masonic Lodge, remarking that she was "afraid it might be something that should be attended to at once." In another letter she called a politician named Buck [Eugene I. Purcell] "as instructed" and reported that "he would see Mr. T. J. [Pendergast] tomorrow sure if he was in town." But there are also glimpses of her dislike for the political way of life. The next day she told Harry she had been invited by a friend to go to a dinner for Senator James Reed. "I was really sorry not to go, so didn't have to fib for once. But I couldn't leave the child."

These negative feelings did not alter her fundamental political loyalty. She was furious when she went down to the post office to mail one of her letters and found it locked. "I had to put your letter in the outside box this afternoon," she wrote. "If it doesn't get there tomorrow, I'll surely be peeved. Whoever heard of a P.O. being closed up so tight you couldn't even get inside to mail a letter? Another example of bum management under this Republican regime."

She could also get a laugh out of politics. The Kansas City *Star* seldom missed a chance to blast the Democrats. A local politician who had recently been worked over sued the paper for $3 million. Bess found this amusing. "If his standing and reputation are worth 3 what are yours worth?" she asked, apparently suggesting that this might be a way to get out of debt.

Once there was an interesting flashback to the Bess Wallace that Harry Truman scarcely knew, the upper-class girl who spent her weekends playing tennis and horseback riding at the Salisbury farm. Harry remarked that Spencer Salisbury and another expert horseman had been selected to represent the unit in a jumping competition. "Fancy Spencer being chosen for his excellent riding," Bess remarked, "when he dislikes it so. I remember tho' that he used to just look like part of the horse and I guess the knack of it must still stick."

In these letters there is also the appearance of what would become a long running worry about Harry Truman's health. Before he left for camp, he had suffered a series of severe headaches. He had had a few of these in the past when he overworked but these were so persistent and frequent, Bess became alarmed. "Have the head-aches quit?" she asked in one of her early 1926 letters. "I surely hope so." But that summer she had a more immediate worry. Lieutenant Colonel Truman (he had just been promoted) was showing an alarming interest in the army's aviation. "Please promise me you won't go up with any of those aviators, half baked or otherwise," she wrote.

In one of his letters, Harry remarked that there were a lot of politicians in camp, and they were having a great time "trying to get our campaign funds out of the poker game." Bess did not show the slightest hostility to what would soon become her husband's favorite recreation. "Bet on you, finding the politicians in the outfit," she replied. "Has your own campaign fund been augmented to any extent? Or depleted? Eh?" She clearly suspected the latter.

These letters also give us a good picture of Mother's day to day life in what might as well be called the Wallace compound on North Delaware Street. She and Natalie and Frank and George and May were constantly together, shopping, going for drives in the country in a new Dodge that all of them seemed to use interchangeably, although I gather it belonged to the Trumans. Scarcely a letter goes by without a comment about Natalie and Frank or George and May taking me on an outing. Once George and May took me golfing with hilarious results. I toddled around the practice tee, picking up everyone's golf balls and refused to stop until they gave me a club and ball of my own.

In a domestic crisis, however, it was Bess who took charge. Her mother came down with intestinal flu and the maid failed to show up. Madge Wallace was being visited by her old friend, Bessie Andrews, who was, Bess remarked to Harry, "worse than no help at all." Bess had to take charge of the kitchen and the nursing and in this letter I shrank to a footnote again. "M. is sound asleep and I will be soon."

At the end of these two weeks of separation a small political crisis gave Bess a chance to demonstrate just how astute she could be in regard to her husband's career. Remember Harry Truman was the unopposed Democratic nominee for presiding judge of Jackson County in the upcoming primary. A local attorney named J. Allen Prewitt, a political outsider, asked him to be on a committee he was hastily putting together for the visit of a St. Louis candidate for the U.S. Senate, Henry B. Hawes. "I'm afraid Mr. Hawes won't get very far under his patronage," Bess remarked.

She promptly checked with Tom Pendergast through an intermediary, and was told that "Mr. Pendergast considered it best for you to keep out of all fights." (St. Louis politicians were never popular in Jackson County.) Bess coolly telephoned Mr. Prewitt and told him Lieutenant Colonel Truman would not be home for another week—a whopping lie—so he could give him no help on his committee. "He said he wanted your moral support more than anything else and I felt like telling him he needed it," Bess reported to Harry.

On August 3, 1926, forty-two-year-old Harry Truman won the Democratic nomination for presiding judge and swept to victory in November, leading a tremendous Democratic comeback in Jackson County. Bess Truman had become a professional politician's wife.

Chapter Eight

The day after the votes rolled in, and dozens of congratulatory telephone calls followed them, Harry Truman was far away from Independence, organizing an offshoot of the Kansas City Automobile Club, The National Old Trails Association. Its goal was to encourage auto travel by persuading local officials to set up historic markers and build tourist facilities. Bess pursued him with complaints. She did not seem able to accept his absence as easily as she tolerated his two weeks' summertime army reserve duty.

Bess reported that Sunday was "poky" without her husband. She had wanted to go to a reception for Queen Marie of Rumania, who visited Kansas City during a world tour. Her majesty was the guest of honor at a musical extravaganza staged on November 5, to raise money to pay for the city's memorial to the dead of World War I. Bess and Harry had been invited. She declared herself unable to go without him.

Harry had wanted her to come with him on the Old Trails organizing trip. "You sure ought to be along. We'd have the time of our lives," he wrote from Great Bend, Kansas. "I've got a trip all arranged to California for next fall if you want to take it."

That suggestion was allowed to pass without comment. Instead, there were more complaints about missing the Queen and about the deluge of telephone calls from jobseekers. "I am ashamed now that I didn't stay home and fight the job hunters and take you to see the Queen," Harry wrote. "I'm afraid I'm not as thoughtful of your pleasure as I ought to be."

She had succeeded in making him feel guilty. Although I think I have made it clear that I love both my parents, I must confess to a certain prejudice in favor of my father as I read these letters. The man was only trying to make a living for himself and his family! I suspect it was his honesty that got him into trouble. Much as he loved his wife and daughter, Harry Truman also liked to get out and see the rest of the country. He poured out his fascination for places such as Dodge City and the characters he met there and elsewhere along the route.

I met Ham Bell, who was mayor of South Dodge at the same time Bat Masterson was mayor of North Dodge. One lies south of the R.R. and the other north of it. They tell me the Hon. Ham was not so pious in those days as he is now. He's a pillar of the Methodist Church and places a bouquet on the altar every Sunday now but they tell it on him that in days gone by, when he ran a dance hall in the part of the city of which he was the presiding officer, he was pitched bodily over into his part of town by the invincible Mr. Masterson when he came across the track to meet some ladies from Wichita who were going to work for him. It seems that inhabitants of the two sections were supposed to stay in their own bailiwicks and if they ventured into strange territory, they did so at their own bodily risk. It seems that Mr. Bell thought he could get over to the train and back without attracting attention, but a long scar on his face shows that he failed. . . .

Bess did not find such pieces of living history as interesting as her husband did. More to the point, he was enjoying himself too much—while he was several hundreds miles away from her.

It did not seem to matter that he had urged her to come with him. "The child" was her excuse to stay home now, although her two sisters-in-law were ready and willing to substitute for her, and Madge Wallace was in the big house with her and quite healthy, except for a sciatic hip. (Mary Paxton had remarked in 1922 when Madge was sixty that she was the youngest looking woman for her age that she had ever seen.) Madge, of course, was always eager to encourage this reluctance to leave home with her subtle manifestations of need for her "dear little girl."

Although Harry Truman was still paying off the debts he had acquired when the haberdashery failed, he was now making enough money to build a house. He even had a bank of his own to give him a mortgage. But the subject seems to have become moot. On the contrary, Bess seemed to want him to become part of the Wallace enclave in the indissoluble, all inclusive way that Natalie Ott, Frank Wallace's wife, and May Southern, George Wallace's wife, had joined the family.

One day around this time, May noticed her sister-in-law Natalie passing her house and asked in her cheerful way where she was going. "To Kansas City," said tiny, frowning Natalie. "But I'm not going to get the streetcar at the corner because if I do, Mother Wallace is going to come out of the house and ask me where I'm going. I'm not planning to do anything wrong. I just want to go someplace without telling her about it!"

Madge Gates Wallace was still largely a recluse who seldom left 219 North Delaware Street except to visit her sister Maud in Platte City and her sister Myra in Kansas City. Inevitably, her family had become her only interest in life, and she devoted almost every waking hour to worrying and fretting over them. Separation from them invariably produced anxiety. Whenever they left the house, she still had to know where they were going and what they were planning to do.

It was difficult for Bess to live day in and day out with such an attitude without absorbing some of it into her own feelings. She could remain independent of her mother on matters that required thoughtful analysis or decisive action, but in matters as indefinite as absence from home or as casual as wanting to see the Queen of Rumania it was easy to slip into disagreement with her traveling man.

Part of this emotional crosscurrent may have come from the awful time that Mary Paxton Keeley was having without a husband. Mike Keeley's mind became affected by his kidney disease, and he was committed to a state asylum in Virginia, where he died. Mary took a job on a country weekly in Missouri and simultaneously tried to raise her child and write a boys' adventure book. A one woman band, she spent most of her time driving over mud roads in all kinds of weather and grew more and more exhausted.

Mary showed up in Independence one day early in 1927 looking like a refugee from a famine. She had a deep cough that alarmed everyone who remembered that her mother had died of tuberculosis. Her father put her to bed and the doctor diagnosed pneumonia. We can be certain that Bess was one of her constant visitors.

In these years, Mother demonstrated an extraordinary devotion to friends when they were struck down by illness or misfortune. Shortly before Mary came home, Bess had received a letter from the mother of one of these friends, thanking her for "the inestimable number of dear things" she had done for her daughter during her fatal illness.

During her convalescence, Mary no doubt discussed with Bess the rise to journalistic eminence of their old classmate Charlie Ross. Charlie had become the Washington, D.C., reporter for the St. Louis *Post-Dispatch* and was building a national reputation. We can be fairly certain that he was on Mary's mind, because we know from her letters in the Truman Library that she and Charlie had seen each other around this time and he had confessed that he still loved her. Since 1913, he had been married to Florence Griffin, a darkhaired beauty from St. Louis, and had two sons. During the year 1926, Mary wrote him a series of passionate letters that she never mailed. "When I think what you have done for me," she wrote in one of them. "I was growing hard. You have softened me. I thought I must harden my heart against every man."

Today these feelings might have led to a sensational divorce. But in the Independence of 1926 the iron rules of respectability were still in force and Mary could only pour out her yearnings on paper. She could not even bring herself to confide her feelings to Bess. But Mother's presence, her loving companionship, had a lot to do with Mary's recovery. When she was well again, Bess joined Mary's father and stepmother in advising her to quit the newspaper business. She simply did not have the physical stamina to work twelve hours a day and try to raise a son and incidentally write a book.

Mary decided to get a master's degree in journalism and become a teacher. A year or so later she was offered a professorship at Christian College in Columbia. It was more than a little ironic that she, who had set out to conquer the newspaper world while Charlie Ross hesitated to leave his teaching job, was now the teacher while Charlie was a big-time reporter.

Meanwhile, Presiding Judge Harry Truman was hard at work building his political reputation. He had an all-Democratic county court and the backing of the Democratic organization, but that was only a necessary prelude to accomplishment, as far as he was concerned. Although I was still considerably short (literally) of being an expert observer, I can add a few bits of reminiscence to these days. I remember happy hours in the family Dodge sitting between Mother and Dad while they drove over every mile of road in Jackson County. Again and again, while I lobbied for a stop in Blue Springs, where they made the best ice-cream sodas in the world, Dad would stop the car and get out and stamp on the edge of the road and see it crumble beneath his feet. These "piecrust" roads had been built by previous administrations and were a disgrace as well as a safety hazard. Judge Truman vowed that his administration would build roads that would last. That sounds easy, but in Jackson County it involved him in all sorts of battles.

He also was determined to cut the swollen county payroll to enable
him to pay for the roads without raising taxes to astronomical
heights. He boldly reduced the number of road overseers from sixty
to sixteen and announced that contracts would be given to the lowest
bidder, no matter whether the contractor came from Jackson County
and was a Democrat or came from Nebraska and voted the straight
Republican ticket. Politicians, contractors, and jobholders went
howling to Tom Pendergast, demanding that he discipline Truman.
But Pendergast liked the aura of honest government Harry Truman
was creating in Jackson County and he refused to interfere.

In some diary notes he made in the early 1930s, Dad paints a gritty
picture of his two colleagues on the county court, Howard Vrooman
and Robert W. Barr. They were both playboys, in politics for what
they could get out of it. Vrooman was a follower of the Rabbit boss,
Joe Shannon, who ordered him, Dad recalled, "to treat me for what I
am in his estimation, that is the lowest human on earth." But
Vrooman was too much of a backslapper to pursue this feud. He
preferred to have a good time, even while the court was in session.

He and Barr used to shoot craps . . . down behind the bench while I
transacted the business. Joe [Shannon] finally had to send his emissaries to
see me when he wanted anything, because when I wanted something done
I'd let Barr & Vrooman start a crap game and then introduce a long and
technical order. Neither of them would have time to read it and over it
would go. I got a lot of good legislation for Jackson Co. over while they
shot craps.

Working under such conditions, Judge Truman's headaches soon
returned to worry Bess. She herself was affected by the turmoil. She
began having what she called "spasms" or "fits" in the middle of the
night, particularly after she had a bad dream. On July 14, 1927, she
wrote to Harry, who was on reserve duty once more: "Your daughter
and I are being extremely lazy while you are gone. It's just what I
need, I guess, because I'm surely feeling better. Haven't had a spasm
since Monday A.M. Had a terrible dream then and it brought on one
of those nervous fits. Isn't that silly?"

With her resolute, willpower approach to life, Bess was trying to
dismiss those attacks of nerves and by and large she succeeded. But
this tight control of her emotions was sometimes experienced by
other members of the family—in particular her daughter—as harsh
and uncaring. "Marg is so cross today," she wrote in another July

1927 letter, when I was three and a half. "We've been continuously at war. No doubt you would lay it to a change in the weather. Personally I think it is the heat and original sin."

Right there is prefigured a pattern that would prevail for most of our family life together. My father unceasingly defended and—in Bess's opinion—spoiled me. She always was ready to lay down the law, reinforced by the hairbrush if necessary.

Sometimes in her determination to drive original sin out of my system, she was unintentionally cruel to me. She simply did not know when she hurt my feelings. In one of her 1927 letters she penned a little vignette of how she dealt with me. "I was giving her the very dickens last night about bedtime as usual and she was sitting down here crying and crying and finally she burst forth with 'When is my daddy coming?' That settled all the discipline. I just had to howl. It was so ridiculous."

I'm sure I was amusing, from an adult point of view. But I was too young to understand why my mother was laughing at me.

There is an interesting glimpse in these letters of the way Bess saw the difference between herself and her husband. She was far more inclined to be hard on people who deserved it. On his way to camp in a borrowed car, Harry had had a flat, which was obviously caused by the owner's failure to repair a slow leak. He was furious and vowed he would cuss out the fellow when he got home. Bess agreed he "ought to hear about it. But you'll calm down before you get home and he'll never know anything about it."

Then she got a fiendish thought. "Maybe it would be a good idea to say nothing and let the same thing happen to him & hope for the worst. That's a Christian spirit, eh?"

Throughout this 1927 tour of reserve duty, Bess kept Harry in close touch with the political situation in Jackson County, sending him a stream of clippings from the Kansas City *Star* about the controversies swirling around the county court. The Republicans tried to torpedo Judge Truman's road program by pushing a law through the legislature calling for a bipartisan commission to supervise the roads of each county. The Jackson County attorney called it unconstitutional and Judge Truman went ahead with his plan to ask the voters to approve a $6.5 million bond issue for new roads. The *Star* reported this as the court's "defi" to the legislature in one of Bess's clippings that have survived the years.

In another letter she reported a visit from an important officer in the DAR (the Daughters of the American Revolution), who gushed over what a wonderful job Harry was doing. "I kept thinking about the marker she wants," Bess wrote.

She even kept an eye on his office. She reported that when she paid a visit, she found three of the staff sitting around having a bull session and the secretary cleaning her nails. "Why didn't you give her a vacation too?" Bess asked. "You might as well have."

She let Harry know she missed him acutely. Her cousin Helen Wallace gave a dinner party in Kansas City and Bess "kept unconsciously looking for you all evening." She bemoaned a "bum Sunday" without him—and without a letter.

It is easy to see how this tangle of emotion and pressure could produce nerves. Bess associated them with being overtired and tried to ration her energy as much as possible. When Eddie Jacobson offered to drive her to Fort Leavenworth and come back the same day, she declined. "A six hour drive would about finish me," she wrote. "The one thing I try to avoid is getting absolutely tired out."

But there were some compensations for being Judge Truman's wife. She told Harry one of them with unconcealed pleasure. She and her mother went shopping for furniture for the downstairs bedroom. Madge Wallace had decided to move to this room, where her parents had slept, because her sciatic hip was making it difficult for her to climb the stairs. The store manager gave Madge "quite a bit off," Bess reported. "He laid great stress on the fact that he knew Mr. Tucker [the owner] would want to do it for you."

That little story emphasizes a new fact in the lives of the Trumans and the Wallaces; 219 North Delaware Street now belonged to Madge Gates Wallace. Her mother, Elizabeth Gates, had died in 1924, about six months after my birth. (It is one of my great regrets that no one had a picture taken of the four generations of Gates-Wallace-Truman women alive for that half year.) She left most of her estate, including the house, to her ailing son, Frank E. Gates, who lived in Colorado Springs. But his health was so frail he could not leave Colorado, so he sold the house to Madge for $10,000.

Those who lived there, including Bess, were constantly aware that it was Madge's house. She made many of the curtains by hand. She bought new furniture and disposed of old pieces she no longer wanted. In the late 1920s, she and her son Fred embarked on an ambitious redecorating program, using money Madge had inherited from Frank Gates, who died a year after their mother. Crystal lamps were installed in the living room and music room, and the chandelier in the living room went to the dump. The mirrors and wood shelving around the big fireplace were removed, and the library was repainted white with red trim, which in retrospect strikes me as ghastly.

Until she decided to move downstairs, Madge Wallace occupied the big master bedroom in the front of the house. Bess and Harry slept in the same east bedroom Bess had occupied since she came to the house in 1904. After two years in a crib in my parents' room, I moved to a bedroom of my own, which was connected to theirs by a passageway built onto the upstairs porch. My uncle Fred, Bess's youngest brother, slept in a room down the hall from me. From my four- and five-year-old viewpoint, he was a cheerful bachelor, boyish for his age, who liked to romp around the house with me.

Dinner always emphasized for me that we were living in Madge Wallace's house. She and my father sat at opposite ends of the table. Whether she sat at the head and he at the foot or vice versa was anybody's guess. I sat between my mother and grandmother, on her left, and Fred sat opposite us, on her right. The atmosphere was always very formal. My manners were expected to be perfect, and so was everyone's costume. I always put on a clean dress, as did Bess and Madge. Fred and my father wore suits and ties.

The conversation was always subdued, even when Fred and my father discussed politics. No one ever raised his or her voice. Nor did Bess ever lose her temper with me, even when I did something as goofy as knocking over a water glass. Under no circumstances were Madge's nerves to be agitated. Bess sometimes offered her opinion of a political problem or a politician (often one and the same), but on that subject Madge maintained a chilly silence.

On Sundays, Mother and Dad and I drove out to the Truman farm in Grandview for a midday meal cooked by Mamma Truman. Here the atmosphere was totally different. The conversation was vivid and salty and full of belly laughs, as Mamma Truman passed judgment on everything from uppity neighbors to the Republicans in Washington. Bess had a wonderful time. She liked Mamma Truman immensely. They were really, behind their very different exteriors, remarkably similar. They were both very hard on people, but Bess, trained to be a lady, usually hesitated to say what she thought. Mamma Truman never hesitated.

To please her husband, Bess also worked at being friendly with her

sister-in-law, Mary Truman. That was a job, as even Harry was ready
to admit. It was now pretty clear that Aunt Mary was going to be an
old maid. She was extremely touchy about her failure to get a man,
which lowered her in her own eyes, and made her demand respect
from everyone in the family in all sorts of petty ways. In a letter Bess
wrote to Harry while he was on reserve duty in 1928, she apologized
for not going to a picnic at the farm, and added: "I'm afraid I missed
Mary again." The implication was clear—Mary would soon be complaining that Bess was ignoring her.

To outside observers, life in the Wallace enclave seemed to be
proceeding serenely. Bess's two older brothers and their wives still
lived in their small houses beside the main house. Madge also bought
these from Frank Gates and sold them to her sons for "one dollar and
other valuable considerations." But inside the family, things were not
so peaceful. Banker Frank Wallace was in constant turmoil over a
quarrel that developed between the Platte City relatives (Aunt
Maud's husband and children) and Boulware Wallace (Aunt Myra's
husband) over the value of their shares in the Waggoner-Gates mill.

Frank still spent a half hour with his mother every day when he
came home from work. But George Wallace had a very different
attitude. Sharp-tongued and high spirited, George seemed to resent
his mother's smothering presence. Although he could not break away
from her, he seldom went near her, and when he did the result was
frequently a quarrel. He worked as an order clerk in a Kansas City
lumber mill.

But these were minor worries compared to the anxiety generated
by Bess's youngest brother, Fred. He was trained as an architect, but
he did not seem able to make enough money at his profession to set
up on his own. Even if he had been able to do so, I doubt if he could
have left his mother. Mary Paxton, in a letter to Bess, remarked that
it was wonderful that Fred and his mother were "pals." But Fred's
life, as it developed over the next few decades, suggests that it might
have been better for him if he had cut Madge's silver cord.

Born in 1900, Fred grew up with the century. Everyone liked him.
He was charming, good-looking, and he loved a party. Of the three
brothers, he was the one who developed the strongest physical resemblance to his father. (That fact alone may explain Bess's nervous
spasms in the night.) By his late twenties, Fred began showing
ominous signs that he had inherited David Willock Wallace's weakness for liquor. Friends carried Fred home completely ossified on

more than one night. As she had done with her husband, Madge Wallace never said a word of reproach to her son. Instead, she often would sit up all night beside his bed and continue the vigil into the next day. It is not pleasant to think of the memories these episodes must have stirred in her mind—and in her daughter's mind.

In her anxiety to help Fred, Bess made one of the few serious mistakes of her life. On May 8, 1928, Harry Truman's forty-fourth birthday, the voters approved a $6.5 million bond issue to improve Jackson County's roads and $500,000 for a county hospital. Bess persuaded her husband to put Fred on the county payroll as the architect in charge of the hospital. Fred's drinking and general irresponsibility soon became a major source of strain in their marriage.

Oblivious to these woes, I was growing into a perpetual-motion and talking machine. On rainy days, I demanded and got permission to ride my bicycle around the house. On sunny ones I zoomed up and down our driveway and around the corner to see my aunts and uncles next door. It took a while for Bess to notice how many of these visits coincided with dinner time and to discover that I was cadging ice cream and cookies, which enabled me to ignore vegetables and any other food I happened to dislike. Directives were instantly dispatched to Aunt Natalie and Aunt May that I was not to be fed anything within three hours of dinner.

One day I dug a marvelous canal through the backyard and filled it with water, which demolished some of my grandmother's favorite flowers. I launched a fleet of boats made from walnut shells, each with a tiny individual sail, and played admiral for several hours before I was discovered. It is interesting that Madge Wallace, although she was very upset, did not say a word to me. The complaint was made to Bess, who ordered me to fill up my miniature version of Suez, or else.

As an ex-athlete, Bess welcomed an active daughter. But she should have been warned by a phenomenon she noticed when I was five: "I've been putting extremely few clothes on Marg and letting her out into the sunshine," she told Dad, "but she just *won't* tan. It's so provoking." It would take Mother years to realize that I was not an outdoors type.

It was around this time that Bess started calling me "Marg" with a hard "g" while my father preferred "Margie." While repeating my disclaimer to be a psychologist, I can only say that Marg still resounds in my ears with orders, impatience, and discipline in it. The other name has none of those things. By five, I was a total Daddy's girl. One night, while out for a ride to Blue Springs for a soda, everyone started improvising lyrics for songs. Harry Truman had been away on reserve duty for nine or ten days. I piped up with a one-line lament: "I saw my Daddy—once he was here." Bess and everyone else thought it was hilarious.

In 1930, the year I began school, I gave Mother a scare that she converted into a lifetime worry. A strange man appeared at school one day and told my first-grade teacher he was calling for "Mary Truman, Judge Truman's daughter." I was registered under my full name, Mary Margaret Truman, but no one, including my teacher, ever used the first name. She decided to call my father. By the time he arrived with the sheriff, the teacher had also called Mother, who rushed to school fearing the worst. In the meantime, the man had vanished. He was later identified as a political foe who wanted to give Judge Truman a scare. The episode wreaked havoc on Mother's nerves. Thereafter she never let me go to school alone, a rule she enforced until I was well into my teens. When it came to worrying, Mother was in a class by herself.

Meanwhile, Judge Truman was pushing ahead with his road program. It was still a struggle. He had to deal with the hatred of the city manager of Kansas City, Henry McElroy, whose bond issue had been defeated at the polls, and the jealousy and greed of numerous crooked contractors from Kansas City, who had bet on McElroy and now wanted to get a piece of the action from Truman. Nevertheless, Judge Truman was on his way to becoming one of the better known politicians in Missouri. He was president of The National Old Trails Association, he was rising steadily in the Masonic Order to the post he was soon to hold, Grand Master of the Grand Lodge of Missouri. Even the normally critical Kansas City *Star* called his administration "extraordinarily efficient."

Behind the scenes, Bess continued to worry about Harry's health. The tensions of his job still gave him terrific headaches, and her letters to him make many anxious references to them. In 1928, when he was again on reserve duty at Fort Riley, she asked: "How did your physical examination turn out? Don't hold anything back!" In 1929, Harry was taking some medicine for his headaches and frazzled nerves. By now Bess had perceived that these reserve tours were really much needed escapes from the political pressure cooker in which he worked. "I was awfully glad to hear your nerves were getting back to normal," she wrote. "Are you still taking your tonic or have you passed the point of needing it? I expect the life you are leading is a better tonic than that green bottle."

Although she still signed her letters "lots of love," they now began with "Dear Harry" or occasionally "Dear Dad." She wrote straight from the shoulder, the way she talked. "You needn't get so upstage [how's that for Missouri slang?] about our coming out [to Fort Riley]. I'd surely like to—but I'll take that money [the train fare] and have our daughter's tonsils out."

That last remark would seem to give us a glimpse of Harry Truman's honesty. He had just spent $7 million in public money and his wife had to scrimp (the train tickets cost $15) to have a much needed operation for his daughter. But that is not the whole story. Partly because of her mother's extravagance, partly because it came naturally to her, Bess was a fierce penny pincher. Her letters in 1929, when she was forty-four, report her doing such money-saving chores as painting the back porch and the front stairs and making a dress for me.

Bess continued to stay in close touch with all aspects of her husband's political career. A stream of clippings from the *Star* went to him when he was away. She smoothly fielded phone calls urging the Judge to attend political funerals or see an importunate jobseeker. In 1929, she calmed Harry's agitation over a threatened investigation of the county farm, about which the Kansas City *Star* had made noises. Bess went straight to the newspaperman who could have done them real damage if he took it seriously, her sister-in-law's father, Colonel Southern, the editor of the *Examiner*. Southern assured her he had no intention of pursuing the story. Bess told Harry this good news. "I'm glad you're not here to be bothered with it and don't let it worry you. There hasn't been another word in the paper and the *Star* has probably realized the foolishness of publishing the story."

She added that he might call the other judges on the court and "tell them what to say. Mr. Ash says those two fools up there don't know what to do."

Fred Wallace remained a worry for both Bess and her husband. In one of those private memoranda Harry Truman wrote at various times in his life, and which have come into my possession, he gives us a glimpse of how he dealt with Fred. As his first term as presiding judge came to a close, he set down several pages of pithy, poignant details about his struggles with the venal crooks around Pendergast and some of the compromises he had been forced to make to deal with them. "I've got the $6.5 million worth of roads on the ground and at a figure that makes the crooks tear their hair," he wrote at the end of this narrative. Then he turned to Fred. "The hospital is up at less cost than any similar institution in spite of my problem brother-in-law, whom I'd had to employ on the job to keep peace in the family. I've had to run the hospital job myself and pay him for it."

Perhaps Bess realized the strain that her brother placed on an already overburdened Harry Truman. Perhaps her intense interest in her husband's political operations, her worry over his headaches, were a way of saying: "I'm sorry."

Chapter Nine

In that same year, 1929, while Bess and Harry tried to cope with their public and private worries in Jackson County, the United States found itself with a worry that rapidly became a national nervous breakdown. The stock market on Wall Street, which had been soaring up, up, up in an ever more dizzying climb, went into a nose-dive steeper than any previous plunge in history. By the time the dazed survivors staggered out of the wreckage in early 1930, the country was in the grip of the Great Depression.

For a while it looked like Harry Truman's bad luck was pursuing him. Not only were he and Bess driven to near distraction with pleas from jobseekers day and night, but the major part of his development program for Jackson County was about to go before the voters in another bond issue—this one for a colossal $7,950,000. He wanted to build new courthouses in Independence and in Kansas City, and complete the network of roads he was weaving around and through the county. Could he persuade voters stunned by the economic paralysis gripping the nation to spend more public money?

Unnoticed except by a few in the mounting turmoil was a political event in Jackson County. On September 3, 1929, a month before the stock market took its historic dive, Mike Pendergast, Boss Tom's brother, died. The political leadership of eastern Jackson County passed to Harry Truman. With his own organization to back him, he hurled himself into the task of persuading the voters to approve the bond issue. First, however, he had to get reelected himself, which he did, handsomely, in 1930, running far ahead of the other names on the ticket.

As part of his plan to sell the bond issue to the voters, Judge Truman, like many other local officials, halved the salaries of everyone on the county payroll, including his own. Bess decided that this policy also had to be enforced at 219 North Delaware Street, and my fifty cents a week allowance was slashed to a quarter. My squawks could be heard in Kansas City, but I got nowhere. I had to rely for a steady supply of candy and ice cream on surreptitious quarters slipped to me by Judge Truman. Whenever he got caught doing this, a quarrel erupted. "How am I ever going to teach that child the value of money?" Bess would storm.

The Judge would feign repentance, but after a decent interval the quarters would start coming again.

As Harry Truman took his case for the second bond issue to the voters, most people saw a politician who was acquiring a state and national reputation. In 1930, he became a director of the National Conference on City Planning. Around the same time he was elected president of the Greater Kansas City Plan Association. But Bess saw a man who drove himself relentlessly to the point of exhaustion and found almost intolerable the barrage of pleas for help that descended on him each day.

A glimpse of his nervous exhaustion comes from several letters in 1931. Early in February, he found the pressure so unbearable he re-treated to Little Rock, Arkansas, for a rest. That he would leave home on the eve of Bess's birthday—and mine—troubled him and he tried to explain it. "I don't know whether you entirely appreciate or not the tremendous amount of strain that's been on me since November," he wrote.

He went on to list the strains. His two fellow judges had been replaced by the voters and in the last months of their term they tried to steal as much money as possible. The county's finances were in deplorable shape, with thousands of people unable to pay their taxes, and Mamma Truman had had to refinance the farm in a way that exposed her to being foreclosed.

Next came a sentence that may have been a reference to Fred Wallace. "You and I had our own difficulties to look after and with it all I was becoming so keyed up that I either had to run away or go on a big drunk. That latter alternative never did have much appeal, so I've taken the other one."

He reported that "my head hasn't ached and I've slept like a baby because I know the phone's not going to ring, and that no one's going to stop me with a tale of woe when I walk down the street."

In July 1931, when he went to reserve camp, Bess was still worried about her forty-seven-year-old husband. "I never did hate so to see you leave for camp as I did this year," she wrote. "I just felt you weren't up to scratch physically and needed somebody to go along with you. But I do hope the decided change in environment and work will make you over."

That year, Judge Truman had to return in the middle of his two weeks for a special session of the court. It turned out to be a lulu, "with every pest in the county there." He emerged from it in a state of nerves and went home to find Bess in a sulk. He had spent the entire weekend visit on politics and practically ignored her. They had a first-class fight.

In a letter from Fort Riley, Harry only semi-apologized. "I was very much surprised at your peeve last evening," he wrote. He described the chaos in the courtroom and said he was "about ready to blow up when another bellows is turned into the balloon (and it's really the only puff that can count) [he meant her peevishness]." Then he added a remark that absolutely amazed me when I read it. "You tell my daughter that the next time you choose to spoil two days in succession, for her please to remedy the situation."

Bess apologized for her "disgruntled spell" and the unpleasant incident was soon forgotten. The bond issue passed in May 1931, all $7,950,000 of it, and Judge Truman was ready to complete his program. A glimpse of his rising political stature comes from two letters he wrote to Bess later in the summer of 1931. One was from St. Louis, where he told of conferring with some of the leading politicians of Missouri, including Champ Clark's son, Bennett Clark, who was planning to run for the Senate in 1932 and urged Judge Truman to run for governor to bolster the state ticket. "I'm receiving more foolish encouragement to run down here than I have at home," he wrote.

From St. Louis he went on to New York, where he addressed a National Conference on City Planning. He had called up Bess just before he left St. Louis and tried to persuade her to take a midnight train from Kansas City and join him. But as usual, she said no. Writing from the Biltmore in New York, he continued his report on his conversations with Bennett Clark and the other St. Louis politicos. "You may yet be the first lady of Missouri," he wrote. "And even a larger position than that isn't beyond the bounds of your ability and good looks."

Alas, the Truman boomlet for governor collapsed when Tom Pendergast announced that he was going to back the man who had run and lost in 1928, Francis Wilson. Judge Truman continued his building and road program in Jackson County. Ever the perfectionist, he decided to erect the best courthouse in the country. This turned him into a traveling man again, to Bess's considerable distress. In the first six months of 1932, he drove 24,000 miles around the country visiting courthouses and conferring with architects and civic planners to see what sort of buildings other officials had put up. He found the model he was looking for in Shreveport, Louisiana, and hired the architect, Edward F. Neild, to design one for Kansas City.

The drafting work, the interior decoration, the nuts and bolts aspects of the job were handled by local architectural firms. They also supervised the rebuilding and modernizing of the much smaller Independence courthouse. Against his better judgment, Judge Truman put his brother-in-law, Fred Wallace, on this local architectural payroll.

In 1930, Fred had married a sweet, pretty girl named Christine Meyer. Like mothers and sisters before and since, Bess and Madge hoped that love and marriage would reform Fred. It did seem to change him for a while. He pretty much stopped drinking and tried hard to find work. But Fred had chosen a discouraging time to try to reform. The Depression made it difficult for men with good job records to stay employed. Fred began drifting back to alcohol for consolation. Once more friends began depositing him on the porch of 219 North Delaware Street after midnight.

Around this time, George Wallace also began displaying signs of instability. Every so often he would drink heavily. With him, Bess did not hesitate to unleash her temper. She gave George some lectures that would have turned Falstaff himself into a total abstainer. George straightened out and with some help from Judge Truman became maintenance superintendent of the Jackson County highway department, a job he held for the rest of his life. But Bess never said a word of reproach to Fred, as far as I know. With him, she followed her mother's example of suffering in silence. Was it Fred's resemblance to his father? Perhaps. Fred also was an artist at displaying remorse. He knew exactly how to play on his mother's and sister's sympathy.

I remained oblivious to this emotional turmoil. I was immersed in my eight-year-old world, which consisted of eight or nine other girls my age who lived on the block. We formed a club called The Henhouse Hicks and connected our houses by a complicated web of wires and string over which we sent messages and gifts. In the abandoned henhouse we staged plays and published a newspaper. Bess watched all this with a tolerance that amazed me. Only when I began exploring her childhood did I realize how much we were repeating her girlhood experiences in the Cadiz Club, where she was the stage manager for Mary Paxton's plays. Now I wonder if there was a kind of catharsis for Bess, watching me grow up as she did in so many ways, but without her burden of sorrow. I am playing amateur psychologist again, but I find it a very consoling thought.

I say this because at the time I often had the feeling that I was a disappointment to my mother. As I have noted, there was a hard as well as a soft side to Bess Wallace Truman, and those closest to her were, alas, the ones who often saw the hardness. I have mentioned the hairbrush and her tendency to laugh at me when I least expected it. She also had a gift for devastating comments. One I particularly remember zinged me when I was eight or nine. For some now forgotten reason, my friends and I suddenly began to wonder if any of us were adopted. It became an enormously important question to me, and I rushed into the house and called upstairs. "Mother, am I adopted?"

"No," Bess replied. "If you were, we would have done better."

One reason for this acerbic tone may have been the way I was rapidly developing into a major worry for both Harry and Bess. In the summer of 1932, Bess wrote to Colonel (another promotion) Truman at Camp Ripley, Minnesota: "Dr. Brick [his full name was Dr. Brickhouse Wilson] was here this morning & said Marg had been doing entirely too much & she would have to quiet down considerably for four or five days & he would be back. [He] said the hot weather alone has a tendency to wear people out. She is so tired today she can hardly move."

That was how I reacted to a Missouri summer. But the winters were my really grim season. If there was a cold or a flu germ floating anywhere in Jackson County, I caught it. My tonsillectomy, paid for by Bess's refusal to spend the money on railroad tickets to Fort Riley, was a failure. One tonsil grew back, guaranteeing me an annual round of sore throats. A major contributor to my problems was, I now realize, 219 North Delaware Street itself. The house's heating system was, to put it mildly, antiquated. There was no heat whatsoever on the upper floor. I can remember awakening on some winter mornings in a bedroom that could have been used for an icebox. During the day, the temperature in many of the big rooms seldom rose above 60 degrees. In spells of bitter cold, the library and music rooms were closed to try to concentrate the heat in the other rooms. But the kitchen was the only room I remember as truly warm.

In 1933, my penchant for the sneezes reached a sort of climax. I went from the flu to pneumonia to rheumatic fever. The weather was atrocious and Dr. Wilson decided he would not have a patient to worry through the summer if he did not get me out of that chilblain palace on North Delaware Street. He ordered Bess to take me south for the rest of the winter.

She chose Biloxi, Mississippi, on the Gulf of Mexico. We rented a cottage on the water, with a big yard for me to play in. My improvement was almost instantaneous. When Bess reported this good news to Harry, he replied that he felt "almost as if a hundred pound weight had been lifted from my head." I was dreadfully bored. I missed my friends and displayed no appreciation whatsoever for my return to health and energy. I did not know it, but Bess was not much happier with Biloxi. In one of her letters to Harry, she referred to it as "this burg." It was not all Biloxi's fault. Bess missed her husband and her mother and other members of the Wallace clan. She had brought along a nurse who complained about everything from the temperature of the water to the character of the local residents.

Although it did not occur to me at the time, I now realize this was the first time in my life that I was alone with my mother for an extended period. We got along pretty well, except for one interesting incident. When a local woman came to do the wash, I joined her in the backyard, where she scrubbed the clothes by hand and then fed them through a wringer. I volunteered to feed them and was having a pleasant time when Bess abruptly called me into the house. "We don't do things like that," she said.

Bess remained a Democrat all her life, but unlike Harry Truman, it took her a long time to become one with a small "d."

While we basked in the sunshine on the Gulf, Harry Truman divided his time between Grandview and Delaware Street. In one revealing exchange, he told Bess that he had "had dinner with your mother who by the way seemed really glad to see me." After reporting on the health of everyone in the family, Harry got down to the important subject, the politics of Jackson County and his future. He told Bess that Pendergast was still backing him and had assured him that when his term as judge expired he could run for Congress in a district recently created in eastern Jackson County or he would support him for county collector. The salary of this post had shrunk to a Depression size $10,000, but it was still the best paying job in the county. "I don't have to make a decision until next year. Think about it," Harry told Bess.

Tom Pendergast was feeling expansive in 1933. After twelve years of Republican rule, a Democrat had returned to the White House and Boss Tom had helped him get there. The governor of New York, Franklin D. Roosevelt, a cousin of the Republican Theodore Roosevelt, had won a landslide victory with his pledge of a "new deal for the American people." To most Missourians, this Hudson River Valley aristocrat was a remote figure, whose accent and background seemed as foreign to them as a British prime minister. But Tom Pendergast had had no trouble recognizing a fellow politician.

Mr. Roosevelt's campaign manager, a genial Irishman named James A. Farley, had come to Kansas City and talked the language Boss Tom understood—a guarantee that a grateful president would reward him for his support. The Pendergast machine had backed Roosevelt down the line, from the nomination to the election, in spite of a sentimental yearning for Al Smith, the Irish-Catholic New Yorker who had stirred a whirlwind of bigotry when he received the Democratic nomination in 1928. When it came to winning elections, sentiment did not play much of a part in Tom Pendergast's calculations.

Before Judge Truman reached the happy turn in the political road that Pendergast offered him, he had some difficult bridges to cross. In Washington, FDR had called Congress into special session to deal with the appalling economic situation. Between Mr. Roosevelt's election and inauguration, the nation had reeled toward collapse. The index of industrial production sank to an all-time low. Banks went bust by the hundreds, taking the savings of millions of middle-class people with them.

While the President and Congress were grounding out a series of programs to cope with the crisis, Judge Truman had to deal with the immediate realities on the local level, where there was simply not enough money to run the county government. The eastern half of Jackson County, mostly farm country, was penniless. The western half, which included Kansas City, was full of empty factories and offices. Tax collections had dwindled. Judge Truman decided that the county payroll would have to be slashed and the tax rate raised to keep the government functioning.

It was not easy to fire a man in 1933. It meant you were putting him on the unemployment rolls. Judge Truman's letters to Biloxi tell Bess his agony. "We are discharging some two hundred people and every one of them and all his friends will try to see me. I was sick last night after the [court] session and lost my supper." In another letter he warned her: "Please be careful about eating anything that comes in the mail. Someone sent me a cake the other day and I threw it away. With these discharges coming off you can't tell what they'll do." The turmoil was so intense, Judge Truman's next few letters came from the Pickwick Hotel in Kansas City, where he was hiding out from this small army of irate job losers and their friends.

During this same period, Bess received a number of letters from her mother. With her marvelous ability to ignore unpleasant realities, Madge Wallace never mentioned the political uproar swirling around her son-in-law. In fact, she never even mentioned him, period. Most of one letter was devoted to more improvements on the house—painting the exterior, the selection of new awnings for the porches. She urged Bess to write George, who had been ill, "often." Bess apparently took her advice, and when George got a letter one day and her husband did not, Harry Truman sent her a scorching complaint.

Bess replied with a scorcher of her own, which has, perhaps fortunately, been lost. I must confess that I am hard put to feel sympathetic with either of them about their insistence on writing a letter every day when they were apart. It is a wonderful testimony of their affection, but it was exhausting for those who were expected to imitate them. In these Biloxi–Independence letters, there begins a fatherly complaint that I was to hear for the next forty years. "What's the matter with my girl? Has she forgotten how to write?"

Before he left for Biloxi to bring us home, Judge Truman made a very important speech to the Kansas City Chamber of Commerce about his new $4 million courthouse. Their support was crucial to its success, and he was enormously relieved to report to Bess that the audience was very friendly. "Everyone seemed to go away sold on the idea that the building should be put up," he wrote. "When I get that job done I can probably retire to a quiet job and enjoy life a little bit with my family."

Bess was in a similar frame of mind after this two month separation. She was so impatient to see him, she disputed how long it would take him to get from St. Louis to Biloxi. He claimed it would take two days, but she noted that "it only took you 36 hours to go all the way home."

In Biloxi, and in the remaining months of 1933, Bess and Harry discussed the choice that Tom Pendergast seemed to be offering them, between county collector and U.S. congressman. Harry deftly pinpointed the differences between the two jobs the first time he mentioned them, in the spring of that year. The congressman's job paid less, but he would have "an opportunity to be a power in the nation." The collector's job had the appeal of more money and one other thing, which he knew was not unimportant to Bess. They could "stay home."

Although Bess's letters for this period have been lost, there are no indications in Harry's surviving letters that she made any immediate declaration in favor of the collector's job. But a good deal can be deduced about her preference from a very emotional letter that Harry wrote to her on the eve of his forty-ninth birthday.

> Tomorrow I'll be forty-nine and for all the good I've done the forty might as well be left off. Take it all together though the experience has been worthwhile; I'd like to do it again. I've been in a railroad, bank, farm, war, politics, *love* (only once and it still sticks), been busted and still am and yet I have stayed an idealist. I still believe that my sweetheart is the ideal woman and that my daughter is her duplicate. I think that for all the horrors of war it still makes a man if he's one to start with. Politics should make a thief, a roué, and a pessimist of anyone, but I don't believe I'm any of them and if I can get the Kansas City courthouse done without scandal no other judge will have done as much, and then maybe I can retire as collector and you and the young lady can take some European and South American tours when they'll do you the most good; or maybe go to live in Washington and see all the greats and near greats in action. We'll see.

My nine-year-old opinion was not consulted on this choice, but my reading of this letter convinces me that Harry Truman was leaning strongly toward Washington. After eight years of tremendous achievements as presiding judge, he was not ready to "retire" into the do-nothing collector's job. As never before, Washington, D.C. was the place where politics was reshaping the nation. It is an index of his awareness of Bess's inclination to stay home that he could offer the two choices as more or less equal.

Meanwhile Harry Truman concentrated on finishing the Kansas City courthouse with an artistic flourish. He had decided to put an equestrian statue of his (and the Democrats') hero, Andrew Jackson, in front of it. Once more he took to the roads, while Bess stayed home in Wallaceville, and soon located the man to do it, sculptor Charles Keck. Judge Truman liked his work so much—Keck had done a magnificent statue of Stonewall Jackson on horseback for Charlottesville, Virginia—he decided to order a second statue for the courthouse in Independence.

On January 1, 1934, he was writing to Bess from New York, where he visited Keck in his Tenth Street studio and saw how the work was coming along. In addition to the statues, Keck was doing friezes of Law and Justice. Satisfied, Judge Truman journeyed on to Washington, D.C., where he planned to confer with various Missouri politicos and "really make up my mind on what I'm to do." Chief among these politicos was Bennett Clark, who had been elected to the Senate in the Roosevelt landslide of 1932. Less than two years ago, he had been urging Harry Truman to run for governor.

Now Clark was very cool to Truman running for anything. The new senator had had to fight a bruising primary battle with a Pendergast candidate for his seat, and he was inclined to think Missouri politics would be much better if Boss Tom and his allies and followers were out of the picture. Clark's loyalty was to the St. Louis bosses who had won him the nomination. The old St. Louis-Kansas City rivalry was once more intruding its ugly snout into Missouri's Democracy.

All Judge Truman got from his visit to Washington was an opportunity to meet Harry Hopkins, one of President Roosevelt's key aides, who appointed him Missouri's reemployment director. He was supposed to handle it along with his duties as county judge. The closer he looked at the job, the less he liked it. "There'll be almost as many rocks heaved at me as there are now," he wrote to Bess.

The year 1934 began badly for Truman, Pendergast, and the nation. In spite of the New Deal's desperate measures, the economic paralysis continued. Bennett Clark persuaded President Roosevelt to appoint Maurice Milligan U.S. Attorney for the Western District of Missouri. He was the brother of Tuck Milligan, war hero and seventerm congressman, an avowed critic of Pendergast. When a fusion ticket tried to contest Boss Tom's control of Kansas City in March, pitched battles erupted around various polling places, leaving four dead and eleven wounded. The new federal attorney rubbed his hands and began doing some gleeful investigating.

To some people, it looked as if an endorsement from Pendergast was the equivalent of those get-well pills Dr. Hyde gave the Swopes. In fact, it was the beginning of Boss Tom's slide from power to the penitentiary. But no one knew that in 1934. He was still Roosevelt's man in Missouri when it came to dispensing the thousands of jobs the New Deal was creating with its public works programs. More to the point, it was clear that other politicians considered Judge Truman untainted by his connection to Pendergast. Governor Guy B. Park asked him to tour the state to drum up support for a $10 million bond issue to rehabilitate mental hospitals, prisons, and similar institutions. Once more Harry went on the road and Bess stayed home.

The more she thought about the future, the more Bess wanted Harry to take the collector's job. Staying home in the accustomed warmth and closeness of the Wallace enclave was enormously important to her. She found it hard to face the guilt she would feel if she went to Washington and abandoned her mother. I am using psychological language here—although I again foreclose any claim to being an expert in the field. In reality, Madge Wallace had a son and daughter-in-law living in the house with her, and in 1934 they presented her with a grandson. But Bess knew, perhaps not in explicit words, that Madge would make her feel that she was abandoned.

Early in the spring of 1934, Eddie McKim, ex-sergeant in Battery D and later a fellow reserve officer, called Harry Truman at North Delaware Street and asked if he could borrow his car. Eddie was working for a Nebraska insurance company and was trying to track down an agent who had absconded with some company funds. His old captain not only lent him the car, but went along with him to Atchison, Kansas, in search of the malefactor. As they drove, they talked politics. Judge Truman described the two jobs he was being offered and asked Eddie what he thought he should do.

Eddie said he thought it would be idiocy to take the collector's job. "When you finish [in eight years] you're still a young man and you're through politically. On the other hand, if you take the congressional job you'll be in the big swim and nobody can tell what will happen."

"You're telling me what I want to hear," Harry Truman said.

What he was not hearing from his wife.

Let me insist, I am only speaking of inclination here. Bess did not try to strong-arm or nag her husband into the decision she wanted. That was never her style. It clashed with her deep conviction that her husband had—and should have—the final say on such a major decision. As a woman, a wife, a mother, I can find ample grounds on which to sympathize with her. She felt a very human inclination to cling to the familiar, the safe, secure world of Independence, where Bess Wallace was somebody in her own right, in contrast to the unknown, threatening world of Washington, D.C., where she was nobody except Harry Truman's wife.

Her mother was not the only person about whom Bess worried. There was also her brother Fred and his drinking bouts. Her fragile daughter was also very much on her mind. How would she react to leaving her squadron of friends on Delaware Street, to dealing with a different school system, to endless car trips between Independence and Washington, D.C.? As the days drew close to the time when Harry Truman had to make up his mind whether to file for the congressional primary, the tension in the big house on Delaware Street was severe.

While Bess and Harry debated, other members of the Pendergast political machine were looking out for number one, as usual. The term political machine is very misleading. It conveys the image of something static, frozen, like a block of metal. Actually a political organization is more like a patch of jungle over which the boss presides as long as he remains strongest. Other jungle creatures are constantly testing him, propositioning him, wheedling favors from him. When Harry Truman went to the Jackson County Democratic Party's caucus in the early spring of 1934, he had made up his mind to choose the congressional seat. He was stunned to discover that Jasper Bell, a Kansas City judge, had talked Boss Tom into giving him the nomination.

Harry Truman was so furious, he vowed to quit politics and go back to the farm. Bess found that idea appalling. She calmed him down and pointed out that there was another choice. He could begin putting the screws to Boss Tom now to pin down the nomination for governor in 1936. This struck her as an excellent compromise between a local and a federal job. Someone was going to run to replace Governor Park. Missouri's governors were limited to a single term. As for getting through the two years between the end of his judge's term and that contest, they would manage, somehow.

The disgruntled, disappointed judge went back to campaigning for Governor Park's bond issue. During the first week in May, a few days before Harry Truman's fiftieth birthday, Bess received a telephone call from Sedalia, Missouri. Harry was supposed to be in Warsaw that night. Her puzzlement was soon solved. Judge Truman had been summoned to Sedalia to talk with James Aylward, chairman of Missouri's Democratic Party, and Jim Pendergast, Mike's son and Dad's biggest backer within the organization. They wanted him to run for the U.S. Senate.

It was astonishing news. Bess could only gasp. Until that moment, she and everyone else in Jackson County had assumed that Aylward would be the Pendergast nominee. But no one gave him much of a chance in the upcoming fight for the seat, because Tuck Milligan, the seven-term congressman and war hero, had announced for it, with Senator Bennett Clark's wholehearted endorsement. As Aylward explained it, he did not want to give up his lucrative law practice for a $10,000 a year senator's salary. But behind that excuse was the unspoken fact that no one thought a Pendergast man could beat Milligan.

According to the newspapers, Pendergast had already asked two aging warhorses, former Senator James Reed and Congressman Joseph Shannon, to run and they had declined. The Kansas City *Star* crowed that Pendergast was "backed into a corner," frantically searching for a candidate that would save him from a humiliating political defeat. Harry Truman told Bess that he had tried to resist the idea. He told Aylward and Pendergast that he thought of himself as an executive, not a legislator. He wanted to wait two years and run for governor.

They had shaken their heads. Speaking for Tom Pendergast, they pounded the furniture and insisted the Jackson County organization needed help now, not two years in the unknown future. If they lost this race, they would be disqualified as the spokesmen for the Democratic Party in Missouri. Those thousands of jobs, those millions of dollars in federal relief money, would be controlled by Bennett Clark and the bosses in St. Louis. They knew Harry Truman could not resist an appeal to his loyalty.

"I said yes," Harry told Bess.

It was a lot like his decision to join the army. When he made one of these rendezvous with history, he acted alone, sensing that it was against Bess's inclination, that it stirred old anguish and doubt about the future in her heart. Yet he was certain, now, that their love would carry them through the difficult feelings.

On May 14, 1934, alone again, Harry Truman paced the floor in the Pickwick Hotel in Kansas City, on the eve of announcing his candidacy for the Senate. He sensed that this was the most important

decision he had ever made. He brought with him memorandums to
himself that he had written at other times when he retreated to this
hotel to escape the political pressure cooker. That night he added over
forty pages to this manuscript, which is known in the Truman Library as the "Pickwick Narrative."

Tomorrow, today, rather, it is 4 A.M., I have to make the most momentous announcement of my life. I have come to the place where all men strive
to be, at my age and I thought two weeks ago that retirement on a virtual
pension in some minor county office was all that was in store for me. When
I was a very young boy, my mother gave me four large books called "Heroes
of History." The volumes were classified as "Soldiers and Sailors," "Statesmen and Sages" and two others which I forget now. I spent most of my time
reading those books, Abbott's Lives and my mother's big Bible. . . . I
remember that there were a number of stories about Biblical Heroes with
what I thought were beautiful illustrations. They impressed me immensely.
I also spent a lot of time on the 20th Chapter of Exodus and the 5th, 6th and
Seventh chapters of Matthews' gospel. I am still at fifty of the opinion that
there are no other laws to live by, in spite of the professors of psychology.

In reading the lives of great men, I found that the first victory was over
themselves and their carnal urges. Self-discipline with all of them came first.
I found that most of the really great ones never thought they were great. . . .
I was not very fond of Alexander, Attila, Ghengis Khan or Napoleon because while they were great leaders of men they fought for conquest and
personal glory. The others fought for what they thought was right and for
their countries. They were patriots and unselfish. I could never admire a
man whose only interest is himself.

He went on to summarize the major events of his life, from meeting Bess Wallace in kindergarten through his struggle on the farm to
joining the army in World War I. Central in these memories were the
figures of his mother and Bess.

My mother and sister came to see me at Camp Doniphan. My mother
was sixty five years old but she never shed a tear, smiled at me all the time
and told me to do my best for the country. But she cried all the way home
and when I came back from France she gained ten or fifteen pounds in
weight. That's the real horror of war.

I believe that the great majority of the country were stirred by the same
flame that stirred me in those great days. I was a Gallahad after the Grail and
I'll never forget how my love cried on my shoulder when I told her I was
going. That was worth a lifetime on this earth.

Next he wrote a history of his political career, complete with vivid
character sketches of Tom Pendergast and the men with whom he

served on the county court. He was unsparing in his description of the corruption of some of them, and what this meant to him philosophically.

I have always believed in Santa Claus I guess. It was my opinion . . . that most men had a sense of honor. Now I don't know. "The Boss" [his first recorded use of this name for Bess] says that instead of most men being honest most of them are not when they are put into a position where they can get away with crookedness. I guess I've been wrong in my premise that 92% are honest. Maybe 92% are not thieves but it is a certainty that 92% are not ethically honest.

I am obligated to the Big Boss [Tom Pendergast], a man of his word, but he gives it very seldom and usually on a sure thing. But he's not a trimmer. He, in times past, owned a bawdy house a saloon and gambling establishment, was raised in that environment, but he's all man. I wonder who's worth more in the sight of the Lord?

Who is to blame for present conditions but swindling church members who weep on Sunday, play with whores on Monday, drink on Tuesday, sell out to the [Big] Boss on Wednesday, repent about Friday and start over on Sunday. I think maybe the boss is nearer heaven than the swindlers.

And now I am a candidate for the U.S. Senate. If the Almighty God decides that I go there, I am going to pray as King Solomon did, for wisdom to do the job.

Although Bess remained at the center of Harry Truman's vision of his life, she was not there at the Pickwick Hotel to share this lonely meditation. I found myself wishing, as I read it, that this was not so. But even the closest, most enduring marriage is not always idyllic. Perhaps the difficulty of perfect union between a strong man and a strong woman, even the impossibility, is an important truth—it might even be the central truth of this book.

Perfect union suggests that there has to be a surrender of one self to the other self—usually the woman to the man. Bess Truman never did that. But she also never forgot that promise she had made to Captain Truman in Trinity Episcopal Church in 1919. When he announced his candidacy for the U.S. Senate, she was there beside him. No one, except the candidate, was aware of the reluctance and doubt in her troubled heart.

Chapter Ten

The campaign was one of the most painful experiences of Bess's life. Until this point, Harry Truman had had his share of verbal rocks thrown at him. But they were mostly hurled from local political platforms, in speeches that were forgotten the day after they were made. The newspapers, even the Kansas City *Star*, had been fairly kind to him. The *Star* had praised him remarkably often, considering the paper's rock-ribbed Republican allegiance.

Now he was running for one of the highest offices in the nation. And he was being backed by a political organization that had suddenly become unsavory to the highest degree. An outburst of gangster violence in Kansas City added to the shock of reading about dead and wounded around the polling places. As a result, the men opposing Harry Truman's Senate candidacy felt no holds—or more exactly, no smears—were barred.

Senator Bennett Clark announced that if Harry Truman was elected to the Senate, he would not have "any more independent control of his own vote than he had as presiding judge of Jackson County." Tuck Milligan sneered that Truman would get "callouses on his ears listening on the long distance telephone to his boss." Reporters gleefully rushed into print with these gibes. To someone as sensitive about her family's reputation as Bess Truman, they were painful reading. These men were saying her husband had been Tom Pendergast's toady, and she knew that this was a dirty lie.

She was discovering the hardest part of being a politician's wife—the problem of swallowing one's rage and disgust at the outrageous lies that other politicians get into print (and now, onto the TV screen) with the eager cooperation of journalists.

The campaign of smear and innuendo went on and on. I think it was Tuck Milligan who said that if elected Harry Truman would be Pendergast's office boy. A third candidate entered the race, Congressman John Cochran, who specialized in violent attacks on the "Pendergast machine" and conveniently ignored the Dickmann–Igoe machine that was backing him in St. Louis.

One of the most dismaying enemies to emerge was a friend of Bess's youth, Spencer Salisbury. He and Harry Truman had quarreled over Salisbury's attempt to seize control of the bank which Truman and he had founded. Now Salisbury leaped into the smear game with the claim that federal employment officials were using their influence with jobseekers to help Truman.

Harry Truman did not take this abuse lying down. Nor did the Jackson County Democrats. Joe Shannon roared that if elected, Tuck Milligan would be Bennett Clark's office boy. As for Cochran, Shannon said he was "the office boy of the St. Louis *Post-Dispatch*." Judge Truman pointed out that he had never voted in Kansas City in his life and had nothing to do with the shenanigans that went on there. He was from Independence, and he dared either of his opponents to point out a single dishonest act in his twelve years in politics. Dad had resigned as federal reemployment director within two days of announcing his candidacy, so if anyone was pressuring jobseekers on his behalf, he had nothing to do with it. As for Pendergast's support, Dad noted that each of the politicians who were attacking him for accepting it had sought Pendergast's help in 1932, when all the congressmen in the state ran at large because of a redistricting dispute with the Republican governor.

A very important backer of Truman's clean image was Colonel William Southern, editor of the *Examiner*, and, as I have mentioned before, the father of Bess's sister-in-law, May Wallace. Along with praising him wholeheartedly in the paper, Colonel Southern inestimably boosted Judge Truman's image as a man of integrity in a less noticed way. In Missouri, Southern was better known as a Sunday school teacher than as a newspaper editor. He introduced Harry Truman to a convention of fellow Bible teachers and preachers in Maryville with the declaration: "I vouch for him, and don't pay any attention to what others say about him."

Through the baking heat of one of the hottest Julys in Missourians' memory, fifty-year-old Harry Truman roamed the state, speaking as often as sixteen times in a single day, and in between doing most of the driving himself. Exhaustion may have had something to do with a collision that left him with two broken ribs and a badly bruised forehead. Bess, always fearful of death on the highway, was distraught. She persuaded him to take a friend with him to do the driving thereafter.

Bess made several platform appearances with her husband at major rallies in and around Kansas City, but she never said a word on his behalf. She already had made it very clear to him that speeches, even brief ones, were not her style. Around this time, she summed up her idea of the wife's role in a comment to Ethel Noland: "A woman's place in public is to sit beside her husband, be silent, and be sure her hat is on straight."

I appeared on the platform with them at one of these shindigs, and someone in the candidate's entourage decided I was "cute" and could be an "an asset" if I showed up regularly. Bess firmly vetoed the suggestion. I doubt if Harry Truman took the idea seriously. Nor did he, knowing how leery Bess was of becoming overtired, even consider asking her to accompany him on the long, hot drives to the dusty small towns and parched hamlets where he did most of his politicking in that blazing summer.

He was convinced that he was going to win the election in the countryside. The St. Louis machine and the Kansas City machine would produce roughly equal numbers of votes for Truman and Cochran. As the campaign mounted in intensity, it rapidly became apparent that Tuck Milligan was running a poor third. Gradually a lot of people began to realize that Truman was pulling into the lead. There were frantic pleas to Milligan to quit the race so that Cochran, who had only a limited appeal to rural voters, could have a chance.

On August 9, 1934 with the temperature still above 100 degrees, the voters went to the polls. Harry Truman's prediction proved almost mathematically correct. The two big city machines fought each other to a standstill. The Truman vote in St. Louis was almost invisible, and the Cochran vote in Kansas City was equally minute. How would the farmers vote? That became the crucial question for the Truman-Wallace clan, as they clustered around the radio in the living room at 219 North Delaware Street. All night the returns dribbled in from the countryside. Finally, toward dawn, it became apparent that Harry Truman had won the election, as one reporter put it, "in the creek forks and grass roots." The final count was 276,850 for Truman, 236,105 for Cochran.

It was an amazing victory, but for Bess it was embittered by the smears and lies that had been flung at her husband. The worst insult was yet to come. The St. Louis *Post-Dispatch*, on its august editorial page, which was read with respect by other papers around the nation, denounced the results of the election. The editorial carped that the winner was "an obscure man . . . scarcely known outside the confines of Jackson County. . . . Judge Truman is the nominee of the Democratic Party . . . because Tom Pendergast willed it so." What made this smear doubly painful was the man who produced it. Charlie Ross was now the editor of the *Post-Dispatch* editorial page.

Although I never heard Bess say a word about it, I am certain she knew Charlie was responsible. Mary Paxton Keeley and she were still in close communication, and Mary would hardly fail to report that Charlie had returned to St. Louis from Washington, D.C.

The sneer was, of course, untrue. Charlie had been out of Missouri politics for fifteen years and did not know what he was talking about. But it was still painful to someone like Bess, who remained so loyal to the friends of her youth.

Harry Truman was not a senator, yet. He still had to beat the Republican incumbent, Roscoe Patterson, in November. Patterson tried to split the Democrats by dividing them into pro and anti Roosevelt voters. But the Democratic nominee refused to let this tactic shake his nerve. He steadfastly insisted he was for Roosevelt and the New Deal. This time, with a united party behind him, Judge Truman rumbled to a smashing quarter-of-a-million-vote majority.

On the day after the election, Bess went to a meeting of her bridge club. As usual they played cards, had lunch, and played more cards. But at this meeting the hostess kept the radio on, and everyone screamed and whooped every time the announcer reported that another county had produced a majority for Harry S. Truman. What amazed everyone was Bess's absolute calm. "That's what twelve or fourteen years of political campaigns will do for a wife," she replied. Another explanation, of course, was her insider's knowledge that her husband was practically certain to win.

There is a third explanation, which can be glimpsed in an interview Bess gave to the Kansas City *Star* the following day. "Of course I'm thrilled to be going to Washington," she told the reporter. "But I have spent all my life here on Delaware Street and it will be a change. I was born on Delaware Street and was married to Harry here sixteen years ago when he came back from the World War. We never have had or desired another home." It is interesting to note that Bess's sense of 219 North Delaware as home was so strong, she forgot she had been born several blocks away on Ruby Street.

The full import of the election only dawned in my ten-year-old brain when Bess explained that we would spend six months of every year in Washington, starting on January 1, 1935. I burst into tears. I realize, now, that Mother was probably tempted to join me. But she concealed her feelings, as usual, and briskly told me there was no point in crying about it. She was trying, in her oblique way, to give me some of the hard wisdom she had learned about the futility of tears. But I am sorry to say I thought she was pretty coldhearted.

Only now, after entering the hidden part of her life, do I realize that leaving Delaware Street was more painful and threatening to Bess than it was to me. The very time of the year probably compounded the pain; 219 North Delaware Street was particularly beautiful in November. The huge maple trees in the yard were fiery red in the glowing sunshine and the full spirea bushes overhanging the porch added an extra touch of glory.

With daughter clutching her battered Raggedy Ann doll, for which Aunt May Wallace had sewed a new dress and some hair, we drove to St. Louis and took a train to Washington, D.C. On January 3, 1935, Mother and I sat in the Senate gallery and watched Harry S. Truman walk down the center aisle and take his oath of office before Vice President John Nance Garner. In his striped pants and swallowtail coat, her husband must have looked almost as strange to her as he did to me. The whole experience must have seemed dreamlike.

We were staying in the Hamilton Hotel, and Bess spent most of her time riding around Washington looking at apartments. The rents struck her as appalling, and so did the prices of everything else, which were roughly twice Missouri levels. It was easy to see that Senator Truman's $10,000 a year salary was not going to go very far. In retrospect, they probably should have stayed in the hotel and shopped a bit longer for an apartment—or "flat," as they called it in their Missouri parlance. But Bess could not stand being crammed into one room for very long. The Senator was equally anxious to get settled so he could concentrate on learning his job. So they took a four-room apartment at 3106 Connecticut Avenue at a rent they could not really afford—$150 a month.

I was the next problem to be solved. Bess decided to send me to Gunston Hall, a private school for young ladies that no doubt reminded her of Barstow. It was located in four handsome old Washington houses, with some modern additions for such necessities as a gymnasium, theater, and laboratories. She took me there every

morning and picked me up each afternoon. It was not easy to enter a
school in the middle of the year, when cliques and friendships have
been formed. Bess listened patiently to my complaints that everyone
in the school hated me (even then, I had an instinct for the dramatic)
and assured me that I would eventually make some friends. To my
amazement, she turned out to be right.

Meanwhile, Bess was feeling her way into the Washington, D.C.
social scene. She had been led by Washington's geographical location
to think of it as an eastern city, which she presumed would be "cold."
She was pleasantly surprised to find the Washington of 1935 was
much more like a small southern city, relaxed, hospitable, informal,
except when the government was playing the official panoply game.
She was also pleased to discover some Missourians who were eager
to be friendly. Jeannette Cochran, the wife of Congressman John
Cochran, Harry Truman's primary opponent, was particularly cordial, and she and Bess quickly became good friends.

Congressman Cochran himself could not have been more cordial,
and so, to Bess's amazement, were Senator Bennett Clark and his
wife. It must have made her wonder about the terrible things both
these gentlemen had said about her husband during the primary
campaign. It gradually dawned on her that name calling was seldom
taken seriously by politicians. It was part of the rough game they
played. But for Bess, with her memory of the price of political
failure, politics could never be a mere game.

Nevertheless, she was surprised to discover that she enjoyed Washington. She had no difficulty coping with the dozens of new people
that she had to meet. Almost everyone is more or less a stranger in
Washington and anxious to make friends. At the comfortable mansion on New Hampshire Avenue that houses the Congressional
Club, she exchanged woman-talk about home and family with the
wives of senators from both parties. Having run a substantial household on Delaware Street, she easily included the five administrative
assistants and secretaries of Dad's office staff in her routine. She
visited the office regularly and soon was on a first-name basis with
everyone.

The staff soon understood that Senator Truman did not call Bess
"the Boss" by accident. She took a very intense interest in their
personal lives, especially if their conduct had any potential political
impact on Senator Truman. One staffer, Edgar C. "Bud" Faris, was
something of a playboy. He ran around with a Washington gossip

columnist, who rewarded his attentions by frequently dropping his
name in her column as one of the guests at various glittering parties.
He was always described as "Senator Truman's top AA." Bess decided that the home folks would not appreciate the idea that the
Senator's staff was living it up in the capital. Dad ordered Bud to
keep his name out of the papers, or else.

With a grandmother, three aunts, and nine girlfriends on North
Delaware Street, I had, until this point, a lot of other people to
distract me from thinking about my mother very much, except when
she was telling me what not to do. In Washington, with no one
around to spoil me—my father was spending fourteen hours a day
learning how to be a senator—her sternness noticeably diminished. I
was ten years old, not exactly the age of maturity but old enough to
appreciate Mother's wry observations on the foibles of neighbors and
politicians. In private she was as irreverent toward the high and
mighty as Dad often was in public. We went sightseeing together at
all the standard places, from the Washington Monument to the White
House. We shopped at Woodward and Lothrop's and other stores,
and feasted at a wonderful old ice-cream parlor on Connecticut Avenue. That year, I think Bess discovered for the first time that a daughter could be a friend as well as a responsibility.

One of our favorite adventures was the time Mother and I came
close to washing the dishes at the Connecticut Avenue soda store. We
had ordered two of their huge chocolate sodas and were sitting there,
smiling at each other in comradely anticipation when Mother exclaimed: "I don't think I have any money with me."

She peered into her purse and discovered she was right. "Do you
have any change?" she asked. I shook my head. I used all my change
to go to the movies. Mother dived to the bottom of her purse and
began dredging up nickels and dimes that had wandered down there.
She finally produced thirty-four cents. The sodas arrived and we
gazed at their foamy, chocolatey, whipcream-topped splendor and
wondered if we should send them back. We could not remember
exactly how much they cost. "Oh let's take a chance," Mother said.

We polished them off and waited breathlessly for the check. It was
thirty cents. We got home with four cents between us, feeling like
conspirators.

On another outing, I was wearing a new crepe dress. We got
caught in a cloudburst and my dress began to shrink until it was
above my knees. Mother understood exactly how I felt. We dashed

into Woodward and Lothrop and she bought a new dress for me so we could go home on the bus without feeling embarrassed. Believe it or not, I was a very shy ten-year-old.

The Washington into which we Trumans settled in 1935 was a contradictory town. It still had much of its sleepy, southern city pace. Traffic was light. It was the depths of the Depression and few people were getting paid enough to own a car. Everybody rode the trolleys and buses, even such personages as U.S. senators. I remember sitting on the bus one afternoon trying to get a head start on my homework. With no warning I was whacked on the head by a folded newspaper. I looked around furiously for the culprit. There sat Senator Truman, laughing fiendishly.

The Washington of 1935 still placed a premium on good manners and the rules of etiquette. I will never forget driving up to the door of the White House with Mother. A butler came out and I solemnly deposited Mrs. Truman's engraved calling card on his silver tray. The butler nodded politely and we drove away. On Thursday, wives of senators were "at home" to pour tea for anyone who chose to visit. Congressmen's wives were at home on another afternoon and cabinet wives had their day. Always, on silver trays were little piles of calling cards with their corners turned down.

Along with this sedate formality, political excitement throbbed through 1935 Washington. It had become the news capital of the nation. Since Franklin D. Roosevelt became president and launched the New Deal to rescue the nation from economic collapse, press associations and metropolitan newspapers had tripled their Washington staffs. The center of the excitement was the President, with his magnetism, his courage, his confidence that Americans could defeat the gray monster, this Depression that was sapping hope and vitality from so many lives. From his electrifying inaugural address, in which he announced that there was "nothing to fear but fear itself," to the whirlwind of reform and political experimentation he unleashed in his First Hundred Days, FDR had acquired almost mythic dimensions. He was "the boss, the dynamo, the works," wrote Arthur Krock in *The New York Times*. Magazine publisher W. M. Kiplinger declared he had never known any president "as omnipotent as this Roosevelt."

FDR's New Dealers had taken control of the capital. From boardinghouses in old brownstone mansions on G Street, R Street, New Hampshire Avenue, and Twenty-first Street, they trooped to the new government agencies with alphabet-soup names, the NRA (National Recovery Administration), the WPA (Works Progress Administration), the CCC (Civilian Conservation Corps). The newspapers were full of stories about these new celebrities, such as Hugh "Ironpants" Johnson, until recently head of the NRA, and Harold "The Old Curmudgeon" Ickes, head of the WPA, and Harry Hopkins, the only New Dealer Senator Truman had met before he came to Washington. A cerebral ex-social worker, Hopkins was supposedly closer to Roosevelt than any other member of the White House "brain trust."

By 1935, other people in Washington were competing with the President and his New Dealers for headlines. Chief among them was a man who had decided he could go Roosevelt one better—Senator Huey Long of Louisiana. A scary, utterly corrupt demagogue, he had his own program, Share Our Wealth, with its own slogan, "Every Man a King." He had broken with Roosevelt. He said he did not like the way the President said "fine, fine fine," to the conservative majority leader of the Senate, Joe Robinson of Arkansas, and "fine fine fine" to Huey. Senator Long wanted, among other things, to limit the fortunes of the rich to $5 million and give every family in the country a "homestead grant" of $6,000 as well as free radios, cars, and washing machines. The Senator held forth on this program to the Senate in speeches that seldom lasted less than four hours.

At the other end of the political spectrum, the American Liberty League began accusing FDR of planning to "Sovietize" America. After two years of relative quiescence, conservatives were beginning to find a lot of things wrong with the New Deal. They had a potent ally in Father Charles E. Coughlin, the Royal Oak, Michigan "radio priest," who claimed 45 million listeners, and received as many as a million letters after a broadcast. Sleek and angry, Father Coughlin headed something called the National Union for Social Justice, which claimed 7.5 million members. He had originally supported FDR, but by 1934 he was starting to attack him, in spite of desperate efforts by Joseph P. Kennedy, father of a future Democratic President, to heal the breach. Father Coughlin had begun to think that two European statesmen, Adolf Hitler of Germany and Benito Mussolini of Italy, had better ways of dealing with the world crisis. He particularly admired the way they had banned freedom of speech in their countries. He called for a similar ban in America as a first step to getting rid of the "Jew Deal."

Buoyed by Democratic gains in the 1934 election, FDR decided on a bold legislative program to counter these assaults from the left and right. He announced a second New Deal, which would be launched by a Second Hundred Days. On the agenda were social security, unemployment insurance, a federal slum clearance program, a national labor relations board, and an inheritance tax. Conservatives in both parties screamed socialism and the battle was on. Roosevelt had to zig and zag to hold together his precarious coalition of southern Democrats, northern labor, big city political machines, and blacks. One of his climactic zags gave Bess a front row seat at a moment of rare political drama.

The President decided to veto the bonus bill, which would have paid $2 billion to World War I veterans. He delivered the veto message in person to a joint session of Congress, and each senator and representative was allowed one gallery ticket. Senator Truman gave his ticket to Bess, and she squeezed into the packed benches to hear FDR argue forcefully against raising the deficit any higher than he was boosting it on his own. Her excitement was intensified by her awareness that her husband disagreed with the President on the issue and had voted for the bill.

Bess also enjoyed meeting Eleanor Roosevelt, who was beginning to emerge as a power in her own right in 1935. The meeting was not an intimate one. Bess was only one of a swarm of senatorial wives invited to the White House for tea. She and the First Lady shook hands and exchanged a few words about the problems of getting settled in Washington. Like most Democratic women, Mother admired Eleanor Roosevelt's energy. She traveled 40,000 miles a year, acting as a roving reporter for her crippled husband. She gave weekly press conferences, wrote a newspaper column, and had a twice-a-week radio show. Bess wondered how she also found time to be a gracious hostess at the White House.

Although Bess enjoyed most aspects of their new life in the nation's capital, the pull of home remained strong. She spent at least an hour every day writing letters to her family, above all to her mother. She even arranged to have a special delivery letter arrive each Sunday so her mother would not be "blue" all day—as Madge Wallace was quick to tell her when a letter did not come.

On June 7, 1935, a day or two after Gunston Hall's term ended, Bess and Harry packed me and most of our possessions (the apartment had been rented furnished) into their car and headed for Independence.

The day after she arrived at 219 North Delaware Street, Bess gave an interview to the Kansas City *Star* reporter that demonstrated her political astuteness. She said she had found Washington, D.C. "warmly social" and yet "home [for the voters, that meant Missouri] was best of all." She praised Eleanor Roosevelt's "graciousness, her ability to say the right thing at the right time," and avowed that no one heard a word of criticism of her in Washington social circles. (Conservatives were beginning to zero in on Mrs. Roosevelt as a prime target of opportunity.) Bess had kind words for the cabinet wives and for Secretary of Labor Frances Perkins, who had "a remarkable memory for names and faces." Then she told of watching FDR deliver his veto of the bonus bill and neatly neutralized her husband's opposition to the President on the bill by declaring this chance to "see and hear" Mr. Roosevelt had strengthened her faith in him.

After a week at home mending a few political fences, Senator Truman went back to Washington, where Congress seemed to be in more or less permanent session. Bess and I stayed in Independence. He was miserable, alone there in the capital. Never before, not even in his courting days, were his letters so full of yearning for Bess, and for me, his daughter, who was having a grand reunion with the Henhouse Hicks on North Delaware Street.

Your card was a lifesaver this morning. I have never in my life spent such a lonesome night. I went "home" at nine-thirty after I'd talked to you [on the telephone] and when I opened the apartment door I thought I heard Margaret say, 'Hello Dad,'—and I asked, well where is mother, as usual, and then I walked all around to make sure I wasn't dreaming, read the Congressional Record, put a sheet on your bed, and turned in. Every time I'd hear that young lady in the next apartment I would be sure my family were coming in. We'll never do it again. . . .

There was no need for us to have returned home so early in June. The lease on the apartment was not due to expire until June 30, when Senator Truman moved to a hotel. There were, as we will soon see, plenty of other apartments that could have been rented on a month to month basis. The weather was not the reason. It was hot in Washington in June, but Missouri was not exactly the place to go if you wanted to beat the heat. Congress was supposed to adjourn eventually, but on June 20, reporting a rumor of a July 10 finish, Dad glumly wrote: "Don't bet on it." He hinted desperately that he would welcome a return.

On June 21, reporting a call he made to one of Bess's friends who had been ill, Dad wrote: "She answered the phone herself and said she was better and that she missed you a lot and wished you were back. I'll meet the train any day."

Bess ignored these hints. Harry Truman was making a painful discovery. There was a limit to how much Bess could give herself to him if it involved separation from her mother. She was a divided woman. Her sense of responsibility for Madge Gates Wallace's happiness went deeper than either of them could understand. It was simply a fact, a fundamental response that was too embedded in Bess's feelings to resist.

Writing more as a biographer than as a daughter, I can see a sort of rough justice at work. There was a part of Harry Truman's soul—where he spoke in solitude to history and his God—that Bess could not reach. Here we are encountering a part of her soul that neither his love for her nor her love for him could touch—that dark, heartbreaking need to console Madge Gates Wallace for the wound fate had inflicted on her.

At times I wonder if it was an even more complex need. As we shall see, Bess was happiest when she could share herself not only with her husband and her mother, but with the rest of the Wallace family. In some primary region of her heart, she endlessly relived their original retreat to 219 North Delaware Street, their drawing together in anguish and grief and consolation after her father's death.

Again I am playing psychologist, stepping outside the circle of love in which I usually view my parents. Love is not synonymous with understanding. Love persisted between Harry and Bess, even while they struggled to cope with their conflicting needs. On June 28, 1935, Bess responded warmly to a sixteenth wedding anniversary letter from her husband. He wondered if she was sorry she married a "financial failure." She told him she did not have a single regret.

They promptly got into a fight over a number of department store bills that the Senator sent her, asking if they were "all right." He apologized for "having to talk money and bills and I wouldn't if I were a millionaire." Bess found this remark extremely irritating.

Her wrath was compounded by a rumor she picked up from Emma Griggs, mother of John Griggs, one of the Senate office staff from Missouri. Johnnie had apparently told his mother that the Senator was miserable without his wife and daughter and spent almost every evening on the town in search of consolation. Mrs. Griggs seemed to have wondered if this involved chorus girls or sultry lady lobbyists. Bess added to these peeves a fierce rebuke because Harry had gone to the office picnic over the Fourth of July. She did not approve of him fraternizing in a bathing suit with his young secretaries while she was in Independence. She warned him that it could lead to damaging gossip of the sort Mrs. Griggs was already spreading.

Money was a frequent source of irritation between them at this time. In mid-July, Bess suggested that instead of renting another apartment, they build a house. Harry said he'd "like very much" to build but the cost daunted him. Bess thought they could do it for $8,500, but he thought $10,000 was more likely to be the figure; then there would be another $2,500 for a lot and at least $2,500 for furniture. "You can see how it piles up," he wrote. There was no need to remind her that his salary was only $10,000 a year.

Their chronic cash shortage made him feel guilty. "Maybe I can make a gamble [in some investment] next fall and hit a pot of gold." He tormented himself for failing to take a chance on an investment opportunity that had come his way in the previous fall. "If I'd played my hunch last fall we'd have enough to build two houses."

Meanwhile, Congress stayed in session. There was a veritable parade of major bills on the agenda from the Social Security Act to the controversial soak-the-rich Wealth Tax Act, which boosted income taxes for the upper brackets and took a big bite out of inheritances. The brawl over this bill alone made the idea of an early adjournment almost laughable.

There was some truth to Mrs. Griggs's gossip about Senator Truman going out almost every night. It was practically unavoidable. Everyone who knew his bachelor status hurled invitations at him. Somewhat defensively, the Senator sent his wife elaborate reports on the outings. One of the more interesting took place at the Virginia home of the chairman of the Securities and Exchange Commission, Joseph P. Kennedy.

The party last night was a real affair. . . . Bilbo [Senator Theodore Bilbo of Mississippi], Burke [Senator Edward R. Burke of Nebraska], and I were the only new ones [new senators] there. It is the finest home I've ever seen. Out west of Washington on the Potomac, a grand big house a half mile from the road in virgin forest with a Brussels carpet lawn of five acres all around it, a swimming pool in the yard, and all the other trimmings. There is a motion picture theater in the sub-basement. It was built by a young Chicago millionaire at a cost of $600,000, then he drank himself to death in two years, and his chorus-girl widow is trying to borrow $40,000 on it and can't. Kennedy has it leased, furniture and all. . . .

Senator Truman seldom enjoyed himself at these parties. Once, in exasperation, he exclaimed that he was "sick and tired of going out to dinner." He wished they could "get enough ahead to go into business in some quiet country seat and get out of the whirl. But I know that will never happen."

If the ordeal was doing nothing for the Truman marriage, it was providing yet another glimpse, this time on a national level, of their intense partnership, even when half the continent separated them. There are hitherto unrevealed glimpses of how Harry Truman was quietly but steadily acquiring a perspective on the Senate. In the following letter, we also get a look at the supercharged political atmosphere of mid-1935, when Huey Long and Father Charles Coughlin cast ominous shadows on America's future.

The Senate convenes at eleven o'clock today to consider the Banking Bill. Senator Nye of North Dakota spoke for four hours after he'd introduced Father Coughlin's bill as an amendment. The priest's campaign manager and the president of the American Bankers Association sat side by side in the gallery. Neither of course knew who the other was. Most of us thought Coughlin wrote Nye's speech. Nye is one of the good-looking egotistical boys who play to the gallery all the time. . . . He never comes to the Senate except to make a speech or introduce a bill to abolish the army and navy or to get more money for more investigations and more publicity. Several so-called people's friends in the Senate would be in a hell of a fix if there were not some good old work-horses here who really cause the Senate to function. . . . There isn't a so-called progressive who does anything but talk.

Dad's readiness to take on legislative chores soon qualified him to join the ranks of those workhorses, who constitute the inner circle of the Senate. A strong signal of acceptance came from Vice President John Nance "Cactus Jack" Garner. He began inviting Dad to his office, known as "the dog house," to "strike a blow for liberty." That was code for sharing some of Cactus Jack's superb Kentucky bourbon. Dad also had won the Vice President's admiration by joining a group of freshmen senators led by Lewis Schwellenbach of Washington who declared their all-out support for the New Deal and their detestation of demagogues who were attacking it, in particular Senator Huey Long.

One day, Senator Long made one of his interminable speeches to a mostly empty Senate. Vice President Garner was among the early departers. He asked Dad to preside in his absence. When Huey finally finished ranting, he asked Dad what he thought of his speech. "I had to listen to you because I was in the chair and couldn't walk out," Dad said. That was the last time Senator Long spoke to Senator Truman.

Senator Truman was also quietly but steadily informing people that he was not the Senator from Pendergast. On June 26, for instance, he went to a dinner for the new senators at which Joe Guffey of Pennsylvania tried to twist everyone's arm into voting for his coal bill, officially known as the Bituminous Coal Stabilization Act, which was aimed at shoring up the coal industry. Guffey, who had, Harry noted, "a desire to be a Senate boss," had taken the precaution of calling Tom Pendergast to insure Senator Truman's vote. "I think I'll vote against it," Harry told Bess, "although I was rather sold on it before that."

On July 9, came another forlorn hint—he was hoping that Bess and Margaret Strickler, my future voice teacher, would drive east. He already had told Bess that he had framed and hung her picture in the Senate office. "You sort of dominate the office in that place," he told her. He kept forgetting to send specials so that she would get a letter on Sunday. "It seems a year since I've been home and I guess it'll be two before I get there," he sighed on July 16.

A week later, he reported that Senator Borah of Idaho had just told him that they would not adjourn until November. This drove the junior senator from Missouri to desperation. Along with endless Senate sessions and committee meetings and a daily deluge of visitors from home seeking favors, he added a search for a temporary apartment, which he would rent on August 1. On July 25, this idea produced two emotional letters. He was thinking of driving to Missouri over the weekend and bringing Bess and her daughter back. In the second letter, he became almost rhapsodic. "The more I think of that temporary apartment idea the more I like it," he wrote.

In the next paragraph, realism took over. He noted the difficulties they faced. "What will you do about Margaret's school? If she's here when it opens she'd have to start here and then you couldn't go home and I'll have to be at home for at least a month after adjournment."

Bess said no. Without qualifications or any attempt to work out a compromise. Senator Truman was left on his own in Washington,

D.C. "I am somewhat disappointed that you don't look with favor on coming back," Harry wrote, surely the understatement of the decade. He admitted that a "sensible survey of the situation . . . would say that you are right. I'm not sensible about it. I couldn't go to sleep until 1:30 thinking about you and home."

Out of this tangle of frustration and disappointment emerged one of Harry Truman's greatest political mistakes. Mother has to share part of the blame for it, I fear. On July 24, 1935, Harry mentioned to Bess that Senator Bennett Clark had told him he had just met three Missourians, all of whom wanted to be governor next year. One of them was Lloyd Stark, a millionaire owner of a vast apple nursery. Earlier in the month, Dad had noted the unexpected arrival of Tom Pendergast in New York. He had returned from Europe a full month early. Senator Truman suspected he was ill, which turned out to be the case.

Soon after the appearance of Lloyd Stark, Harry began telling Bess that he was considering a trip to New York to see Pendergast. On July 28, after warning Bess to tell no one, he made the trip and told her why. He had found out that Charles Howell, who had run against Bennett Clark for the Senate in 1932 and had earned his enmity, was going to announce for governor, presuming on Boss Tom's backing. Clark was certain to oppose him with a candidate of his own, and the Missouri Democratic Party would be in smithereens again. Dad proposed Stark as a compromise candidate. He was rich, he was honest, and he was begging for Pendergast's support.

It was clever politics, at that time. It held the state party together when President Roosevelt was coming under increasingly fierce attack by conservative Democrats, who were numerous in Missouri. But we shall see that for Harry Truman personally, it was a horrendous mistake. If Bess had been in Washington, D.C., and had met Lloyd Stark, I think she might have persuaded her husband to be a bit more cautious about backing the man. I don't attribute any superior ability to read character to her, but her general approach to life was warier, more pessimistic about human nature and the future than Harry Truman's. She might have thought Lloyd Stark's vows of eternal gratitude and warm tributes to Senator Truman's political acumen were a little too good to be true.

Suddenly she had a letter from her husband informing her that he was coming home to line up the state for Lloyd Stark. He zoomed through Independence, spending only a single day with her, and then whirled around the state and back to New York a week later, where he told Tom Pendergast that everyone now agreed that Stark was an excellent candidate for governor. Harry Truman was acting as the de facto leader of the Democratic Party in Missouri—at a time when the newspapers were still calling him the boss's errand boy. In her letters, Bess cheered him on; she particularly enjoyed the way he was pulling the whole thing off without a line of it getting into the newspapers.

But the long separation continued to be a sore point between them. In his first letter after his return to Washington from his meteoric trip around Missouri, the Senator noted that Bess had failed to kiss him goodbye when they went out to the car. He had wanted her to come back to Washington with him for the next few weeks and she had refused. Bess heatedly reminded him that she had given him a very serious kiss in the house and was not in favor of public embraces in the first place. The lonely Senator apologized, and for the last two weeks of the session they debated where to go for a vacation.

The fifty-one-year-old Senator was badly in need of one. Always proud of his ability to digest enormous amounts of facts and remember them, he was shocked by a late August lapse. He had gotten a bill on the Interstate Commerce Committee calendar for Senator McCarran of Nevada, and the day it came up he forgot what it was all about. He had to read the original proceedings in the Senate to recall the whole business—it had to do with putting airlines under the commerce committee. "That ought not to happen and wouldn't have ten years ago," he wrote. "Maybe I need a holiday."

Mother concurred. She was not finding 219 North Delaware very restful. For the first time she began criticizing some of her Wallace relatives. As we have seen, her sister-in-law Natalie chafed at living under her mother-in-law's omnipresent eye. Natalie was difficult in other ways, too. On August 14, Bess wrote Harry: "Natalie and Frank are thinking about driving to Santa Fe about the 10th of September & asked if we would be interested in coming. I think *she* thinks the car would be too full tho' with Marg along so I don't see how we could go for I wouldn't leave her here at home for that length of time."

Bess concluded they had better do their own traveling. "It would probably be more satisfactory anyway. They are both of them so old & crotchety."

As homecoming neared, Bess resumed her partnership role. She went down the list of the office staff and discussed with the Senator who should come home with him and who should stay in Washington. She still maintained a very proprietary interest in the staff. When John Griggs fell in love during the summer, Bess wanted to know all about it. She fretted, along with the Senator, about secretary Mildred Latimer's boyfriend, William Dryden, who was an alcoholic and went berserk on a bus in late August. The Senator took the time to visit him in the hospital. He told Bess how expertly Dryden played on Millie's sympathy, perhaps hoping that the message might be applied closer to home. "He's like all alcoholics—undependable," he wrote.

Bess preferred to discuss the legislative struggle in Washington, which she had been following closely. She thought it would be better if they did not pass the controversial wealth tax bill. "The Dem. party would probably profit considerably (& each one of you, personally) [she meant they would finally adjourn] if the thing doesn't come to a vote this session." Huey Long enlivened the closing days of the session by announcing that he was going to run for president in 1936. Bess wanted to know if he had "made any sort of stir" when he declared for the highest office, as if Franklin D. Roosevelt did not exist.

In the last week in August, the Senate passed a staggering number of major bills. The Banking Act reorganized the Federal Reserve System, the Public Utility Holding Act transformed that industry, the Guffey-Snyder Coal Act did likewise for the miners, and a modified version of the Wealth Tax Act passed on the last day. Senator Truman voted for the utility bill in spite of a plea from Tom Pendergast and a warning from the Kansas City *Journal Post*, the only local newspaper that regularly supported the Democrats. The paper happened to be owned by an oil magnate who violently opposed the bill. The *Journal* castigated the junior Senator on its editorial page as a "tool of the Roosevelt administration."

Earlier in the summer, discussing their finances, Harry had told Bess that he hoped to build a reputation as a senator that would "make the money successes look like cheese." But he warned her that she would have to put up with a lot "because I won't sell influence and I'm perfectly willing to be cussed if I'm right." In spite of their differences in the ragged summer of 1935, on this crucial point Bess Wallace Truman was in complete agreement with the junior Senator from Missouri. There was not a word of reproach for his defiance of the big boss and the newspapers. When he finally got home, I am quite certain that there were words of praise.

I suspect, however, those words came somewhat later. The first
thing on both their minds was some time together, away from everyone. In a matter of days they were in the car heading for Colorado,
accompanied only by their eleven-year-old daughter, who was still
blithely unaware of the drama that was swirling around her.

Chapter Eleven

When Senator Truman returned to Washington early in December of 1935, Bess and daughter remained in Independence. Bess refused to consider the possibility of celebrating Christmas any place but at 219 North Delaware Street. For the Senator, this was not good politics. Every time he came home from Washington, he got his picture in the paper and was deluged with pleas for jobs and favors. The Depression was still rampant, in spite of all the things President Roosevelt was doing to fight it. "I dread the trip home," he wrote to Bess, "because I know what they'll do to me."

In fact, the fifty-one-year-old Senator had found the three months he spent in Missouri almost as exhausting as the previous year in Washington, D.C. "You've no idea how tired I was," he wrote in another letter. "I'm not starting home until Dec. 21st if that suits you. It'll take me until then to rest up."

Meanwhile, the same lament that had dominated his letters in the summer began to reappear. "If you and Margey had just come on [to Washington] with me everything would be perfect." There was an unintended dividend from his loneliness. He spent his evenings reading the interstate commerce law and all the relevant court decisions and became an expert on the transportation business, which in those days mostly meant the railroads.

During the day, the Senator spent a lot of his time looking for an apartment. He found one for $130 a month and was so elated he could not sleep. There was no lease, but they could definitely have it until June. Alas, Bess did not go back to Washington with him after Christmas. I had a cold, and she, fearing the worst as usual, decreed I was too ill to travel.

This left the Senator adrift in the heavy seas of the Washington social season. His tension headaches returned, and he went to a fancy party at Senator Guffey's house in mufti and discovered almost everyone in white tie and tails. He and Sherman Minton of Indiana, who was also out of uniform, commiserated on their wifeless state. "He said never, never would he come to town again without Mrs. Minton," Harry wrote.

My cold refused to go away and Bess refused to budge until I was in perfect health. One day I had a fever, the next day I didn't. On January 14, I had recovered and Bess began packing. But on the 15th, the chilblain palace on Delaware Street struck again and I had another cold. The expedition was canceled. The Senator said he had not been so disappointed since he lost the 1924 election for eastern judge of Jackson County. "I honestly believe that house is infected with cold germs or something," he wrote, obliquely putting his finger on the real problem. "If you ever arrive, I'll never let you out of my reach again."

When we finally arrived the following week, there were more problems. Nettie, the maid of all work and sometime cook who had been a big help the previous year, was getting married, and this made her very unreliable. She began disappearing for several days at a time. From Independence came advice that ignored the Trumans' tight budget. "Let the house go and take your dinners out," Madge Wallace told Bess.

I rediscovered my old friends at Gunston Hall and met a few new ones, so Bess was soon able to assure her mother that I was perfectly content—news that Madge seemed reluctant to believe. Along with the usual Washington whirl of parties and receptions, Bess undertook to shepherd two younger relatives, Elsie and Oscar Wells, who were living in Washington. He drank too much and Bess tried, pretty much in vain, I think, to comfort her.

Even more time consuming were another couple, Harriette and Leighton Shields, who were about the same age as Harry and Bess. She was the daughter of a St. Louis businessman who had been a Truman supporter—one of the few in that city. But it was sentiment, not politics, that attracted Bess to Harriette and Leighton. This was another marriage mangled by alcohol. Harriette was sweet and pretty; Leighton was a lawyer who had drunk his way out of a promising legal career in St. Louis and had a minor job, probably arranged by his father-in-law, with the Reconstruction Finance Corporation.

The Shieldses decided that jointly they could convert the Trumans into a meal ticket. Bess felt so sorry for Harriette she could not resist urging her husband to do something for Leighton. While Bess could be very hard on those who needed no help, sympathy overwhelmed her judgment when she saw a woman afflicted with a drinking husband. One does not need a Ph.D. in psychology to understand why.

The Shieldses had her feeling sorry for them in the spring of 1935. That summer, they had showered the bachelor Senator with dinner invitations, and he reluctantly accepted one of them, after which he wryly reported to Bess that for once Leighton was sober. In December, he remarked that Leighton was coming into the office to see him. "I fear he is going to become a nuisance," he warned. But he continued to put up with Shieldses, because he sensed that Bess's deepest feelings were involved.

Leighton Shields wanted the Senator to make him an assistant U.S. attorney. Instead, with a shrewdness that he always concealed beneath his plain farmer manner, Harry Truman found him a job that got Leighton and Harriette far away from Bess. He persuaded the Roosevelt administration to appoint Leighton the district attorney in Shanghai, China. There was a United States court there that handled cases involving United States residents of several Chinese ports at which Americans had treaty rights.

Politics were relatively tranquil in the early months of 1936, in Congress, at least. Most of the action was in the U.S. Supreme Court, which began declaring unconstitutional much of the New Deal legislation that Senator Truman and his confreres had sweated over in the preceding summer. The outrage within the Roosevelt administration was immense. But most of the politicians' thinking was focused on the presidential election that was coming in the fall. Roosevelt, wary about offending the party's conservatives and stunned by the court decisions, did not try to pass much innovative legislation.

Once more, with hindsight to bolster us, we find it hard to believe that the Democrats were worried about the 1936 election. But most of the nation's newspapers had swung sharply against Roosevelt, and the business community had also lost faith in his social engineering, which had failed to end the Depression. Father Coughlin had declared himself an all-out foe of the New Deal and launched a third party movement with a galaxy of assorted extremists in his retinue. Huey Long had been killed by an assassin's bullet in the lobby of the Louisiana State House in the fall of 1935. But no one knew where or how his discontented followers would vote.

Harry Truman continued to work for a unified Democratic Party in Missouri, pushing the election of Lloyd Stark as governor as the best guarantee of this goal. Early in May, he dashed back to the state Democratic convention in Joplin, Missouri, where he continued to line up backers for Stark's candidacy. He told Bess all about it in a letter crowded with names of forgotten politicians. He stopped in Independence to see Mrs. Wallace, and she told Bess what a pleasant surprise that was. Madge was beginning to look with a little more favor on her son-in-law.

But Madge was still unreconciled to separation from Bess. On April 16, when Bess had been in Washington less than three months, her mother began asking her when she was coming home. This became a regular feature of succeeding letters that spring. Bess tried to defend herself by sending Madge a rundown of her schedule. "What a world of things you have to do this week!" Madge exclaimed. "How do you keep it up? I imagine you will enjoy the quiet and rest when you come home." Underlining each word, she added: "How much longer will it be before you are here? We are growing very impatient."

By June 15, Bess was back in Independence again, and Senator Truman was wandering around their empty apartment, telling her how lonesome he was. Again he took up the subject of buying a house. Their big fear was the possibility that they would not be able to sell it if he lost his bid for reelection four years hence. "I'm sick of this two-time move every year," he wrote. "It costs more than we get for the stay in Washington no matter what we do, and that rent if we were smart enough, could be an investment."

His main political concern was the way the Roosevelt administration was ignoring him on patronage and giving Bennett Clark all the plums. This was standard Roosevelt tactics, to woo opponents with favors and presume that loyal supporters would stay loyal no matter what was done to them. What made this policy especially irritating in Clark's case was his spoiled-boy approach to his job. Because his father, Champ Clark, had once been the most powerful Democrat in the country and almost became president in 1912, Clark seemed to think he could get away with anything. He drank too much, constantly broke appointments, and still wanted everyone in Washington to acknowledge his importance as Champ Clark's son.

Nevertheless, Clark was important in Missouri, and Harry Truman urged Bess to remember this in one of the few rebukes he

ever gave her. When Myra Colgan, a Truman cousin who was working in Washington, asked Harry if Bennett was the only heavy
drinker in his family, he blamed Bess. "Apparently there must have
been cause for the question," he wrote. "Now that's nothing but
plain gossip, and I'm not in the habit of telling it to you or anyone
else."

While I had twelve-year-old fun in Independence and Bess played
bridge and cleaned house, Senator Truman went to the Democratic
Convention in Philadelphia. From there he wrote letters full of wry
politics and laments about how much he missed her.

Well the second day is gone. Mr. Barkley [Senator Alben Barkley of
Kentucky] raised the roof with his keynote speech. I didn't hear it but all say
it was fine. I sneaked off and went to bed when he began talking. Was that a
proper thing to do after I'd heard him probably forty times?

The crowds are immense and the National Committee is selling everything. Delegates couldn't get tickets until all the purchasers had been satisfied. . . . I may run out on them tomorrow and go back to Washington,
pack up and start home.

The next day he was still thinking about Bess and regarding the
convention with an even more disenchanted eye.

Myra [Colgan, his cousin] came down again and I borrowed a [delegate's]
badge and let her sit with the delegation while Robinson [Senator Joe
Robinson of Arkansas, the majority leader] made his speech. . . . Mrs.
Clark [Senator Clark's wife] was there and sat with the delegation—quite a
concession as she had a box seat on the stage. I was given one for you but
gave it to T. J. [Tom Pendergast].

There is only one paper here that is nice to us. All the rest are violently
against the administration. They have drawn out the meeting two days too
many. That's to pay Phila back its $750,000 [the city's contribution to the
convention] by letting merchants and hotels take war time toll from us. I
guess it's all right but the delegates have a right to growl about it because
they had to come. Idle spectators should take their medicine. Hope to see
you *very* soon.

The next day, June 26, his thoughts were almost exclusively about
Bess.

Well you'll get this one the great day [June 28, their wedding anniversary]
and I'll be away again. I think I said last year I'd never do it again, but the
devil has a hand in most things. Do you seriously regret that action seventeen years ago when you promised to "love honor and obey?" I know that

you have had a difficult time, sometimes, particularly when the income wouldn't and doesn't meet the outgo, and I sometimes wish I'd gone after things [taken graft] like other men in my position would have but I guess I'm still fool enough to like honor more. I hope you believe I'm right.

The only regret I have about [it] today (the twenty-eighth) is that it didn't happen in 1905 instead of 1919. You were, are, and always will be the best, most beautiful and sweetest *girl* on earth.

Senator Truman stayed at the convention until President Roosevelt and Vice President John Nance Garner were renominated and then drove back to Washington, where he listened to FDR's acceptance speech on the radio and wrote another letter to Bess on their seventeenth wedding anniversary.

I was so lonesome last night I just had to spend four dollars to call you up. If I'd stayed in Philly, it would have cost me five for a hotel and I'd gotten wet besides. [FDR made his speech outdoors at Franklin Field and it rained during it.] *The New York Times* said this morning that everyone got soaked but they stayed anyway, 105,000 of them, to hear and see the President. . . . His speech was a masterpiece I think. The convention was like all such gatherings, just one grand yell from start to finish, and in order to find out what went on it was necessary to read the papers or go down to a hotel and listen to the radio. You couldn't tell what was happening by being on the floor. When they nominated Roosevelt I left after an hour. Jim Pendergast [Boss Tom's nephew] got the leg of his pants ripped down the front on a railing during the demonstration. Lucky he had another pair—it was a Ted Marks suit [Ted was their best man].

I hope you are enjoying the day. It's just about as hot here as it was in Independence June 28, 1919. I wish I had a gray-checked suit to celebrate in but I haven't so put on a white one. There is no special prize for seventeen years of married life that I could discover, so you'll have to make out without any. I'd like to be there to take you to dinner though. Lots of water has gone under the bridge since then. War heroes are no longer that. They are now looked upon as a sort of nuisance and are considered fools to have gone. [Bennett] Clark made the statement that if his pa had been President, there'd have been no war at all. Oh well!

I think my sweetheart is better looking today than ever, if that is possible and you know it is not fashionable now to think that of the same one. Please kiss Margie and I hope I get that letter tomorrow. It wasn't in the mail this morning.

Love to you and I hope for at least seventeen more.

Reading Dad's letters from Philadelphia, I found myself wishing we had gone with him instead of traipsing home. Although I was

only twelve, I would have loved to have been there at Franklin Field
to hear FDR's acceptance speech. Historians agree with Dad's contemporary estimate, that it was a masterpiece. The President called
on his fellow Americans to accept the fact that "there is a mysterious
cycle in human events. To some generations much is given. Of other
generations much is expected. This generation has a rendezvous with
destiny." Marquis Childs wrote that the huge crowd cheered "as
though the roar out of the warm sticky night came from a single
throat."

Madge Wallace and the pull of 219 North Delaware were not the
only reasons Mother and I stayed home. Money was also a problem,
as Dad's remarks about income and outgo make clear. Bess's replies
to all these letters have been lost, but I'm sure she told Dad she had
no regrets about him putting honor above a fast buck. She also may
have reminded him that the word obey was not in the Episcopal
wedding service.

Back in Missouri, Senator Truman went to reserve officers' camp,
largely to stay out of sight until the Democratic primary in August.
He wanted to avoid intramural brawls at political picnics with the
temperature more than 100 degrees. Thereafter, virtually all Missourians above the age of seven hurled themselves into the presidential election campaign, which pitted Governor Alfred M. Landon of
Kansas against FDR. The mere thought of a Kansan in the White
House was enough to raise hackles on the necks of Missouri
Democrats.

They had nothing to worry about. FDR won an enormous victory, carrying every state except Maine and Vermont. Lloyd Stark
won handsomely in his race for the governor's mansion, and for a
month or two it was bliss to be a Democrat. But events soon revived
the truth of comedian Will Rogers' witticism, "I don't belong to an
organized political party. I'm a Democrat."

Before we get into that disaster, the Trumans had to cope with the
renewed travails of Washington versus Independence, husband versus
mother in Bess's psyche. Once more Senator Truman came to Washington without his wife. They had decided they could not afford
another move and another round of rent payments. But this decision
came unglued within a week of the Senator's arrival in the capital.

On January 5, an invitation to a White House luncheon with Mrs.
Roosevelt arrived in the mail for Bess. "You are supposed to be there
on January 13. I *want you to be* present," Dad wrote. "I'm going out

with Vic [Victor Messall, one of his Senate office staff] tonight to get an apartment. . . . I just can't stand it without you. If we are poorer than church mice, what difference does it make? There is only one thing on earth that counts with me and that is you and Margie."

Bess responded with a telegram abjuring him not to rent an apartment under any circumstances. They simply could not afford it. "Your telegram rather unseated me," Harry wrote. "I was under the impression that if I found a bargain in a place to stay, you would still come." He then told a story about a fellow senator whose wife said he was away so much, she was beginning to prefer the company of a jackass she had just bought for her grandchild. "Maybe I'm in the jackass class," Senator Truman wrote.

The next day he took an even tougher line. "I am terribly distressed that you are not here and getting more so all the time." He was going to keep on looking for a bargain apartment and "if I find one *you are coming*."

Bess rushed a special delivery letter to her husband, informing him that the real reason she did not want to come was my health. I was succumbing to the chilblain palace again, and it probably would have done me some good to get out of it and into a warm Washington apartment but that is hindsight. Mother could find no fault with dear old 219 North Delaware Street. I was simply a germ factory, in her opinion.

I now think the real reason for Bess's adherence to 219 North Delaware Street in these early months of 1937 was never stated, at least in their letters. She may have been sincere about blaming my health—people can easily use one legitimate reason to conceal another one perhaps not quite as legitimate or acceptable. Christine, Fred Wallace's wife, was pregnant with her second child, and Bess felt she would be needed when she gave birth. She was not sure how Fred would handle the tension and was even more worried about her mother.

The Senator accepted my health as an explanation for the delayed departure. "I guess I'll have to quit being a baby and go to work," he wrote. "But it's hell, I tell you." He once more found himself adrift socially. He went to another party given by Senator Guffey and wore a "hickory" shirt when everyone else was in evening clothes. With malice aforethought, I suspect, he reported that Miriam Clark, Bennett's wife, offered to chaperone him until Bess arrived. Bess did not particularly like Mrs. Clark, who had almost as many pretensions as her husband.

Complicating the Senator's life even more, if possible, was the presidential inauguration on January 20. He was going to have to cope with swarms of Missourians who were heading for the capital on a special train with Governor Stark. Many of them were women, and he badly needed Bess on his welcoming committee. But she stayed home and watched me wheeze. The Senator frantically rounded up extra tickets for the visitors, and then it rained and no one went to the ceremony. But he enjoyed meeting the home folks.

Few words have more sharply defined the difference between Harry and Bess on this point than four sentences that he wrote in his letter of January 16, 1937. "It is just too bad you aren't here. What a time you'd have!" Then, writing at top speed as always, he seemed to remember how she felt about such things. Without a break for a paragraph or even a phrase such as "On the other hand," he added: "You should be glad you're AWOL this week, I'm going to be a worn out dishrag by next Saturday but I guess I can take it."

Meanwhile, he was being pestered at long range by Leighton Shields, who wrote to him asking for a $2,000 raise, after having barely landed in Shanghai. Bess had also persuaded him to get her brother Fred another job. Harry dutifully reported on his meetings with the head of a cement company, who offered Fred work in Chicago. But Fred did not want to go so far away from home and Mother, and the Senator wearily tried to persuade the executive to get him into the company's Kansas City offices.

Much more worrisome was the camaraderie that developed between Bennett Clark and Lloyd Stark during the inauguration festivities. Bess had gone to the governor's own inauguration in Jefferson City and Stark had been polite enough. But in Washington he more or less ignored Senator Truman. There was a reason for this, aside from the man's egotism. Federal Attorney Maurice Milligan was beginning to make headlines with his investigation of the Pendergast machine in Kansas City. Stark was already showing strong signs of joining him in this crusade.

Harry shared all these worries with Bess, but she continued to ignore the one thing he wanted her to notice. "I sure wish you were here but maybe you are happier where you are," he wrote after reporting on another try to get Fred a job and noting the numerous women visitors he had met at a lunch given by the Missouri House delegation.

After the inauguration, Bennett Clark pulled a fast one on his fellow senator from Missouri. When Harry Truman went down to

Union Station to see Governor Stark and his entourage off, he found
Bennett ensconced in the governor's car. He was going to ride home
with him—and spend two days sweettalking him into playing the St.
Louis Democrats' game. Senator Truman's suspicions became facts
when he made a hasty trip to St. Louis at the end of January to find
out why Stark was not appointing any Jackson County Democrats to
jobs. He got nowhere with the governor, and nowhere with Bess,
whom he telephoned urging her to return to Washington with him.

The lonely Senator returned to the capital, where the national
Democratic Party soon began coming apart. When Congress reconvened on January 3 with huge Democratic majorities in both houses,
the exultant President and his advisers announced that their primary
political target was the U.S. Supreme Court. They were going to
expand the number of justices to fifteen and give the President an
opportunity to appoint men who would outvote the anti-New Deal
coalition then in control. This core idea was unfortunately buried in
the middle of a lot of verbiage about improving the Court's efficiency
and allowing the present justices to retire at seventy and adding fifty
federal judges in the lower courts and requiring instantaneous hearings for New Deal laws.

"Packing the Court," as Roosevelt's critics called it, instantly split
the Democratic Party's conservatives and liberals, and created a personal nightmare for Senator Truman. After intense study of the history of the Court, he decided that there were numerous precedents
for raising the number of justices—the size of the Court had fluctu-
ated over the years—and he would vote for the bill. His mail soon
revealed that his constituents were 20 to 1 against it, but that only
intensified Harry Truman's commitment to it. What he disliked was
Roosevelt's devious approach to the problem. "There are plenty of
good reasons for increasing the Court without going around the barn
to do it," he told Bess.

In Missouri, Bess was exposed to the mounting storm of hostility
to Senator Truman's stand on the Court. She warned him in several
letters that the newspapers and critics were painting him as a tool of
Roosevelt. They were saying that he had been opposed to the bill and
then switched under pressure from the President. Bess wondered if
Harry should try to explain his position to the home folks.

He declined to get into a ruinous debate. Instead, he calmly and
coherently explained his position to her in a number of remarkable
letters. "I have never changed my mind on the Court and have never
made but one statement on it and that was to *The New York Times*

. . . and they printed it as I sent it and the [Kansas City] *Star* copied it word for word," he told her. "They'd like to make me out to be a know nothing but I don't believe they can."

Bennett Clark, seeing a chance to bank some credit for a presidential run in 1940, was one of Roosevelt's most outspoken Senate opponents. With public opinion in Missouri so heavily on his side, many of Harry Truman's friends warned him that he had "better line up with Bennett," he told Bess in another letter. "What would you do if you believed the plan is right but the approach is wrong?" he asked Bess. He lamented Roosevelt's deviousness. "He should have just said the court is fossilized on an 1884 basis and then said let's give it some new blood by appointing two or three young men on it. That's what the issue is and that's all it ever will be. Harlan, Holmes, Stone—all the great dissenters warned of this very situation."

Still worried, Bess reported that Harry was in danger of losing the support of such loyalists as the editor of the Independence *Examiner*, William Southern. He was angry at Roosevelt's minimum wage laws and applauded the Supreme Court for striking them down. In one of his previous letters, Senator Truman had described how he had "burned to a cinder" one of his condescending critics, the president of a local power and light company. He now proceeded to give Colonel Southern the same treatment. If ever a letter showed Harry Truman shaking off the limitations of his Missouri background, this was it.

Mr. Southern is of course against the President. He always has been. Whenever labor and hours come up he's against labor and for unlimited hours. My father was the same way. They honestly believe that every man ought to have to work from daylight to dark and that the boss ought to have all the profit. My sympathies have been all the other way, and that is the reason for my lack of worldly goods. I just can't cheat in a trade or browbeat a worker. Maybe I'm crazy but so is the Sermon on the Mount.

These letters are important because they show how intensely and completely Harry Truman shared his widening political horizons with Bess. She participated in this process by questioning him and forcing him to think out his positions on issues more thoroughly. Writing and talking to her, he could let off steam and say things he could not say publicly. To Bess's eternal credit, she did not yield to her fears and join the "smart alecks" (as Dad called them), who were telling Harry Truman to line up with Bennett Clark to save his political skin.

In the midst of this upheaval, which dominated the headlines of the nation's newspapers the way the war in Vietnam did in the late sixties, Harry wrote Bess a very interesting birthday letter. He told her she would be getting a small package from Mr. Julius Garfinckel along about Saturday, "your seventy-second birthday or maybe it's your thirty-second—I haven't kept very close count on it. It would make no difference if it was your one hundred and fifty-second [it was her fifty-second]—to me you'd still be the prettiest, sweetest, best and all the other adjectives girl on earth—in heaven or in the waters under the earth. You are not only Juno, Venus, Minerva all in one but perhaps Proserpina too. (You'd better look that one up.)"

Proserpina, for those who don't have a classical dictionary handy, was a goddess who spent six months of each year with her husband in Hades, separated from her grieving mother. Was the Senator suggesting a certain resemblance to their own situation? I can't be absolutely certain, but he did not ask Bess to look up Juno, Venus, or Minerva.

Nevertheless, their political partnership continued to deepen. Dad began sending her weekly copies of the *Congressional Record* so she could follow the debates on the Court bill. As the argument raged in Congress and around the nation, Senator Truman began to think FDR wanted to split both the old parties. "He, you know, reads a lot of history and I think would like to be a Monroe, Jackson and Lincoln all in one—and is probably succeeding. Only history will tell."

In the midst of the uproar, Harry Truman quietly began working on his first major task in the Senate. Senator Burton K. Wheeler, chairman of the Interstate Commerce Committee, was one of the most violent opponents of the Court bill. Before it appeared on the docket, he had begun an investigation of railroad finances, setting up a subcommittee with himself as chairman and Dad as vice-chairman. The Court bill absorbed all Wheeler's time, and Dad was left to conduct the railroad investigation pretty much on his own.

Just as he was about to begin work, he learned that the chilblain palace had gotten to Bess. She had been sick in bed for several previous days, she told him in late February. Dad replied that if he had known this he would have come home, "Senate or no Senate, committee or no committee." Bess had a bad case of the flu. In an earlier letter, Dad noted that flu had been traveling around Washington, but it was not the "fatal kind." He was remembering the virus that had almost killed Bess in 1918. This memory alone was enough to touch off all the alarm bells in his system. When she did not recover fast enough to suit him, he decided they should retreat to warmer weather in their old haven, Biloxi. They took me out of school and spent ten days there, letting Roosevelt, the Supreme Court, the committee go hang.

When the Senator returned to Washington, their correspondence had echoes of the first years of their marriage. "I'm glad you missed me," he wrote in response to one of Bess's letters. "It is awful to be reaching for you and you're not there. They have changed my room [in the Carroll Arms Hotel] and have given me a double bed instead of twins so I'll have the same trouble."

On March 31, the Senator reported that he and Bess had been invited to dinner at the White House on April 6. Could she come? The answer was no, but there is graphic evidence of a renewed wish to be with her husband. She was alarmed when Dad remarked in a letter two days before the event that he was tempted to call FDR and refuse to go. Bess wanted him to go, and shine. On the day of the dinner, she sent him a telegram, warning him not to wear a blue shirt. The next day he was telling her that he went in the proper getup and it was a "very spiffy" affair.

More important, he had found an apartment for only $115 a month. The lease would run until September 1, but that was all right because he was sure Congress was going to be in session all summer. "What do you say?" he asked, in the manner of a man who was pretty sure what the answer would be.

Before April 1937 was over, Bess and I headed for Washington. A typical thirteen-year-old, I was pretty upset to be transferred from my hometown milieu with so little warning. Now, thanks to that wonderful biographical-historical tool called hindsight, all I can say is: three cheers for Biloxi. Let's throw in one for Proserpina, for good measure.

Chapter Twelve

Shortly before Mother and Dad and I went to Biloxi, Fred Wallace's wife, Christine, had given birth to a daughter, Marian. In her daily letters to Bess, Madge Wallace reported in detail on how the baby and Christine were doing as well as on other matters, such as the antics of Chris's first child, David, and troubles with the help. She called her regular maids "two of the slowest mortals that walk." She said they reminded her of the time that her father had pointed to their Negro handyman, Luke, and asked Fred to sight him on a tree to see if he was moving. These plaintive letters probably helped to delay Bess's departure to Washington for several weeks.

All her life, Bess felt a responsibility for her brothers. It was a feeling that went beyond the ordinary loyalty of an older sister. She was the acknowledged leader of the family. All her mother's power over her daughter and her sons came from not leading, from a refusal or inability (take your pick) to accept responsibility, from sweet, pathetic passivity. Fred Wallace was the brother who most evoked Bess's sense of responsibility for reasons already made clear. Bess transferred it to his wife and children. So it was a great tribute to Biloxi (and Proserpina) that she tore herself away from 219 North Delaware to come to Washington.

Another young family on North Delaware Street also claimed her sympathy. Sometime in the mid-thirties, Josephine Ragland Southern moved into the home of Dad's cousins, the Nolands, with her two young sons. She was Ethel and Nellie Noland's niece. Jodie, as everyone called her, had married James Allen Southern, nephew of the Independence *Examiner*'s William Southern. The marriage had not worked out and the couple had separated. Jodie was a lively, pretty girl on whom Nellie and Ethel doted. They were even fonder of the two little boys. Early in May, Jodie developed appendicitis which was misdiagnosed. The operation was performed too late. She developed peritonitis and died.

Dad flew out for the funeral. Mother and I remained in Washington, because she did not want me to miss any more school. But Bess was terribly shaken by the death of someone so young, someone who was so needed by her children. It evoked memories of another baffling death on Delaware Street. Her mother's letter, describing the tragic scene, seemed almost calculated to evoke such feelings, although I know this was not the case.

Madge reported that the Nolands were deeply grateful for Dad's visit. They said "nobody but Harry would have come so far to help them." She told Bess that Mrs. Noland, Nellie's aging mother, was shattered by the death and Nellie was almost as bad. "I keep thinking of the dear little home that Jodie and James Allen [Southern] planned and built and were so happy in it. It is all so hard to *understand*," Madge wrote.

That summer, Bess wrote to Ethel and Nellie, revealing her own anguish. "I have tried three times to write to you but I couldn't. To me there is no rhyme or reason to Jodie's going—and I have had such a feeling of bitterness about it. I surely hope with your great faith you have found some measure of comfort *somewhere, somehow*."

I almost wept when I read this letter. It gave me such a flash of insight into the deepest, most hidden part of Bess's life. The wound inflicted by her father's suicide was still visible here, thirty-four years later.

I suddenly understood why it was Dad, not Mother, who insisted I go to Sunday school. "I am sure hoping you get the daughter properly started on her religious education," he wrote, early in 1937. "I don't care whether she's an Episcopalian or a Baptist but she ought to be one or the other and the sooner she starts the better. . . . I've tried to give you a free hand in this and I hope you are going to get started." I had just celebrated my thirteenth birthday when he wrote this letter, so there were some grounds for his sense of urgency.

Mother had enrolled me in Sunday school when I was seven or eight, but I complained so loudly that she accepted my offer of a compromise. If I went to church with her and sat absolutely still, I could abandon Sunday school. Since she seldom went to church (her mother never went) this was tantamount to an escape clause. Now, in response to Dad's prodding, she enrolled me in the Episcopal choir, which I enjoyed. I was beginning to think I wanted to have a career as a singer. "I hope she'll get interested in the church end of it," Bess added in a later letter. This was as far as she could go on my religious education.

The Trumans had other much more immediate worries in the spring of 1937. Early in April, the intense emotions stirred up by President Roosevelt's Court-packing bill and Dad's support of it in the teeth of his constituents' overwhelming opposition produced a death threat. It arrived at the Senate office, postmarked Independence, on April 19. Addressed to "Dear Rat and Other Rats," it announced that Senator Truman would be assassinated in Washington on April 22. The assassin seemed to be unaware that the Senator had gone home to give a speech on the Court bill.

Bud Faris, Dad's administrative assistant, notified the police, who in turn notified the Independence police, who promptly stationed guards at 219 North Delaware Street. The Kansas City police gave him an escort when he made his speech that night. You can imagine the consternation this stirred among the highly strung Wallace clan. Dad was furious with Bud for overreacting. He said that if he had seen the letter first, he would have thrown it away. Mother and I were inclined to side with Bud. Having survived those thousands of German shells fired at him in France, Harry Truman was almost too inclined to feel indestructible.

Dad told a crowded meeting at the Kansas City Music Hall that in his opinion the Constitution was not in danger. The Supreme Court could not be "packed" by anyone, not even FDR. It was a political, not a constitutional, issue, he insisted. I doubt if he changed many minds in Missouri, which has a conservative streak about as wide as the state. But he made his position clear.

Meanwhile, in Washington, D.C., Senator Wheeler, Dad's mentor, had organized a coalition of western and southern Democratic senators that was demolishing the President's bill. They were not all conservatives. Wheeler was a liberal on almost every other issue before the Congress. Many liberals saw the bill as an insult to eighty-year-old Louis D. Brandeis, the great dissenter on the Court. The Republican minority sat on the sidelines, gleefully watching the Democrats destroy themselves.

Mesmerized by his landslide victory, President Roosevelt had become dangerously arrogant. "The people are with me," he snapped, when advisers such as Vice President Garner told him to settle for two or three extra justices instead of six. As early as February, Dad saw that the President was beaten and the bill would probably never reach a vote. "Some sort of compromise will be reached I think where some of the Court will retire," he told Bess.

While the Senate brawled over the Supreme Court, Senator Truman spent most of his days and many of his nights slogging through reams of documents gathered by the staff of his subcommittee investigating the railroads. In 1937, President Roosevelt called the sorry state of the nation's rail carriers "the most serious problem" his administration faced. In 1926, American railroads had employed 1,779,000 men with a payroll of $2,946,000,000. Ten years later, 840,000 of these men had lost their jobs and an incredible 10,000 miles of track had been abandoned, destroying any hope of prosperity in countless small towns and medium-sized cities. Senator Truman was trying to find out why a business that was handling 75 percent of America's internal freight traffic could go bankrupt on such an appalling scale. Not even the impact of the Great Depression explained it.

The more he studied the problem, the more convinced Dad became that the answer lay not in the money squeeze of the Depression, but in the manipulations of a small group of greedy men on Wall Street. To prove this contention and to write legislation preventing a repetition of this financial crime, Senator Truman was taking on some of the biggest bankers and tycoons in the country, and he was determined to know as much as all their high-priced lawyers, accountants, and public relations men put together. It was hard work, complicated by the mountains of mail he was receiving on the Court bill. When he returned from Biloxi, he told Bess he found 1,000 letters on his desk.

For Bess, the drama of the Court bill reached a climax with the death of Joe Robinson, the Senate majority leader. Against his better judgment, he had led the fight for the bill after Vice President Garner went home to Texas in disgust. It was widely rumored that FDR had promised Robinson a seat on the Court, which would have fulfilled a lifelong ambition. In the suffocating heat of one of the hottest Washington summers in memory, Robinson continued to exhort and lecture and beg his colleagues to follow the President's lead. The bill was dead but he refused to believe it.

Many of Robinson's friends became alarmed as they watched him, his face a deep purple, his breath coming in gasps, struggling to repel opposition hecklers. A few days after New York's Senator Royal S. Copeland, who was a doctor, begged him to get some rest, Robinson was found dead in his apartment, a copy of the *Congressional Record* in his hand. This promptly inspired Bess to insist that Senator Truman check into the Bethesda Naval Hospital for a physical examination.

He obeyed and breezily told her they had found nothing wrong with him. But something about his offhand manner made her suspicious. He continued to work fourteen hours a day. In a letter to his cousin, Ethel Noland, Bess revealed her continuing worry. "The weather here is ghastly and we are most anxious to get out of it. H. is worn out and is not well and will simply have to have a good rest or he will be really ill. Margaret and I have each lost ten pounds which is a break for me." As you can steadily conclude by glancing at my picture at this age, it made me almost invisible. It was around this time that Dad invented my least favorite nickname, "Skinny."

After burying Joe Robinson, the senators got into an ugly fight about his successor as majority leader of the Senate. FDR wanted Alben Barkley of Kentucky, whom he thought he could manage. The anti–Court-bill people were determined to shove a more conservative and independent senator, Pat Harrison of Mississippi, down FDR's throat. Dad had promised Harrison his vote and refused to change his mind, in spite of a Roosevelt engineered call from Tom Pendergast. Dad not only voted for Harrison, he sent a message to FDR via his secretary, Steve Early, that he resented being treated like "an office boy." This earned him a round of applause from his wife, who was beginning to grow disillusioned with Mr. Roosevelt. Barkley won by a single vote.

The exhausted lawmakers finally passed a pathetic echo of the original Court bill, which provided for some modest reforms in lower court procedures, and went home leaving the Supreme Court intact. The same could not be said for the Democratic Party. Probably no president in the history of the country, except perhaps Lyndon Johnson and Richard Nixon, ever dissipated a landslide more rapidly than FDR in 1937.

Bess persuaded her exhausted solon that he really needed a rest and another checkup. We went home to Independence and Dad retreated to the U.S. Army hospital at Hot Springs, Arkansas. He was so tired he slept twelve hours a day on the trip down. Bess's letters reveal the wide range of her worries. She wanted to know everything that the doctors reported about Dad's heart, lungs, teeth. She asked if they had discovered a diabetic condition.

When the Senator failed to write (proof of how tired he was) she telephoned the hospital, but they told her no such person as Senator Harry S. Truman was registered there and refused to believe she was

Mrs. Truman and not a nosy reporter. She wrote that she was going to "send a searcher" to Hot Springs if she did not get a letter.

Dad responded with a hasty scrawl in which he casually remarked that the army doctors disagreed with the navy doctors, there was nothing wrong with his heart after all. Bess pounced on this slip. "I'm afraid you have been holding out on me," she wrote. "The *Navy* Dr. told you something unpleasant about your heart—and you swore he said it was ok after promising to tell me exactly what the report was! I guess I'll have to write the hospital to get the correct dope on you this time." Perhaps wanting to reassure him that she was not really mad, she added: "Here's hoping it's all fine."

A sunny spirit pervades Bess's letters during the early fall of 1937. She had taken up horseback riding again, and persuaded me and Natalie and May Wallace to join her. "I feel more limber already," she told Harry. She wondered if he would be home from Hot Springs in time for a moonlight ride she was planning. In another letter she wrote that if she had the money she would hop a train and head for Hot Springs to join him. When Dad mentioned that the doctors were giving him a diet, she told him that she hoped it would let him eat as much as he wanted, "even if you develop a senatorial front."

Almost as if the doctors were responding to Bess's hopes, they reported that everything about Senator Truman was A-1. But there was nothing A-1 about the Democratic Party that confronted him when he returned from Arkansas.

The self-inflicted wounds of the Court fight were visible everywhere in Missouri. But no place was as acrimonious and chaotic as Kansas City. There, Federal Attorney Maurice Milligan had been investigating vote frauds in the 1936 election and was hauling Pendergast Democrats before special grand juries from which Jackson County citizens were barred. He was using a law passed during Reconstruction to protect Negro voting rights in the South. As far as Harry Truman was concerned, it was lynch law justice, in which the accused men had not a prayer of defending themselves. More important, it was destroying the Democratic organization in Kansas City. Worse, Governor Stark was cheering Milligan on, and the White House was doing nothing.

This was a major worry that Bess and Harry discussed and analyzed when they were reunited at 219 North Delaware Street. But it was hard to decide on a course of action in the aftermath of the Court bill turmoil. No one was sure where anyone stood in the hierarchy of aides around Roosevelt. Senator Truman was friendly with Postmaster General Jim Farley, who had managed Roosevelt's winning campaigns and handled most local political problems. Dad hoped he could persuade the President, with Farley's help, to put the brakes on Milligan, who was up for reappointment in 1938.

For Bess, the President's unpredictability was underscored by his announcement on October 12, 1937 that he was calling a special session of Congress on November 15. This wrecked her expectation of three months at home with her husband. It produced one of the angriest explosions she ever permitted herself, at least in her letters. Dad left for Washington on October 15 to prepare his railroad subcommittee to hold hearings during the session. "We sure missed you last night," Bess wrote. "I never did hate so to see you leave. It's a h——— of a way to live—the way we do."

Alone in Washington, D.C. again, Senator Truman agreed wholeheartedly with his wife's unladylike epithet. He tried to be philosophic about it. "It is a most unsatisfactory way to live but nearly everyone has some sort of difficulty and all life is." The trick lay in "beating the difficulties and making things as pleasant as possible. Perhaps if we were rich we would be crazy or some other handicap would obtain."

The Senator immediately began looking at apartments, and this time his wife all but cheered his search. She also reported rather acerbically on the situation in Kansas City, where the papers printed columns about Federal Attorney Milligan and ignored what Senator Truman was doing in Washington. Dad remarked that the Washington papers "all noted my arrival in town and the why of it." From Independence, Bess reported more alarming news. Tom Pendergast was showing signs of radical instability. He was firing old and trusted members of the organization. "Mr. P. certainly has gone completely loco," Bess wrote, after lunching with the wife of one of the victims.

Bess enclosed a clipping from the St. Louis *Star* indicating that the St. Louis Democrats could not resist relishing the ruin of the Kansas City Democracy and were rallying behind Maurice Milligan's reappointment. Dad somehow found time to search for an apartment while launching his railroad investigation. Thanks to his painstaking preparation, he took on the best brains Wall Street could find and dissected their fraudulent finances in session after scathing session. It won him headlines in newspapers across the country—and barely a line in the Kansas City *Star*. Their Washington reporter, Duke

Shoop, was not even in the capital. He was in Kansas helping Governor Alfred Landon write a speech.

During this hectic fall of 1937, Bess began to be troubled by a physical problem that was to plague her for the rest of her life. She developed arthritis in her right hand. It was extremely painful. She told Dad it was giving her "Hail Columbia" day and night. He urged her to consult a doctor. But she had grown very distrustful of the family physician, because when he called early in the previous week he had been "tight."

Dad suggested consulting her old school chum, Dr. Elmer Twyman, but Bess demurred. She was afraid he would want to take out her tonsils or her teeth. This gives us a glimpse of the medical practice of the thirties, when doctors believed in a "locus of infection" and took out all sorts of organs believing that would cure the patient's ills. Bess's common sense stood her in good stead here. The theory has long since been discredited.

Bess reported there was a rumor sweeping Missouri that Governor Stark was developing senatorial ambitions and was thinking of running against Bennett Clark. Senator Truman became so worried about the Missouri Democratic Party that he rushed to St. Louis to confer with trusted friends there, such as bankers John Snyder and Jake Vardaman. Typical of his ability to do (or think) two things at once, he rode the Chesapeake and Ohio, one of the railroads he was investigating. He wrote to Bess on the way back and she replied that if she had known he was in St. Louis, she would have taken a train down there immediately.

Bess continued to keep a sharp (and then some) eye on local politics. She reported that gossipy Emma Griggs had finally wangled a government job and someone else was taking the credit for it, after all Senator Truman's efforts on her behalf. "She didn't say who," Bess wrote, "but I'd let whoever it is take care of her in the future, too, because you know darn well that twenty four hours after she goes to work the complaints are going to start coming in."

Still worried about the Missouri situation, Senator Truman rushed to New York to see Tom Pendergast, who was under medical treatment there. He returned furious with Governor Stark. He told Bess that Jim Pendergast had gone to Jefferson City and personally given Stark names of Kansas City Democrats who deserved appointment to state offices under the governor's control. Stark had not appointed one of them. It was virtually a declaration of war.

With his marvelous ability to mingle the personal and the political, Dad shared another memory of his New York trip with Bess. He had turned on the radio and heard someone singing "They'll Never Believe Me." He was flooded with the memory of the day they had seen *The Girl from Utah,* just after Bess had told him she cared for him. "I hope you remember," he wrote. Bess replied somewhat tartly that of course she remembered. "Why should I forget any more than you?" she asked.

The railroad committee hearings ground on, and by now Dad was really digging up steamy dirt. Some of the steamiest emerged from the books of the Missouri Pacific. This great railroad system, which had no less than seventy-nine subsidiaries, had been taken over by a Cleveland holding company, the Alleghany Corporation, using money supplied by J. P. Morgan. The financiers proceeded to declare dividends out of capital instead of earnings and fired thousands of workers to cut the payroll and provide cash for still more phony dividends, most of which went into their pockets. They cut maintenance to near zero and did not put a nickel into improvements. In a few years the Missouri Pacific was bankrupt.

The Alleghany Corporation had had to persuade the Missouri state legislature to let them buy the Missouri Pacific. A lot of businessmen and politicians in Missouri wanted the details of this persuasion to remain as invisible as possible. Senator Truman was deluged with telegrams and telephone calls urging him to take it easy. His response was predictable, for those who knew the man. He told Max Lowenthal, the general counsel of the committee: "I don't want you to ease up on anything. You treat this investigation just as you do all the others." Mr. Lowenthal later said he did not know a half dozen senators who could have withstood that kind of pressure from their home states.

Dad did not let the so-called financial experts who appeared before his committee to defend the Alleghany Corporation get away with anything, either. George O. May, senior partner of Price Waterhouse and Company, the accounting firm, tried to defend the practice of carrying an uncollectible debt of $3.2 million on the books of the Missouri Pacific as an asset. This allowed the Alleghany swindlers to pretend the railroad was in the black when it was actually on the brink of financial collapse. Mr. May haughtily declared the practice was "misleading in effect but not misleading in intent." Dad angrily told him it was misleading in both respects, and before the hearing ended, Mr. May, chastened by a stinging rebuke from the Interstate Commerce Commission, humbly agreed.

What made Dad's performance especially remarkable was the mood of the country. Throughout 1937, business and labor were locked in alarming combat. The sit-down strike, in which workers seized plants, had enraged conservative executives and their supporters. Open warfare had erupted between police and strikers outside Republic Steel's South Chicago plant, leaving ten dead and ninety wounded. Conservatives—and I will remind you again that most Missouri Democrats proudly wore that label—did not want to hear any more bad news about the ethical lapses of American business. Even President Roosevelt was careful not to side with the workers. "A plague on both your houses," was his response to the South Chicago massacre.

Harry Truman went before the U.S. Senate and told them and the American people what he had found from his railroad investigation. He drew on his knowledge of Jackson County history for his text. He compared Jesse James and his gang, who used guns and horses to hold up trains, with the tactics of the holding companies, who used the slick accounting tactics condoned by Price Waterhouse. "Jesse James held up the Missouri Pacific in 1876 and took the paltry sum of $17,000 from the express car," Dad said. Holding companies such as the Alleghany Corporation had looted railroads of sums in the neighborhood of $70 million. "Senators can see what pikers Mr. James and his crowd were alongside of some real artists."

Along with the railroad uproar, Dad was simultaneously conducting a less publicized but no less burdensome investigation into the aviation industry. This was a business that was in chaos, not from financial corruption but from unrestrained, unregulated competition. He decided that this competition had to be regulated for a few decades, in order to protect the industry until it was mature enough to operate as part of an integrated national transportation system. Only a few experts appreciated the care with which Dad and his staff drafted the bill that created a Civil Aeronautics Authority Board and gave the airline industry the stability it needed at that time.

Mother worried about the strain of these multiple hearings and major speeches, but for the moment she was absorbed by a major event closer to home. Mrs. Roosevelt was coming to Kansas City to give a lecture, at the invitation of the St. Teresa's College Guild. The head of the guild was the wife of an old Truman supporter, and Dad agreed to come home and introduce the First Lady. Governor Lloyd Stark hustled up from Jefferson City to horn in on the welcoming committee.

We chatted briefly with Mrs. Roosevelt before the lecture. By this time Bess had been to several White House receptions and felt more relaxed with the First Lady. Mrs. Roosevelt did most of the talking, as I recall it—mostly about the hectic schedule her lecture bureau had worked out for her. An obedient thirteen-year-old for once, I said nothing.

Mother and I sat on the platform while Mrs. Roosevelt delivered her talk, which urged everyone to participate more vigorously in the life of their community. Bess gave me such a ferocious warning not to move, mug, or even blink while I was on display, I was virtually paralyzed. I concentrated so hard on not moving, I barely heard a word. After the speech, when I tried to stand up, I discovered my arms and legs had gone to sleep, and I had to be all but dragged off the platform.

The Trumans were obviously hoping that by being extra nice to Mrs. Roosevelt they might gain some leverage with the President. Neither they nor anyone else outside the White House circle in those days realized how estranged the Roosevelts were.

Politics dominated the first letter Bess wrote to her husband after his return to Washington. "I hope you make a point of finding out exactly where Mr. R. and Mr. Farley stand on K. C. politicians, if you can depend on what they say. Because if they think they can get along without us in '40—we'll show them a thing or two."

Getting even angrier, Bess pointed out the inconsistency of Roosevelt's support of Milligan. "Is the Pres. trying to wreck Sen. Guffey too? It seems to me you are in the same boat, as far as bossed organizations are concerned." Machine politics were pretty much the rule in both parties in Pennsylvania.

Bess continued to follow the war between Milligan and Stark and the Pendergast machine, unqualifiedly rooting for the home folks. In November, she applauded when the Missouri state supreme court struck down an attempt by the governor to invalidate a ruling by a previous state insurance commissioner who had been a Pendergast man. "I'm surprised the *Star* did not say they [the judges] were picked men," she wrote to Dad, using an epithet designed by the paper to discredit any Pendergast loyalist.

Bess's partisanship proves one thing about the Trumans. Although she had warned her husband about Boss Tom's growing instability, neither she nor Dad had any idea of the moral rot that was developing in Tom Pendergast's troubled soul during these years. In particular they did not realize that the brawl over the state insurance commissioner was connected to a huge bribe that the insurance companies had paid Boss Tom to get favorable rulings from his appointee.

In Washington, D.C., Dad went back to grilling the railroad looters, garnering headlines by the dozen. Even the St. Louis *Post-Dispatch* praised him, which made him wonder, he wryly remarked to Bess, if "I'm doing right." Meanwhile he kept in close touch with the situation in Missouri. His old army buddy, Jim Pendergast, Tom's nephew, told him he was sure Stark was planning to run against Bennett Clark. Dad went to Jim Farley and urged him not to support the governor, and Farley assured him that the President would stay out of the developing brawl. But in his next letter, the Senator reported that he had heard that Roosevelt and Farley were "on the outs" because Farley had opposed the Court bill. So the suspense about the President's position continued.

Harry Truman was helping Bennett Clark in this imbroglio, and Bennett Clark was grateful. He began having second thoughts about Governor Stark. Senator Truman hastened this process by coming to Clark's aid in an unrelated incident in the Senate. Tom Connally of Texas, one of the titans of the upper house, was filibustering against some Roosevelt bill when Clark tried to interrupt him. Connally turned on him like a lion about to swallow an antelope whole. Dad happened to be presiding at that moment—a chore Vice President Garner had begun handing him regularly. Senator Truman ruled Connally out of order, rescuing Clark from humiliation.

Dad urged Bess to read the account in the *Congressional Record*, which he was still sending her. She loved it. "It certainly is something to squelch one of those old timers who have been at that game for twenty years or so. Connally probably thought more of you for doing it," she wrote. (She was right.) Bess understood exactly what her husband was really doing. Harry Truman was working to end the "Clark-Stark hookup," as he called it. He was thereby strengthening his own position with the St. Louis wing of the Democratic Party in Missouri. He was soon telling Bess that he had pretty much succeeded. She was delighted and wrote: "I'm dying to know [the details of] how you broke up the Clark-Stark combination."

In an answering letter, Dad gave her some juicy details. He had dinner with Bennett Clark, who told him that the last time he and Maurice Milligan met, they had almost come to blows over Clark's refusal to condemn Pendergast. Clark said he had heard that the President was thinking of running Milligan against him, with Stark's backing. "The governor and the President would like to be heroes and boss busters," Dad observed. So far as he could see, "my position gets better all the time."

Fueled by this sort of delicious inside information, Bess's interest in national politics intensified during 1937. Apropos of the rift between Roosevelt and Postmaster Farley, the strategist behind the election victories in 1932 and 1936, she remarked: "The Pres. isn't very smart if he thinks he can get along without James A. Farley. But he *is* about that 'cocky.' "

Senator Truman used this interest, and other devious means to lure his Proserpina to Washington. While Bess wrote him a guilty letter, worrying about the lonely Thanksgiving he would have, the Senator used the four tickets he got by virtue of his seat on the Military Appropriations Committee to organize an expedition to the Army-Navy game. He took along two of his aides and one of his favorite Missouri characters, Fred Canfil, a bulky bearlike man with a foghorn voice. Fred was somewhat short on brains but had a super-abundance of loyalty to Harry S. Truman. Dad sent Bess the following report on the outing.

Well I had a grand wet day yesterday. . . . Canfil was on the train and as pleased as a ten year old boy to go to the game. He had a blanket, hunting jacket, muffler, rain coat, overcoat and overshoes. It was a spring day with April showers and fog so the raincoat was all that was needed. Took him around and introduced him to the V.P. [Vice President Garner] who made his usual hit. Sens. Guffey & daughter, Burke & wife, Schwellanbach and wife and Chavez and wife were on our car along with a lot of Senate employees. . . .

The game was a soggy affair. Too wet for the parade and show. The Army outplayed the Navy though. The Navy's mascot is a goat & the Army's a mule. They have two mules, one a regular mule & the other a South American donkey given them by the Peruvian Ambassador, whose son is at the Point. They dressed the donkey up like a goat and unloaded him from an ambulance in front of the Navy stands, mounted an army man in an admiral's uniform on him and had a fellow on the mule in army uniform chase him around the area and shoot him. The "Admiral" and the donkey both fell in front of the Naval contingent much to the pleasure of the Army boys.

It probably wouldn't have been so funny if they hadn't won afterwards. Canfil yelled himself hoarse. When the Army was about to score and failed he shouted: "More brutality Army—what are you being trained for any way." He entertained the spectators for acres around. . . .

I hope you can see one of those games someday but I hope it won't be in the rain. I want to see one when they have all the trimmings. We'll do it someday.

This letter had a devastating effect on Bess. She sighed that she would "give my store teeth" to see an Army-Navy game. A few days later she issued Senator Truman marching orders on their quarters for the coming winter in Washington. She did not want to rent a house. "I don't want to spend the whole winter working, and I don't want to have to have a maid and *I don't want an extra bedroom*."

The way she underlined that last sentence made me wonder if this was the most important point. Back in Independence, Fred Wallace and his wife were thinking of moving out of 219 North Delaware Street. I suspect Bess was trying to avert the possibility of her mother joining us in Washington, D.C. At this point in the long struggle between mother and husband, Harry Truman was in the ascendancy.

A few days later Senator Truman rented an apartment and Bess began getting ready to end their two-and-a-half-month separation. She commissioned Harry to furnish the apartment, an assignment that made him nervous. He feared Bess would not approve of his extravagant tastes. "I'd like to have rugs and carpets from Bokhara and Samarkand, pictures by Frans Hals, Holbein and Whistler and maybe a Chandler pastel and a Howard Chandler Christy or two with Hepplewhite dining room, mahogany beds (big enough for two) etc."

But politics remained at the center of their lives. Bess continued to report the newspapers' exaltation of Maurice Milligan. Dad used this fact for a mordant reflection on the press. "He's a drunkard, libertine and a grafter but he's helping them now so he is a great man." Then he added, with that indestructible optimism which Bess did not share. "But it will work out in the end."

Meanwhile, his railroad committee hearings roared to a climax, in which he uncovered skulduggery between the Wall Street looters and a federal judge. Supreme Court Justice Louis Brandeis, who had dug up a fair amount of financial dirt in his time, was so impressed, he invited the Senator to tea and spent most of the afternoon talking with him. To Bess, Dad dismissed it with his usual modesty. "It was a rather exclusive and brainy party," he wrote. "I didn't exactly belong but they made me think I did." Dad ended his investigation with a fiery speech that more than lived up to the advance billing he gave Bess. He said it would "blister some very outstanding lawyers." It parboiled them and their financier clients for legally looting a long list of railroads with complete indifference to the public's safety or the nation's needs.

A few days before Christmas 1937, Harry Truman strode through the door of 219 North Delaware into Bess's arms. Within moments he stirred an echo of the surprise she had felt in 1910 when she encountered the husky, windburned farmer who had replaced the bookish boy she had known in school. There was new confidence in his voice, new pride in his eyes. He had proved to himself and to a watching world that he belonged in the U.S. Senate. At least as important, he had a wife who was growing more and more eager to help him play that great American game, politics, in Washington, D.C.

Chapter Thirteen

The Washington to which we Trumans returned in January 1938 was a troubled city. In the White House, the President sulked and fumed over his humiliating Supreme Court bill defeat. FDR's massive spending had dismally failed to end the Depression. In fact, unemployment had soared to a new record—19 percent. In Congress, the split between Democratic liberals and conservatives remained unhealed. The conservatives teamed up with the Republicans to defeat one Roosevelt measure after another. It was an alliance that would torment Democratic presidents for the next thirty years.

Even more alarming, in some ways, was a bloc of congressmen who thought Americans should isolate themselves from a world that was growing more and more ugly. Over in Europe, a man named Adolf Hitler was rearming Germany and persecuting Jews and bullying English and French politicians into letting him do pretty much as he pleased. On the other side of the world, the Japanese were going insane in their own unique way, repudiating the rule of law and adopting a weird mixture of totalitarian state worship and militarism which inspired them to attack China and cast greedy eyes on other nations in Asia.

President Roosevelt announced that we needed a strong national defense program to cope with these clear and present dangers. The isolationists responded by tightening the neutrality laws and, for a topper, proposed the Ludlow Resolution, which called for an amendment to the Constitution requiring a national referendum before Congress could vote the United States into a war. A poll purportedly showed 73 percent support for this crackpot idea. President Roosevelt denounced it but, grim evidence of his declining popularity, it almost passed the House of Representatives (where the Democrats had a 328 to 107 majority), losing by only twenty-one votes.

Harry Truman continued to support the President, especially on the issue of national defense. But isolationism, combined with the conservative revolt, made it clear that as 1938 began, the Democrats were in trouble, and nowhere more so than in Missouri, where they continued to inflict awful wounds on themselves. Federal Attorney Maurice Milligan was still putting Kansas City Democrats in jail for padding the voting rolls. Governor Stark was gleefully collaborating in the assault on the Pendergast machine.

A glimpse of Mother's state of mind is visible in a letter she wrote to Dad when he was at reserve officers' camp in the summer of 1938. She was awakened in the middle of the night by a man who sounded drunk. He berated Harry Truman for failing to go to the wake of one John Maloney's wife. Bess tried to explain that Senator Truman was out of town. The caller demanded a telegram from her to that effect to show the grieving husband. Bess decided not to send it, fearing, as she said, that there was a "catch" in it somewhere. The tireless attempts to link her husband to the Pendergast machine made her justifiably wary.

In this same letter, Bess also enclosed a clipping from the Independence *Examiner*, endorsing Judge James M. Douglas for renomination to the state supreme court, and Bennett Clark for the U.S. Senate. She referred to them wryly as two "touching" editorials. The Bennett Clark endorsement was proof of Colonel Southern's by now inveterate opposition to President Roosevelt. But in many ways the praise for Douglas was more significant.

Judge Douglas was being backed by Governor Stark. Tom Pendergast and the Kansas City Democracy were backing Judge James Billings from southeast Missouri. It was a test of strength and loyalty within the party and Democrats such as Colonel Southern were deserting Tom Pendergast left and right. Stark used every crooked tactic in the book to win a narrow victory in the August primary, the only election that mattered. It was the beginning of the end of Tom Pendergast's power. Henceforth, FDR ceased to regard him as the Democratic spokesman for Missouri. Instead, to Dad's and Bennett Clark's fury, the President began consulting Governor Stark on federal appointments.

This only deepened Bess's dislike of FDR. She did not have Dad's gift for entertaining two points of view simultaneously. He could approve of FDR's policies, which he thought were good for the country, and deplore his devious, capricious personality. Bess simply disliked the man for the tricky, inconsistent way he played politics.

But she never passed over into that tribe of people who hated the President. That was a phenomenon to which we have been exposed in more recent years, when waves of hatred engulfed Lyndon Johnson and Richard Nixon. It was just as bad in 1938, when the hatred of FDR and Eleanor Roosevelt peaked.

For a while, this hatred all but poisoned the air of Washington. Some people said they preferred Stalin to Roosevelt. Others concocted genealogies to prove his name was "Rosenvelt," and thereby Jewish. A national news service actually circulated a backgrounder that claimed the President had syphilis. They only whispered the other half of the story, that he had caught it from Eleanor. Bess heard (or heard about) Eleanor Roosevelt derided as a Communist, a Negro lover, a prostitute. She saw the Roosevelt children assaulted with similar slanders. It did not incline her to view the presidency as a desirable job.

Back in Missouri that summer, Mother tried to escape the local acrimony by teaching me to play tennis. This proved she could be optimistic about some things or maybe it just confirmed that love is blind. She simply refused to believe that she had a fourteen-year-old daughter who was one of the world's worst athletes. "I tried to show M. how to serve but it was a washout," she wrote Dad.

Let me explain, for my own self-respect, if nothing else, why the serving session was a washout. Mother tried to teach me by demonstration. She served to me. The ball bounced reasonably close. I swung and missed by several feet. Instead of coming toward me, it bounced backward, toward the net! "See what a little spin can do?" she said. After about five more serves that bounced backward, or with corkscrew twists to the right or left, I threw down my racquet and quit. I knew I could never learn to serve that fiendishly, and what was the point in trying to hit it? I think Chris Evert Lloyd might have had some trouble with Mother's serve.

Mother doggedly insisted I had "the makings of a good player." She added a wry middle-aged observation: "I am convinced the courts are about a mile longer than they were when we played."

She continued to keep her part-time soldier in touch with politics. Senator Bennett Clark was almost sunk when some enterprising reporter found out he was taxing Democratic jobholders in his St. Louis bailiwick 2¼ percent of their salaries to pay for his reelection campaign. "The receipts had B's picture on them!" Bess gasped. But Governor Stark, the newspapers' current white knight, was taxing state employees 5 percent of their pay to elect Judge Douglas, so the story was allowed to fizzle.

Bess also dealt with the petty annoyances. Emma Griggs appeared on our doorstep with her son John, who was out of a job again. Bess had to listen to their woes. "They're down on everybody on earth except the Griggses," she wrote. By the time they left she was "boiling" and had all she could do to remain a lady.

She also reported acerbically to her husband on the progress of one of President Roosevelt's less astute political maneuvers. He had written a letter to Senator Alben Barkley in the spring, to help him fend off a serious primary challenge from Kentucky's governor A. B. "Happy" Chandler. In the letter he told "Dear Alben" that Chandler was "a dangerous person . . . of the Huey Long type, but with less ability." FDR then persuaded John L. Lewis to put his CIO muscle and money behind Barkley and looked the other way while WPA administrators turned their employees into Barkley campaign workers. In the summer of 1938, Mr. Roosevelt went to Kentucky to speak on Dear Alben's behalf. The contrast between this solicitude and the President's apparent indifference to Harry Truman's political welfare only confirmed Bess's disillusion with him.

All this was a prelude to the 1938 midterm elections. Roosevelt supporters went down like tenpins all over the country. The Republicans won a dozen governorships, eighty House seats, and eight Senate seats, without losing a single incumbent. It did not require a crystal ball to conclude that this was bad news for Senator Truman, who was up for reelection in 1940.

It was now more or less taken for granted that Governor Stark, who could not succeed himself, was going to run against Dad. This worry haunted Bess and Harry throughout 1939. On the one hand, a great deal still depended on the capricious President. Harry Truman was the last man in the world to change his political principles to get elected, and he believed in what Roosevelt was doing. He remained a Roosevelt man. The question was, would Roosevelt remain a Truman man? Governor Stark tirelessly wooed the President, flattering and fawning on him the way he had soft-soaped Senator Truman and Tom Pendergast in 1935. Soon they were on a "Dear Franklin"–"Dear Lloyd" basis in their letters. Bess and Harry—and almost everyone else in Missouri—soon heard about this development.

Then the bottom fell out, the roof caved in, the political walls tumbled down in Kansas City. The FBI, the IRS, and a swarm of other government investigators tracked down the bribe the insurance companies had paid to Tom Pendergast. Worse, they discovered that Boss Tom had been cooking the books of eight companies that he owned, to avoid paying a million dollars in income tax. Only then did the Trumans and most other people learn that he was a compulsive gambler who bet as much as $100,000 day on horse races around the nation. The bribes and the unpaid taxes were necessary to support this habit.

Boss Tom was indicted on April 7 and pleaded guilty on May 22, 1939. He stood before the federal bench, a humbled hulk of his former self, and was sentenced to fifteen months in the penitentiary. This was enough all by itself to give the Trumans political nightmares. But investigators soon revealed that Henry F. McElroy, the city manager of Kansas City, had his own unique brand of bookkeeping, which concealed a $20 million deficit. McElroy died before they could put him in jail, but other Pendergast loyalists, such as the former state insurance commissioner, Emmett J. O'Malley, and Matt Murray, who had succeeded Dad as Federal Reemployment Director and went on to head the state WPA, joined Boss Tom in the hoosegow. Reading about these disasters from distant Washington, Bess remarked to her mother, "the whole town seems to have gone haywire."

The Trumans had no illusions about what this meant. "The terrible things done by the high-ups in K.C. will be a lead weight to me from now on," Dad told Bess, a few months after the collapse. Having the Kansas City *Star* and the St. Louis *Post-Dispatch* against him did not help matters. The *Star* gloatingly referred to him as "the last survivor of the once dominant Pendergast organization to hold high office." The *Post-Dispatch* published an editorial which declared that Harry Truman was "automatically disqualified" from serving another term because he was a Pendergast man.

In late September, Bess reported from Independence that the *Star* was accusing Dad of holding up the appointment of two deputies to Federal Attorney Maurice Milligan. The story implied that he was seeking petty revenge against the man who had put Tom Pendergast in jail. Dad had told Duke Shoop, the *Star*'s capital reporter, that the White House would not consult him about the deputies and if they did, "they wouldn't mean it." Shoop—or the rewrite men in Kansas City—twisted this statement into the story they printed. Mournfully, Dad concluded: "It doesn't make much difference what you say and you can rest assured that from now on they'll willfully misconstrue everything I do."

The situation made Roosevelt's opinion of Lloyd Stark all the more important. Bess's heart leaped when Dad reported that FDR had told Senator Clyde L. Herring of Iowa that Stark was "an egotistical fool," and he wanted to see Senator Truman reelected. She asked if she was free to repeat that to everyone she knew in Missouri. Dad's reply suggests that he had acquired some of her dislike of FDR. "Go ahead and say what the President told [Herring] about Stark. It won't hurt anything. They are about alike."

A few weeks later, Dad saw FDR himself, and the President insisted on talking Missouri politics with him. "I do not think your governor is a real liberal," he said. "He has no sense of humor. He has a large ego." The President said he was planning a swing around the country and urged Dad to get on his train when it entered Missouri. "You can rest assured your governor will without any invitation." From there, Dad went to see Bennett Clark, who was "cockeyed [drunk] but very affectionate." Bess had recently sent Dad a clipping from a St. Louis paper in which Clark had predicted Senator Truman would not run for reelection. Now Clark said he was going to announce he was supporting Senator Truman as soon as he got back to Missouri. Of course he did no such thing.

Adding further strain was the worsening international situation. Dad threw himself into the President's struggle to get the neutrality laws changed so that the United States could deal with Germany and Japan. As the laws then stood, the President was forbidden to sell arms or munitions to either side in a war. It made the United States a spectator in world affairs and gave the dictators the illusion that they could get away with anything.

When Japan attacked China in 1937, for instance, the President could do nothing but make disapproving noises. When FDR asked Hitler for assurances that he would not attack the weaker nations of the world, the Führer contemptuously replied that he would be glad to promise not to invade the United States. Roosevelt haters in the Senate and elsewhere chortled almost as much as the Nazi deputies in the Reichstag.

Dad got into this neutrality fight even though it endangered the Wheeler-Truman Transportation Bill on which he and Senator Wheeler had spent four years of work. The bill incorporated reforms of the abuses Senator Truman had found in the finances of the railroad industry, after his months of hearings, as well as other reforms needed to restore vitality to the nation's transportation system. Pushing this bill through the Senate and House was a frustrating, exhausting business. It was also extremely important to his survival as a senator. To have one's name on a piece of major legislation was the best proof that Harry Truman had been a productive, hardworking lawmaker.

Whether she was in Washington or Independence, Bess kept in close touch with every facet of Senator Truman's ever more complicated career. When he threw a party in his office as the Senate neared adjournment in the summer of 1939, she provided a ham that "went over big." More to the point, Dad recited a list of names at the party, a wild mixture of isolationists and interventionists, liberals, and conservatives, and remarked that from Bess's reading of the *Congressional Record*, she would no doubt wonder how they ever got along. They all wished him luck in his reelection campaign, which everyone knew had already began.

Happily, not everything in these years revolved around the dread of defeat in 1940. Bess's enjoyment of life in Washington, D.C. continued to grow. By 1937, Dad was an established member of the Senate's hardworking inner circle. He was a close friend of Vice President Garner. This growing prominence made Bess feel more socially secure—as well as more proud of her husband. Invitations to lunches, teas, and dinners multiplied. She even liked the way politics intertwined with these social occasions. For instance, when she told her mother that the Trumans had been invited to tea at Justice Brandeis's home, she noted the invitation could not have arrived at a better time, with the Pendergast mess in all the papers.

In another letter around this time, she made it clear that she had not lost her feet-on-the-ground Missouri approach to Washington high life. She told her mother of going to a "very high-brow dinner" at which a Chinese diplomat made a speech. "It was mostly propaganda," she remarked. Bess was far more interested in an Indian girl who had practiced law in London for five years and was going back to India "to try to do something for the country. I imagine she'll *do* it." She summed up the rest of the company as "strictly a bunch of brain trusters (minus the Trumans) and a number of top columnists and state department people."

Bess became active in the Congressional Club, where wives of senators and representatives mingled for lunch and tea. She and

Miriam Clark gave a tea for the wives of the Missouri delegation there and invited a national committeewoman to give a talk. Several months later, she told Dad with obvious pride that she had been asked to pour at another tea. She ran a Missouri bridge party for the benefit of the club and raised a whopping fifty-eight dollars. (Remember, these were the days of the three-cent stamp!) When the Daughters of the American Revolution came to town for their convention, she gave a highly successful tea for the Missouri delegates.

For sheer enjoyment, however, nothing quite equaled the June 1939 visit of the King and Queen of England. I was in a near frenzy over it, and Mother was pretty enthralled herself. I had followed with anguish and fascination (I was now fifteen and a complete romantic) the drama of the royal house in recent years, culminating in the abdication of Edward VII to marry American-born Wallis Simpson. I implored Mother for a chance to examine their successors close-up, to see if I could transfer my allegiance.

We went down to the Capitol the day the royal couple was presented to Congress. Mother wrote Grandmother Wallace a vivid letter about it. "The whole of the capitol plaza was filled with chairs and it was the hottest place I ever got into. We sat there from 10–11:45 and just broiled. I wouldn't have stuck it out but Marg had had such a *glimpse* of them the day before [as they whizzed by in a car]. When they came out they walked the whole length of the plaza thru the middle aisle and we were within fifteen or twenty feet of them so she got a *good* look. And she still prefers the Duke & Duchess!"

Later Bess went to a garden party for the royals which "was even nicer than anybody thought it was going to be—and plenty interesting," she told her mother. "I got myself into the second row when the Queen went thru the garden so got a good look and saw the King from the same vantage point." She thought the Queen was beautiful but rated the King as only "fairly good looking." But both passed another, more crucial test. They were "very democratic."

Bess observed that the King and Queen "had made a terrific hit in Washington." She did not say it but she was well aware that the visit was more than mere pageantry for the benefit of their American cousins. They had come to try to influence Congress and the American people to join their country's stiffening stand against Adolf Hitler's rearmed Germany. Throughout the following summer, Dad played a key role in the struggle to repeal the neutrality laws.

The first round was not encouraging. In midsummer of 1939,

Senators Truman, Minton, and Guffey informally polled the Senate on the question for Majority Leader Barkley and the result was 52 against repeal, 33 for, and 9 doubtful. "You should have seen his [Barkley's] lip go down," Dad told Bess.

On August 23, 1939, Adolf Hitler stunned the world—in particular the liberals who persisted in seeing a difference between Nazi Germany and Communist Russia—by signing a nonaggression pact with Josef Stalin. After a decade of spewing hatred at each other, the two gangster states revealed to the world their essential similarity. The agreement was actually an aggression pact against Poland. On September 1, with Stalin's tacit consent, Hitler invaded that hapless country, and Britain and France were bound by treaty to declare war. Now it was the turn of the isolationists in Congress, who had insisted there was no need to do anything about the neutrality legislation because there was no danger of war, to be stunned.

Dad was gloomy over the odds England and France faced. He discussed the situation with General Robert M. Danford, under whom he had served in France, and they were both "mighty blue," he told Bess. "Neither of us think that England and France can lick the Germans and Russians. They were beaten in the last war when we got in. If Germany can organize Russia and they make England give up her fleet, look out—we'll have a Nazi, or nasty, world."

FDR had reconvened Congress for another special session after little more than a month's recess, and the battle over the neutrality legislation resumed. "We are in the midst of a terrific struggle and I hope we answer it for the country's welfare," Dad wrote to Bess. I doubt if there was a woman in the country, including Eleanor Roosevelt, who was more intimately involved with this crisis. In letter after letter Dad gave her the insider's view of the brawl. He told her that FDR had made his "best speech" to the joint house on September 21, urging them to repeal the neutrality laws. But Senators Nye and Walsh [leaders of the isolationist bloc] and Bennett Clark "looked down their noses all the time he was speaking and never applauded once."

Back in Independence, Bess kept the Senator in touch with his ongoing struggle for political survival. She sent him clippings of *Examiner* stories and editorials that showed their hometown paper was leaning toward Stark. The more she thought of anti-Roosevelt types like Colonel Southern, the less she liked them. She told Harry she had become an FDR supporter again. "I am most happy you are

. . . back in line," he wrote. "You should not have gotten out seriously. My patronage troubles were the result of the rotten situation in Kansas City and also the jealous disposition of my colleague [Bennett Clark]. While the President is unreliable, the things he's stood for are, in my opinion, best for the country."

I found myself envying Mother as I read Dad's letters over the next month. To be in on such an enormous drama, with the fate of the world at stake! I never had a clue to what was going on. I remained immersed in my fifteen-year-old world, which was pretty exciting from my point of view. I was acting in Shakespeare at Gunston Hall and singing over the radio with other congressional children in a broadcast that some enterprising media men had set up. Mother kept the home folks in closer touch with my doings than she did with Dad's. Everyone at 219 North Delaware Street was glued to the radio when I performed, and they all predictably declared me the best.

The neutrality fight raged on. The isolationists, with a liberal sprinkling of German American Bund types from St. Louis, deluged Dad with letters. He ignored them and flew to Caruthersville in the heart of rural Missouri to make an antineutrality speech to the most conservative voters in the state. Talk about profiles in courage! He was buoyed to discover that there were four political factions in that part of the state and they all hated Lloyd Stark.

Dad topped this one by giving a speech sponsored by Moral Rearmament (MRA) calling on Americans to resist the amoral dictatorships of the left and right. The MRA people told him they were going to distribute 3 million printed copies of the address.

On November 4, the neutrality struggle came to climax in Congress. By hefty majorities the lawmakers repealed the embargo and authorized the President to sell arms and munitions to the belligerents on a cash and carry basis. This left Senator Truman and his wife free to concentrate on his struggle for reelection.

There were other matters that flew back and forth between them. Oscar Wells, Mother's cousin, finally drank himself out of his job— and almost off the planet, wrecking his car as well as his career and ending up in jail. Harry told Bess that his government employers "just could, and would, not take him back again. . . . It's a mess but I don't see any way to help him." He was relieved to discover that Bess was inclined to let Oscar solve his own problems. She was realistic enough to see that the Truman reelection was the only problem they should take seriously.

Not even my Uncle Fred, who was out of a job again, claimed much of Mother's attention. She reported it to Dad, along with an unfortunate accident in which Fred injured his eye, but there was little he could do for Fred in late 1939. He could not even protect his own brother, Vivian, and friends for whom he had gotten jobs in the Federal Housing Authority. They were all getting fired in an anti-Pendergast purge that White House subordinates were gleefully pursuing, presumably with (or simply presuming on) FDR's approval. Even more humiliating, politically, was Dad's attempt to get his most loyal supporter, Fred Canfil, named federal marshal in Kansas City. This was an appointment that traditionally belonged to a senator. The White House ignored Senator Truman.

Perhaps the most interesting development as 1939 drew to a close occurred on a Sunday afternoon Dad spent at Charlie Ross's house. Charlie had returned to Washington earlier in the year to resume his job as the St. Louis *Post-Dispatch*'s chief capital reporter. During the visit, Charlie got out a copy of their 1901 graduation ceremony program and passed it around to several other *Post-Dispatch* staffers. Then, with considerable emotion, he told Dad that he had not written the vicious editorial against him in 1934. But he had had to publish it or get fired. Dad told Bess about this confession in an ebullient letter, which included some warm remarks in his favor from other *Post-Dispatchers*. The man who covered foreign affairs, no doubt reflecting his knowledge of Senator Truman's fight for the repeal of the neutrality laws, told him he was one of the few men in the Senate who was "honest of purpose." All the newsmen said they disliked Stark and Milligan.

That letter made Bess's heart soar. Charlie Ross's Independence roots guaranteed him a special place in her affection. But a few days later, she received a letter that sent her emotions plunging in the other direction. Not even Harry Truman's optimism could withstand the rotten things that were being said about him in the newspapers in Missouri, especially in the Kansas City *Star*. The drama of the neutrality crisis was over and his loneliness [Bess and I had been in Missouri since August] reasserted itself. "I'm so homesick I'm about to blow up and have been for two months," he wrote on December 15, 1939. "It's a miserable state of affairs when a man dreads showing up in his home town because all his friends are either in jail or about to go there."

Bess saw that 1940 was going to be a long year.

Chapter Fourteen

I wish I could tell you that Bess wrote Harry Truman a marvelous letter in response to that outburst of gloom, telling him that she believed in him if no one else did. But she was probably more discouraged about his chances, at this point, than he was. She was in Missouri, reading the slams and smears and digs in the newspapers every day. But that strong will, which kept her turbulent Wallace emotions under firm control, stood her in good stead during these trying days.

It was a moment in Harry Truman's career when a panicky wife could have wrecked him. Not long after he wrote that downcast letter, FDR sent him a message, telling him that he did not think he could win renomination next year and offering him a job on the Interstate Commerce Commission.

I mentioned this offer in my biography of Dad. Now, the most interesting aspect of it seems to me is its absence from his letters to Bess. Would a man who was in the habit of telling his wife everything (except news that would upset her, such as a diagnosis of heart trouble) omit such an offer? It was honorable retirement, a safe haven that paid far more than a senator's job. There are only two explanations: (1) Senator Truman did not trust FDR to keep his word; (2) this was another of those lonely moments when Harry Truman confronted his rendezvous with history. I think both explanations are right.

Senator Truman sent a message back to the White House. He was going to run for a second term as senator from Missouri, if the only vote he got was his own. It is a fascinating political moment, that exchange. Two totally different men confronted one another. Franklin D. Roosevelt, the supreme manipulator, the man whose word was definitely not his bond, who slivered and sliced the truth until it looked like macrame. Harry Truman, who believed a political promise was a binding contract and preferred to tell the truth, bluntly, totally, whenever possible.

Back in Missouri, there was no doubt about which man Bess Truman preferred. She accepted her husband's decision and put her shrewd political brain to work on the campaign. Dad was inclined to apologize to Charlie Ross for all the rotten thoughts he had had about him since that 1934 editorial. Bess advised him to wait until the campaign was over. She saw that it would do the Trumans no harm to let Charlie feel like the guilty party for the next nine months. Dad reluctantly agreed. "I guess maybe it would be well to wait until after the campaign to apologize," he wrote. "Newspapermen have to act as if they have no heart and no friends."

For the next six months, Bess and Harry and their sixteen-year-old daughter went back and forth to Washington, D.C. so often, those bankrupt railroads Dad had been investigating should have been able to declare a dividend. Bess decided to try the trip by bus when she and I were traveling alone. It was a disaster. We were a couple of dishrags when we reeled into the terminal in Kansas City. No human being should be required to spend two days on a bus. Even two hours is too much in my opinion.

It was totally confusing. More often than not, Bess was in Washington while the Senator was whirling around Missouri, trying to rally his discouraged friends. In mid-March we went home for a visit that combined Easter and politicking. Bess and I returned to Washington without Dad. "I wired Mother this morning as soon as we got here," Bess wrote. (The wire to Madge was written into the budget of every trip.) "But I didn't know *where* to wire you." She added that it was going to be "right lonely for the next ten days" but she hoped "things were working out in St. Louis."

Building some kind of a base of support in St. Louis was crucial to Dad's strategy, now that he could not rely on a massive vote from Kansas City. He involved his fellow reserve officer, banker John Snyder, in his political fate by persuading him to come to Washington as head of the Defense Plants Corporation. In Washington, Bess assured him that she would do her best to make Mrs. Snyder, who was not thrilled to leave St. Louis, feel at home.

In another letter Bess told her traveling man that she did not mind in the least when he called her at 2 A.M. to tell her things were starting to look brighter. She also reported that Senator Tom Stewart of Tennessee "thinks he can get things fixed up so he can go tonight [he was coming to Missouri to speak for Dad]." She was "anxious to know about the St. Joe [St. Joseph's] meeting." This was another step in the campaign's strategy, building strong "outstate" support in cities and towns beyond the influence of Kansas City and St. Louis. With a sigh Bess added that "it sure was lonesome last night."

With no money to pay for a Missouri campaign staff, Dad drew on his Senate office staff for help. In April he traveled with his administrative assistant, Vic Messall, Vic's wife Irene, and his secretary Millie Dryden. Bess worried about this arrangement. By now the newspapers had more than demonstrated their readiness to spread any smear about Senator Truman they could find. She sent Dad a letter while he was en route to another meeting in St. Louis advising him not to bring the women to any of the conferences he was having with the city's politicians. "Don't give any of that St. L. outfit a chance to talk about you and Vic being with the girls down there," she wrote. "No one is going to miss seeing Mildred!"

She was right about that. Millie Dryden was a dear woman, but she was no beauty.

Bess wanted the inside story on everything that was happening in Missouri. Her letters sometimes read like a list of questions. Did Maurice Milligan (who was thinking of joining the senatorial race) get the reception the *Star* said he got at the Young Democrats meeting? Was Dad pleased that Senator Stewart was going to speak in Kirksville? She commiserated with him about more and more bad news from Kansas City. On April 2, in the city elections, the Pendergast organization got trounced, carrying only five of the city's sixteen wards. "It was rotten luck about the KC election," she wrote.

For a little while Bess got deep into the tangled web of the insurance company bribe that had put Tom Pendergast in jail. She reported to Dad that a man who worked for one of the companies thought he had information that Senator Truman might find useful. He was prepared to go to Missouri and speak to him. Dad decided that the less said about that matter, the better, and Bess so informed the informer.

Bess also reported assiduously on the political climate at the White House. She noted with glee that Lloyd Stark, in town to solicit FDR's support, got exactly ten minutes with the President, while Senator Truman had recently spent two hours in the Oval Office discussing legislation and other matters. On the eve of the Missouri State Democratic Convention, she all but whooped at the news that the gathering was completely in the hands of Harry Truman's friends. They were going to pick delegates for the National Democratic Convention, and she wondered if they would go so far as to keep Governor Stark off the slate.

Dad decided this would be unwise. It might enable Stark to portray himself as a martyr, persecuted by vengeful Pendergastites. The governor was voted a place on the delegation but he was the only Stark man in sight. Dad got the Missouri seat on the resolutions committee, one of the most important jobs at the national convention. The word went out that Stark had made an obnoxious ass of himself at the state convention, and he proceeded to confirm this report by his conduct at the national convention.

Already running for the Senate, the governor announced he was also a candidate for the vice presidency! He handed out Stark Delicious apples to people and actually organized a Stark for vice president parade. Bess laughed uproariously when Dad told her how Mary Chinn Chiles, a six-foot amazon, invaded the procession with a big sign that read TRUMAN FOR SENATOR. Mary was the chairman of the Truman campaign's woman's division.

Stark's behavior drew Senator Bennett Clark into the race on Harry Truman's side. Bennett remarked that the governor seemed to be running for everything in sight, and wondered if this included the archbishopric of Canterbury and the emirate of Afghanistan. Bennett and Dad teamed up to make sure Stark did not even get the votes of the Missouri delegation when the convention chose Henry Wallace as vice president at FDR's request.

It took Bennett a while to break his silence and deliver on his promise to back Dad. By the time he spoke, the Truman campaign was well launched, with a big rally on June 15 in Sedalia, shrewdly chosen because it is almost equidistant between St. Louis and Kansas City. Mother and I were on the platform and Mamma Truman sat in the front row of the audience. The crowd was big and enthusiastic, and I pounded my hands black and blue while Democrats from all parts of the state said nice things about Harry S. Truman. Before and after the rally, I watched Mother and Dad "work the crowd," shaking hands with at least half the 4,000 people that were on hand. I pitched in wherever I thought someone wanted to shake hands with a sixteen-year-old.

A few days later, the Senator wrote an emotional letter from Washington, telling Bess he had been "reaching for you all night long." He apologized for not letting her "and Miss Margie" know how much he appreciated our help in Sedalia. "Both of you did untold and yeoman service, and the more I think of that day's work, the more pleased I am."

In another letter, he had a private laugh with Bess over the latest development in the race. Maurice Milligan, Tom Pendergast's prosecutor, had decided to run. He did not know it, but Dad's friends had taunted him into it by inflaming his jealousy of Lloyd Stark. The object was to split the anti-Pendergast vote between them. Dad and Bess enjoyed the confusion this produced in the Kansas City *Star's* editorial writers. "That awful paper had an editorial on Stark and Milligan in which you could see much anguish," Dad wrote.

All this Missouri turmoil took place in the shadow of dreadful news from Europe. Hitler's legions had launched their blitzkrieg against the French and English, and by the time Dad spoke in Sedalia, the storm troopers were goosestepping through Paris. The threat of war had a lot to do with FDR winning his nomination for a third term in July. Even with this in his favor, he had to throw himself into the arms of Boss Frank Hague of New Jersey and Boss Ed Kelly of Chicago to carry his divided party. For the Trumans, the ironies of that political move were almost too heavy to think about.

Dad's letters to Mother during July and the first week in August read like local train schedules. On Thursday I'll be in Keytesville at 2, Brunswick at 4 and Carrollton at 8. At times both sets of nerves got a little frayed. Bess lost her temper over the way Dad was barking orders and Dad apologized for offending her. "Guess I'm getting cranky," he wrote.

Dad zoomed back to Washington and reported every senator and office boy seemed to be rooting for him. He organized a few verbal uppercuts to Governor Stark's jaw from his fellow solons. Senator Gillette, in charge of investigating campaigns, issued a blast accusing the governor of repeating his dirty trick of forcing state employees to contribute 5 percent of their salaries to his campaign. A half dozen other senators, including Majority Leader Barkley, came to Missouri and endorsed Senator Truman.

Finally, with Mother and I feeling numb and Dad completely exhausted, we got to August 5, primary day. That night we crowded around the radio in the living room at 219 North Delaware Street and listened to the returns. It was unquestionably one of the worst nights of Bess's life. The early returns gave Stark a 10,000-vote lead, which he held for several hours. Dad astonished her (and me) by announcing that he was sure he was going to win and in the meantime would get some badly needed sleep. He went to bed, leaving us and Grandmother Wallace and Fred and Christine up to our chins in gloom.

I can still see the tears streaming down Bess's face as we went to bed. A lot of salt water was running down my cheeks too. But I realize now my disappointment did not come close to the anguish Mother was feeling. She had tried so hard to help Dad. She wanted him to win with a fierceness, an intensity that transcended anything else she had ever desired. She had come to love her life in Washington, D.C. She had become a success in her own right as a senator's wife. To have it all demolished by the collapse of Tom Pendergast and the blindness, the simplemindedness of a few newspapers!

Bess went to bed, but I am sure there was no sleep for her. She lay in the darkness listening to Harry Truman's steady breathing next to her. She wanted him to hold her, she wanted to hold him but she knew how much he needed the sleep he was getting. She lay there, weeping bitter, lonely tears.

About 3:30 A.M., the silence in the old house was shattered by the clang of the telephone. Bess groped for the black noisemaker in the dark bedroom. "This is Dave Berenstein in St. Louis," said a cheerful voice. "I'd like to congratulate the wife of the Senator from Missouri."

"I don't think that's funny!" Bess snapped and slammed down the phone.

Only as she sank back on her pillow did Bess remember that Mr. Berenstein was the Truman campaign manager in St. Louis. She charged into my room and shook me awake. "Marg," she gasped. "I hope I'm not dreaming. I've just heard the most incredible news. Do you think it could be true?"

I was too sleepy to make much sense out of Mr. Berenstein's call. But that eager gentleman was soon back on the line, asking why Mrs. Truman had all but punctured his eardrum with that slam of the receiver. He had presumed that everyone would still be awake, rejoicing over the good news. Dad had carried St. Louis by 8,000 votes and was now ahead of Governor Stark.

That meant there was no sleep for Mother or me for the rest of the night. We spent the morning glued to the radio, while Dad's lead went up and down, sometimes sinking to a nerve-shredding handful of votes. Not until 11 A.M. was he declared winner by 7,936 votes.

By that time he was up, full of glowing, I-told-you-so ebullience. Bess and I sat there like two polio victims in need of respirators.

When Dad learned what Mother and I had gone through during the night, he was very upset. It troubled him all the way back to Washington, where the Senate was still in session. "I'll never forget Tuesday night if I live to be a thousand," he told Bess. "My sweet daughter and my sweetheart were in such misery, it was torture to me." He found himself wishing "I'd never made the fight."

Then he reached out to the fighter in Bess, the athlete's competitive spirit that she never lost. "But it was a good fight." He listed all the people who had been against him, the newspapers, the state and city employees. He told her that Les Biffle, the secretary of the Senate, had said that in all his years in Washington he had never seen a victory like it. Finally, Dad appealed to what mattered most to Mother, loyalty. "We found out who are our friends and it was worth it for that."

Then he added a familiar question: "When do you want to come on here?"

Bess decided she had better remain in Missouri, because the Trumans had another election to win in November. It was a good thing she did, because lack of money, a quarrelsome staff, and a formidable Republican opponent soon gave everyone the heebie-jeebies. In St. Louis, Dad's administrative assistant Vic Messall and other Senate staffers got into a brawl with local politicians and called Bess to straighten it out. At another point, Dad had to implore Bess to protect him from Mary Chinn Chiles, head of his woman's division, who was turning into a female Lloyd Stark in front of his eyes. She was demanding a post on the National Democratic Committee. "Next thing she'll want to be senator or governor," the candidate growled. Lloyd Stark did not help matters by sitting out the campaign without a single word or gesture of support.

In Washington, the Senate sat far into the night, quarreling over the military conscription bill, the first ever proposed in peacetime. Prominent Americans such as John L. Lewis, head of the CIO and William Green, head of the AFL, denounced it, along with dozens of clergymen, college professors, and isolationist politicians from both houses of Congress. Dad fretted about the Wheeler-Truman Transportation Bill, which was still struggling against the international turmoil. Hitler was bombing London, and FDR was proclaiming the United States the arsenal of democracy. The conscription bill, providing for a one-year draft and requiring all men between twenty-one and thirty-five to register for military service, finally passed. In Missouri Mary Chinn Chiles was in a sulk and Jim Pendergast, commanding the remnants of the old organization, was in a rage because Dad had decided, in the interest of party unity, to recommend Maurice Milligan for reappointment as federal attorney to serve out his term. He had had to resign to run for the Senate.

"If I can just do something to make the state chairman and McDaniel [Larry McDaniel, the Democratic candidate for governor] angry I'll be batting 100%," Dad wrote. Bess, the family baseball fan, knew he meant 1000 percent. Getting mad himself, Senator Truman made a very significant declaration. "I don't care much of a damn what they do or don't from here out. I'm going to do as I please and they can like it or not as they choose. I've spent my life pleasing people, doing things for 'em and putting myself in embarrassing positions to save the party and the other fellow. Now I've quit. To hell with 'em all."

When Bess read this in Missouri, she could have had only one comment. "Hurray." She never had much patience with the egotism and power plays of the politicians who swirled through her life. But she never gave the public a glimpse of this side of her mind. Even more to her credit, she had let Dad deal with them his way.

To make things completely cuckoo, Harriette Shields and her alcoholic husband, Leighton, whom Dad had shipped off to be U.S. attorney in Shanghai, showed up in Independence. Harriette's health had broken down, either from Shanghai's climate or from Leighton's drinking or both. Bess could not resist feeling sorry for them. She sent them on to Washington with her blessing. There, Leighton grandly informed Dad that he wanted an appointment with the President. It is not clear whether he wanted to advise FDR on the situation in the Far East or simply ask him for a transfer. Senator Truman told Leighton that he had trouble getting an appointment for himself.

This episode was not a total loss. It prompted another one of those declarations of independence that Senator Truman began issuing around this time. "I'm not going to see the President any more until February," he told Bess, "and then he's going to want to see me. I rather think from here out I'll make him like it."

That one definitely got a hurrah from Bess. She never completely forgave FDR for the cynical game he had played with Lloyd Stark in 1939–40. She thought—and I agree with her—that Harry Truman

deserved better treatment from the President for the support Dad had
given his domestic and international policies.

The topper in this endless series of headaches was the Truman
farm. A vindictive county court judge, elected on an anti-Pendergast
"reform" ticket, foreclosed the mortgage of $35,000 Mamma
Truman had borrowed from the county school fund, and after eighty
years of struggle and heartbreak the land was lost. The only motive
was an attempt to embarrass Dad. In hard times, such mortgages
were routinely extended and the unpaid interest added to the principal. Dad and Vivian had to move Mamma Truman to a small house
in Grandview. Bess did her best to help with the transition, for which
Dad was grateful. "I'm glad you went to see Mamma," he wrote.
"No matter how much front she puts on, she hates to leave the farm."

By the end of September, the combination of campaigning and
getting bills through the Senate had the candidate frazzled. "I was
never so tired in my life," he wrote to Bess. "My desk looks like a
cyclone had piled up all the unanswered letters in the world. The
Senate will not adjourn." He found himself wishing he had just
bundled her up and taken her back to Washington with him. "I need
somebody I can tell my troubles to most awful bad—and it looks like
you are it."

In spite of these fits of gloom, the Senator was soon home in
Missouri, and if he stopped long enough to tell his troubles to Bess,
no one except her noticed it. Once more there was a whirlwind
campaign, but this time election night was a celebration instead of a
sob session. Dad coasted to a relatively easy victory over his Republican opponent, winning by more than 40,000 votes. It was a campaign that attracted national attention. Harry Truman won without
the support of a single major newspaper or political organization. He
had proved he was a political power in his own right.

For Bess this was a source of pride in itself. But from her woman's
point of view, this 1940 victory also meant something equally important. After almost twenty years of political and economic peril (one
writer described Dad as a man who had been doing a high-wire act
without a net), the Trumans had achieved safety, permanence, security, and—not unimportant to Mother—just the right amount of
prestige. She liked being the wife of the Senator from Missouri. She
looked forward to playing that pleasant role for the rest of her life.

Chapter Fifteen

Our Christmas on North Delaware Street in 1940 was one of the happiest of many happy holidays in that stately old house. We had the usual huge tree and no one felt any need to scrimp on the presents. Little more than a week later, on January 3, 1941, Mother and I were back in Washington to see Dad sworn in for his second term, while the entire U.S. Senate rose to give him a standing ovation.

In our five-room apartment at 4701 Connecticut Avenue, Bess tackled redecorating with the air of a woman who was thinking of the place as home, now. I remember one exhausting day when we moved every piece of furniture in the house from one side of the room to the other for about five hours before she decided things looked right. No. 4701 was a pleasant place to live. We had a second-floor apartment with French doors that opened onto a small porch. Writing to her mother, who did not want to hear anything nice about Washington, Bess described the porch as "2 × 4." It was a little bigger than that. In the spring, irises and azaleas bloomed on the lawn around us. It was hardly the equal of 219 North Delaware Street, but it was several dozen degrees nicer than your ordinary city apartment.

Another nice thing about 4701 was a nearby restaurant to which the Trumans could take guests. Although Bess did our everyday cooking, she had neither the inclination nor the talent for major efforts in the kitchen. In this respect she remained her mother's daughter. One day, in the fall of 1941, someone sent us a couple of ducks. "I guess I'll have to experiment on them tomorrow," she told her mother. "It sure will be an experiment."

It sure was. The result probably accounts for my lifelong hatred of duck. I was seventeen years old at this point and rapidly acquiring my own opinions about everything from entrees to escorts. I had a lively circle of friends at Gunston Hall. We tooled around town on our own, going to the movies or visiting back and forth. For me,

Washington had become a second home, too.

With less need to worry about entertaining me, Bess plunged into the capital's senatorial social life. In mid-January, she gave her mother a rundown of her schedule. It included three teas and a supper on Sunday, a luncheon, a tea and a dinner at the Mayflower on Monday. It made me tired just reading it.

In February, she went to a dazzling formal dinner at the White House and, as the third-ranking woman present, sat next to young Grand Duke Jean of Luxembourg. He and his parents had been invited to Washington to demonstrate American disapproval of the Nazi seizure of their small country. "He is just twenty one and is as nice and attractive and democratic as any young American," Bess told her mother. On her left sat Senator Maloney of Connecticut. "He's lots of fun so I really enjoyed it," she wrote.

A few days later she took Ernestine Gentry, a youngish sister-in-law of her friend Mary Shaw, to a Congressional Club tea for Mrs. Roosevelt. Ernestine, who could be rather uppity to people Bess's age, was properly thrilled. Although by this time Eleanor Roosevelt had come under fierce attack for her support of people and causes that conservatives considered left wing, I never heard Mother say a word of criticism against her. She particularly admired the way she tried to give women a stronger voice in American politics.

Although she stayed behind the scenes, Bess's interest in politics remained intense. Congress was still divided between isolationists and interventionists. But both sides agreed that the United States needed a strong national defense. They voted stupendous sums to build a two-ocean navy, to expand steel, aluminum, and other defense-related industries, and to build training camps for the men being drafted into the army. The total appropriation came to something like $25 billion, and no one seemed to know or care how it was being spent.

Across Dad's desk in those first weeks of 1941 came a lot of letters from Missourians telling him of the shocking waste and corruption visible even to a casual observer in the construction of Fort Leonard Wood, in Pulaski County. What made him even angrier was the discovery that 90 percent of the defense dollars were going to giant corporations, most of them in the Northeast. One night he sat down and discussed the situation with Bess. He did not want to embarrass the President at this crucial period, when the isolationists were looking for ammunition to smear him. But he was convinced that the corruption and misdirection of the defense program could wind up wrecking the Democratic Party. Bess reminded him that Harry Truman had quite a reputation as an investigator of large, complex businesses, and he had promised her—and himself—that after his reelection he was not going to worry about what FDR thought.

On February 10, 1941, Dad made a fateful speech in the Senate proposing the creation of a committee to investigate these enormous defense expenditures. That was the moment when history, that faceless, unpredictable force which kept butting into Bess's life, began making mincemeat of her hopes for a serene existence as a senator's wife.

The game began with some typical Roosevelt maneuvers. The President told the press he warmly welcomed Senator Truman's idea and simultaneously had his man on the Senate Audit and Control Committee bottle it up. But FDR was finally forced to swallow the proposal in order to head off a dedicated Roosevelt hater, Georgia Congressman E. Eugene Cox, who was putting together a similar committee in the House. The President next tried to cripple the investigation before it started by having the Audit and Control boys vote the Truman Committee a munificent $15,000—to investigate $25 billion!

This time FDR was dealing with an old pro who had vowed to do things his way and make the President like it. Dad promptly hired a staff and arranged to pay them by stashing them on the payrolls of various government agencies, an easy thing to do if you have senatorial clout. Dad made sure he had that vital ingredient by refusing to let Majority Leader Alben Barkley and Vice President Henry Wallace shove a lot of Roosevelt yes-men onto his committee. Instead, he chose Carl Hatch of New Mexico and Mon Wallgren of Washington, who shared Harry Truman's fondness for hard work and his dislike of grandstanding. He also chose Tom Connally of Texas and James Mead of New York, two veteran senators with tremendous influence in the government. They were Roosevelt supporters, but not yes-men.

For his first target, Dad went after the new army camps. The dirt he turned up stunned Washington and the country. The government was letting architects and contractors earn as much as 1,669 percent above their average annual profits. Time-and-a-half and double-time wages at Fort Meade in Maryland cost $1,803,280. Soon Dad had documented $100 million worth of waste in the $1 billion camp-building program.

When Mother and I went home to Independence for a visit during my spring break from Gunston Hall, Dad wrote Bess that a procession of Roosevelt appointees had "come down to tell me how to run my committee." He ignored them and went back to the Senate to ask for more money to continue his investigations. This time he got $85,000.

At home, Bess found herself coping with several crises. Mamma Truman had fallen in her unfamiliar new house and broken her hip, inspiring Dad to wrathful commentary on the local politicians who had forced her to sell the farm. Christine Wallace was also ill, and we had to pitch in with the care and feeding of her two children. Dad had gotten Fred Wallace a job at the Federal Housing Authority, but he still preferred to live at home with his mother, to his wife Chris's considerable distress.

The spring visit had become a necessity to calm and console Madge Wallace. She was now in her eightieth year and was becoming childishly dependent on Bess. Once in January 1941, Bess telephoned when Madge was lying down. Later in the day, Bess telephoned again and Madge told her she was "about to have a good cry" because she did not get a chance to talk to her. Swelling in her ankles forced her to stay in bed, and she "lay there all day thinking of you and Margaret." Even phone calls did not help much. In May, she told Bess that one had made her "homesick."

Bess responded by turning up her worry machine several notches. Her letters were a series of inquiries about her mother's ankles, Christine's inflamed arm, Frank's bad back. This was not entirely new. Thanks to Madge, she had been kept in touch with every cold, sore throat, toothache, and aching back that anyone in the Wallace enclave suffered. Bess tried to manage things from a distance of a thousand miles, warning Chris against taking her son David to school and her mother against cleaning the house until they were well again.

Back in Washington, just as the Truman Committee began to pick up steam, the Senator provided Bess (and me) with a worry that temporarily obliterated the minor ills of Delaware Street. At 4 A.M. on April 13, Dad awoke in agony, with excruciating pains shooting through his abdomen and up into his chest. Bess was sure he had fibbed about the army doctors' examination too, and that he was having a heart attack. A doctor was summoned and he turned out to be a good diagnostician. He said the fifty-six-year-old Senator was probably having a gallbladder attack. It was a very common Washington disease, brought on by too many lavish banquets. "The doctor says rich fat food is the principal cause of it," Bess told Madge.

The Senator rested for a few days and then went over to Walter Reed Army Hospital, where X-rays confirmed the gallstones. The doctors put him on a very strict diet, and he went back to work.

The arsenal of democracy was going full blast all over the country. Other senators were getting reports from their constituents about chicanery here, there, and everywhere, and called on the Truman Committee to investigate them. One of the worst odors was coming from the Aluminum Company of America. When Alcoa's president tried to defy the Truman Committee, Dad chewed him into little pieces and got headlines all over the country. "We're getting somewhere," the Senator told Bess.

Somehow, along with all this politics and social life, Bess managed to keep her seventeen-year-old daughter in focus. We frequently trotted off together to a movie or a concert or opera. Once or twice she persuaded me to join her for a round of golf. She was not a phenom at that sport, having started late, so I could go along as a fellow duffer. Toward the end of the spring, she helped me give a luncheon for about twenty-five friends from Gunston Hall at Pierre's, an inexpensive downtown restaurant. I never knew, until I read her letter to her mother, where she got the lovely floral centerpiece. She was shocked to discover the local florist was going to charge $12 for it. She went downtown and bought it from a flower cart for $4 and brought it to Pierre's herself. Mother never lost her ability to pinch a penny.

She and I also conducted a running battle over the athletic program at Gunston Hall. She insisted I participate. I strenuously maintained it was a waste of time. In one letter she wearily remarked that for once she had gotten me off to gym without an argument. This imbroglio was temporarily resolved when I discovered fencing, which I liked. But the battle resumed after I graduated from Gunston Hall in 1942 and began George Washington University, where there was no fencing coach and some form of athletics was also required. Mother suggested swimming. I said I hated to put my face in the water. She could not understand that, either, and told me to do it or else. "Marg floated the width of the pool with her head under water today, so there's some hope for her," she told Dad, making me sound like a paraplegic.

Having raised four sons into near-adulthood, I can now view these skirmishes as more or less standard maneuvers in the eternal war between parents and children. Mother, having had somewhat quieter but in some ways more severe tussles with her mother, did not let them disturb her affection for me in the least. But she did not let my resistance change her maternal style, either. In July 1941, I was shipped home to stay with Grandmother while Fred and Christine and their children vacationed in Colorado. Mother's letters to me are a good summary of that style.

I was ordered to stay close to home. She never abandoned the fear that someone would try to kidnap me. "Dad told me to tell you not to go anywhere [underlined three times] with Perry. If you can think of an excuse, alright, but if you can't, just tell him you can't go." This reduced me and Perry, my boyfriend of the moment, to sitting on the porch swing eating enormous amounts of candy, which he brought me by the two-pound box. Bess also wanted to know where Grandmother and I were sleeping and was relieved to learn we had both moved upstairs. She wrote that now she would "feel much easier about you."

She sent me separate amounts of money to pay for my music lessons and for my allowance. With the latter came a warning that I had to "make it go a long way." We had a good laugh over one of these letters, which she inadvertently signed "Bess." I liked it and threatened to call her that from now on—but of course I did not have the nerve. It was just habit, she explained.

A crisis was triggered when I received an invitation to a church picnic in Excelsior Springs, about forty miles from Independence. I wanted to go. Mother decided I could, if I followed her instructions exactly, to reduce the strain on her worry machine. I was to take Route 10, but I was told to drive slowly because it was "very twisty and narrow." I was also to avoid getting sunburned and I had to take a reliable girlfriend with me. But Mother could not figure out how I could get home if the picnic lasted until after dark. Night driving was absolutely banned. She summed up this tangle of instructions and prohibitions by telling me to "call me collect after you get back and if you don't go call me in the morning" (so she could turn off her worry machine). I was so exasperated I abandoned the idea.

In another letter in this 1941 series, Mother wrote with genuine enthusiasm that it was "swell about your voice improving." When she returned to Independence in mid-August, at least half her letters to Dad were written while sitting behind the wheel of her car, waiting for me to finish a singing lesson with Mrs. Strickler. This was the summer in which I began to think I might really want to be a singer. I worked extremely hard at it, day after day (unlike my piano playing, which I had pursued mainly to please Dad, and which usually involved more arguments with Mother than practicing). At the end of the summer, Mother wrote Dad that "M. [Margaret] Strickler says Marg is making remarkable progress and she wants her to sing for that tall hat teacher of hers in N.Y. around Easter, when she will be there!"

By this time Congress had voted to stay in session until the national emergency ended. Since that might last a decade, Mother and Dad decided we had better become full-time residents of Washington, D.C. Instead of doing my usual split-year schedule at two schools, Bess enrolled me at Gunston Hall and headed for Washington in mid-September. Her mother was predictably disconsolate, but Bess did not let Madge's sighs change her mind. There was another reason for this decision. In July, the Senator had put Bess on his office payroll at a salary of $2,400 a year.

For all practical purposes, Bess had been working as a member of the staff since 1934. She visited the office regularly and signed letters for him and read and handled routine correspondence. More than a few other senators and congressmen had relatives on the payroll to make ends meet. It was risky because a snide opponent or newspaper critic could make it seem corrupt, although it was perfectly legal and even necessary for men who had to live on their inadequate salaries. The Trumans had not felt secure enough to chance it until Dad's reelection.

The war news continued to be awful, from America's point of view. In the spring of 1941, Germany had overrun Greece and Yugoslavia and then launched a massive assault on Russia, adding another customer to the arsenal of democracy. This meant more work for Senator Truman—and it soon became apparent that all of it could not be done in Washington. He was from the Show Me state, after all, and had a long established habit of seeing things for himself close up.

The Senator spent most of August and September 1941 rampaging up and down the West Coast, forcing defense plant managers from San Diego to Spokane to tell him the truth about their labor troubles and production bottlenecks.

Looked over the new marine base camp and then got another walk around a plane plant, the Consolidated [in San Diego]—said to be the biggest of 'em all. The managers are all such liars you can't tell anything about the facts. Each one says he's having no trouble and everything is rosy but that the other fellow is in one awful fix. By questioning five or six of them separately I've got an inkling of the picture, and it is rather discouraging in some particulars but good in others. We are turning out a very large number of planes and could turn out more if the navy and army boys could make up their minds just what they want.

Labor is a problem. The same brand of racketeer is getting his hand in as he did in the camp construction program. Some of 'em should be in jail. . . .

To save time he flew everywhere, and Bess did a lot of worrying about his flight schedule. As we rode toward Independence on the B. & O. in mid-August, Bess kept watching the thick clouds to the south and southwest. She knew Dad was in a plane heading for Dallas. "It was a tremendous relief to get your phone call last night," she wrote the next day. Those clouds "didn't look so cheerful."

When the Senator added to his investigatory trips a political swing through Missouri that occupied the better part of two weeks in the fall, things grew a little tense. The familiar situation was ironically reversed. Now Bess was in Washington, D.C., complaining about how much time the Senator was spending in Missouri. Bess was never shy about letting him know when she was displeased. A telephone call made it clear, as Dad wrote the next day, that she was "not in the happiest frame of mind." He admitted he had been away a long time but vowed "I haven't wasted one minute."

In spite of her wifely complaints, the politician in Bess enjoyed the letters Dad wrote her from Missouri that fall. He reveled in the contrast between the treatment he was getting and what they had gone through in 1940. The St. Louis *Star-Times* and *Globe Democrat* both ran stories about the Truman Committee on their front pages "exactly as I said it," he wrote. "Last year that would have been impossible." In Kansas City, he saw over 1,000 people in two days at the Muehlebach Hotel, members of every faction and age group, all seeking favors and asking his advice as the ruler of the party in Missouri. "What a difference from last year this time and what a kick there is in it," he chuckled.

Around this time, Dad started writing letters to me. He decided I was too old—I was seventeen and a half—to be satisfied with a "kiss

Margie for me" at the end of his letters to Mother. I was amused to note on the first one that he had not abandoned the argument he had had with Bess Wallace Truman about my name. (You will recall it took them four years to agree on it.) The letter—and all subsequent ones—was addressed to "Miss Mary Margaret Truman."

Some of Dad's early letters were lectures on the history of ancient Greece or the Civil War, subjects I was studying in school. But some of them were intensely personal. This one, written in early October 1941, is one of my favorites.

Dear Margie,

I have a hotel radio in my room. The co-ed singing program is now on, and the charming young lady who is the "Charming Co-ed" hasn't half the voice of my baby.

You mustn't get agitated when your old dad calls you his baby, because he always will think of you as just that—no matter how old or how big you may get. When you'd cry at night with that awful pain, he'd walk you and wish he could have it for you. When that little pump of yours insisted on going 120 a minute when 70 would have been enough, he got a lot of grey hairs. And now—what a daughter he has! It is worth twice all the trouble and ten times the grey hairs.

Went to the Baptist Church in Caruthersville this morning and the good old Democratic preacher spread himself. He preached to me and at me. . . . Last week I had dinner in Trenton and the Chinese Consul General was on the program with me and he made a corking speech to the United States Senator present and not to the audience at all. It's awful what it means to some people to meet a Senator. You'd think I was Cicero or Cato. I'm not. Just a country jake who works at the job.

Less than a month after he returned from Missouri, Dad was off again, prowling through defense plants and watching army maneuvers in Tennessee. Everyone thought we were close to war with Germany. President Roosevelt had U.S. destroyers escorting British merchant ships as far as Iceland, and on October 16 the USS *Kearny* took a torpedo that killed eleven men. Two weeks later, the USS *Reuben James* was sunk and 100 sailors died. The isolationists were unimpressed. When the President tried to get some changes in the neutrality laws that would permit American merchant ships to be equipped with cannons, the brawl was stupendous, and the measure passed both houses by narrow margins.

Unquestionably, FDR was trying to provoke a war with Germany, something that would get a President impeached these days. But

Hitler declined to accept the challenge. The President was being equally hostile to Japan, slapping an embargo on oil shipments and scrap metal after they seized French Indochina earlier in the year. Everyone knew that the Japanese could not survive more than a year without American oil. They were consuming their reserves at the rate of 28,000 tons a day. But the Japanese too seemed disinclined to give the President the incident he needed to break the power of the isolationists in Congress and among the American people. Instead, a team of bowing, smiling diplomats arrived in Washington to negotiate a compromise settlement.

On his November trip to Tennessee, Dad was already getting worried about his growing fatigue. He was on the Appropriations Committee, the Military Affairs Committee, and several other major committees in Congress, besides running the Truman Committee. He confessed, some eighteen months after the fact, that he had had a scary episode at the 1940 convention. He almost had passed out during the vice presidential nomination fight. "I had to hang on a railing for fifteen minutes until somebody got me a cup of water," he wrote. That was enough to set Bess's worry machine going full blast. She began urging him to take a rest.

He did not get a chance to pay much attention to her for the next few weeks. A tremendous battle erupted in Congress over a bill to prohibit strikes in defense plants. Early in December, fate intervened. Senator Alva Blanchard Adams of Colorado died, and a large contingent of lawmakers felt obligated to go to his funeral. As the Senator from a nearby state, Dad went along. It was a pleasant two-day trip. During this expedition, the House of Representatives passed the antistrike labor bill, and Dad wryly noted to Bess that many of the Congressmen were congratulating themselves for being away with a good excuse. No Democrat wanted to support the bill, because it was violently opposed by organized labor. But privately, a majority favored the idea.

Obeying orders from the White House, the Senate announced it would hold hearings on the House bill. Everyone knew this was part of a plan to emasculate it, a decision that was bound to deepen the split between Democratic liberals and conservatives. Nothing else of any importance was on the congressional agenda for the rest of the year, and most of the lawmakers on the funeral train headed for their native states instead of returning to Washington. Senator Truman did pretty much the same thing. He stopped off in Missouri to do a little politicking prior to attending a Democratic statewide "harmony" dinner in Jefferson City, scheduled for December 9.

On Sunday, December 7, 1941, the Senator called Bess from the Pennant Hotel in Columbia, where he had decided to hole up for the day reading the papers and getting some extra sleep. Bess heartily approved of that idea. They chatted about the pleasant visit he had just had with the Wallaces and the Trumans in Independence. Later in the day he wrote her a letter, noting with amusement that he was on the front page of four major Missouri papers, including the Kansas City *Star*.

In Washington, D.C., it was a gloomy, chilly day and I had a cold. As usual, Mother insisted I stay indoors. I groused, also as usual, but obeyed. I fiddled with my homework for a while, and then turned on the New York Philharmonic. Mother did some light cleaning and then wrote some letters. With most members of Congress going home imminently, the Washington social season was pretty much over, and she had nothing on her schedule.

Suddenly an excited voice interrupted the orchestra to report that Japanese planes were attacking Pearl Harbor. I never was very good at geography, and I thought that was some port in China. When Mother looked in to see how I was breathing, I complained about the way the music was being ruined by bulletins about a Japanese air raid that could just as easily have waited for the six o'clock news.

Mother, in closer touch with the international situation, asked me what the Japanese were bombing. When I said Pearl Harbor, she did a vanishing act. I sat there blinking while she raced to the telephone and frantically demanded a long-distance operator. She awoke Dad from his snooze in the Pennant Hotel and told him what was happening. He dashed across the road and found a small plane whose pilot volunteered to fly him to St. Louis. There he wangled a night flight to Washington, which soon turned into one of his more harrowing journeys.

The weather was atrocious. Every landing was a breathstopping descent through a soup of fog and rain. In Pittsburgh, they sat on the ground for three hours while the pilots and the control tower debated whether they should take off. Bess shared almost every minute of this awful trip, because she spent the night calling the airline to keep track of the plane. Finally, she drove out to National Airport at dawn and waited in a continuing murky drizzle for Dad to land. The plane circled overhead for a half hour before the pilots came in on a radio beam, unable to see a thing.

Dad was so tired he all but fell into the car. Mother drove a lot faster than usual to our apartment, where the Senator shaved, bathed, and put on fresh clothes. Dad and I then raced to the Capitol for the joint session of Congress. He barely made it to the floor in time to vote for a declaration of war on Japan.

I sat in the press gallery for this historic moment, having talked my distracted mother into giving me her ticket to the joint session and tricking her into thinking I had no temperature by playing games with the thermometer. I feel a little guilty, now, thinking of the way I got to relish this momentous scene, while Mother, who had done so much to get Dad there on time, sat home. But she may have been grateful for a chance to be alone and get a grip on her nerves. Dad's horrendous plane trip had been pure anguish for her.

There was nothing special about the waves of applause that greeted the President as he slowly made his way to the rostrum of the House of Representatives' chamber. That was the standard tribute Congress always paid the Chief Executive. But I will never forget the hush as he seized the lectern and prepared to speak. The silence was full of tension, foreboding; it was almost funeral. Mr. Roosevelt already had met with the congressional leaders and told them about the damage the Japanese had inflicted on our fleet and air force at Pearl Harbor. The news had spread through the rest of Congress. They sat there, fearing the worst.

Then the President's voice rang out. "Yesterday, December 7, 1941—a date which will live in infamy—the United States of America was suddenly and deliberately attacked by naval and air forces of the Empire of Japan."

I felt those words go through Congress, through me and everyone in the galleries, like a jolt of electricity. This speech was not going to be a report of a terrible defeat. It was going to be a summons to battle—angry, proud battle. But the silence persisted. Congress was still waiting for the bad news. The President continued, speaking so slowly each word might have been transcribed by hand.

"It will be recorded that the distance of Hawaii from Japan makes it obvious that the attack was deliberately planned many days or even weeks ago. During the intervening time the Japanese Government has deliberately sought to deceive the United States by false statements and expressions of hope for continued peace."

He told us that the navy and the army air force had suffered "severe damage" at Pearl Harbor. He reported that the Japanese had also launched attacks against Malaya, Hong Kong, Guam, the Philippines. As Commander in Chief of the Army and Navy, he had directed that "all measures be taken for our defense."

Still the silence persisted. The President's voice rose, regaining the anger of his opening words: "No matter how long it may take us to overcome this premeditated invasion, the American people in their righteous might will win through to absolute victory."

That did it. Congress exploded into cheers and applause. I could see Dad clapping with the rest of them, even though he knew through his chairmanship of the Truman Committee how unprepared we were to meet this crisis.

A hush descended again—no longer funereal but full of pent-up fury—as we listened to the President's final, fateful words. "I ask that the Congress declare that since the unprovoked and dastardly attack by Japan on Sunday, December 7, 1941, a state of war has existed between the United States and the Japanese Empire."

On December 18, my mother and I went home for a very different Christmas from the one we had expected. Every day the government seemed to proclaim a shortage of something crucial, such as rubber or sugar. The Japanese seemed to be winning everywhere. Dad stayed in Washington to defend the Truman Committee against an all-out assault from the White House and the armed forces. Secretary of War Robert Patterson had announced on December 13 that the committee ought to go out of business because it would "impair" the war effort to give the members information.

On December 21, the Senator wrote to Bess that he was waiting for a call from the President about the committee, but he did not expect it to come through and he would probably have to rush back to Washington to see him right after Christmas. "He's so damn afraid that he won't have all the power and glory that he won't let his friends help as it should be done," he wrote. If Roosevelt refused to see him and persisted in trying to destroy the committee, Senator Truman was prepared to tell him "to go to hell."

In Independence, Bess spent a lot of her time visiting the dentist and the doctor, because she doubted if she would be returning home for a long time. In a week we were on our way back to Washington. Bess apologized to Ethel Noland for failing to get "even another glimpse of all of you but Heavens—how fast the week went. It seems to me I saw more of Dr. Hull [the dentist] and Dr. Andrews than I did of anyone else."

From Washington, Bess apologized to her mother for the brevity of our stay. Speaking for herself and her daughter, she wrote: "We both hated to leave home, we had such a nice visit. But I imagine we are all going to have to do a lot of things we hate doing in the next few years."

She had no idea how prophetic those words would soon become.

Chapter Sixteen

As 1942 began, Washington, D.C. became the headquarters of a global war. The city started losing the polite, easygoing atmosphere Bess had known and liked. Thousands of people arrived to staff the government agencies that were organizing American industry for the mightiest production effort in history. The District, as the locals called it, was on its way to becoming the rude, crowded metropolis of today. There was one striking difference. With the government rationing rubber and gas, the traffic, already light, became almost nonexistent. All three Trumans took buses to work and school, leaving on separate schedules. Grandmother Wallace became alarmed when she heard about this. Although I was about to celebrate my eighteenth birthday, she thought I was incapable of crossing Connecticut Avenue alone without getting squashed by a wayward army truck. Bess had to reassure her that the traffic was so light, there was nothing to worry about.

The year began with a visit that gave Bess great pleasure and hope. Fred Wallace wrote to tell her that he was coming to Washington to talk to some of his government superiors about his future. Bess promptly urged him to bring Christine with him and orchestrated the entire operation by mail. She persuaded Vietta Garr, the part-time cook and maid, to move into 219 North Delaware Street to help Grandmother Wallace with "the imps," as Mother fondly called David and Marian Wallace. She told her mother to "let Vietta take the brunt" and not overdo on the child-care business. Fred and Christine arrived in Washington, and Bess took an entire week out of her busy schedule to show them the sights. I also was pressed into service as a guide and hostess. We had a lovely time and Fred and Chris seemed to enjoy themselves every minute.

The visit was important to Mother because when she was home in Independence for the Christmas holidays her mother told her that

Fred seemed to have licked his drinking problem. Bess reported the good news to Dad, who replied: "I hope you're right about Fred but I doubt it." This only redoubled Mother's wish to do everything in her power to make Fred happy—and, presumably, sober. She loved this big, ingratiating youngest brother for his own and for her mother's sake.

Although the war was absorbing most people's time and attention, social Washington continued to operate, thanks to a few resident millionaires. Bess told her mother about a spectacular dinner she attended at Friendship, the mansion of Evalyn Walsh McLean. A year younger than Bess, Mrs. McLean was the daughter of a Colorado mining tycoon. In 1902, she had married the son of the owner of *The Washington Post*, and their combined wealth reportedly topped $200 million.

"She has the most tremendous place," Mother wrote. "We went through three rooms before we even got to the dining room and the drawing room still had some bare spots with over a hundred people in it. We were seated at tables of ten. I sat between the Australian minister (Casey) and J. Edgar Hoover." Also at the table was Mrs. McLean, who examined Mrs. Truman through huge horn-rimmed spectacles that gave her, someone once said, an expression that was half astonished, half inquisitive. Her presence was proof of Senator Truman's growing importance.

A few days later, Bess told her mother about attending a luncheon at which Mrs. Maxim Litvinov, wife of the Russian ambassador, spoke. Like her husband, Bess was unimpressed by the love affair between Russia and the United States that some people were trying to promote on the strength of the alliance against Hitler. In a recent letter, Senator Truman had told Bess he considered the Communists "as untrustworthy as Hitler and Al Capone." Several months later, Bess remarked to her mother that they were attending a reception at the Soviet Embassy to celebrate their "October Revolution—whatever that was." They had skipped it the previous year, and she was inclined to do it again, but Senator Truman decided they had better go.

Like several million other American housewives, Mother began fretting about shortages of such staples as potatoes and coffee. At one point, she reported to Dad that there was not an Irish potato in any store in town. She told her mother about seeing frantic housewives grabbing bananas out of a bin as if they were in a bargain store. More ominous sounding, at first, was her letter telling her mother she was having blackout curtains made. "We are to have a ten hour blackout beginning at 8 o'clock Tuesday night," she wrote. "It's for checking up purposes and will probably be as much of a fizzle as all the rest of the OCD orders have been."

Bess had it in for the Office of Civilian Defense because they had banned awnings on all Washington apartments and houses. They feared an incendiary bomb attack. Mother thought this was silly (which it was). She was no doubt among several thousand influential housewives who got the OCD to abandon this prohibition before the hot summer weather began.

Other aspects of Washington and the world brought the war home to Mother this year. She became deeply involved in the anguish of her cousin, Maud Gates, who was married to a brigadier general, Charles Drake. He had the misfortune to be stationed in the Philippines when the Japanese invaded. Cousin Maud begged Mother for some inside information on what was happening to him, but all Senator Truman could get was a mishmash of rumors. One day Charlie was on Cebu, another day on Corregidor, another day on Mindanao. In fact, he was trapped on Bataan with other regulars and Filipino troops. Bess reported to her mother on her growing concern for Cousin Maud. She neither ate nor slept and began to look as if she might break down. But like other army wives, she somehow managed to keep a grip on herself.

Other friends and relatives went into the army and moved toward the battlefronts. From Mary Paxton Keeley came a letter telling Bess that her only son, Pax, true to the Paxton family tradition, had enlisted in the infantry. A Paxton had fought in every war since 1776, often getting killed in the process. Harry Vaughan, Dad's 1940 campaign treasurer who had become one of his key Senate aides, was an Army Colonel in Australia, which the Japanese seemed intent on invading. An Independence friend, Julia Rice Latimer, had a son who had lost a leg at Pearl Harbor and was in a California hospital. Mother asked Dad to inquire for him when an investigation took him to the West Coast.

The fifty-eight-year-old Senator and his committee zoomed around the country, making headline after headline. Bess stayed in Washington, D.C., running the office, signing letters, dealing with jobseekers, and visiting Missourians. She found it hard to resist old friends who came to town expecting her to play tourist guide. When

Ketura Harvey, sister of her former boyfriend, Julian Harvey, arrived, Bess groaned to her mother that she would have to use some of her precious gas to take her to Arlington, or "I'll never hear the end of it."

Every Wednesday, without fail, Bess spent five or six hours at the Washington, D.C. USO, handing out doughnuts and coffee and chatting with the lonely soldiers and sailors who were working in the capital. Her own experience in World War I made her tremendously sympathetic to servicemen separated from their homes and families. She may also have remembered the vivid reports Mary Paxton Keeley sent her from France about her canteen work over there in 1918.

The war continued to go badly for our side. Although we had won a crucial (and very lucky) victory at Midway in the struggle with Japan, elsewhere around the world the Allies were fighting desperately on the defensive, and frequently losing. Hitler continued to chew up the Russians and simultaneously rampaged across the North African desert toward Cairo. Rumors that the British might make a deal with Hitler to save their empire upset many people in Washington. Harry Truman was one of them. Here he reports his thoughts to Bess on April 30, 1942, after a bad night's sleep in Durham, N.C.

Got awake and began fighting the war, and running the [Truman] committee, and finally got started on a mystery story by Mary Roberts Rinehart, and then fought the war some more and by that time most of the night was gone. But I feel all right now. That German peace offensive worries me. If Britain were to run out on us, or if China should suddenly collapse, we'd have all that old isolation fever again and another war in twenty years. We must take this one to its conclusion and *dictate* peace terms from Berlin and Tokyo. Then we'll have the Russians and China to settle afterwards.

Bess responded with similar worries about the British. "Looks as if we had better send some smart American over there to run the war for them. Not that we have done too well ourselves." In July 1942, she commented: "I can't see any hope but a second front. The psychological effect would be great, even if they could not wade all the way to Berlin in 15 or 20 minutes."

The urgency of the job confronting the Truman Committee soon had its chairman working himself to the brink of exhaustion. Dad had to cope with bruised egos on his own committee and jealous senators on other committees who wanted to win a few investigatory headlines of their own. He took on Donald Nelson, head of the War Production Board (WPB), with a critical blast that shredded the WPB performance. Nelson had been given sweeping executive powers by the President, but he failed to exercise them to coordinate the war effort.

Nelson was furious, but his wrath was mild compared to the choler of the mossbacks at the Navy Bureau of Ships, who refused to give a contract to a genius named Andrew Jackson Higgins for a landing craft that the army and the marines desperately needed. By the time Dad was through with the spluttering admirals, Higgins had his contract. (And by the time we invaded North Africa in November 1942, the army had the boats, which inspired a telegram from General Eisenhower thanking the builder.) Secretary of the Navy Frank Knox, the Republican in FDR's war cabinet, was so mad he tried to foment a Senate investigation of Truman. "That ought to be good," the Senator wrote Bess.

To muster public support, Senator Truman began speaking regularly over the radio about his committee's work. Bess's comment on a speech he made in June of 1942 is an interesting glimpse of their partnership at this time. "Your speech last night was really 'somethin'," she wrote. "I think it was the best radio speech I have heard you make. Ethel [Noland] said your consonants were all pronounced just as her speech teacher taught her. In your 'spare time' [she put it in quotes by way of wryly noting it did not exist] it really would be a good idea to take a few speech lessons if you are going to be on the radio from now on. But if you keep on doing as well as you did last night you won't need any."

Bess reveled in the excitement Senator Truman was causing. She even enjoyed his clashes in the Senate with jealous fellow solons. When she was in Independence she continued to receive and read the *Congressional Record*, and she loved the way Dad "made a monkey" out of Senator Tom Connally of Texas when he made a sarcastic, ill-informed speech about the way the Truman Committee's reports had become the final word on everything in the war effort. Connally was on the committee but he seldom came to hearings. "I read the record of the 18th [of June] yesterday and enjoyed it hugely," she wrote. "It's somebody else getting the headlines that's bothering Tom C."

For their twenty-third wedding anniversary Dad sent Mother twenty-three roses and one of his most heartfelt letters. "Twenty three years have been extremely short and for me altogether most happy ones. Thanks to the right kind of a life pardner for me we've come out reasonably well. A failure as a farmer, a miner, an oil promoter and a merchant but finally hit the groove as a public servant—and that due mostly to you and lady luck. The lady's best roll of the dice was June 28, 1919." She was still his sweetheart, "as good looking and loveable as when she was sixteen."

Bess replied that "it always amazes me that you can write a so called love letter when you have had so little practice." She told him she was particularly pleased to get roses on her twenty-third wedding anniversary. "It doesn't seem at all possible it has been that long but I'm pretty sure it has."

Mother telephoned Dad on their anniversary eve, and the next day he apologized for his sluggish conversation. "I was so tired I could hardly sit up." That started the Wallace worry machine churning. She suggested he invite his Man Friday, Fred Canfil (who had become a committee investigator), to live with him until Congress adjourned, knowing that when Fred was around Dad was more likely to play poker than work. Failing that, she implored him to let Fred do all the driving on the trip to Independence, and make sure the driving was *slow*. This was a plea she never tired of making, but this time she had a good argument for it. "You'll get a sort of rest by taking the time on the road," she pointed out.

On the eve of his return home, Mother urged Dad to take a month-long summer vacation. She found a quote in, of all places, the Kansas City *Star*, recommending it. But he did not feel he could let the committee run without his supervision. After little more than two weeks in Independence, he was back in Washington again, doing battle with the admirals, Donald Nelson, and assorted other characters, including the leaders of the steel industry.

Bess continued to enjoy the headlines he was making. In mid-August she wrote that he had been mentioned on the radio again yesterday. "Don't you ever skip a day?" she asked teasingly. She sent him an editorial from the Kansas City *Times*, praising his investigation of the Higgins contract mess, and remarked that she "had to read it twice to make sure I wasn't seeing things." Two years earlier, the *Times* did not have a single kind word to say for Senator Truman.

Dad's growing national fame did not diminish Mother's interest in local politics. When Independence's Mayor Roger Sermon fielded an anti-organization slate in the August 1942 primary and won, Mother steamed. "Geo. [her brother George Wallace] says a lot of Republicans voted in the Dem. primary so that explains some of Boss Sermon's success. Don't you think Mother can stop trading with that skunk after we leave? [Mayor Sermon ran the local grocery store.] Why, now, should he get a 100 a month out of our family?"

When that Wallace temper got loose, it too was "somethin!"

Dad took a somewhat cooler view of Mr. Sermon. He declined to jump on him with both feet. "I know how you feel about Roger," he wrote. "But I can still get some political mileage out of him." He meant in Missouri politics, which he was too busy to think about for the time being. He continued his battle royal with the steel industry, which had been allocating too much of its output to favored eastern customers.

In spite of his often fierce criticism of politicians and businessmen, Dad told Mother he was surprised and pleased at the respect the committee was getting from "people in high places." If he could avoid major mistakes, he was beginning to think he could "really help win the war. . . . That means fewer of our young men killed and a chance for a more honorable settlement. So you must pray for me to go the right way."

This was one of the few times Dad spoke to Mother so seriously in religious terms. Usually when they mentioned religion in their letters, they joshed each other about their failure to go to church very often, or commented on the hypocrisy and inconsistency of so-called religious people. But the mounting intensity of the war, the tragedy it was bringing into so many lives, stirred my father's fundamentally religious nature. Few people can resist religious feelings when they encounter the awesome power of history.

These feelings undoubtedly had something to do with Dad's growing distaste for social Washington, where guzzling and gorging continued while American soldiers and sailors were dying overseas. He told Bess he had ducked two major dinner invitations, one from Washington's premier hostess, Evalyn Walsh McLean.

"Too much society to suit me," he wrote. "Maybe I'm nutty but I can't see anything to those people but a bunch of drunks and parasites, most of whom would be better off in some institution." He did not like being invited to their parties "as one of the animals for display purposes." He was more interested in trying "to save the country for our grandchildren."

Mother let this blast pass without comment, but she was soon expressing her awe at the headlines the Truman Committee was gathering for its investigation into the steel shortage. She also worried about how hard Dad was working. "I am sure I should be in W. [Washington] to help out at the office," she wrote, proof, if any is needed at this point, of how closely she was identifying with Dad's personal war effort.

The global conflict continued to absorb them on both a personal and a public level. Mother's oldest brother, Frank Wallace, begged Dad for help when it became almost impossible to compete with the government to buy grain for the Waggoner-Gates mill. "Frank is on the verge of losing his mind over the mill," Mother wrote. Dad threw his weight around a little and kept the business going. He flew up to Maine to inspect shipyards, giving Mother the airplane jitters.

Harriette Shields and her husband Leighton reappeared in the headache department. He and several thousand other Americans were interned in Shanghai, and Harriette thought the Trumans should be able to get him out. Leighton finally managed it without their help and began camping in the Senator's office, demanding another job. Dad referred to him as "our persistent and pestiferous friend from China." In response to Mother's pleas, he finally got Leighton a job in the Attorney General's office, so he could get on with the business of saving the country.

The war began going better. The Americans landed in North Africa in November 1942, joined the British in wiping up the Afrika Corps, and then surged on to Sicily and Italy. In Russia, the Soviets captured an entire German army at Stalingrad early in 1943 and went over to the offensive. This only inspired Senator Truman to work harder to keep America's defense plants pumping out planes and ships and tanks in ever more stupendous numbers.

By April 1943, he was exhausted, and Mother insisted on another retreat to the army hospital in Hot Springs, Arkansas for a round of tests and X-rays. She demanded to know the results of each examination. She was determined not to let Dad play any cute games on her. "What did the heart man say?" she wrote. "I noticed you skipped that report." All the doctors could find was an acid stomach. The man was simply working too hard!

In the spring of 1943, a family crisis absorbed a lot of Mother's attention. Fred Wallace and his wife and children moved to Denver, where the government offered him a better job. The family decided they could not leave Grandmother Wallace alone at 219 North Delaware Street and moved her to a small apartment on nearby Maple Avenue. She hated it. She missed her garden, her spacious kitchen, the big old house that enabled her to feel she was still Madge Gates, in spite of her sorrow. Mother tried to manage things from Washington, writing worried letters asking whether Natalie and May Wallace were helping her shop, urging her not to overdo anything. She no doubt remembered what happened to Mamma Truman when she moved to unfamiliar quarters. This only multiplied her worry quotient.

After a flurry of long distance calls, a new plan was drawn up. Grandmother would live with Fred and Christine in Denver. I doubt that this thrilled Christine, but Mother and I went out to Independence in June and took Grandmother and a lot of things Freddy and Chris had not been able to ship, such as bed linen, to Denver. We stayed for the better part of two months, giving me a chance to dip my toe into show business. I got a part in a local production of the operetta, the *Countess Maritza*. I was one of 365 gypsies who tripped about the outdoor stage (almost freezing to death) and sang our heads off about the joys of Romany life.

Dad was stuck in Washington, up to his eyeballs in committee and legislative business. He wrote me a rueful letter of apology for missing my debut in Denver. He also wrote to Mother around the same time saying that he was getting ready to head for Colorado. But it took him the better part of three weeks to get there. The delays involved a drunken member of the committee staff, car breakdowns en route, and several days of politicking in Kansas City.

While she waited, and I performed, Bess did a slow burn. There are times when every woman feels neglected and unappreciated, and this was one of them. Senator Truman seemed to be putting everything in the world ahead of his family. When the Senator finally reached Denver, Bess let him have it with both barrels.

Dad was so upset, he told Mother he almost wished he had never become a senator. But he did not fight back. That was never his style in arguing with anyone, and especially with Mother. He simply put us on a train to Independence and headed for an investigation in Nebraska. From there he wrote hoping Bess was "all thawed out from Colorado."

My neglected debut and her worries about her mother may not have been the only reason for Bess's angry outburst in Denver. In the midst of his delayed departure from Washington, Senator Truman wrote her one of his most important letters, from an historical point of view. It began with a report on his brother Vivian's visit to the capital, and Dad's efforts to show him a good time.

Dad praised the way Vivian's children had grown up to be solid citizens. "It's a remarkable job in this day not to raise a jitterbug or a zoot suiter." He added that Vivian had had some very complimentary remarks on his niece (that's me). "He thought she had real character to be as nice and unaffected as she is under the handicap of her dad—then he said, 'I guess her mother ought to have credit for that.' "

With no warning Dad switched to a meeting he and Vivian had had with Senator Guffey of Pennsylvania.

He [Vivian] told Mr. Guffey a horse trade story that caused the Senator from Pennsylvania to tell me today at lunch that perhaps that farmer brother of mine could tell me how to make some high-up people here behave. The Senator from Pennsylvania took me out into his beautiful back yard (garden in the capital) and *very confidentially* wanted to know what I thought of [Vice President] Henry Wallace. I told him that Henry is the best Secretary of Agriculture we ever did have. He laughed and said that is what he thinks. Then he wanted to know if I would help out the ticket if it became necessary by accepting the nomination for Vice President. I told him in words of one syllable that I would not—that I had only recently become a Senator and that I wanted to work at it for about ten years.

This letter marked the first appearance of an idea that was going to wreak havoc in Bess's life. The more I think of it, the more I am convinced that it was the real reason for her wrath in Denver. She did not realize it, of course, but she was taking on an opponent far more formidable than husbandly neglect. Her old foe, history, was stalking her again.

Chapter Seventeen

Senator Guffey was not the only Democrat who was troubled about Vice President Henry Wallace. He represented the extreme left wing of the Democratic Party in all its high-minded looniness. He was an example of FDR's tendency to place ideology above competence in many of his appointments. As a vice president, Wallace had been a disaster. That is no mean trick, to gum up that job. All a veep has to do is preside over the Senate and ingratiate himself and the administration with its leaders. Henry Wallace did the precise opposite, ruffling feathers, rarely appearing to preside.

Even worse was his performance as Chairman of the Board of Economic Warfare. It was probably an impossible job, but he proceeded to get into a public shouting match with Jesse Jones, head of the Reconstruction Finance Corporation and idol of the Senate conservatives. FDR had to publicly rebuke both of them.

Another worry that emerged in whispers among Democratic Party leaders as 1944 began was Franklin D. Roosevelt's health. His body already crippled by polio, he was showing ominous signs of the strain of running a global war. In 1943, exhausting trips to international conferences in Casablanca, Quebec, and Cairo had added to the stress. The toll on his health became more and more visible. For a while some people wondered if he would run for a fourth term, especially as the momentum of the war shifted in favor of the Allies.

But most people believed FDR's leadership would be needed to carry the war to a successful conclusion and to construct a lasting peace. One of the first politicians to make this point was Harry Truman, in a Jackson Day Dinner speech in Florida, early in 1944. He made the same speech three or four more times in the next few months. Simultaneously he began pushing other candidates for vice president.

Almost all these candidates were critical—or at least indepen-

dent—of Roosevelt. As he did on most issues, Dad was reflecting the
mainstream of the Democratic Party. The politicians sensed that
roughly half the Democrats now disliked or distrusted Franklin D.
Roosevelt. The President's zigs and zags on countless issues, his habit
of dumping or humiliating loyal supporters, had accumulated a host
of disillusioned enemies within his party. *Time* magazine quoted a
prominent Washington Democrat as declaring: "I haven't an ounce of
confidence in anything Roosevelt does. I wouldn't believe anything
he said." Southern Democrats were especially restive. They threatened to organize a new party that might back a Republican for president and deny Roosevelt reelection in 1944.

The President's attempts to outmaneuver his enemies only added
to the disenchantment. As 1944 began, he announced that the New
Deal was dead. It was no longer needed to doctor America's ills. "Dr.
Win-the-War" was now in charge. Two weeks later, in his economic
message to Congress, he made some of the most radical proposals of
his career, calling for an "economic bill of rights" that would guarantee jobs, housing, medical care, and education to every American.
The message, to quote one of FDR's biographers, "fell with a dull
thud into the half-empty chamber of the United States Congress."
But it convinced his conservative opponents that Roosevelt was still
determined to destroy the free enterprise system.

Next came a ferocious brawl over a tax bill. Roosevelt wanted to
boost taxes to combat inflation. The lawmakers declined to go along
and sent a tepid compromise to the White House. The bill had been
passed by FDR's fellow Democrats, who controlled both houses of
Congress. Yet the President vetoed it and used scathing language to
defend his action. He called it "relief not for the needy but for the
greedy." Senate Majority Leader Alben Barkley resigned in protest
and castigated the President for his "calculated and deliberate assault
upon the legislative integrity of every Member of Congress." For the
first time in the history of tax legislation, the bill was passed over the
President's veto.

These nasty episodes help explain why the Democratic leaders in
1944 felt that the man they put up as vice president had to be opposed
to, or at least distinctly independent from, Franklin D. Roosevelt.
Henry Wallace, who identified himself totally with FDR, would cost
the Democrats 40 percent of the vote at the precinct level, the party
leaders warned.

Senator Barkley was Harry Truman's first candidate for vice president. That boomlet collapsed when "Dear Alben" accepted reelection as majority leader and made his peace with the President. Dad turned to another prospect, Speaker of the House of Representatives Sam Rayburn of Texas. He took Mr. Sam to Missouri and presented him to the people as an ideal vice president. Everyone liked him—Texas and Missouri have always had kinship feelings—but that boomlet too collapsed when conservative Democrats seized control of the Texas state convention and humiliated Sam by refusing to endorse him as a favorite son because he was a Roosevelt supporter.

Meanwhile, Senator Truman was getting more and more letters from friends in Missouri urging him to enter the race himself. To each of these letters, he wrote an earnest negative reply, giving as his chief reason the one he had given Senator Guffey—his desire to stay in the Senate.

Unquestionably, Mother and Dad discussed the vice presidency during the first months of 1944. It was inevitable, because the Senator now had a friend very close to the President. Early in 1944, Dad had proposed Robert Hannegan, a St. Louis politician who had given him crucial support in the 1940 election, to be Chairman of the Democratic National Committee. When Bob got the job, the St. Louis *Post-Dispatch* promptly declared that this appointment moved Truman into prime consideration for the vice presidency.

We now know something even more important. Mr. Hannegan, who began seeing FDR regularly, became convinced that the President would not live out a fourth term. The choice of a vice president thus became considerably more than a matter of winning the 1944 election. It involved the future of the United States of America.

Dad undoubtedly heard about the President's declining health from Bob Hannegan and others. When friends and staffers such as Max Lowenthal urged him to accept the vice presidency, Dad used me as his first line of excuse. Later, Mr. Lowenthal recalled that he said he had "talked it over with the Mrs. and he had decided not to be a candidate. Also, he had a daughter and the White House was no place for children." Bess undoubtedly pointed to the awful smears and rumors that had swirled around the Roosevelt children and asked Dad if he wanted to subject me to a similar ordeal, at the age of twenty. She also stated her own antipathy to the idea for reasons we shall soon discuss.

In the spring of 1944, the Independence *Examiner* suddenly published an editorial, grandly informing the world and the state of

Missouri that Harry Truman did not want to be vice president. I have no hard evidence, but I would be willing to bet a lot of money that the source of that editorial was Bess Truman. She did not have to use any clandestine device to get it in the paper. She may have told the paper's editor, Colonel Southern, himself. Or told her sister-in-law, May Southern Wallace, with the implicit confidence that the news would soon reach her father's ears.

A Missourian sent Dad a copy of the editorial and asked him if it was correct. Dad said it was. He had worked nine years to become an influential senator and did not want to throw it away. "The Vice President . . . is a very high office which consists entirely of honor and I don't have any ambition to hold an office like that," he wrote.

Mother had every reason to assume that the matter was settled by the time the D-Day landing on June 6, 1944 pushed political news off the front page. In mid-June the entire family, including Dad, left Washington and headed for Denver, where again Mother planned to leave Grandmother Wallace for the summer. They now had a new worry in that locale. Fred Wallace's wife, Christine, was pregnant again and the doctor was predicting twins.

June 28, 1944 was the Trumans' twenty-fifth wedding anniversary. It is an index of her brother Fred's importance to Mother that she celebrated this day not at 219 North Delaware Street or at our apartment in Washington, either of which place might legitimately be called home, but in Freddy's rented house in Denver. Nevertheless, Harry Truman made it a memorable day. He gave Mother twenty-five roses and a chest of Gorham silver in the Fairfax design. If anyone doubts that this ex-farmer had good taste, a look at this silver (it is now on display at 219 North Delaware Street) would change that opinion. It is exquisite.

I had been collaborating with Dad on the silver since Christmas time, when I helped him buy it. Two days before the anniversary, I bought the chest in which he gave it to Mother. So I was almost as excited as she was when she saw it. The set was not only beautiful, it was complete. Along with eight place settings, there were sixteen teaspoons, ladles, and salad forks. Bess was overwhelmed. Her two sisters-in-law had sets in this design, which Dad had long admired. Mother had chosen another much simpler design for her wedding silver.

That anniversary was one of the happiest days in the Truman marriage. But Bess found it difficult to sustain her happiness in the anxious weeks that followed it.

The Senator returned to Washington, where the push to make him vice president resumed with furious intensity. Now that the Second Front was established, President Roosevelt was certain to be renominated for a fourth term. (It may surprise some readers to learn that he did not announce he was a candidate until July 11, 1944.) In Denver, I had seen a newspaper story about Dad becoming vice president and asked Mother about it. She dismissed the idea as a "plot" by Robert Hannegan and other ambitious politicians and assured me Dad did not want the job. I wrote him a letter, remarking offhandedly that I hoped he would continue to continue to keep the "plotters" at bay.

I was startled by the seriousness of his reply. "Yes they are all plotting against your dad. Every columnist and prognosticator is trying to make him VP against his will. Bill Boyle, Max Lowenthal [Senate staffers], Mr. Biffle [Secretary of the Senate] and a dozen others were on my trail yesterday with only that in mind. Hope I can dodge it. 1600 Pennsylvania is a nice address but I'd rather not move in through the back door—or any other door at sixty."

In my biography of Dad, I quoted that letter to demonstrate his reluctance to accept the nomination. While that is still visible, a lot of other things are now much more visible to me. One is the assumption, already firm in Dad's mind, that the Vice President was going to become President. The other is the extraordinary frankness of the letter. Dad was not in the habit of discussing the inner secrets of his political career with me. If anything, he and Mother had gone to extreme lengths to keep politics out of my life. I am now convinced that this letter was meant for Mother. He was certain I would show it to her—which I did. She frowned, shook her head, and reiterated her disapproval of these plotters. She told me and her mother that Dad was definitely not a candidate.

A few hours after he wrote that letter, Dad left Washington, D.C. and drove to St. Louis, where he paused to pick up some tires from a man who was a close friend of Robert Hannegan. With Fred Canfil, he drove up to Kansas City to do some Missouri politicking. Roger Sermon was running for governor in the August 1 primary and Bennett Clark was up for renomination to the Senate. Dad wanted to help both men, but he reported to Mother that they looked like lost causes—a grim comment on the divisions in the Democratic Party.

The Senator wrote a very significant letter to Bess from Kansas City. He said it was "good of her to stay at home" the previous night because she was certain he would call. "Wouldn't I have been some sort of heel if I hadn't?" Dad asked, and then added: "I hope I never do get into the real heel class."

He was obviously nervous about the possibility that he was going to do something that would make Bess very angry. I am quite certain that during that telephone call the Senator convinced Bess that she should come to Chicago and bring me along. He was still assuring her that he did not want the vice presidency, and was doing everything in his power to avoid it (which he was). But he was beginning to get some idea of the juggernaut that was coming toward him.

The next day, he wrote Mother another letter, reporting a "tough interview" he had had with Roy Roberts, managing editor of the Kansas City *Star*, informing him that he did not want the vice presidency. "Also told the West Virginia and Oklahoma delegations to go for Barkley. Also told Downey [Sheridan Downey, Democratic senator from California] I didn't want the California delegation. Mr. Roberts says I have it in the bag if I don't say no—and I've said it as tough as I can."

This was only a warmup for the pressure Dad faced in Chicago, where the Democratic National Convention was slated to begin on July 19. Thanks to FDR's deviousness, a veritable covey of politicians arrived at the convention, each thinking he had the President's backing for second place on the ticket. Henry Wallace was one of them. Jimmy Byrnes, senator from South Carolina and "Assistant President" for the war effort, was another one. Alben Barkley of Kentucky was a third. Wallace represented the left wing, Byrnes the right wing of the party. Barkley represented the middle, but his age and previous identification with Roosevelt made him a very weak contender.

Robert Hannegan and a group of other party leaders told FDR it had to be another younger man of the center, Harry Truman. Mr. Roosevelt agreed with this analysis and gave Mr. Hannegan a letter stating that he would be happy to run with either Truman or William O. Douglas, the Supreme Court justice. His name was added to avoid the appearance of dictating to the convention. He had no support whatsoever in the party.

How much Dad knew about this conference, which took place in the White House on July 11, I can't be sure. He left Kansas City on the 14th and drove to Chicago, arriving there on Saturday, the 15th. Almost immediately, he confronted a phalanx of party leaders who informed him that he was FDR's choice. Bob Hannegan flourished the letter the President had given him.

Still Dad resisted. Jimmy Byrnes, who was as devious as FDR, had called Dad just before he left for Chicago and told him he had the President's blessing, and asked for Senator Truman's support. Dad had given it to him without hesitation and now, he insisted, that message superseded Hannegan's letter.

In his desperation, Dad had summoned two of his closest friends, Tom Evans and Eddie McKim, to come to Chicago to help him fend off the nomination. Tom was the owner of Station KCMO in Kansas City. Eddie, whose name I have mentioned before, was his old army and reserve officer buddy, who had become a prominent insurance executive in Nebraska. Both were baffled by his reluctance to accept the vice presidency. It was to Tom Evans that Dad revealed—or half revealed—his real reason for refusing it. Here is how Tom later recalled their conversation.

"I don't want to drag a lot of skeletons out of the closet," Senator Truman said.

"Wait a minute. I didn't know you had skeletons," Tom Evans said. "What are they? Maybe I wouldn't want you to run either."

"I've had the Boss on the payroll in my Senate office and I'm not going to have her name dragged over the front pages of the papers and over the radio."

"Well Lord," Tom said. "That isn't anything terrible, I can think of a dozen senators and fifty congressmen that have their wives on the payroll."

"Yes, but I don't want them bringing her name up," Dad insisted. "I'm just not going through that."

After repeatedly declaring myself out of the running as a psychologist, I am afraid I am forced to assume the role here. You have just read the words of a man who is yearning to tell his friend the whole truth—but can only tell him part of it. The metaphor Dad used is especially, sadly, revealing. The skeleton he was trying to keep in the closet was not Mother's name on his Senate payroll. It was David Willock Wallace's suicide.

Having seen the cruel way the newspapers had exhumed Mr. Roosevelt's ancestors and used them to try to smear the President, Harry Truman's fears—which were Bess's fears—were not completely unreal. But they were somewhat hypothetical. Dad's anguish revealed Mother's anguish—her extreme sensitivity about this trag-

edy, forty-one years later. If her mother had died during these intervening years, Bess might have been less sensitive. She dreaded the
impact of the story on Madge Wallace far more than on herself.

Meanwhile, at Dad's request, Eddie McKim had been touring the
state delegations trying to tell them that Senator Truman did not
want the nomination. The more Eddie talked to the delegates, the
more convinced he became that his old friend's nomination was not
only inevitable, it was necessary.

On Monday, July 17, Eddie, John Snyder, and several other friends
tackled Dad in his hotel room. They barraged him with arguments.
He was the only man who could prevent the Democratic Party from
splitting down the middle. If Byrnes got it, the liberals would take a
walk. If Wallace got it the South would defect en masse. Dad continued to shake his head. "I'm still not going to do it," he said.

"Senator," Eddie said, "I think you're going to do it."

Dad furiously demanded to know where in #$J%@ Eddie got the
nerve to say that.

"Because there's a ninety-year-old mother down in Grandview,
Missouri, who would like to see her son President of the United
States," Eddie said.

Dad walked out of the room and did not speak to Eddie for
twenty-four hours. With uncanny intuition, Eddie had invoked the
name of the one woman who could challenge Harry Truman's devotion to Bess.

That same day, Mother and I left Denver for Chicago. Mother
seemed perfectly calm to me at the time. But my research for this
book discovered a sign of her inner agitation. She did not tell her
mother where we would be staying in Chicago, and Grandmother,
having no other address, wrote to the empty house in Independence
for the rest of the week.

We arrived in Chicago on the night of the 18th and the convention
started the next day. Dad continued to resist the nomination for the
next two days, but he found no support for his reluctance from
anyone. The AFL and railroad labor leaders said they would not
consider anyone else. Even Sidney Hillman, the left-leaning CIO
leader, told him he was that union's choice, if Wallace could not be
elected.

I spent most of these two days touring Chicago's department
stores with Marion Montague, a school friend from Washington
whom I had invited to join me. Mother remained in our hotel, the

Morison, and discussed the situation with Dad when he returned from the Stevens Hotel, where Robert Hannegan and the other heavy politicos were staying. She had invited an old Independence friend, Helen Bryant Souter, who lived in Evanston, to join her. Helen fended off numerous reporters who wanted to talk to Mother as it became more and more evident that Dad was the probable vice presidential nominee.

In Denver, Grandmother Wallace and Freddy and Chris listened to the radio and read the newspapers with growing puzzlement. On the 20th, Grandmother wrote a letter telling Mother that she missed her and was fighting off a "homesick spell." She added that "F and I listened to several talks over the radio last night. They don't seem to think Harry is not a candidate."

The climax to the struggle was a telephone call Bob Hannegan put through to FDR, who was in San Diego, about to depart on a Pacific inspection tour. Hannegan held out the phone so Dad could hear the President declare that Truman was his choice. "Why the hell didn't he tell me in the first place?" Dad snapped, furious at Roosevelt's deviousness, which had already given him so many headaches and, in 1940, near heartbreaks.

At this point, Bess still could have forced Harry Truman to issue an absolute, unshakable no, a refusal on the order of General Sherman's historic turndown of the presidential nomination in 1884. She could have told him that the whole idea of him becoming President and her becoming First Lady was intolerable to her. He would have said no, even if he really believed that his refusal might, in FDR's words, "break up the Democratic Party in the middle of a war."

But there was an invisible line in their partnership that Bess never crossed—a line that divided a wife's power over her husband between influence and control. Bess never hesitated to try to influence Harry Truman's decisions. But she never attempted to control him—especially in those lonely moments when he confronted his deepest self, the instinct that drove him to risk the pain and sacrifice of meeting history head on. This was the most awesome of those moments. Bess allowed him to accept its inevitability, even though she dreaded the pain it might cause her.

For the next few days, the nomination did not look inevitable. The Wallace backers in the party were numerous and vocal, and they put up a vigorous fight for their candidate. They packed the galleries and staged earsplitting demonstrations in the sweltering convention hall.

On July 20, they came within a whisker of stampeding the convention into renominating Wallace by acclamation. After a night of furious politicking, the Truman forces met the wild-eyed Wallace devotees in a tremendous brawl the next day.

Mother and I were in a box looking down on the floor, where the state delegations sat like regiments waiting to be hurled into battle. Helen Souter was with us, still doing her best to keep reporters at bay. Several thought she was Mrs. Truman and tried to interview her. Dad remained on the convention floor with the Missouri delegation, of which he was the chairman. Ignoring his pleas, they already had voted unanimously to make him their candidate.

Henry Wallace led on the first ballot, mostly because favorite sons controlled a dozen delegations and were hoping for a deadlock that might have made one of them a compromise candidate. In the second ballot Dad edged ahead. Suddenly delegation after delegation switched to him, and the final result was a landslide 1,031 to 105. Pandemonium exploded as exultant Truman supporters cavorted in the aisles.

Take a look at the picture in the middle of the book showing Mother and me as the final count was announced. I am cheering my head off. Mother was barely able to muster a smile. At twenty, of course, I reveled in the pandemonium and was relatively unbothered by the suffocating heat. I also had been having a good time in Chicago while Mother suffered through anguished days and sleepless nights.

I can sympathize with her now. I can see what she saw, what she felt. It was not only the fear of her father's suicide returning to haunt her and her mother. She was losing the serene, comfortable life of a senator's wife, which she had worked so hard to master. She was fifty-nine years old, and all her life she had been making sacrifices for people, putting herself and her concerns second to her mother's peace of mind, her brothers' welfare, her daughter's health, her husband's career. She had a right to eight or ten years of serenity and fulfillment—and she had to sit there and watch that wish annihilated by these whooping, howling maniacs who were determined to put her husband in the White House.

Her personal fears and desires were only part of Bess's opposition to the nomination. She knew Harry Truman's tendency to overwork. If he pushed himself to the brink of breakdown as a senator, what would he do as a president? Everyone was talking about the toll the presidency had taken on FDR. She envisioned an equally deadly impact on Harry Truman, who had recently celebrated his sixtieth birthday.

Mother's political instincts were even more opposed to the nomination. She foresaw that anyone who succeeded FDR, especially through "the back door," as Dad put it, was going to have a terrible time becoming president in his own right.

All in all, hindsight tempts me not only to sympathize with Mother, but to say she was right. On a rational, reasonable estimate of the situation, Dad should have said no!

But Mother was confronting—she and Dad were both confronting—something deeper, stronger than reason, logic, or common sense.

A phalanx of policemen helped Dad fight his way to the platform. An exultant Bob Hannegan held up his arm, as if he were a prizefighter who had just won a knockout victory. The delegates continued to go berserk in the aisles. Dad finally seized the chairman's gavel and banged for order. The celebrators sat down and listened to one of the shortest acceptance speeches in the windy history of political conventions.

You don't know how very much I appreciate the very great honor which has come to the state of Missouri. It is also a great responsibility which I am perfectly willing to assume.

Nine years and five months ago I came to the Senate. I expect to continue the efforts I have made there to help shorten the war and to win the peace under the great leader, Franklin D. Roosevelt.

I don't know what else I can say except that I accept this great honor with all humility.

I thank you.

As he left the platform, Dad commandeered another cordon of police and fought his way through the frenzied crowd to our box. There we were blinded by the flashbulbs of a hundred photographers. Men pounded and pawed us, screaming congratulations. Women wept and flung their arms around us, all but fracturing our spines. Dad told the police to get us out of there as fast as possible. Clinging to each other like shipwreck victims on a raft in the middle of a hurricane, we let Chicago's finest batter their way through the mob to a waiting limousine.

As we got into the car Bess glared at the nominee. "Are we going to have to go through this for the rest of our lives?" she asked.

It was not a good beginning.

Chapter Eighteen

The next morning, the reporters were after us like a brigade of hunters gunning for quail—or sitting ducks. Bess had a press conference in which she did not try very hard to disguise her lack of enthusiasm for her husband's nomination. She frankly admitted she had been opposed to it but now said she was "almost reconciled." When asked why she had felt that way, she replied that her reasons were "perhaps selfish." She liked the calm of a senator's life and disliked the "pressures" she foresaw in the vice presidency.

In her oblique way, Mother gave the reporters a glimpse of how her political partnership with Harry Truman operated, although no one paid much attention to it at the time. She said that she "understood the issues" but had no intention or desire to comment on them. That was "the Senator's job." With shrewd political instinct she omitted the source of her understanding: her intense scrutiny of the newspapers, her daily reading of the *Congressional Record*, her discussions with her husband. She sensed that if she sounded too knowledgeable, the hostiles among the reporters would instantly churn out stories portraying Harry Truman as his wife's yes-man.

Asked if she had any relatives who had been in politics, Bess said that her grandfather, Benjamin Wallace, had been one of the first mayors of Independence. She coolly short-circuited further questions about her family by saying that "as far as she knew" she was not related to Henry Wallace, but she considered him "a very fine man." Then she summed up the Truman-Wallace contest with a remark that gave the reporters another insight into Bess Wallace Truman. "It's nice to win," she said.

Bess patiently answered a lot of nonsensical questions about Dad's favorite foods (beefsteak and fried potatoes) and what she did with her spare time. I put in a plug for her fried chicken and her chocolate pie, two of her best dishes, and had to answer a lot of even sillier questions about my spare time. I had just finished my freshman year at George Washington University, majoring in history. Studying is not a momentous activity, nor is going to the movies and concerts and taking voice lessons. I spent most of my time doing these things, and I found it hard to understand why the reporters were interested. One of them, Margaret Alexander of the Kansas City *Star*, began following me around. That I distinctly disliked.

We started home to Independence later in the day, stopping in Peoria overnight. Outside, the weather was July in the Midwest at its most broiling; inside the car the atmosphere was close to arctic. Dad tried to be cheerful and philosophical simultaneously. Mother said little. At home, we felt strange entering the old house after it had been closed for the winter. Although May Wallace had opened it up, the rooms still had the dank, musty smell of abandonment, which could not have raised Bess's spirits.

Nevertheless, she smiled gamely as her brothers Frank and George and sisters-in-laws Natalie and May Wallace rushed to congratulate Dad, followed closely by his cousins, the Nolands, and other neighbors. The following day, July 24, we had a reception in the front yard. Some 3,000 friends from Independence swarmed onto the grounds and the Trumans had their first experience with marathon handshaking.

Greeting that many people as a hostess was far different from working a crowd at a political rally. There you have a chance to vary the pace of the handshakes or skip them entirely if your hand starts to ache. About halfway through the procession, Bess had to stop. She was in excruciating pain. She had not yet mastered the quick shake and withdrawal before the mashing can take place.

For the next few days we all tried to rest. Dad was staying until August 1 to organize support for Roger Sermon, whose run for the governorship was looking more and more dubious, and Bennett Clark, whose chances of winning renomination to the Senate were growing even dimmer. The vice presidential nominee spent most of his time huddling with politicos in Kansas City. When Mother went out to several luncheons, I retreated to my Uncle Frank Wallace's house at 601 Van Horn Road, just behind 219 North Delaware Street. Frank's wife, Natalie, was good company, and I was leery about staying alone in the big house when almost anyone was liable to show up at the door wanting to see the nominee. Aunt Natalie had a piano, and I could practice my scales or otherwise amuse myself on it.

During one of these retreats, Aunt Natalie and I got talking about the effect that the nomination might have on the family. She feared it would give Fred Wallace dreams of glory. Then she tried to find out how my mother felt about it. When I was not very informative (mainly because I did not know very much) Aunt Natalie frowned and said: "I suppose it will all come out now, about the way your grandfather died. The reporters will dig it up. I'm sure it's going to upset your mother and grandmother terribly."

I did not have a clue to what she was talking about. "What do you mean?" I asked. "I thought he died of a heart attack or something like that."

Aunt Natalie smiled sardonically. "He shot himself," she said. "Frank found him."

I could not have been more astonished if she had told me that she had seen David Willock Wallace ascend into heaven. I stumbled back to the big house and found Vietta Garr in the kitchen. She had been working for us for decades. I told her the story and asked her if it was true. Vietta nodded. She blamed it on a growth which (she had heard) David Wallace had discovered on the back of his neck. According to that version, he had been afraid of dying of cancer.

Mother came home, but some shred of my father's good judgment told me not to say anything to her about Aunt Natalie's revelation. I waited until Dad arrived later in the evening, and I asked him what he knew about it. I have never seen him so angry and upset. He seized my arm in a grip that he must have learned when he was wrestling calves and hogs around the farmyard. "Don't you *ever* mention that to your mother," he said.

He rocketed out of the house and down through the backyard to Aunt Natalie's house. I have no idea what he said to her, but it is not pleasant to think about, even now. I was too shaken to think about it in 1944. Now I can see that Aunt Natalie had been living much too long in what amounted to her mother-in-law's backyard. She was obviously striking back for twenty-eight oppressive years with Madge Wallace breathing down her neck, sweetly inquiring what she was doing, where she was going every time Natalie left the house. Childless, Natalie had also grown to resent the hours Frank spent with his mother. It was not her sister-in-law Bess that Natalie was out to get with her revelation about David Willock Wallace, it was her mother-in-law. Everybody has a mean streak, I'm afraid, and when circumstances exacerbate it, watch out.

Harry Truman was one of the few people I have ever met who did not have a mean streak. But he could be very, very tough when he felt it was necessary. That night, I fear Aunt Natalie saw that side of him. She never mentioned David Willock Wallace again to me, or, I presume, to anyone else.

I wish I could tell you that years later I asked Mother if her anxiety about her father's death was the hidden reason for her opposition to Dad's nomination. But to the end of her life, I never felt free to violate the absolute prohibition Dad issued on that summer night in 1944. More than once, in these later years, I had hoped Bess would talk to me about her father, but she never did.

In the course of researching this book, I changed my mind about Mother's silence on this subject. As I explored Mother's early life, I realized that she should not be judged by the standards of our talkative century, where with the help of legions of psychiatrists we try to ventilate away our woes. Mother was born and grew up in the nineteenth century, and she handled the lifelong burden of David Willock Wallace's suicide with the psychological strategies of her own time.

When Theodore Roosevelt's first wife, Alice Lee, died following childbirth in 1884, he was devastated by the loss. For the rest of his life he never mentioned her again in his diaries or letters—or even in conversations with his daughter Alice, who bore her mother's name. This great man and great president, almost the prototype of the courageous American, could only deal with the pain of this loss by putting Alice Lee out of his mind and heart by an act of the will. This tactic may strike us as almost cruel; at the very least uncaring. But it worked. Theodore Roosevelt and Bess Wallace Truman survived their grief and lived full, satisfying lives.

If this resolute silence was necessary to enable a man to survive the loss of a wife in childbirth, hardly an unusual event, think how much more urgent it was for Bess Wallace Truman to consign David Willock Wallace to the silence.

Early in August 1944, after Grandmother Wallace had absorbed the shock of Dad's nomination, she wrote Bess a touching, surprisingly perceptive letter. It began on the usual melancholy note. It was a lonely Sunday in Denver; Fred and Christine and the children had all gone to church, and she was sitting on the terrace thinking about us. "I somewhat realize what a task is before you, and Margie, dear," she wrote, "and I wish in some way I could help." As always, Grandmother was being oblique. But I think that she was trying to tell Bess in this letter that she wanted her to face the future without worrying about her.

Bess was determined to minimize the task, for the time being. She announced that she and I were going to stay in Independence for the summer. She also made it very clear to Dad that she would not campaign with him on a day-to-day schedule. She would make a few appearances at major rallies and nothing else.

The candidate headed back to Washington, having done everything he could to help Roger Sermon and Bennett Clark in the upcoming primary. From the capital he filled Bess in on conferences with John Snyder and other friends. Already Dad was concerned that FDR was going to ignore him and he would commit political blunders. But John Snyder reminded him that he had plenty of friends inside the administration who would enable him to "get the truth."

Dad was very disturbed by Mother's reaction to the nomination. It accentuated his own natural, normal feelings of apprehension about the step he had taken. When he went to the Senate and informed the other members of the Truman Committee that he had decided to resign as chairman, he found himself swept by deep, almost uncontrollable emotions.

Yesterday was a hectic day. The train [from Missouri] was late. Fulton [Hugh Fulton, the Truman Committee counsel] met me at Martinsburg, West Virginia and we talked over every angle of the committee and came to the decision that for the best interests of all concerned I'd better quit. I had made my mind up that when the nomination was forced on me. I have never in my life wanted to sit down and really blubber like I did when I told 'em I was quitting. I didn't do it—but they did. Connally, Mead, Kilgore, Brewster, Benton, Ferguson were there—so were Fulton, Halley, and one or two others of the staff. . . .

Dad was saying farewell to his ten years of senatorial life, and it was as painful for him as it was for Bess.

A few days later, Dad wrote me a letter in which he tried to cope with that deeper, more hidden worry, David Willock Wallace's suicide.

This is going to be a tough, dirty campaign and you've got to help your dad protect your good mama. Nothing can be said of me that isn't old and unproven—so this little district attorney [the Republican candidate, Thomas E. Dewey] will try to hit me by being nasty to my family. You must remember that I never wanted or went after the nomination—but now we have it (to save the Democratic Party—so the Southerners and AF of L and RR Labor say) we must win and make 'em like it. . . . But you must help me keep all the family in line. Most of 'em on both sides are prima donnas and we must keep our eyes on the ball.

In this letter Dad was strengthening the bond of silence he had forged with me on the night of my encounter with Aunt Natalie. He was also sending Mother a message. He was certain that I would show her the letter or she would ask to read it after I opened it. He was trying to say that he understood her anxiety and he cared deeply about it.

From Independence came only silence. On August 10, the Senator telephoned Bess, and to his immense relief he saw that his letter to me had done some good. They had a pleasant chat. "I'm sure glad I called you last night," he wrote on the following day. "I was so lonesome and feeling sorry for me—which is no good for me or anyone else. But there has been no letter for three whole days."

For the rest of the letter he tried to reassure Bess that things were looking better and better. He had been to the White House and had "a most happy session with Jim Byrnes and afterward with Harry Hopkins." He also reported—and dismissed—the first attacks on him in the Republican-controlled press. The Chicago *Tribune* and its "Washington echo sheet," the *Times Herald*, had declared that Senator Truman was running against himself because he had criticized the administration fiercely in his committee reports and now had joined it. "They are surely desperate for an issue," Dad wrote.

The next day, the Senator reported that he was "feeling much better this evening," thanks to a "nice long letter" from Bess (unfortunately among the lost). A few days later, FDR returned from his Pacific inspection tour and invited his running mate to lunch at the White House. Dad wrote a long letter to Bess about this meeting.

Wish you'd been here for the White House luncheon today. . . . I went in about five to one and you'd have thought I was the long lost brother or the returned Prodigal. I told him how I appreciated his putting the finger on me for Vice President and we talked about the campaign, reconversion, China, post-war employment. . . .

Then lunch was announced and we went out into the back yard of the White House under an oak tree planted by old Andy Jackson, and the movie men and then the flashlight boys went to work. He finally got hungry and ran 'em out. Then his daughter Mrs. Boettiger [Anna Roosevelt], acted as hostess and expressed a lot of regret that you were not there. I told the

President that you were in Missouri attending to my business there, and he
said that was O.K. He gave me a lot of hooey about what I could do to help
the campaign and said he thought I ought to go home for an official noti-
fication [of the nomination] and then go to Detroit for a labor speech and
make no more engagements until we had another conference. So that's what
I'm going to do. Hope to get things in shape here so I can start home
Sunday evening. . . .

Well this is strung out too much. But the President told me that Mrs. R.
was a very timid woman and wouldn't go to political meetings or make any
speeches when he first ran for governor of N.Y. Then he said, "Now she
talks all the time." What am I to think?

Dad was telling Mother, with that sly final paragraph, that he was
hoping she might get over her reluctance to become the First Lady.

What Dad left out of that letter is almost as significant as what he
put into it. He did not say a word to Bess about President Roosevelt's
appalling physical condition. The Pacific inspection trip had exhausted him. His speech was slow and halting, like a phonograph
record played at the wrong speed. His hands shook so badly he could
not get the cream into his coffee. His skin was ashen, his lips colorless. His mind remained keen, but his body was obviously close to
disintegration. He did not even try to pretend that it was a temporary
decline. When Dad told him that he was thinking of using an airplane
to campaign, Mr. Roosevelt shook his head. "One of us has to stay
alive," he said.

The campaign picked up steam, and Bess began to participate in it.
While I spent a fun-filled week in Columbia, Missouri as the guest of
the Pi Beta Phi Chapter at the university, Mother joined Dad for a
speech he was making to the American Legion Convention in Chicago. "You should have seen your mother getting off the train in
front of about a half dozen photographers," Dad wrote to me. "She
stood up exceptionally well." They paid a visit to Eugene and Helen
Souter, who had been so helpful during the convention. "I'm going
to speak at 11 A.M. and your ma and Helen are going to listen—
maybe," Dad wrote. Obviously, Mother had not entirely overcome
her reluctance.

At the end of September, we closed the house in Independence and
went back to Washington, taking Grandmother with us. Christine
Wallace had all she could do, with her difficult pregnancy, to keep
house for her own family. I went back to George Washington University, and Mother stayed out of sight at 4701 Connecticut Avenue.

On the pretext that the war demanded most of the President's attention, FDR did not campaign very heavily. But in his few appearances he went out of his way to refute rumors about his failing health. Bess, no better informed on this point than the rest of the country, was impressed by newspaper stories of Roosevelt's jaunty ride through New York City in a cold autumn rain with the top of his touring car down.

Meanwhile, Senator Truman toured the country aboard a two-car train. His schedule was brutal; he frequently did not have time to eat his meals. Even his habit of a daily letter to Bess went by the boards. "I suppose you'll be off me for life," he wrote from Spokane, Washington, in late October. The following day he was apologizing for failing to telephone from Seattle. "They simply had me so full of appointments. . . . I couldn't even eat my dinner," he wrote. "They seem to think I'm cast iron and I am in a campaign, I guess."

These letters may have soothed Bess's feelings of neglect, but they did not contribute to her peace of mind. She began wondering if she and not Eleanor Roosevelt would be a widow before the end of the campaign.

Both Trumans were grateful for the elimination of another worry. The campaign was not as nasty as Dad feared it would be. In the final days, the Hearst press revived the old canard that Harry Truman had been a member of the Ku Klux Klan. He refuted it with eyewitness evidence and a demand for even a shred of proof—which was, of course, not forthcoming. Making light of it to Bess, he wrote: "Hugh [Fulton, counsel of the Truman Committee] says we have him [Hearst] for a million dollar libel suit. Be nice to tour South America at his expense, wouldn't it?"

At the end of October, we went to New York and joined Dad for a joint speech with Henry Wallace before a huge crowd in Madison Square Garden. Back in Washington, D.C., we boarded the nominee's special train and headed for Missouri by a route that might best be described as political. We wound through Pennsylvania, with Dad making about ten speeches a day, and then debarked for a spectacular motorcade through Pittsburgh. In Kansas City, we settled into a penthouse suite in the Muehlebach Hotel and regrouped for one more big rally and speech in Independence.

Election night at the Muehlebach lacked the tension of previous Truman contests. Everyone was pretty sure the Democrats were going to win. Mother announced she was tired and went to bed early. I declined to join her, and she was loath to issue orders to her twenty-year-old daughter in front of so many people. So I stayed up while Dad played the piano and kidded with his fellow politicians. I was too excited to notice at the time the way Mother was boycotting one of the biggest nights in Dad's life. Her antipathy to a sojourn in the White House obviously remained intense.

For a while Dewey startled everyone by running ahead, but his lead began to dwindle rapidly around midnight and by 3:45 A.M. he had conceded. Then the liquor really began to flow, and soon a lot of politicians were gaga. I was shocked. Dad got rid of the boozers and urged me not to say anything about them to Mother. I can see now that he was still worried about her negative feelings and was trying to avoid an argument.

In spite of his wife's disapproval, Harry Truman enjoyed himself that night. He was tremendously proud of being the first Missouri politician elected to a national executive office. He also was proud of having made a major contribution to the future of the United States and the world. This was evident in the telegram he sent President Roosevelt:

I AM VERY HAPPY OVER THE OVERWHELMING ENDORSEMENT WHICH YOU RECEIVED. ISOLATIONISM IS DEAD. HOPE TO SEE YOU SOON.

For Dad, the euphoria of victory was soon followed by exhaustion. The full impact of his eighteen-hour-day campaign effort hit him. Mother (and I) struggled with an avalanche of congratulatory letters from old friends and acquaintances. After a few days, we all went back to Washington to meet President Roosevelt when he returned from Hyde Park on November 11.

It was another cold, rainy autumn day and FDR again decided it was a chance to show there was nothing wrong with his health. He ordered the Secret Service men to take down the top of his Packard. Flanked by Dad and Henry Wallace, he rode up Pennsylvania Avenue while 300,000 soggy DC'ers cheered their heads off. Watching this performance, and fearing the worst about its effect on her exhausted husband, Bess could only conclude that the reports of Mr. Roosevelt's imminent demise were greatly exaggerated.

At this point, she was still much more worried about Vice President-elect Truman. She saw that he would never get any rest in Washington, with everyone from hostess Evalyn Walsh McLean to the Ambassador from Honduras putting him at the top of their guest lists. She decreed that he would have to get out of town, pronto, and he agreed with her. He fled to French Lick, Indiana, for some intensive resting and restorative treatments at the spa there. But he insisted on breaking this badly needed vacation to come to Kansas City to be on hand when his sister Mary received a new title from the Eastern Star. She had made this women's branch of the Masons her career.

On Thanksgiving Day, Bess wrote to Dad's cousin, Ethel Noland, describing in the frankest terms what she thought of all this. "Harry was a wreck after a week here so we simply dumped him on the train for French Lick and he is feeling much better already." She cautioned Ethel not to tell anyone where Dad was, "unless it is broadcast," and then issued her opinion of the visit to Kansas City. "He will be in K.C. on the 29th. Some silly Eastern Star performance. He has no business breaking into the treatments he is taking."

Bess did not let her absent husband keep her away from that year's Army-Navy game. We went with Colonel Harry Vaughan and almost froze to death. But Mother loved every minute of it. I vowed that she would not get me to another game without a detailed weather forecast from navy or army intelligence.

After his visit to Kansas City for Mary Truman's Eastern Star ceremony, Dad segued south for more rest and relaxation, and we all regrouped in Independence for Christmas. Mother and I spent most of our time in Kansas City frantically shopping for dresses to wear to the inauguration. I only had to buy one or two, but Mother had to acquire a wardrobe to survive the round of parties that were scheduled.

These started on December 30 with a tremendous bash at Friendship, Evalyn Walsh McLean's estate. In spite of having denounced her circle as parasites, Dad went and allowed himself to be displayed, because Mother wanted to go. She liked Evalyn's kooky, unorthodox personality and admired the way she had tried to help Washington's poor during the Depression. But she had no illusions about her fondness for publicity. "A few headlines and she is on the job," Bess told her mother.

A glimpse of the Trumans' schedule emerges from a letter Dad wrote his mother on January 13. He gave her a list of the receptions, dinners, and meetings he and Mother had to attend between January 18th and the 21st. "Some of 'em are at the same time and blocks apart and I'm supposed to be at all of them," he wrote. Bess undoubtedly agreed with Dad's advice to FDR, to use the war as an excuse and abandon the inauguration. "He should have boarded his automobile and driven to the Supreme Court and been sworn in and I should have taken the oath at a regular Senate session," he wrote.

Instead, politics as usual had the Trumans swamped with demands for inaugural tickets from half the state of Missouri. Wallace and Truman relatives had priority, of course, but Bess could not hope to board them all in our five-room apartment. We took in Grandmother Wallace, naturally, and stowed a few more with cooperative neighbors, but most of the relatives were parked in hotels. Nevertheless, they all regarded our apartment as their headquarters and showed up expecting coffee and a sandwich at all hours. Between racing home to change for the next party and playing short-order cook, Bess was exhausted by the time January 20 finally arrived.

It turned out to be another awful day. It is creepy the way bad weather pursued FDR during the last year of his life. This time sleet mixed with rain on a cutting wind. For warmth I had planned to wear a new fur scarf. Mother took my school coat out of the closet. "Put this on," she said. "And no arguments." I went into a colossal sulk but Dad backed her up, and off we went to the religious ceremonies at St. John's Church that began the inauguration.

President Roosevelt had decided to scale down the festivities out of respect for the men still fighting and dying in the Pacific and in Europe, and to conserve his own strength. Instead of taking the oath on the steps of the Capitol, he began his fourth term on the south portico of the White House.

Dad was sworn in first, by the departing vice president, Henry Wallace. Then FDR was helped from his wheelchair by his son James, in his marine uniform. Bess studied the President as he stood at the podium and was not reassured by what she saw. There were dark circles of exhaustion under his eyes. His skin had the grayish tinge that many people had already noticed.

On the other hand, Bess had seen Harry Truman in more than a few exhausted states, and he had recovered his vitality after a decent rest. She was more impressed by the way the President insisted on defying the weather again, to demonstrate his good health. He stood coatless and hatless in the freezing wind to take the oath and give a brief speech.

Bess did not have much time to fear the worst, anyway. After the ceremony, FDR retreated to his bedroom. Bess had to join Eleanor Roosevelt in trying to cope with 1,805 damp, frozen VIP's who had stood in the slush on the White House lawn for the ceremony. All those hands had to be shaken before everyone lined up for a buffet lunch. This first horde had scarcely departed when a second wave of 678 appeared for a tea. Dad left Mother and Mrs. Roosevelt to deal with these minor-league VIP's. All in all, it was an exhausting day for a woman only a month away from her sixtieth birthday.

Two days after the inauguration, FDR sailed off to Yalta to confer with Stalin and Churchill. The war was going well. In Europe, the western Allies had beaten back Hitler's last desperate gamble in the Battle of the Bulge and were now across the Rhine and smashing their way into the heart of Germany. The Russians were pounding into the collapsing Reich from the east. In the Pacific, the Philippines were close to liberation, and B-29's were battering Japan from newly captured bases in the Mariana Islands.

For Bess, the possibility of an early victory had a very personal dimension. She presumed it would take much of the crushing weight of responsibility from President Roosevelt's shoulders, which meant that there was a good chance that he would live considerably longer than the pessimists were predicting.

While the President dickered with Stalin and Churchill at Yalta, the Vice President was not exactly idle. Before FDR left, he handed Dad one of the messiest jobs ever. He had fired Jesse Jones, his Secretary of Commerce and the darling of the Senate's conservatives, and appointed Henry Wallace in his place. It was up to Dad to get the Senate's consent to this highly political move. What made it truly explosive was the Secretary of Commerce's control of the Reconstruction Finance Corporation (RFC), which loaned billions of dollars each year to large and small businesses to fuel the war effort. That made the Secretary of Commerce one of the most powerful men in the U.S. government.

After endless hours of conferring with key senators, Dad worked out a compromise. The RFC would be severed from the Commerce Department, and the job would be given to someone more acceptable to conservatives and moderates. Mr. Wallace would then be approved for the now toothless commerce appointment. Wallace angrily insisted he wanted both jobs, until Dad bluntly informed him that he had better settle for half a loaf or get nothing. Even with this compromise, Dad had to use all his skills at parliamentary maneuver to push the deal through the Senate without letting FDR's original two-job appointment come to a vote that would have humiliated the President. The Senate's opinion of Mr. Wallace was all too visible in the vote to take the RFC away from him: it was 72 to 12.

Bess did not pay much attention to this internal Democratic squabble. She was far more worried about the way the press continued to belittle Harry Truman. During the campaign, they had constructed a straw man, a gray little mediocrity that FDR had tolerated on the ticket to keep the party bosses happy. Henry Wallace's frustrated supporters in the Democratic Party were helping to perpetuate this myth.

One of the leading protagonists of this make-Harry-Truman-look-dumb school was Duke Shoop, the Kansas City *Star*'s Washington reporter. He wrote a snide, sneering story about Bess and the Vice President attending that party at Evalyn Walsh McLean's, emphasizing the gorgeous furniture, the expensive silver and gold plate, and describing Mother and Dad awed by it all, as if they were a couple of bumpkins.

Even supposed friends, carried away by the discovery that they now knew someone authentically famous, got into the act. Henry Bundschu, their Independence neighbor, wrote a reminiscence of Harry Truman in which he compared him to Calvin Coolidge! Henry was a Republican, which excuses him slightly, but with that kind of friend around, Harry Truman did not need enemies.

Bess was appalled. So was her old friend, Mary Paxton Keeley, watching this media auto-da-fé from her post as a journalism professor at Christian College in Columbia, Missouri. She wrote Bess a shrewd letter in mid-February 1945, urging her to tell the Vice President to hire an expert to handle his publicity. "I wrote to Henry Bundschu giving him the devil for comparing Harry with Calvin Coolidge," Mary added. But she thought Shoop's story on the McLean dinner was a more serious matter. "I know it is all right to go to that dame's dinner," she wrote. "But it shouldn't get in the paper as if Harry was a wide eyed country boy who had left the plow handles to eat off the gold plate."

With a nice compliment to her old friend, Mary got to the main point of her letter. "I know you are not impressed by anyone in Washington any more than Harry is, but these fool stories can give the wrong impression of Harry." The Vice President needed a good press secretary to "put out stuff to overbalance this social poison."

Bess's answer showed how concerned she was. "I . . . quite agree with you that Harry has had some pretty bad press notices lately. If we had to run for the Senate in '46 they'd be terrible. They mostly stem from that skunk of a Duke Shoop. 'Snoopy' Shoop, they call him back here. He isn't allowed to blast him politically now so he does the next best he can. Like Pegler [Westbrook Pegler, the Hearst columnist] he can't possibly write anything kind about anybody.

"We have eaten off the 'gold plate' once or twice a month (or have been asked to—we don't always go—) for the last four or five years," Bess continued. "But D.S. is never there so he wouldn't know." She added that she "sure would like to have heard Henry B. [Bundschu] stuttering over your letter!"

Not long after this exchange, Vice President Truman got himself the worst piece of publicity yet. He went to a party at the National Press Club at which someone suggested he play the piano. He sat down to do no more than riffle the keys when—presto—the actress Lauren Bacall was sitting on top of the piano, with her gorgeous gams on full display. The picture made several hundred magazines and newspapers, and Bess was furious. It was exactly the kind of publicity she had been warning against since Harry Truman arrived in the Senate.

Bess would have been even more upset about this publicity if she had thought Vice President Truman might soon become President Truman. She continued to doubt an early entrance into the White House. Late in March, she received a letter from Ethel Noland informing her that the editor of the Boston *Globe* had sent a reporter to Independence for background on Harry Truman, because he was convinced that FDR was going to die soon. Bess replied that she hoped "the Boston *Globe* man is a mighty bad prognosticator." She then offered proof that he was, in her opinion. "F.D. looks fine to me. I sat by him at a W.H. dinner last week & had a good chance for close observation. He's a little deaf—but that's not going to wreck him. So am I!"

Bess had encountered FDR on one of his good days. We know, now, that he even baffled his doctors by seeming to be on the brink of dissolution one day and the next day be brimming with vitality and good cheer. The letter also suggests that Dad continued to avoid discussing Mr. Roosevelt's health with Bess.

Ten years later, in his memoirs, Dad told of going to see the President a week after he returned from Yalta.

I . . . was shocked by his appearance. His eyes were sunken. His magnificent smile was missing from his careworn face. He seemed a spent man. I had a hollow feeling within me for I saw that the journey to Yalta must have been a terrible ordeal.

Dad tried to think how he could help the President conserve his strength.

I recalled the expressions of pain I had seen on the President's face as he delivered his inauguration speech on January 20 on the south portico of the White House. Apparently he could no longer endure with his usual fortitude the physical pain of the heavy [leg] braces pressing against him.

I urged that he address Congress [on the results of the Yalta Conference] seated in the well of the House, and I explained that I had already cleared this unusual arrangement with the congressional leaders. He had asked for no such consideration, but he appeared relieved and pleased to be accorded this courtesy.

This arrangement did not produce the hoped-for effect. Even though FDR was freed of the burden of his braces, his speech was lifeless and rambling. He infuriated the Senate by telling them no more about Yalta than they had read in the newspapers. A few weeks later, Dad was even more shocked by the President's dazed, vacant manner at the annual dinner of the White House Press Association. But he did not say a word about these impressions to Bess.

One worry he did share with her was the President's disinclination to bring him into the inner circle of the administration. He saw FDR in private only twice after he returned from Yalta. They discussed domestic political problems, none particularly important. Mr. Roosevelt invited Dad to sit in on the few cabinet meetings he called during this period. But he soon learned that nothing important was discussed there. FDR preferred to hold detailed discussions with individual members before and after the meetings.

The cabinet meetings did give Dad a chance to see the games FDR liked to play with his followers. "He took a great deal of pleasure in getting one member of the cabinet to argue against another and in then hearing what they had to say," Dad later recalled. "He would beam when Ickes jumped on Hopkins or Hopkins on Ickes. He sometimes seemed amused when Morgenthau [Secretary of the Treasury] raised mischief with the Secretary of State on how he was handling things."

At neither the cabinet meetings nor their two private sessions did the President say a word to Dad about foreign policy, which was absorbing 90 percent of Mr. Roosevelt's exhausted mind. The Yalta agreements were collapsing in front of his eyes, as Stalin ruthlessly imposed a Communist regime on Poland.

FDR was getting telegrams from Winston Churchill asking bluntly: "Poland has lost her frontier. Is she now to lose her freedom? I do not wish to reveal a divergence between the British and the United States Government, but it would certainly be necessary for me to make it clear that we are in the presence of a great failure and an utter breakdown of what we settled at Yalta."

For all Vice President Truman knew about this momentous development, it might have been taking place on another planet.

As far as Bess could see, except for those spasms of bad publicity, things were going well. She told Mary Paxton Keeley that even her mother seemed "contented" about living in Washington. "It becomes harder and harder for her to get around so it's a good thing for her to be here on one floor—and with plenty of heat." To Ethel Noland, she wrote: "Harry looks better than he has for ages—is really putting on a little weight." Her only worry was Chris and Fred Wallace, who were struggling to recover from the loss of the twins to which she had given birth in November. The babies had only lived a day.

The Trumans even began planning a summer vacation, something they had never been able to do while he was running the Truman Committee. One of Dad's closest Senate friends, Mon Wallgren, had become governor of Washington. Dad and Mother accepted an invitation to join Mon and his wife for a July cruise up the Pacific Coast to Alaska.

In another letter to Ethel Noland, Bess conveyed a charming picture of domestic contentment. "Marg. has gone to a picture show and Harry to a poker party. Mother is practically asleep in her chair—so it's very peaceful."

The day after Bess wrote that letter, FDR went to Warm Springs, Georgia, for a badly needed rest. She knew nothing about the way the crowd at the Warm Springs station had gasped when they saw the President's condition, how he had sagged in his wheelchair, his head bobbing out of control. For Bess it was another piece of encouraging news, like the headlines reporting Allied armies gaining as much as fifty miles a day inside the crumbling Third Reich. She hoped—and believed—that two or three weeks in Warm Springs and a daily diet of good news from the battlefronts would restore Mr. Roosevelt.

After church on Easter Sunday, April 8, Mother and Dad took special delight in ignoring critics such as Duke Shoop and going to a luncheon at Evalyn Walsh McLean's home. It was one of the pleasures of being a new vice president, with no worries about an imminent reelection campaign. They went to many other parties in the same carefree spirit during these first months of 1945. I remember being stirred by how happy and handsome they looked as they left our apartment in formal clothes. Bess's blue eyes sparkled. She looked regal. The Vice President cut quite a figure too in white tie and tails.

I particularly remember how spiffy they appeared on the way to a party given in their honor by Perle Mesta. An heiress to two fortunes, one from her father, the other from her husband, she had been a Republican most of her life. She switched her allegiance in 1941 and moved to Washington, D.C., where she became not only a social lioness but a major contributor to the Democratic Party. She was a shrewder, more aggressive woman than Evalyn Walsh McLean. Mrs. Mesta relished power as much as the limelight. Dad—and a lot of other Democratic politicians—admired her far more for her ability to raise money than for her glittering parties. Mother enjoyed her effervescent personality. Perle was exactly like the woman in the musical Irving Berlin wrote about her, *Call Me Madam*.

There was still plenty of politics for Bess to discuss with the Vice President. The Senate was in a swivet over FDR's failure to tell them anything about the agreements he had made at Yalta, and Dad had a daily struggle to prevent the southern Democrats from joining the Republicans in humiliating the President. They balked at almost everything the administration submitted to them, even a treaty with Mexico on water rights along the Rio Grande.

In a letter to his mother and sister, Dad described a typical vice presidential day. He got to the office about 8:30 A.M. and with the help of Reathel Odum, one of his Senate staffers who had followed him to this new job, he waded through a foot high stack of mail.

By that time I have to see people—one at a time just as fast as they can go through the office without seeming to hurry them.

Then I go over to the Capitol gold plated office and see Senators and curiosity seekers for an hour and then the Senate meets and it's my job to get 'em prayed for and goodness knows they need it, and then get the business to going by staying in the chair for an hour and then see more Senators and curiosity people who want to see what a V.P. looks like and if he walks and talks and has teeth.

Then I close the Senate and sign the mail and then maybe go home or to some meeting, usually some meeting and them home and start over. . . . I am trying to make a job out of the Vice President and it's quite a chore.

Bess spent the first week of April working with the VP on a Jefferson Day speech he was giving over network radio on April 13. By this time Dad had gotten in the habit of having Mother read all his speeches in advance. This one was important, because the President was also scheduled to speak from Warm Springs. Dad was going to introduce him.

April 12 was another rainy day. Dad was flying to Providence the following morning to give his speech to the Rhode Island Democrats, and Bess eyed the lowering clouds, worried as always whenever her husband took to the air. I was getting ready to go to a birthday party for my friend and next-door-neighbor, Annette Davis. A nice young man was escorting me and I was feeling ebullient.

About six o'clock, the telephone rang and I answered it. In an odd, tight voice, Dad asked to speak to Mother. When I tried to kid with him in our usual style, he cut me off and ordered me to put Mother on the line. I obeyed and went back to putting on my makeup, wondering if I had done something to offend the Vice President.

"Bess," Harry Truman said. "I'm at the White House. President Roosevelt died about two hours ago in Warm Springs. I'm sending a car for you and Margaret. I want you here when I'm sworn in."

Bess's old antagonist, history, was in command of her life now.

Chapter Nineteen

For a moment Bess was engulfed by tears. She could not think or see. She put down the telephone and groped her way down the hall to my bedroom, where her mother was chatting with me about my date. Grandmother Wallace always wanted to know the background, the personality, of my beaus.

We both looked up at Bess as she appeared in the doorway. By now she was crying so hard she could not speak. I rushed to her and put my arm around her. "Mother, what's the matter, what is it?" I said.

"President Roosevelt is dead," she gasped, through her tears.

"Dead?" I echoed. I simply could not believe it. FDR had been president for most of my life. I found it even harder to believe what it meant. My father was now the President of the United States.

The sight of me standing there wide-eyed in my new party dress and dancing slippers and white gloves—an outfit so wildly inappropriate to the occasion—seemed to restore Bess's self-control. "You'd better change your clothes," she said. "Pick out something dark. A car will be here in a few minutes to take us to the White House."

Bess rushed to her room to dress. She paused long enough to call Mrs. Davis, mother of my friend Annette, and ask her if she would come over to our apartment and look after her mother. I managed to locate a brown suit, and we were ready when the Secret Service men arrived. They took us out through a rear entrance to avoid a crowd that was gathering outside the apartment. But a lot of shrewd newsmen anticipated this move, and dozens of flashbulbs exploded in our faces as we emerged into the rainy dusk. Bess ignored them and steered me into the car.

At the White House, Bess asked if she could see Mrs. Roosevelt. This thoughtful gesture showed how thoroughly that strong will had regained control of her turbulent Wallace emotions. It would have been understandable if a woman who had just received such stunning news had simply reeled to her husband's side and awaited orders. But Bess demonstrated in what might be called her first official act as the new President's wife her ability to find her own distinct role.

I think that Mrs. Roosevelt appreciated our visit. She was with her daughter, Anna. Both were grave but composed. Bess expressed our deep sympathy and sorrow. She meant every word of it. Although Mother had been critical of President Roosevelt's political tactics, she had been charmed by him when they met face to face. Mrs. Roosevelt thanked her and said: "I just told Harry I am ready to do anything I can to help. That of course applies to you, too." Bess thanked her and we hurried down to the Cabinet Room, where cabinet members and congressional leaders had assembled to see the new President sworn in.

If ever I have felt the awesome dimensions of history, it was in that room, that night. It was not a very large room. It was dominated by the huge, odd-shaped table at which Mr. Roosevelt had conferred with his cabinet members. That night, the barren table and its cordon of empty leather-upholstered chairs seem to be making a silent statement about the dead President. Everyone in the room was standing. Faces were universally funereal. I recognized some of them—Speaker of the House of Representatives Sam Rayburn, House Majority Leader John McCormack, Secretary of State Edward Stettinius (one of nine cabinet members present). There were only three women—Mother and I and Frances Perkins, the Secretary of Labor. Oddly, although we were in the midst of the greatest war in history, there were only two men in uniform, Fleet Admiral William D. Leahy, FDR's White House Chief of Staff, and General Philip B. Fleming, who had served Mr. Roosevelt as Public Works Administrator.

We gathered at the front of the room, before a mantelpiece surmounted by a portrait of Woodrow Wilson. A fitting touch, I realize now. Wilson was the President whose idealistic war messages had inspired Harry Truman to join the army and begin his rendezvous with history. Dad was in profile, facing Harlan Stone, the Chief Justice of the Supreme Court. I remember glancing at Mother as Dad raised his hand to take the oath of office. Her eyes were red from weeping. But her face was calm, her lips firm. I find that amazing, now. If the scene was dreamlike to me, who had more or less grown up in Washington, D.C., it must have seemed incredible to Bess, remembering the night in 1910 when she had invited that shy but strangely self-confident young farmer into her living room on North Delaware Street.

Dad picked up the small red-edged Bible in his left hand. It was the only Bible the White House aides had been able to find after a frantic search. Beneath his thumb he held a small piece of paper on which the presidential oath had been typed. Chief Justice Stone began: "I Harry Shippe Truman—"

Where the Chief Justice got the idea that Dad's middle name was Shippe no one has ever found out. Dad calmly corrected him. "I, Harry S. Truman, do solemnly swear that I will faithfully execute the office of the President of the United States and will, to the best of my ability, preserve, protect, and defend the Constitution of the United States."

"So help you God," added the Chief Justice, revealing his own deep emotion. These words are not part of the official oath but they were added spontaneously by George Washington when he took his first oath as president.

"So help me God," Dad said, and solemnly raised the Bible to his lips.

This, too, was something George Washington had done. The time on the clock beneath Woodrow Wilson's picture was 7:09 P.M.

Dad turned and kissed Mother and me. He explained that he had decided to call a cabinet meeting and sent us home. While we returned to 4701 Connecticut Avenue with an escort of Secret Service men, Dad told the cabinet members that he intended to continue FDR's domestic and foreign policies. But he also warned them that he intended to be "President in my own right." He urged them to be frank and forthright in expressing opinions, but they should understand that he was going to make the final decisions.

At our apartment, Mother and I discovered the Davises had brought along the cake and a lot of the food from Annette's party, including a turkey. Bess and I nibbled haphazardly at the cake and other goodies. Dad arrived home about 9:30 P.M. He did not say much to us. I realize now that he did not feel he could talk freely with the Davises in the apartment. When he remarked that he had nothing to eat since noon, Mrs. Davis made him a turkey sandwich. That was the extent of the Truman dining for the evening.

Dad retreated to the bedroom and telephoned his mother. Mamma Truman had heard the news. With Vivian's help she was fending off dozens of phone calls from reporters. Dad told her he was going to be very busy for the next few days. But he would write her as soon as possible and tell her everything. Mamma Truman, ninety-two, was perfectly calm. "Be good, Harry," she said. "But be game, too."

Next Dad called his friend John Snyder, who was at a monetary conference in Mexico City. He told him that he felt like he "had just been struck by a bolt of lightning." Mr. Snyder was planning to leave government service for a very good job at St. Louis's biggest bank. Dad told him this was out of the question now. He needed friends like him in his administration. He asked him to become the Federal Loan Administrator, a job loaded with political dynamite.

The new President went to bed and was asleep in five minutes. Much later in the night he awoke to find Bess sobbing beside him. He tried to comfort her, but there was little he could do or say. He knew she was weeping over the loss of her happy senatorial years and for the eighty-two surprisingly happy vice presidential days. She feared the worst for me, her brother Fred, and other members of the family who were liable to be unbalanced by having a relative who was president.

But it was the politics of the situation that she dreaded the most. It would have been bad enough for Harry Truman to have inherited the presidency from Franklin Roosevelt a year or two after the war. To come into office now, when our armies were on the brink of victory, when the President was revered as a triumphant, charismatic leader, was the worst possible time.

Even more unnerving was the knowledge that FDR had continued until the hour of his death to keep most of the secrets of his presidency in his head. Mother's feelings on this point were summed up in the first thing she said to John Snyder, when she saw him the following day. "This is going to put a terrific load on Harry. Roosevelt has told him nothing."

Exhausted and depressed, Bess sometimes wondered if she would survive during the next few days. President Roosevelt's funeral, on Saturday, April 14, 1945, was the major item on her agenda. That was a physically wearing ordeal—and emotionally trying, too. Bess grieved for the dead President along with her fellow Americans. But when she looked out at the tearstained faces in the crowd jamming Lafayette Square in front of the White House as she and I arrived for the service, she found herself wondering if these people would accept her husband as president.

It was an extraordinarily hot, muggy day, and the East Room of the White House had flowers covering every inch of the four walls.

Their overpowering scent seemed to devour what little oxygen there was left over from the dozens of government officials and foreign dignitaries in attendance. The service seemed to last for an eternity, although it was in reality only about an hour. That evening, Mother and I joined Dad aboard the seventeen-car train that took FDR's body to Hyde Park.

Mother sent me to bed and sat up with the new President as he labored on a vitally important speech that he was to give to Congress on Monday. It was an eerie journey. All along the right of way, flares illuminated the faces of tens of thousands of Americans who gathered for a last tribute to Franklin D. Roosevelt. I doubt if Bess or her husband got more than two or three hours sleep that night. With nothing to do but sleep, I found it impossible.

After the touching funeral service at Hyde Park, we returned to Washington. With Mother's strong approval, Dad had told Mrs. Roosevelt that she could stay in the White House as long as she felt it was necessary. Both Trumans thought we would continue to live in our Connecticut Avenue apartment. Within twenty-four hours of FDR's death, it became obvious that they were wrong. The Secret Service found the place a security nightmare, and the other tenants in the building rapidly grew weary of having their identities checked and their parcels examined every time they came home.

Dad decided we would move to Blair House, just across the street from the White House. It was a lovely old Washington residence, donated to the government by the Blair family, a powerful political clan since the days of Andrew Jackson. Bess instantly fell in love with the place. It was full of early American and French antiques, Aubusson rugs, crystal chandeliers and about two dozen sets of exquisite china. We moved into this refuge on Monday, April 16, 1945.

On that same day, Dad gave a highly successful speech to a joint session of Congress and the nation. Mother and I sat in the gallery, listening and applauding. I have always loved Dad's closing words.

I have in my heart a prayer. As I have assumed my heavy duties, I humbly pray Almighty God, in the words of King Solomon:
"Give therefore Thy servant an understanding heart to judge Thy people, that I may discern between good and bad: for who is able to judge this Thy so great a people?"

Behind the scenes, Dad was making it clear that he meant it when he said he intended to be president in his own right. He spent long hours with Mr. Roosevelt's top aides, getting a grasp on both domestic and foreign problems as seen from the White House. One of the first men he summoned to the Oval Office was Jimmy Byrnes. Few men had been closer to Mr. Roosevelt. As head of the Office of War Mobilization, Mr. Byrnes had wielded vast domestic power. Moreover, he had gone to Yalta with FDR.

After talking with Mr. Byrnes, Dad decided to make his first cabinet change. He asked him to become his Secretary of State. As Dad recalled it later, Mr. Byrnes "practically jumped down my throat" to accept the job. Dad had another reason besides Mr. Byrnes's intimate knowledge of Roosevelt policy. Under the law as it then existed, Mr. Byrnes as Secretary of State would be next in line to succeed him as president. Dad felt strongly that the president should be an elected official, not an appointed one. Mr. Byrnes had been a senator from South Carolina for many years before going to the White House. The incumbent secretary, Edward Stettinius, on the other hand, had never been elected to anything.

This appointment was Dad's first mistake—another example of his otherwise admirable tendency to expect and hope for the best in people and events. Mr. Byrnes was still seething over FDR's failure to back him for the vice presidency in Chicago. He thought he should be president and immediately started acting as if he had the job. One of his first moves was to present Dad with a complete speech, written by him and his staff, to make to the joint session of Congress. He read the entire opus aloud to Dad in the Oval Office and left, satisfied that he had turned Harry Truman into his mouthpiece. Dad threw the speech in the wastebasket ten seconds after Mr. Byrnes departed. Too late, he realized Mr. Byrnes was going to be a giant headache.

Another Roosevelt adviser with whom Dad spent a lot of time was Harry Hopkins. His attitude was a heartening contrast to Jimmy Byrnes's. He and Dad had known each other since the early 1930s. You will recall he was the only member of the Roosevelt administration Dad had met before he became a senator. Hopkins left the Mayo Clinic, where he was being treated for a painful stomach problem that had reduced him to a skeleton, and put his mortally ill body and all the insider's knowledge in his large and generous mind at the new President's disposal, without the slightest attempt to upstage him. Perhaps his most valuable contribution were his assessments of Winston Churchill and Joseph Stalin. He had served as Mr. Roosevelt's personal envoy to both men and had gotten to know them well.

Toward the end of his first crowded week as President, Dad confronted the largest crowd of reporters in White House history, 348, for his first press conference. He impressed everyone with his direct and forthright replies when he thought that questions could be answered without endangering the nation's security. When he did not think so, he said as much, in his same direct way. It was a startling contrast to Mr. Roosevelt, who was fond of playing hide-and-seek with reporters, tantalizing them with half answers and evasions.

Swiftly, calmly, Dad affirmed his support of Negro voting rights and fair employment practices, declined to say when he would dispose of the nation's synthetic rubber factories, and said he expected to confer with the Russian foreign minister, Vyacheslav Molotov, on his way to the upcoming conference in San Francisco to create the United Nations. One reporter asked if Mrs. Truman was going to hold press conferences too. Dad said he did not want to comment on that for the time being. He pointed out that Mrs. Roosevelt was still living in the White House and was planning to have a final press conference soon.

Dad's smooth reply gave no hint that from his point of view, he was handling an explosive question. In those chauvinistic days, women reporters usually covered the First Lady's side of the White House. They had a separate organization with which Mrs. Roosevelt had held weekly press conferences. Mother had already received a message from Mrs. Roosevelt suggesting that she continue this custom. It goes without saying that the newspaperwomen were extremely anxious for her to do so.

Mother said no. The squawks from the frustrated reporters were tremendous. But Mother stood her ground. She had no desire to compete in the public mind with Eleanor Roosevelt. This did not mean she had changed her mind about Eleanor Roosevelt. She remained an admirer of her energy and idealism. But Mother felt, quite rightly I think, that admiration did not necessarily require imitation. Bess Wallace Truman was determined to chart her own course as First Lady.

We have seen how traumatic Mother's memories of newspaper publicity were. They went back to the anguish of her father's death, the agony of her close friends, the Swopes, during those grisly murder trials. Even more influential was the low opinion of reporters' tactics and ethics that Mother acquired during Dad's political struggles in Missouri.

All of these things entered into Mother's decision. But the bottom line, I think, was a simple fact. Bess Wallace Truman was a different woman from Eleanor Roosevelt. She did not want to be a public personality. She had reasons, strong, even heartbreaking reasons, for wanting to preserve her private self. She also had the courage to insist on it, in the face of violent disapproval.

Mother agonized over the decision. At one point during the first presidential week, in spite of enormous reluctance, she agreed to a press conference. At the last moment, she canceled it and decided to go her own way.

This decision did not mean that Mother put newspapers and reporters out of her mind. On the contrary, she was concentrating in those first days on something she regarded as supremely important for the success of Harry Truman's presidency—the choice of a good press secretary. She had not forgotten the letter that Mary Paxton Keeley had written to her about the need for one when Dad was vice president. Now it became trebly urgent. The White House correspondents had had a very negative reaction to Leonard Reinsch, a radio newsman whom Dad had appointed on a temporary basis.

Bess was particularly upset about this situation because Duke Shoop, the Kansas City *Star* reporter, was running all over Washington telling everyone that he had the appointment as press secretary in the bag. He had also printed a nasty paragraph about Bess in his column: "It's far too early to say that Mrs. Truman will not enjoy being the first lady of the land, but it's violating no secret to report that she doesn't like her new position thus far. President Truman said today [April 13] 'Bess cried most of the night and it wasn't for joy, either.' "

That put Mary Paxton Keeley on the warpath. She told Bess she was outraged by the insinuation "that you could not do the job." Mary reported that she had written to the *Star*'s managing editor, Roy Roberts, and had received an apologetic letter. "I hope I did some good," Mary wrote. "I notice he [Shoop] has not had a signed column since and I hope he never has."

Mother urged Dad to give top priority to finding a new press man and recommended as the ideal choice their old Independence classmate, Charlie Ross. President Truman agreed and asked Charlie if he would take the job. After some anguished hesitation—he was giving up a salary of $35,000 a year to take a job that paid $10,000, and he knew the brutally demanding hours he would have to work— Charlie said yes.

Not long after, Bess wrote triumphantly to Mary. "Don't worry about Duke. He's made an ass of himself the way he broadcast the fact that he was going to be H's press Sec'y. Even went down to the press club and spread it there of all places. If there is anybody on earth that H. has absolutely *no* use for it's D.S."

Mary replied that she was "very happy about Harry putting Charlie in. Charlie can be a great help to him. He has a splendid background for it and he and Harry talk with the same Missouri accent."

Other aspects of Bess's correspondence with Mary during these first White House weeks are extremely interesting. Mary assured Bess that she was confident Harry Truman would do a good job. She said it was a task "more important to us all than any job any man has had." Then she spoke, as only a friend can speak, to Bess. "Yours is the hardest job I have ever known any woman to undertake but I have never known you to do anything that you did not do well."

Bess's reply to those consoling words is the most revealing statement she ever made about Harry Truman becoming president. "I think you have sized up the situation pretty well. We are not any of us happy to be where we are but there's nothing to be done about it except to do our best—and forget about the sacrifices and many unpleasant things that bob up."

Regretfully, lovingly, I must disagree with one word in that statement: "we." In his deepest self, Harry Truman found it impossible to resist the chance, the challenge, to be president, once he realized the door to the White House was open. He did not want to become president at the time and in the manner that he inherited the job. He did not want it because he knew Bess did not want it. But he could not turn his back on this opportunity to confront the history of his time, just as he could not evade World War I or the decision to run for the Senate in 1934, although he knew he was making Bess unhappy both times. His whole life pointed toward these rendezvous with destiny. This was something Mother found hard to accept or understand.

I am not writing as a daughter here. I am using that historian's tool—which can so easily become a wicked, judgmental weapon—hindsight. As a daughter I know—because I too went through the experience—that history is not something you think about while you are part of it. All Bess could think of was, the way this decision to become vice president, which we knew meant becoming president, was tearing her life apart. Day and night, her mind was filled with foreboding. Was she going to watch another man whom she loved, another man to whom she had entrusted her happiness, stumble into catastrophic defeat, this time with the whole world watching?

As I have already said—and spelled out the reasons for it—Mother was never an optimist. Now all her pessimism about human nature, about life itself, rushed into her feelings. All her fears about Dad's health, his tendency to overwork, his (in her opinion) tendency to trust people too much, added to her anxiety.

During these same emotion-filled days, Harry Truman was confronting problems and making decisions that would shape the postwar world. On his first night as president, he decided that the San Francisco conference to create the United Nations must proceed as scheduled, in spite of FDR's death. He found out from men such as Harry Hopkins and W. Averell Harriman, the U.S. Ambassador to Moscow, that our relationship with Russia had begun to deteriorate months before Franklin Roosevelt's death, when Stalin started ignoring or distorting the Yalta agreements. From Secretary of War Henry Stimson he learned about the most awesome secret of the war, the project to build an atomic bomb.

Dad selected not only a new press secretary, but a new appointments secretary, a genial, witty former Truman committee staffer named Matthew Connelly. For his military aide, Dad chose his friend, Harry Vaughan, who had become a major general with some help from Harry Truman. He named Fred Vinson, a tall, genial Kentuckian who had succeeded Jimmy Byrnes as head of the Office of War Mobilization, his Secretary of the Treasury.

"Poppa Vin," as Mother and I soon called Fred Vinson, had been in Washington since 1924, when he was elected to Congress. He later became a federal judge, a position he held until President Roosevelt drafted him to serve as a key White House war administrator. Few people could match his insider's knowledge of national politics.

For another politically sensitive post, Secretary of Agriculture, Dad chose Senator Clinton P. Anderson of New Mexico, a good friend from the Senate years. He saw that it was absolutely necessary to surround himself with his own team, loyal to him, not Franklin Roosevelt.

On April 18, the thirteenth and last truck loaded with the Roosevelts' personal possessions rolled away from the White House. Mrs. Roosevelt stopped at Blair House to say goodbye to the Trumans. She was somewhat apologetic about the condition of the White House. The war and her heavy travel schedule had never given her time to do much decorating or housekeeping. She also warned us that the place was infested with rats. A big rat had run along the porch railing when she was lunching with three friends on the south portico a few months earlier.

On April 19, the seventh day of the Truman presidency, Mother and I went over to inspect our new quarters. The expression on Mother's face when she saw the dingy, worn furniture and the shabby white walls, unpainted in twelve years, was more expressive than a paragraph of exclamation points. I am referring to the private rooms, upstairs, where first families spend most of their time. The splendid first floor rooms, which every visitor to Washington lines up to see, were polished and glowing as always. But the private quarters were far below the level of the furnished apartments Bess had lived in during her first years in Washington, before we settled into 4701 Connecticut Avenue. In my diary, I wrote: "The White House upstairs is a mess. . . . I was so depressed when I saw it." If that was the way a casual twenty-one-year-old felt, you can imagine Mother's feelings.

We fled back to Blair House's elegance, and Mother ordered a major redecoration before we moved in. To allow me some privacy and a place to entertain friends, she gave me a suite that included a sitting room, bedroom, and bath. She let me pick out my own color scheme—wedgwood blue for the walls, flowery chintz curtains, rust-red sofas. For her suite, she chose lavender in the bedroom and gray in the sitting room.

Meanwhile, she was grappling with her own staff problems. She persuaded Reathel Odum, a petite, attractive young woman who had worked in the Truman Senate office since 1936, to become her personal secretary. Reathel was bright and willing, but she did not know any more about the way First Ladies operated in the White House than Mother. Yet it did not seem a good idea to retain anyone from Mrs. Roosevelt's staff. Like Dad, Mother felt she needed her own team. Discussing this with me in Blair House, Mother decided to bend this principle somewhat. "I'm going to ask Mrs. Helm to stay on. I think I can work with her," she said.

Edith Helm was the White House social secretary. The widow of an admiral, she was a dignified, charming woman who could hold her own with any of the so-called best people of Washington, because she was one of them. She knew everything about everything when it came to protocol, the press, the pressures on a First Lady. Moreover, she had perspective. She had begun working in the White House during Woodrow Wilson's administration, so her memory went back to those distant days when the First Lady was not named Eleanor Roosevelt and did not give press conferences. I was there when Mother asked Mrs. Helm to stay on the job. She was delighted by the offer, and Mother was delighted with her prompt acceptance. With her on the team, Mother's worries about diplomatic or political gaffes subsided.

We moved into the White House on May 7 so that Dad could celebrate his birthday there the following day. Instead, we found ourselves celebrating the surrender of Germany, along with the rest of the country. Dad wrote his mother and sister a lively letter describing the big event.

I am sixty-one this morning and I slept in the President's room in the White House last night. They have finished the painting and have some of the furniture in place. I'm hoping it will all be ready for you by Friday [when they were coming for a visit].

This will be an historical day. At 9:00 o'clock this morning I must make a broadcast to the country announcing the German surrender. The papers were signed yesterday morning and hostilities will cease on all fronts at midnight tonight. Isn't that some birthday present?

It was a wild day, in Washington and in the country at large. Mobs of people poured into the streets to cheer and yell and kiss. At the end of his brief talk, Dad reminded everyone that "our victory is only half over." We had another war to win with Japan, an empire bigger and far more fanatic than Nazi Germany. He added a plea to Japan's leaders to lay down their weapons and tried to soften the terms of unconditional surrender that Mr. Roosevelt had decreed. "Unconditional surrender does not mean the extermination or enslavement of the Japanese people."

No one wanted a swift, bloodless end to the war with Japan more than Harry Truman. He had the grim statistics of recent battles on his desk. It had cost 25,489 marines, a third of the landing force, to capture eight square miles of volcanic rock known as Iwo Jima. On Okinawa, a larger island south of Japan, the toll had been 49,151 Americans. Kamikazes—suicide planes—had sunk 34 U.S. ships and damaged another 368. His military experts were telling him it would cost a minimum of 1,250,000 American casualties and God knows how many ships to invade and subdue the main Japanese islands.

For Bess, the German surrender had a very strong personal mean-

ing. Unlike many of his ancestors, Mary Paxton Keeley's son had
survived the war. "I thought about you mighty early on VE day," she
wrote to Mary a few days later. "It must be almost beyond belief to
you that Pax isn't, now, constantly in danger." Pax had already selected a wife, a young woman Mary described as "better than I could
have picked if he had asked me to find a girl for him—which he did
not ask me to do. She is tall and blonde like Margaret." Mary hoped
Bess could come to the wedding. Bess said she would love to come,
if she was in Missouri when it took place.

To keep the women reporters from exploding in frustration, Mrs.
Helm suggested that Bess invite them to tea in the upstairs rooms, so
they could at least give their readers a few details about how the
Trumans were living. Bess agreed, but requested Mrs. Helm to make
it clear that she was not going to answer questions. Everything that
was said had to be off the record. The women eagerly accepted this
arrangement, and I was drafted to help the conversation flow
smoothly. But Mother found it very hard to relax. She disliked being
required to invite these inquisitive people into her private life.

Two days later, on May 28, the Trumans gave a formal reception at
the White House for the Prince Regent of Iraq. It was Bess's first
encounter with the incredible minutiae involved in these official visits. She and the President received a six-page memorandum detailing
every step of the affair, from the moment the prince regent's three
cars came through the White House gate until he departed.

Here is a sample of these marching orders. "After a suitable interval, the President will take the Regent into the White House and
present him to Mrs. Truman. The Acting Secretary of State will
introduce Nuri Pasha [former prime minister and political boss of
Iraq] to Mrs. Truman. She will then be escorted by a White House
aide to the Red Room. The President, with the Regent on his right,
will proceed to the Blue Room." The next paragraph went into
equally intense detail about who would not be introduced to whom
until they got to the Red Room, where Bess was to serve the Regent
a cup of tea.

This was pretty trying stuff to people used to the informal hospitality of Missouri.

Missouri was where Bess decided to go, not long after this reception. She had a good excuse: 219 North Delaware Street was being
painted, renovated, and overhauled on its way to becoming "the
Summer White House." For a while the newspapers had called it
The Hyde Park of the West and other silly names, such as The

Gates Victorian Mansion. Bess maintained she would be there to supervise the work. I suppose there was some truth to that, but the job was being done by a good Independence contractor, and the U.S. government, which was paying the bills, would have been happy to send a team of army engineers to supervise things, if she had requested it.

My point is, Harry Truman needed her a lot more in the real White House. But Bess was reverting to those early Senate years when she yielded to the impulse to retreat to 219 North Delaware Street, that original refuge from life's harsh blows. I am sure that she also told herself that I would be better off out of the glare of the White House's publicity for a few months. Her mother had even more to do with this decision. Grandmother Wallace was not happy in the White House, and a summer in her own house would, Bess hoped, cheer her up. But these reasons were essentially rationalizations for Bess's retreat from the White House, the presidency, the whole rigamarole of playing First Lady.

Without Bess and his daughter, Harry Truman found the White House a "lonesome place." At night, he sat up reading cables and memos and reports until he was too tired to focus his eyes. He fretted over the Roosevelt loyalists still in various government posts. He called them "the palace guard." He tried to assure Bess that he was mastering the job. Early in June, he told her he was getting a grip on the various government departments. "There'll be no more to this job than there was to running Jackson County," he wrote.

But when he cited the "big headaches"—foreign relations, national finances, postwar military policy, reconverting the wartime economy—he obviously was asking for support. "Things get tougher and tougher," he wrote a few weeks later after a meeting with General Eisenhower and other military advisers. The soldiers told him, as they had told FDR, that they needed the cooperation of the Russians in the final assault on Japan. A Russian attack would tie down millions of Japanese soldiers in Manchuria. Without it the Americans would have to fight the entire 5-million-man Japanese Army on its home islands. That meant the United States had to keep trying to deal with Joseph Stalin, who was becoming more and more brazen in his determination to impose communism on everyone within range of a Russian gun.

There were times when the President sounded more than a little discouraged. In this letter he sees himself competing for a place in history with previous White House winners and losers.

Just two months ago today, I was a reasonably happy and contented Vice
President. Maybe you can remember that far back too. But things have
changed so much it hardly seems real.

I sit here in this old house and work on foreign affairs, read reports and
work on speeches—all the while listening to the ghosts walk up and down
the hallway and even right in here in the study. The floors pop and the
drapes move back and forth—I can just imagine old Andy and Teddy having an argument over Franklin. Or James Buchanan and Franklin Pierce
deciding which was the more useless to the country. And when Millard
Fillmore and Chester Arthur join in for place and show the din is almost
unbearable. But I still get some work done. . . .

Write me when you can—I hope every day.

In Independence, Bess soon discovered that she could not escape
the public. A crowd of 200 people greeted us at the depot. A traffic
jam soon developed on Delaware Street, and the Independence police
department had to put a man on duty full time to deal with the
hundreds of cars that drove slowly by the house. More hundreds of
well-wishers and curious trooped past on foot, making the Secret
Service jittery.

Bess's reaction to this public scrutiny was demonstrated on June 5,
when moving vans took away the furniture Fred and Christine Wallace had left in the house and a team of workmen delivered the
furniture she had shipped from Washington, D.C. Mother ordered
the blinds pulled and the lights turned on in the middle of the day, so
the gawkers on the street saw nothing.

The renovation of 219 North Delaware did not go smoothly. The
plumbers' slow pace particularly irked Bess. She complained to the
President, who wrote to her in mid-June that "the plumber troubles
make me tired also—but we are up against it and will have to put up
with it. Hope you can get caught up on it in a reasonable time."

Somewhat naively, Mother asked Dad what he thought of a proposition that floated in from Fred Wallace in Denver. A well-to-do
friend in that city had offered Fred a house, free of charge, which the
President would use as a summer White House when he and Mother
came to visit Fred and Christine.

"I don't believe it would be good policy to let Fred take that house
in Denver," Dad wrote. "We should only have the one in Independence on the basis I outlined to you." (The basis was the government's willingness to pay for the improvements.) Dad was worried
about giving columnist Drew Pearson, whom he particularly detested, material for a scandal. "If we should go to Colorado we

should stay at a hotel and *pay* for it," he wrote.

Bess was disappointed by this decision, although she found it difficult to argue against it. Fred had recently quit his government job and gone into the real estate business. He was not making much money. But that did not justify the risk he was asking Dad to take.

Some badly needed comic relief was provided by Vietta Garr, our long-running cook and maid, who had left the Wallace-Truman payroll to manage a luncheonette. Bess had asked her sister-in-law May Wallace to persuade Vietta to return. Somehow reporters got wind of this negotiation and asked Vietta if she had made up her mind yet. "I don't know," Vietta said. "They're a nice family to work for but I'm sort of on the outs with the cooking right now." She gave the newsmen a rundown of the Delaware Street kitchen, speaking with special fondness of the outsized old-fashioned icebox. "I don't think they will ever have an electric icebox in the house," she declared. "Mr. Frank owns some stock in the Independence Ice Company."

Along with some other pertinent comments, a letter to Reathel Odum provides the denouement of Vietta's performance. "This house is bedlam and I wish I had never come home," Mother wrote. "There is someone working in almost every room in the house and a horde of them on the outside. I don't see any end to it. . . . Vietta came today so that will help. At least I don't have to cook."

In another letter to Reathel during these same weeks, Mother summed her policy in regard to reporters, who were pestering Reathel and Mrs. Helm for stories. "Just keep on smiling and tell 'them' nothing."

Gawking curiosity seekers, slothful plumbers, hammering carpenters, were not the only upsets Bess encountered in Independence that summer. When she went to the first meeting of her bridge club, the members all stood up as she walked into the room. It was a half humorous, half serious gesture. They were trying to tell her how proud they were that she had become First Lady. They were also expressing some of the awe Americans feel for the presidency.

Dad had had a similar experience with Eddie McKim. When he came to the Oval Office the day after Dad took over, Eddie started calling him "Mr. President" and could not bring himself to sit down in his presence.

Mother dealt with the bridge club in her own direct way. "Now stop it, stop it this instant," she said. "Sit down, every darn one of you."

Late in June 1945, the President flew to San Francisco to address the

closing session of the UN conference. On the way back he stopped in
Independence. He had promised Bess that he would "do as I'm told"
while he was there. She hoped that these words meant she would
enjoy his company for a few quiet days. But he brought the presidency with him, and instead of a peaceful interlude, the visit was
four days of continuous uproar. As Mother put it in a letter to Reathel
Odum, "The place has been running over with all sorts of people."
Both Trumans were learning that a president could not go anywhere
without an army of reporters and aides and Secret Service men in
his wake.

In this case, Dad should have realized that the first visit of Missouri's first president would inevitably be a circus. The biggest crowd
in the history of Jackson County roared a welcome at the airport.
Dad loved every minute of it, especially the part where he issued a
proclamation declaring Kansas City part of "Greater Independence."
On his last day, Dad tried to arrange twenty-four hours at home
without intrusions. But he yielded to reporters' pleas and granted a
picture session on the front porch at 3 P.M. He had no trouble persuading me to join him, but after a few minutes of click-click they
naturally asked for Bess. Dad went into the house to get her. A few
minutes later he came out looking unhappy. "Take a few more of us,
why don't you, boys," he said. Mother had flatly refused to join us.

After Dad returned to Washington, Mother declared her independence from the Secret Service on her home turf. She called in our
resident agents and informed them that under no circumstances was
she going to tolerate anyone trailing her when she went shopping or
visiting friends. She would put up with surveillance in Washington,
D.C., where she could see it was necessary. But not here. Thereafter,
when she went anywhere, I or one of my aunts was her only escort.

Bess's dark mood may have been worsened by bad news from
Denver. Fred Wallace was starting to drink again. But Harry Truman
felt, accurately, I fear, that he was the chief cause of her woe. On July
5, on the eve of leaving for a summit conference with Churchill and
Stalin in Potsdam, Germany, he telephoned her from the White
House. The conversation was so unpleasant, he was still upset about
it the next day, when he wrote her this farewell letter.

I'm on the train, bound for Norfolk, to take the boat ("ship" is navy) for
Antwerp. [It was the cruiser USS *Augusta*.] I am blue as indigo about going.
You didn't seem at all happy when we talked. I'm sorry if I've done some-
thing to make you unhappy. All I've ever tried to do is make you pleased

with me and the world. I'm very much afraid I've failed miserably. But there is not much I can do now to remedy the situation.

Tonight I sat in the front row with Vaughan, Vardaman, Snyder and others and listened to a most beautiful band concert by the Air Corps Band—a million dollar organization. They were most pleased to play for *me!* Why I can't understand.

Now I'm on my way to the high executioner. Maybe I'll save my head. Let's hope so. George VI R.I. sent *me* a personal letter today by Halifax. [The British ambassador, Lord Halifax.] Not much impressed. Save it for Margie's scrapbook.

As President, Dad was deeply concerned about the potential impact of this venture in diplomacy on his standing with the American voters. He remembered that Woodrow Wilson had ruined his popularity at home by letting European statesmen out-negotiate him at the Versailles Peace Conference in 1919. Dad was skeptical of what could be gained from any agreement with Stalin, who already had proved himself to be a double-dealer. But he was at least as worried about Bess's reaction to the presidency. He tried to remedy the situation by writing the frankest imaginable letters to her from Potsdam, in the hope that she would feel a part of this history-in-the-making, even though she was 6,000 miles away.

This letter describes the opening of the conference.

I've only had one letter from you since I left home [on July 6]. I look carefully through every [diplomatic] pouch that comes—but so far not much luck. . . .

The first session was yesterday in one of the Kaiser's palaces. I have a private suite in it that is really palatial. The conference room is about forty by sixty and we sit at a large round table—fifteen of us. I have four and they each have four [seats], then behind me are seven or eight more helpers. Stalin moved to make me the presiding officer as soon as we sat down and Churchill agreed.

It makes presiding over the Senate seem tame. The boys say I gave them an earful. I hope so. Admiral Leahy said he'd never seen an abler job and Byrnes and my fellows seemed to be walking on air. I was so scared I didn't know whether things were going according to Hoyle or not. Anyway a start has been made and I've gotten what I came for—Stalin goes to war August 15 with no strings on it. . . . I'll say that we'll end the war a year sooner now, and think of the kids who won't be killed. That is the important thing. . . .

Wish you and Margie were here. But it is a forlorn place and would only make you sad.

Dad also reached out across 6,000 miles to talk to Mother in Independence by a special telephone hookup. The phone had a "scrambler" device which prevented anyone from eavesdropping on the conversation. This next letter was written after one of these calls. Potsdam, for those who, like me, never did well in geography, was a suburb of Berlin, and Dad's comments reflect a recent tour of the shattered Nazi capital.

It was an experience to talk to you from my desk here in Berlin night before last. It sure made me homesick. This is a hell off place—ruined, dirty, smelly, forlorn people, bedraggled, hangdog look about them. You never saw as completely ruined a city. But they did it. I am most comfortably fixed and the palace where we meet is one of two intact palaces left standing. . . .

We had a tough meeting yesterday. I reared up on my hind legs and told 'em where to get off and they got off. I have to make it perfectly plain to them at least once a day that so far as this President is concerned Santa Claus is dead and that my first interest is U.S.A., then I want the Jap War won and I want 'em both in it. Then I want peace—world peace and will do what can be done by us to get it. But certainly am not going to set up another [illegible] here in Europe, pay reparations, feed the world and get nothing for it but a nose thumbing. They are beginning to awake to the fact that I mean business.

It was my turn to feed 'em at a formal dinner last night. Had Churchill on my right, Stalin on my left. We toasted the British King, the Soviet President, the U.S. President, the two honor guests, the foreign ministers, one at a time, etc. etc. ad lib. Stalin felt so friendly that he toasted the pianist when he played a Tskowsky (you spell it) piece especially for him. The old man loves music. He told me he'd import the greatest Russian pianist for me tomorrow. Our boy was good. His name is List and he played Chopin, Von Weber, Schubert, and all of them.

When Dad got a letter from Mother, his day was made, even in Potsdam.

The letter came last night while I was at Joe's for dinner. . . . I can't get Chanel No 5 . . . not even on the black market. But I managed to get some other kind for six dollars an ounce at the American PX. They said it is equal to No 5 and sells for thirty five dollars an ounce at home. So if you don't like it, a profit can be made on it. I bought you a Belgian lace luncheon set—the prettiest thing you ever saw. I'm not going to tell you what *it* cost. You'd probably have a receiver appointed for me and officially take over the strong box. But I came out a few dollars to the good in the game of chance on the boat [he means poker], so it's invested in a luxury for you. . . .

But I seem to have Winnie and Joe talking to themselves and both are being exceedingly careful with me. Uncle Joe gave his dinner last night. There were at least twenty five toasts—so much getting up and down that there was practically no time to eat or drink either—a very good thing. Being the super-duper guest I pulled out at eleven o'clock after a lovely piano and violin concert by a dirty-faced quartet. The two men play the piano, the two women the violin. I never heard better ones. . . . It was real music. Since I'd had America's No. 1 pianist to play for Uncle Joe at my dinner he had to go me one better. I had one [pianist] and one violinist—and he had two of each.

He talked to me confidentially at the dinner and I believe things will be all right in most instances. Some things we won't and can't agree on—but I have already what I came for. Hope I can break it off in a few days.

Three days later, they were still at it.

We have accomplished a very great deal in spite of all the talk. Set up a council of ministers to negotiate peace with Italy, Rumania, Bulgaria, Hungary, Finland and Austria. We have discussed a free waterway program for Europe, making the Black Sea straits, the Danube, the Rhine and the Kiel Canal free to everyone. We have a setup for the government of Germany and we hope we are in sight of agreement on reparations.

So you see we have not wasted time. There are some things we can't agree to. Russia and Poland have gobbled up a big hunk of Germany and want Britain and us to agree. I have flatly refused. We have unalterably opposed the recognition of police governments in the Germany Axis countries. I told Stalin that until we have free access to those countries and our nationals had their property rights restored, there'd never be recognition. He seems to like it when I hit him with a hammer.

In a final letter, Dad summed up what he and Stalin had failed to agree on.

The whole difficulty is reparations. Of course the Russians are naturally looters and they have been thoroughly looted by the Germans over and over again and you can hardly blame them for their attitude. The thing I have to watch is to keep our skirts clean and make no commitments.

The Poles are the other headache. They have moved into East Prussia and to the Oder in Prussia, and unless we are willing to go to war again they can stay and will stay with Bolsheviki backing—so you see in comes old man reparations again and a completely German-looted Poland.

There was one subject that Harry Truman did not mention in these letters from Potsdam. Throughout the last weeks of July, he got a stream of reports from the test of the first atomic bomb in New

Mexico. In the opening paragraphs of his letter summing up the conference, he made an oblique reference to it. He remarked that he had "an ace in the hole" if Stalin refused to reach an agreement Obviously, Bess knew about the existence of the bomb. But it is also clear that Dad did not discuss with her the decision to drop it.

This omission does not imply a guilty conscience on his part. On the contrary, it underscores the virtually unanimous conviction among America's leaders that there was no alternative to dropping it. In the preceding weeks Harry Truman had studied reports from committees of scientists and military men, all of whom voted by large majorities to use the weapon. The idea circulated by some of Dad's third-rate biographers that he spent hours reading and rereading the "To be or not to be" soliloquy from Hamlet, agonizing over the decision, is utterly absurd. To put it in the negative, no American president, including Franklin D. Roosevelt, could have refused to use this weapon. He could never have defended a decision to go ahead with an invasion of Japan that would have cost American lives, whether the final casualty figure was 10,000 or 1,000,000.

After a final conference with his advisers and with Winston Churchill, Dad authorized the Army Air Force to drop the bomb to end the war swiftly. The "Little Boy," the code name for the first bomb, was dropped on August 6, 1945, while Dad was on his way home from Potsdam. Bess was on a train to Washington, D.C. at the time. She was alone (except for her Secret Service detail), having left me in Independence with Grandmother Wallace. Three days later, John Snyder escorted her from the White House to meet the USS *Augusta* at Norfolk, when it arrived on August 9. That same day, according to the plan recommended by Dad's military advisers, a second bomb smashed Nagasaki. Major General Leslie Groves, the head of the Manhattan Project that created the bomb, had predicted (with amazing accuracy, as events proved) that a second bomb would be necessary to convince the Japanese that the first one was not a fluke.

John Snyder recalls that Bess was deeply disturbed by this new weapon. "What do you think of it?" she asked him. "Should we have dropped it?"

John told her it was necessary to end the war and save American—and Japanese—lives. Bess accepted the explanation without comment. But she found herself wishing that Harry Truman had consulted her on this momentous decision. I am not suggesting she would have changed his mind. However, she did not like the way the news had taken her by surprise. It underscored what she felt as she read Dad's letters from Potsdam, describing decisions on issues that he had never so much as mentioned to her before. She was forced to face a very unpleasant fact. She had become a spectator rather than a partner in Harry Truman's presidency.

That made her very, very angry.

Chapter Twenty

What had happened? Depending on your point of view, you can blame it on history, on Bess, or on Harry Truman. I am inclined to blame history, that maddening, mysterious tangle of people and events which Abraham Lincoln mournfully reminded Americans that they could not escape.

History had been accelerating at such a tremendous rate of speed since April 12 that Harry Truman had had no time to discuss with Bess dozens of major and minor decisions. There was no *Congressional Record* to read and reflect on, none of the leisurely give and take of the Senate, where a wife could analyze issues and personalities and make shrewd observations, helpful suggestions.

Instead, Bess felt like she was suddenly watching the man she loved driving a supercharged car at suicidal speed around the Indianapolis raceway for eighteen hours a day. Occasionally, he glanced her way and she was able to shout a suggestion, such as "HIRE CHARLIE ROSS." But most of the time he was too busy trying to keep the car on the track. She felt more and more superfluous. This feeling combined with her original opposition to Harry Truman becoming president to build a smoldering anger that was tantamount to an emotional separation.

I stayed in Independence during these tumultuous final days of World War II. Bess wrote me a number of letters, which are a study of her attempt to ignore the kettledrums of history. On August 10, the day after the second atomic bomb exploded and the Japanese tottered, her entire letter dealt with paying a new maid, Leola, $5 each Wednesday without fail and using the balance of the check she enclosed to pay for my music lessons. Her only comment on Washington, D.C. was: "It's plenty sticky here today and looks like rain."

The return address on the envelope was also a comment in itself. She wrote: "1600 Penn. Ave, Wash. D.C." She still could not bring herself to write that fateful phrase, "The White House."

On August 14, Bess shared in the general exultation over the Japanese surrender. She joined President Truman on the north portico to wave to the huge crowd in Lafayette Square. That same day she wrote a letter to Mary Paxton Keeley. Her only acknowledgment of history being made was a parenthesis under the word "Tuesday" in the upper right-hand corner, "(I hope V-J Day)". The letter began with a lament that "the weeks at home went so horribly fast." Then Bess turned to Mary's son, Pax. "I hope Pax is back in this country and is on the verge of a wedding." She asked Mary for news of a play she had written about Lincoln. It was being considered by a New York producer. (Alas, it did not make it to Broadway.)

"I left Mother and Marg at home," Bess serenely continued, while Washington, D.C. and the rest of the country celebrated. "Marg [is] working hard at her voice lessons & has really made some progress this summer. . . . If you get up to Indep. be sure to go see the family. [I] am still planning to read the Sandburg Lincoln as you suggested. Will probably have plenty of time this month. Not much doing except callers. Please let me know about Pax. I think of him so often."

Mother's subsequent letters to me were mostly chitchat about my friends inquiring for me, the activities of an ex-beau. In this same period, Dad was giving his mother and sister a very different version of what was happening.

I have been trying to write you every day for three or four days but things have been in such a dizzy whirl here I couldn't do anything but get in the center and try to stop it. Japan finally quit and then I had to issue orders so fast that several mistakes were made and then other orders had to be issued. Everybody has been going at a terrific gait but I believe we are up with the parade now.

Not until August 18 did Bess tell me what was going on—and that was after the excitement was over.

"Everything has quieted down around the White House," Bess wrote. "Dad had the Chiefs of Staff of Allies to dinner last night. Just twenty eight altogether. The table was lovely, with small white dahlias and deep rose and violet asters—four large bowls of them & tall candlelabs between them. The Marine Band played all evening and [we] enjoyed it in the upper hall."

The sum total of my reaction to this letter in 1945 was: I wish I were there. Now I see it as a summation, an image of the distance between Bess and the presidency. Harry Truman was downstairs giving elegant stag dinners, and she was watching and listening in the upper hall.

But Bess was still a woman who cared deeply about people she knew and liked. On August 31, she joined twenty other "Wed. USO workers" who journeyed fifty miles to Winchester, Virginia to offer their sympathy to a fellow USO'er whose son had been killed on VJ day on Mindanao. On a happier note, she was enormously pleased that her cousin Maud Louise's husband, General Charles Drake, had been rescued, alive and relatively well, from a prison camp in China. She sent me a news clipping about it in one of her letters and commented on how happy she was.

There is a glimpse of her feelings in another letter, written on board the presidential yacht, *Potomac*, during a Sunday outing on the river of the same name. Bess told me that the navy was going to turn over to us a bigger, more seaworthy ship, the *Williamsburg*. "Captain Kuver [the commander of the *Potomac*] says we can go round the world in it! Shall we?"

She was still yearning to escape the task that was facing her, somehow.

A letter to Ethel Noland displayed similar sentiments, focusing on 219 North Delaware Street this time. On September 4, after she had been in Washington less than a month, Bess wrote: "I've been wondering how all of you are. . . . I am getting anxious to go home again. I was sick to miss seeing Chris and Marian [who visited Grandmother and me in Independence] but there was nothing I could do about it." She ended this letter with a glimpse of her view of the White House. "The Ambassador of Guatemala and his gal are calling this afternoon so I must get on down there. It's always something!"

Meanwhile, President Truman was grappling with the problems of postwar America. As he remarked to his mother in one of the many letters he wrote to her at this time, it was the "political maneuvers" that he had to start thinking about now. On September 6, he made a bold move to assume the presidency in his own right. He sent a twenty-one-point program to the members of Congress, calling on them to join him in a series of programs that would make sure the United States did not collapse into another depression. He called for a massive housing program, an unemployment compensation program, and generous aid to small business. The Republican-southern

This picture of me and Mother was taken just after Dad was elected to the U.S. Senate in 1934. Neither of us looks happy about going to Washington. (*Courtesy of the Truman Family*)

Every Wednesday throughout World War II, Mother worked at the Washington, D.C., USO. Here she seems to be doing a little housecleaning. I don't know the names of the other women. (*Courtesy of the Truman Family*)

Here we are in 1944 at the convention in Chicago, where Dad was nominated for vice president. Mother's opinion of this move is visible on her face. I was young enough to think it was a great idea. (*Courtesy of the Truman Family*)

A glimpse of the happy all too brief vice-presidential days. Dad and Mother are enjoying a joke at a National Press Club party. (*ACME Newspictures—UPI*)

As Dad takes the oath as president, Mother's expression again reveals her feelings. She had already gone upstairs to express her sympathy to Eleanor Roosevelt—her first act as First Lady. (*Harris & Ewing Historical Pictures Services Inc.*)

The First Lady's Spanish class in session at the White House. Mamie Eisenhower is seated at the far left. Mother studied hard. Others, to her vexation, goofed off. (*UPI*)

Mother liked football as much as baseball. She dragged me to several Army-Navy games where I almost froze. Dad enjoyed this one, in 1948, because Army won, 38–0. As president, of course, he had to pretend to be neutral. (*Courtesy of the Truman Family*)

The Trumans leave Union Station in Washington, D.C., to hit the 1948 campaign trail. Note the absence of a crowd. Mother never entirely forgave Washingtonians for failing to give us a decent send-off. (*Abbie Rowe—National Park Services. Courtesy of Harry S. Truman Library*)

In the presidential box, we greet celebrators at the 1949 inaugural ball. We were the first to have more than one ball to keep the throng of well-wishers happy. (*ACME Newspictures—UPI*)

Here's Mother hard at work First Ladying, as I grew to call it. She is entertaining several hundred women Democrats at a White House tea. (*AP*)

This was one formal party that Mother enjoyed. Here the Trumans entertain the future queen of England, Princess Elizabeth, and her husband, Prince Philip, when they visited in 1951. (*Harris & Ewing Historical Pictures Services Inc.*)

The First Lady and I are looking pretty spiffy here, on our way to opening night of the Metropolitan Opera in 1950. I was always after her to take time off to enjoy herself. (*Courtesy of the Truman Family*)

Why does Mrs. Truman have such a pleased expression on her face? Because President Truman has just said: "I shall not be a candidate for reelection in 1952." A friend said she looked like a poker player with four aces in her hand. (*International News Service—UPI*)

Democrat coalition in Congress screamed as if he had asked them to surrender their wallets. It was the beginning of a three-year brawl.

On September 14, Dad and Mother flew to Independence to bring me back to Washington for my final year at George Washington University. By this time Bess had made it extremely clear to the President that she did not want a repetition of his first visit. This one was supposed to be quiet and private. The local folk were asked in advance to cool it on fanfare and celebrations. But Americans have never been inclined to obey such edicts. A crowd of 200 swarmed around 219 North Delaware Street as the presidential car arrived.

The next day, when Dad dropped into his old Kansas City barbershop for a haircut, the crowd blocked traffic and almost broke the windows trying to get a look at him. Swarms of drivers and a small army of walkers streamed past the house, making it difficult for any of us to sit on the porches or enjoy the grounds in our usual way without giving the Secret Service men heart attacks.

Dad flew back to the White House after two days, leaving Mother considerably less than happy with his "quiet" visit. She stayed in Independence for another two weeks, ostensibly to help me shop for a fall wardrobe. From Washington came letters from a troubled president.

It's a lonesome place here today. Had Schwellenbach [Senator Lewis B. Schwellenbach of Washington] over for lunch and heard all the pain in the labor setup. Hope to fix it tomorrow. Should have done it 60 days ago. Snyder is also having his troubles too. But I guess the country will run anyway in spite of all of us. Saw Rayburn, McCormack, Barkley and McKellar on the state of the Congress this morning—it's in a hell of a state according to all four. . . .

Hope you and Margie are having a grand time—I'm not.

Two days later, he reported that he had replaced Frances Perkins as Secretary of Labor. She had told Dad soon after he became president that she wanted to leave the job, which she had held since 1933. He took the opportunity to get rid of some troublesome Roosevelt loyalists in the Labor Department.

Well I got the job done as I told you I would. But I'm not sure what the result will be. Lew Schwellenbach is now Secretary of Labor sure enough and I got rid of some conspirators in the "Palace Guard". . . . I'm sick of having a dozen bureaus stumbling over each other and upsetting the applecart. I'm either going to be President or I'm going to quit. . . .

I am hoping things will straighten out now and we can go to work. I don't know what else I can do if they don't. It surely will be good to have you back here. This is a lonesome place.

Three days later, on September 22, he told her about an acrimonious cabinet meeting.

We . . . had a stormy Cabinet meeting discussing the atomic bomb. Lasted two hours and every phase of national and international politics was discussed. It was very helpful. I must send a message down [to Congress] on it soon.

The funny part of the meeting was that those on the right of me were "Left" and the others on the left were "Right." Stimson, Acheson, Interior (Fortas for Ickes) Schwellenbach, Wallace, Hannegan, McNutt were arguing for free interchange of scientific knowledge, while Vinson, Clark, Forrestal, Anderson, Crowley were for secrecy. Anyway I'll have to make a decision and the "Ayes" will have it even if I'm the only Aye. It is probably the most momentous I'll make.

The message—the plea—in these letters was unmistakable. He was trying to get Bess back into the partnership. But she could not manage it. Her anger continued to smolder.

Meanwhile, Bess was the First Lady, whether she liked it or not. When she and I returned to Washington at the end of September, she tackled the job with dogged resignation. The ladies of the press were still clamoring for more information. Bess decided that Reathel Odum and Mrs. Helm would hold a press conference for her. They gamely obeyed, and met the assembled women reporters looking, Mrs. Helm later wrote, "like condemned criminals." One of the reporters wrote that "their attitude toward this part of their duties clearly was that there must be an easier way to make a living."

Basically, all Miss Odum and Mrs. Helm did was distribute copies of the First Lady's schedule for the coming week. The still-dissatisfied reporters, nothing if not ingenious, used these schedules to ferret out more information.

Reathel Odum remembers taking calls in Bess's second-floor office, while the First Lady sat a few feet away, scribbling memos on letters to be answered. "What will Mrs. Truman wear to the tea for the United Council of Church Women today?" the reporter would ask.

Reathel would pass the question to the First Lady, who replied: "Tell her it's none of her damn business."

Reathel would pick herself up off the floor and say: "Mrs. Truman hasn't quite made up her mind."

Anyone who was too pushy ran straight into Bess's hard side. One day Mrs. Merriweather Post, one of Washington's grande dames, showed up at the White House without an appointment and demanded to see the new First Lady. Bess sent Reathel Odum out to talk to her in the lobby. Mrs. Post did not even get invited to sit down.

Another woman pestered Bess with letters and phone calls to get her husband appointed a federal judge. Bess told Reathel Odum what she thought of her. "If she thinks I can get a federal judgeship for her fat Overton she is completely out of her mind. It's very embarrassing to be put on the spot like that. I'm sending [you] her most recent 'spasms' . . . keep them for Mr. T's private file."

Bess's determination to avoid publicity extended to her staff. One of the more ingenious women reporters announced she would like to do a profile of Reathel. After all, she had had an interesting Washington career. She had followed Harry Truman from the Senate to the vice presidency to the White House. Reathel was, understandably, thrilled when the reporter called to tell her that a leading magazine had accepted the idea. Reathel went to Bess and asked for her approval. "Absolutely not," she said, and that was the end of it.

Bess was not going to let anyone around her contract Potomac fever, a Truman term for those who get carried away by the Washington limelight. President Truman was encountering some serious cases of it on his side of the White House. First Eddie McKim, whom he had hoped to make his chief of staff, came down with it and had to be sent back to Nebraska. Dad managed this task without losing Eddie's friendship.

Commodore Jake Vardaman was a more difficult case. Dad was very fond of Mr. Vardaman, who had been a big help in the 1940 senate campaign. He made him his naval aide, a job with more honor than responsibility. (Mr. V. had gone into the navy during the war and risen to the rank of captain.) Not having very much to do, the Commodore decided that the First Lady needed help. He proceeded to try to "organize" Bess's correspondence and to tell Mrs. Helm and Reathel Odum that they were doing all sorts of things wrong. Bess had a rather warm conversation with the President about Mr. Vardaman. He was instantly recalled to the executive side of the White House and eventually kicked upstairs to the Federal Reserve Board.

During these months, Bess was short-tempered with Dad, some-times in front of me and even in front of White House staffers. One day, George Elsey, a naval aide, soon to become assistant to White House counsel Clark Clifford, was riding in the limousine with Mother and Dad on the way back from a reception at the Congressional Club. The President began complaining about Congress's refusal to let him expand the executive wing to add more offices. There was a fence blocking the path of this expansion and Dad said: "If they don't give me permission in a few days, I'm going to get a bulldozer in here and knock that damn fence down and go ahead without their permission."

"Harry," Bess said, waving her fingers under his nose, "you will do no such thing!"

Bess had scarcely gotten rid of Commodore Vardaman when she found herself embroiled in one of the nastiest political crossfires of the Truman presidency. It started with her acceptance of an invitation from the Daughters of the American Revolution to a tea in her honor at Constitution Hall on October 12. The announcement of this forth-coming event raised the hackles of Congressman Adam Clayton Powell of New York, a thoroughly unpleasant demagogue on race and anything else that could get him a little publicity. Powell an-nounced that his wife, pianist Hazel Scott, had been refused permission to perform in Constitution Hall because of her color.

This stirred memories of an ugly incident in 1939, when the singer Marian Anderson had been barred from Constitution Hall by the DAR because of her race. Mrs. Roosevelt had resigned in protest from the DAR, which stubbornly refused to change its biased policy regarding the use of the hall.

Congressman Powell sent a telegram to Bess the day before the tea, urging her not to attend. He went out of his way to compare what she was doing with Eleanor Roosevelt's protest. "I can assure you," he wrote, "that no good will be accomplished by attending and much harm will be done. If you believe in 100 percent Amer-icanism, you will publicly denounce the DAR's action."

Bess stood her ground. She was not a segregationist, but she was also not a crusader. She wired back that "the invitation . . . was extended prior to the unfortunate controversy which has arisen. . . . In my opinion the acceptance of the hospitality is not related to the merits of the issue. . . . I deplore any action which denies artistic talent an opportunity to express itself because of prejudice against race origin."

President Truman backed up Bess with a telegram of his own, which reminded Mr. Powell that we had just won a war against totalitarian countries that made racial discrimination their state policy. He said that he despised such a philosophy, but in a free society neither he nor Mrs. Truman had the power to force a private organization to change its policy.

In his heart, Dad knew this telegram was a mistake. He was far more inclined to condemn the DAR. He already was formulating plans for one of the great breakthroughs against discrimination, the integration of the armed forces. But Bess had decided she was not going to let a congressman tell her where she could have a cup of tea. She still was not quite able to accept the idea that she too was a public figure as much as the President.

Bess went to the tea. Adam Clayton Powell retaliated by calling her "the last lady." Dad was furious and forthwith banned the Congressman from the White House. Mr. Powell was right about one thing. Much damage was done, not to race relations but to the Truman partnership. There could not have been a worse beginning to her first ladyship, as far as Bess was concerned. She had been maneuvered into a comparison with Eleanor Roosevelt and had come out a dismal second on the public opinion charts.

In the midst of this brawl, Bess received a letter from Mary Paxton Keeley, urging her to jettison the DAR. Bess's answer revealed her stubbornness—and her wrath. "I agree with you that the DAR is dynamite at present but I'm not 'having any' just now. But I was plenty burned up with the wire I had from that _____ in NY."

Mother left that word blank, not I. Even when she was steaming, she remained a lady.

On another matter during this first fall in the White House, Bess demonstrated her normally sound political instincts. The American economy was having a difficult time readjusting to peace. There were shortages of everything from steak to coffee, and prices were rising at an alarming rate. Americans had saved something close to $134 billion during the war and were itching to spend it. A New York *Daily News* headline read: PRICES SOAR, BUYERS SORE, STEERS JUMP OVER THE MOON. Bess decided it would be a grave political mistake to launch a formal social session at the White House, with elaborate dinners and receptions. Instead, she announced that she would hold a series of teas and ladies luncheons, beginning on December 1.

Official Washington grumbled. Nothing is more desired by the ambassadors and bureaucrats and congressmen than an invitation to a White House formal dinner. But the decision was warmly approved by the rest of the country.

As she approached this truncated social season, Bess wrote another letter to Ethel Noland that again revealed her unhappiness. "I meant to answer your note at once," she wrote. "But I seem to get very little done that I *want* to do. . . . I get so homesick some days. Think about you all often."

This acute homesickness makes no sense for a woman who had spent most of the previous eleven years in Washington. Bess was suffering from the White House blues, a disease whose symptoms are the opposite of Potomac fever.

All these negative feelings came to a boil at the end of December 1945, when we went home for Christmas. Mother and I and Grandmother Wallace departed on December 18. Dad stayed in Washington waiting to hear from Secretary of State Byrnes, who was involved in heavy negotiations with the Russians in Moscow. He also decided, he told his mother, that he wanted to let the family have at least part of their holiday without a presidential invasion. So he waited until Christmas Day to fly home. The weather was awful; every commercial plane in the nation was grounded. After waiting four hours, Dad ordered the *Sacred Cow* aloft. It was one of the wildest flights of his life.

The New York Times, *The Washington Post*, and other guardians of the republic castigated the President for "taking chances with his personal safety." Bess's comments when he got to 219 North Delaware Street were not much more cordial. In the privacy of their bedroom, the conversation went something like this.

"So you've finally arrived," Bess said. "I guess you couldn't think of any more reasons to stay away. As far as I'm concerned, you might as well have stayed in Washington."

To ruin his Christmas completely, on December 27, Dad received an urgent call from Charlie Ross, informing him that Secretary of State Byrnes wanted to deliver a "fireside chat" to the nation on the Moscow conference before he said a word about it to President Truman. It was not the first time, but it was close to the last time that Mr. Byrnes revealed his inclination to treat Harry Truman like a puppet.

Dad rushed back to Washington to deal with this crisis. But he was so furious with his wife, he could not think about anything else until he wrote her a letter, telling her exactly what he thought of her rotten temper and insulting words. He mailed it special delivery that night.

The next day, I received a telephone call in Independence. "Margie," Dad said, "I want you to do something very important for me. Go over to the post office and ask to see Edgar Hinde [the postmaster]. Tell him to give you a special delivery letter that I mailed to your mother, yesterday. It's a very angry letter and I've decided I don't want her to see it. Burn it."

I did as I was told. Postmaster Hinde naturally made no objection. He handed me the letter, which had just arrived. I took it home and burned it in the backyard incinerator. I felt terribly guilty. I had made such a fuss as a teenager about Mother's tendency to read my mail. If Mother had ever looked out the window and asked me what I was doing, I would have had hysterics.

That day, December 28, 1945, a calmer Harry Truman sat down at his desk in the Oval Office and wrote Bess one of his most important letters.

Well I'm here in the White House, the great white sepulcher of ambitions and reputations. I feel like a last year's bird's nest which is on its second year. Not very often I admit I am not in shape. I think maybe that exasperates you, too, as a lot of other things I do and pretend to do exasperate you.

You can never appreciate what it means to come home as I did the other evening after doing at least one hundred things I didn't want to do and have the only person in the world whose approval and good opinion I value look at me like I'm something the cat dragged in. . . . I wonder why we are made so that what we really think and feel we cover up?

With those latter words, Harry Truman was telling Bess that he had known since the day he became president eight months ago that this explosion was coming. Now at least her anger was out in the open and they could begin to deal with it, and the presidency.

This head of mine should have been bigger and better proportioned. There ought to have been more brain and a larger bump of ego or something to give me an idea that there can be a No. 1 man in the world. I didn't want to be. But, in spite of opinions to the contrary, Life and Time say I am.

If that is the case you, Margie and everyone else who may have any influence on my actions must give me help and assistance; because no one ever needed help and assistance as I do now. If I can get the use of the best brains in the country and a little bit of help from those I have on a pedestal at home, the job will be done. If I can't . . . the country will know that Shoop, the Post-Dispatch, Hearst . . . were right."

Twenty-seven years later, when Harry Truman died, this letter was found in his desk at the Truman Library. It is the only one of the 1,600 surviving letters that he wrote to Bess that he kept there.

After Christmas, Madge Wallace departed for Denver with her son Fred and his wife Christine. Mother and I and Vietta Garr returned to Washington on New Year's Day. We had a private Pullman compartment, which Drew Pearson expanded into a private car. This viper in a reporter's disguise (he made Duke Shoop look like St. Francis of Assisi) wrung his hands at the thought of "the Truman women" traveling like Vanderbilts while "GI's had to travel in day coaches." At his next press conference, Dad pulled Pearson aside as he was leaving and threatened to punch him in the nose if he wrote anything like that again.

Next came an incident that takes on new depth and significance when told in the context of the troubled Truman partnership. Although Bess had canceled the formal White House occasions, Dad decided that it would be a good idea to have a diplomatic dinner. Americans would not object to seeing foreigners eating heartily at the White House, and the bonus in improved relations with the home countries might make it worth the time and trouble.

At the last moment, the Russian ambassador, Nicolai V. Novikov, had someone call and say he was ill. An investigation revealed he was healthy and happy in New York. The cause of his illness, it soon became apparent, was his proximity at the White House table to the envoys of Estonia and Latvia, two countries that the Soviet Union had swallowed at the end of the war, although their governments in exile were still recognized by the United States.

The dinner went off smoothly enough, but the next day Dad stormed into his oval office breathing fire. He summoned Dean Acheson, the Undersecretary of State who was running the State Department while Jimmy Byrnes was in Moscow, and informed him that he wanted Novikov declared persona non grata and thrown out of the country.

"Why?" asked the aghast Acheson, who could see the headlines blossoming, the army and navy going to full alert.

"He insulted Mrs. Truman by turning down that invitation at the last second." Dad stormed. "I'm not going to let anyone in the world do that."

Outside the Oval Office, Matt Connelly put through a hurried phone call to Bess and told her what was about to happen. Was she as

angry as the President? he asked. Matt, a shrewd Irishman, was
pretty sure she was not.

"Let me talk to him," Bess said.

Matt connected the call to Dad's telephone, and Mother told him
to calm down. She urged him to discuss the matter with Dean
Acheson, whom she had already met and liked.

"I'm talking with him now. He agrees with you," the President said.

He handed the telephone to Mr. Acheson, and Bess expressed her
abhorrence of the move. "His critics will have a field day," she said.
"We've already given them too much ammunition."

"What do you—er—suggest," Mr. Acheson said. He was only a
foot or so from the steaming President.

"Tell him you can't do anything for twenty-four hours, something
like that," she said. "By that time he'll be ready to laugh about it."

At this point, Mr. Acheson did something very clever. He put
words in Bess's mouth. He repeated aloud things she was not saying.
"Above himself—yes. Too big for his britches—I agree with you.
Delusions of grandeur."

Dad snatched the phone away from him. "All right, all right," he
said to Bess. "When you gang up on me I know I'm licked. Let's
forget all about it."

He hung up and reached for the photograph Bess had given him
when he left for France. He kept it on his desk in a gold filigree
frame. "I guess you think I'm an old fool," he said, "and I probably
am. But look on the back."

The acting secretary of state read the inscription Bess had written
there so many years ago. "Dear Harry, May this photograph bring
you safely home again from France—Bess." He understood a little of
what Dad was feeling.

But Dean Acheson could not know the deeper levels of emotion
that were swirling around the photograph during those early months
of 1946. In my biography of my father, I have written whole chapters
of solid evidence that Harry Truman was not, normally, a hotheaded,
hair-trigger man. On the contrary, he rarely lost his temper and
preferred to give his decisions long, cool, analytical thought before
making them. His behavior in the Novikov incident only revealed
how profoundly his quarrel with Bess was disturbing him.

Meanwhile, up on Capitol Hill, it was politics of the nastiest kind.
Harry Truman took on the whole industrial establishment by de-

284   MARGARET TRUMAN

manding another year of price controls to beat back inflation until the
servicemen came home and the economy returned to a peacetime
footing. The National Association of Manufacturers, the U.S.
Chamber of Commerce, and every other spokesman for business in
the country deluged Congress with a demand to "strike the shackles"
from the American economy. Congress, caught between a hard rock
and campaign donations, waffled, and the Office of Price Administration went down in flames, along with a good chunk of the
Truman administration's credibility. When a president is repudiated
by Congress, tie down your hat. Everyone starts running amok.

Meanwhile, on the First Lady's side of the White House, the job
continued to be done with a minimum of enthusiasm. I was now
twenty-two—old enough to sense that something was wrong even if
I did not know exactly what. We were not the same relaxed family at
dinner. For a while I thought it was the upper-class style in which we
dined, with a butler and servants hovering around us. They were
Mother's bailiwick. And I noticed something else. She did not seem
to be coping, or trying to cope, with our housekeeper, Mrs. Nesbitt,
who planned the White House menus, supposedly in consultation
with the First Lady.

Early on, I had met one of the Roosevelt sons, and he had asked
me: "Has Mrs. Nesbitt begun starving you yet?" I shook my head,
and he laughed and said, "Don't worry, she will."

Mrs. Nesbitt's ideas on food reflected Eleanor Roosevelt's, which
can be summed up in one word: awful. I could not understand why
Mother did not take charge of the situation. Then, suddenly, I was in
charge of the situation. In mid-March, Mother received a frantic
phone call from Denver. Fred Wallace had begun to drink in a desperate, self-destructive way. He was hiding bottles all over the house,
behind books, in closets. Chris could not deal with him. Grandmother Wallace was frantic.

Although Mother had barely recovered from a bout with the flu,
she instantly departed for Denver. A day or two later, Mrs. Nesbitt
served brussels sprouts for dinner. Dad pushed them aside and I
informed Mrs. Nesbitt that my father did not like brussels sprouts.
The next night we got them again. Somewhat tensely, I informed
Mrs. Nesbitt, again, that the President did not like that vegetable.
The next night we got them again. I exploded and put through a
long-distance telephone call to Denver. "If you don't come back here
and do something about that woman, I'm going to throw a bowl of
brussels sprouts in her face!" I raged, displaying a combination

Truman-Wallace temper that I scarcely knew I possessed at that point.

"Don't do anything until I get there," Mother replied.

I believe that contretemps was a turning point in Mother's feelings about the White House and the presidency. Out in Denver she faced the sad fact that Fred Wallace was forty-six years old, no longer her baby brother, but a sick man whom she could not cure. Her real task was back in Washington, where her daughter and her husband needed her.

Bess brought her mother back to the White House and dealt with Mrs. Nesbitt in very short order. She vanished from the scene, and on May 2, the rest of the staff learned that our beloved housekeeper was retiring. Her successor was a pleasant woman who quickly grasped the Trumans' likes and dislikes. Bess seldom had to revise the menus that were submitted for her approval each week.

Before this happy announcement, Mother had done something else that helped her view the White House in a more positive light. She invited her entire Independence bridge club for a four-day weekend. The ten ladies, including her two sisters-in-law and old friends such as Mary Shaw, arrived on April 12. Mother had a schedule lined up for them that would have wilted the iron campaigner, Harry S. Truman himself.

They raced from Congress to the Smithsonian to a luncheon in the State Dining Room to the circus. They had dinner each night at the White House, with Dad presiding, and played bridge aboard the *Williamsburg* as it cruised the Potomac. When the yacht rounded the bend at Mount Vernon, the ship's bell tolled, and the crew and passengers came to attention as taps were sounded in honor of George Washington.

At the circus occurred the only sour note in the whole weekend—although even Mother laughed about it eventually. A clown figured out that Bess was the First Lady and proceeded to sit in her lap. The look he got froze his funny bone. A Secret Service man went backstage and told the joker not to do that again.

The ladies had a spectacular time, and Bess, watching their wide-eyed enjoyment of it all, began to get a little perspective on the life she was leading. Maybe there was something wonderful as well as something awful about it. She was also discovering that the life of a First Lady was not necessarily all ceremonial chores. She could do a few things in the White House that pleased her first.

Coincidentally, Bess's bridge club weekend was manna to the ever more desperate women reporters. In fact, it was a media coup. "The girls," as they called themselves, got the kind of press coverage that movie stars and politicians would kill to achieve. They were photographed and interviewed from the moment they stepped off the plane. *Life* magazine did a six- or eight-page spread on them. It was one of the few positive stories the press wrote about the Trumans in 1946, although Bess did not have an iota of politics in mind when she issued the invitation.

As far as the President of the United States could see, everything in the world seemed to be going wrong at once. Half the labor unions in the country were out on strike, and the other half were threatening to join them. The Russians were becoming more and more impossible. Agitators in the armed forces stirred "I wanna go home" riots from Manila to Berlin. Naturally, the press and public were blaming the President for everything. Americans have always expected their presidents to be combination uplifters, hard-boiled politicians, and miracle men.

Although the world was definitely out of joint, something very important was happening at the White House that made the mess a lot easier for the President to bear. Around this time, Bess began joining Harry Truman in his upstairs study each night for a long, quiet discussion of the issues, the problems, the personalities with which he was grappling.

Bess had returned to the Truman partnership.

Chapter Twenty-one

That summer, Bess left me and her mother at 219 North Delaware Street and spent the entire month of July in the White House. To help her tolerate the Washington humidity, Dad had air conditioners installed in her suite. They spent the Fourth of July at Shangri-La, the presidential retreat in Maryland, now called Camp David. She wrote me a cheerful letter, describing "the most peaceful Fourth I have any recollection of." Dad had gone for a long walk and a swim in the pool, "But [it's] not for me! I've been reading or just sittin'." During the afternoon they were going to explore the place in a jeep. "Won't we be sore tomorrow?"

She teased me about the movies I was missing, especially *Anna and the King of Siam*. But the Marx Brothers' *Casablanca* drew a negative comment. "That will be the night I go to bed early." Although Bess loved a good laugh, the Marx Brothers never amused her. I think she identified with Margaret Dumont, that dignified matron they were always tormenting.

Bess lured the Chief Executive home for a brief vacation in August, one that actually achieved some of the quiet that she thought they were still entitled to enjoy, even if they were Mr. and Mrs. President. With all the Wallaces, including Fred and Christine, on hand, we had a lovely family picnic in the backyard, beyond the scrutiny of the public.

On this visit, they also enjoyed a foray into local politicking. Roger Slaughter, a Jackson County congressman, had voted against, and loudly criticized, almost every proposal President Truman had sent to Congress. Dad decided to put this ornery Democrat out of action in the August primary. Bess bet him $10 that he could not do it. That aroused the shrewd Missouri politician still very much alive inside the President of the United States.

He invited Jim Pendergast, now the leader of the county's Democrats, to the White House to discuss Mr. Slaughter. How the conversation went can be glimpsed from a paragraph in a letter Dad wrote to Jim before the visit. "If the home county organization slaps the President of the United States in the face by supporting a renegade Congressman, it will not be happy for the President of the United States or for the political organization."

Mr. Slaughter lost, surprise, surprise. Dad's first letter to Mother, when he returned to Washington, began: "Where's my ten dollars? You just can't believe in your old man's luck and judgment, can you?" The best part of the whole thing, he added, knowing Bess would love it, "is that Mr. Roberts [managing editor of the Kansas City *Star*] is very much put out."

That casual remark reveals another aspect of Bess's feelings about Harry Truman becoming president. She was not sure he could do the job. That was partly Dad's fault. He shared so many of his moments of doubt and discouragement with her. This frankness combined with her natural pessimism to produce a lack of confidence. But this feeling too was abating, as the Indianapolis Speedway version of the presidency subsided into the politics that we post–World War II Americans have come to accept as usual.

Bess sent the $10 and not one but two warm letters. The President was ecstatic at this evidence that they were in basic harmony again. He told her the letters had made the day "bright and happy." Perhaps pushing a little too hard, he continued: "You know that there is no busier person than your old man—but he's never too busy or too rushed to let his lady love, the only one he ever had, hear from him every day no matter what portends. It hurts just a tiny bit when he finds that trips uptown, time to dress etc interfere with letters from his lady love."

Dad thanked her for sending the Wallace family doctor to examine Mamma Truman, who was ninety-three and beginning to fail rapidly. "She is on her way out," he wrote. "It can't be helped but I wish it could. She's a trial to Mary and that can't be helped either. Wish you could be more patient with both. But I can't ask too much I guess."

Bess responded to this hint by going to a family party at Vivian Truman's farm. Dad told her he was "most happy" about the visit. "I have a terrible time with my immediate family about which you, of course, know not a thing. But that visit will help a lot."

That last sentence stirred Bess's ire. Was he implying that the Tru-

mans were mad at her because she did not visit them often enough? I
suspect that was what Dad meant but he denied everything. He
labored through an explanation of various Truman family feuds and
ended by asking Bess not to play newspaper reporter and "begin
putting hidden meanings on my remarks."

Dad's letters kept Bess in touch with daily doings in the White
House, as well as matters of state. He was becoming more and more
convinced that the Great White Jail was haunted.

I slept well but hot, and some mosquitoes bit my hands and face. Night
before last I went to bed at nine o'clock after shutting all my doors. At four
o'clock I was awakened by three distinct knocks on my bedroom door. I
jumped up and put on my bathrobe, opened the door, and no one there.
Went out and looked up and down the hall, looked into your room and
Margie's. Still no one. Went back to bed after locking the doors and there
were footsteps in your room whose door I'd left open. Jumped and looked
and no one there! The damned place. is haunted sure as shootin'. Secret
service said not even a watchman was up here at that hour.

You and Margie had better come back and protect me before some of
these ghosts carry me off.

Mother tended to be skeptical about the White House ghosts. So
was I, and I said so in one of my letters to Dad. Back came this reply.

Now about those ghosts. I'm sure they're here and I'm not half so
alarmed at meeting up with any of them as I am at having to meet the live
nuts I have to see every day. I am sure old Andy [Andrew Jackson] could
give me good advice and probably teach me good swear words to use on
Molotov and de Gaulle. And I am sure old Grover Cleveland could tell me
some choice remarks to make to some political leaders. . . . So I won't lock
my doors or bar them either if any of the old coots in the pictures out in the
hall want to come out of their frames for a friendly chat.

By this time the White House staff had stopped marveling at the
down to earth way the Trumans treated them and were just enjoying
it. Here, along with a report on a cleanup campaign, is some repartee
Dad exchanged with Mayes, a tall, cadaverous White House butler,
who, except for his color, had a striking resemblance to Abraham
Lincoln.

The Blue Room is torn up now. They have been washing windows,
cleaning Venetian blinds, cleaning the chairs and scrubbing the floor. There
is no carpet in the State Dining Room and the third floor looks like an attic.
I go up there for sunbaths on the days I can get them in. I told old Mayes

when I started up there that a few more days would make me as brown as he is. He said, "You'd better not get that brown, they won't let you stay in a first class hotel."

Dad was still worried about giving Drew Pearson any ammunition, as this letter makes clear.

I failed to answer your question about your car. It seems to me that if you can get a good price for it you may as well sell it and buy a bond and then when we leave the great white jail a new car can be bought. The new cars won't have the bugs out of them for two or three years anyway. Be sure though that no regulations or price ceilings are in any way infringed, no matter how good you may think the friendship of the person you sell to may be. The temptation to take a crack at the first family for pay is almost irresistible and so far we've escaped any factual misdemeanor and I'd like to finish with that reputation. Save the number. . . .

Many more of Dad's letters in the fall of 1946 kept Mother in touch with his ongoing problems with the recalcitrant Congress, Secretary of State Jimmy Byrnes, and the man who was becoming the biggest headache of all, Secretary of Commerce Henry Wallace. Among Mr. Byrnes's many defects was his tendency to hog the conversation, even when he was talking to the President. "Jim Byrnes came in for one drink," Dad wrote in December, "and stayed for dinner! You can't beat that." The next day Mr. Byrnes brought the Prime Minister of Greece to see the President and met his match.

Saw the Greek Prime Minister with Byrnes. Almost had to throw him out of the office. Even Byrnes, as great a conversational pig as he is, was out-talked and after a half hour I began ushering him to the door—and he was still going at top speed and finally had to have the door shut in his face.

Dad's clash with Henry Wallace was a far more serious matter. The Secretary of Commerce decided that he was FDR's heir apparent and began issuing pronunciamentos on foreign policy, strenuously criticizing the President's tough attitude toward the Russians. Henry had been making disapproving noises ever since Dad escorted Winston Churchill to Fulton, Missouri, on March 3, 1946, to receive an honorary degree from Westminster College. With President Truman's obvious endorsement, Churchill told the local audience—and the world—that Russia was ringing down "an iron curtain" across Europe. In Henry Wallace's confused mind, this made Churchill and Truman warmongers.

Mr. Wallace was launching a tradition that has become a knee-jerk reaction in certain parts of the academic world and in the media. He blamed the United States for our difficulties with the Russians. He saw nothing wrong with letting Moscow do what it pleased in Poland and the rest of Eastern Europe. He wanted to reduce our defense spending to the brink of unilateral disarmament. Things came to a boil when Henry gave a speech voicing most of these sentiments to a Soviet-American friendship rally in Madison Square Garden in mid-September. He had brought the speech to the White House and gotten Dad's approval of a version that criticized both the Russians and the British. He then gave an entirely different version, eliminating almost all criticism of the Soviets. He ended his jeremiad by claiming that Harry Truman agreed with every word he had just said.

When reporters rushed to the White House and asked Dad if this was true, he confirmed it, without realizing the double cross that had been pulled. The result was a major fiasco. Mr. Byrnes, who was talking tough to the Russians in Paris, threatened to resign. Editorial writers heaped abuse on Truman's two-headed foreign policy. Dad poured out his woe to Bess, who was still in Missouri. He did not receive much comfort from her. "It was nice to talk with you [last night]," he wrote on September 16, "even if you did give me hell for making mistakes."

The mistake was trusting Henry Wallace. Nevertheless, Dad still struggled to come to an understanding with him.

Henry came to see me last night and stayed from three-thirty to six. He finally agreed to make no more speeches until Byrnes comes home. I don't think I ever spent a more miserable week since Chicago.

I simply had to tell Henry that he could make no more speeches on foreign affairs. He didn't want to quit the Cabinet because I told him he had the right to do as he pleased outside the Cabinet. He finally agreed to stop talking. This affair . . . is one of the worst messes I've ever been tangled up in and I hope another one doesn't come up again soon but it undoubtedly will.

The crackpots [left-wing Democrats] are up in arms and we'll probably lose the Congress and New York and then we'll have a time sure enough. But it can't be helped. I hope we can manage to get over the next two years without too much trouble. The world picture is none too bright. Looks like Marshall will fail in China [General George C. Marshall, Army Chief of Staff during World War II, was trying to negotiate a truce between the Communists and the Nationalists]. I'm not sure that with Henry muzzled, Byrnes will bring home the bacon [an agreement with the Russians]. We're

staring another round of strikes in the face. The army and navy are at each
other's throats again and my Cabinet family just keep bickering all the time.
But you'll say, well you brought it on yourself and so I have no consolation
whatever.

I don't suppose I deserve any! Well anyway, it's only five days to Tuesday.

He was referring in that last sentence to Bess's scheduled return to
the White House. As you can see, their quarrel over the presidency
was not completely resolved. But it was out in the open now and
they could face it as partners.

Meanwhile, the Wallace imbroglio continued to boil, with the
Secretary of Commerce revealing the ugly side of his personality, as
well as some devious ideas about the presidency that he had acquired
from FDR.

I have written a letter to Henry asking for his resignation. After our long
talk of day before yesterday he evidently held a session of his help and every
word of our two-hour conversation was quoted in the [Washington] *Daily
News*. I told Henry in the confidential letter that I could never talk frankly to
him again, therefore it was best he resign. I also told him that I didn't believe
he could work on a team, particularly a team as important as the President's
Cabinet. I expressed the opinion that he would undoubtedly be happier out
of the Cabinet than in it.

We [had] agreed on exactly what he would say to the press. He said just
what he agreed to and then answered questions which completely nullified
his agreed statement. Then when I saw the news piece I hit the ceiling.

So now I'm sure I've run the crackpots out of the Democratic Party and I
feel better over it. Henry told me during our conversation that as President I
couldn't play a square game. That I shouldn't let my right hand know what
my left did, that anything was justified so long as we stayed in power. In
other words, the end justifies the means.

I believe he's a real Commy and a dangerous man. If I can't play square I
won't play. It's four days!

The next day, the President was feeling a lot better about getting
rid of Mr. Wallace.

The reaction to firing Henry is terrific. The stock market went up twenty
points! I've had an avalanche of telegrams from Maine to California agreeing with the action. I've also had some from New York, Detroit and California calling me a traitor to F.D.R. and a warmonger. But I think I'm right.
Charlie Ross told me I'd shown I'd rather be right than President and I told
him I'd rather be anything than President and Clifford [Clark Clifford,
White House counsel] said, "*Please* don't say that."

Anyway it's done and I feel like Mon Wallgren's Swede. This Swede owned a fine retail business and was doing fine, but according to Mon he became somewhat intimate with a lady named Gina Olson. Gina came to his store one day and told Ole (Mon's Swede) that she thought she was due to produce a child but that she wasn't sure. Well Ole walked the floor, kicked and cussed himself for a fool and wished he'd behaved. Gina came back shortly and told Ole that the Doc could not see her until the next day. So they decided to take a walk and discuss the situation. The walk led them to the town reservoir. Gina said to Ole with Mon's Swede accent, "You know if what I believe is true is confirmed by the doctor tomorrow, I shall come up here and jump into that reservoir." Ole threw his arms around her and said, "Oh, Gina, you don't know what a load you take off my mind!" Also in Mon's Swedish dialect.

Well Henry's demise makes me feel like Ole did—but not for the same reason, thank God.

That reminds me, I had a telegram from Steve Early [FDR's press secretary] which said, "Thank God, Steve." Just three days.

Three days later, Bess arrived on schedule and went to work as First Lady. A letter she wrote to me in October gives us a good idea of how frantic some days could be. Dad was speaking at the UN in the late afternoon. Bess stayed in Washington to attend the Community Chest luncheon, keeping a promise she had made to one of her close friends among the Senate wives. "I had to leave before Elsa Maxwell's talk to catch the plane at 2:30. We got to NY at 3:40 and were whisked to the UN Bldg & rushed into a reception room where Lie [Trygvie Lie, Secretary General] and someone else greeted us. Then to [the] auditorium where Spaak [Henri Spaak of Belgium] made a speech in French & then Dad's speech.

"Then about 75 motor police took us to the Waldorf where I had to hurry & dress for the reception. . . . We shook hands with 835 (according to H. Vaughan) [General Vaughan, Dad's military aide] & then rushed to dress to make the train at 8:25. The Byrneses [the Secretary of State and his wife] came home with us so we had to be polite and sit up and talk all the way when I had planned a good nap."

Later in the fall of 1946, Bess launched the first full-fledged White House social season since 1941. It was, to quote Edith Helm, "pressed down and running over" because there now had to be two of everything where only one had done the job before the war.

In 1916, when Mrs. Helm went to work for Mrs. Woodrow Wilson, there were only thirty-five chiefs of mission (diplomatic jargon for ambassadors) in Washington. In 1946, there were sixty-two. The official guest lists (VIP's of all stripes and nationalities) had doubled from 1,000 to 2,000. The State Dining Room, which seated 104, could not hold all the Chiefs of Mission and their wives at one dinner so there had to be two dinners. The official receptions, which, believe it or not, could handle 1,000 guests in the good old days, also had to be twinned to keep everyone happy.

Here, from Mrs. Helm's records, is a list of the Trumans' official entertaining for that first season.

November 26, Tuesday, Diplomatic Dinner, 8 P.M.

December 3, Tuesday, Diplomatic Dinner, 8 P.M.

December 10, Tuesday, Judicial Reception, 9 P.M.

December 17, Tuesday, Cabinet Dinner, 8 P.M.

January 7, Tuesday, Diplomatic Reception, 9 P.M.

January 14, Tuesday, Dinner to the Chief Justice and the Supreme Court, 8 P.M.

January 21, Tuesday, Reception to the Officials of the Treasury, Post Office, Interior, Agriculture, Commerce and Labor Departments and Federal Agencies, 9 P.M.

January 28, Tuesday, Dinner to the President Pro Tempore of the Senate, 8 P.M.

February 4, Tuesday, Army and Navy Reception, 9 P.M.

February 11, Tuesday, Speaker's Dinner, 8 P.M.

February 18, Tuesday, Congressional Reception, 9 P.M.

These, of course, were only the highlights of a schedule that included innumerable teas, luncheons, and personal appearances to cut ribbons and to beam on various groups from the Washington Committee for National Civilian Rehabilitation to the Girl Scouts.

For the official dinners and receptions, Dad and Mother decided to revive the "Little Procession," which had been dropped during the Roosevelt years because of FDR's crippled condition. Here is how it went on one of the most spectacular evenings, the Diplomatic Reception. At about 8:30 P.M. the ambassadors arrived in splendid uniforms or full evening dress, their coats ablaze with decorations. They marched into the East Room, four abreast. Meanwhile, the Cabinet members and their wives were being greeted by Dad and Mother in the President's study on the second floor.

At 8:45 P.M., four young servicemen, led by an officer, came to the door of the study and asked permission to remove the colors. These were the flag of the United States and the President's own flag, flanking his desk. The President gave his permission, and two of the young men removed the flags. They saluted and marched down the stairs and took stations to the right and left of the door leading to the Blue Room.

As the clock struck nine, the President and the First Lady began the "Little Procession." They descended the stairs, followed by the Cabinet members and their wives. Dad and Mother, looking marvelously dignified (my friend Drucie Snyder and I were practically falling over the upstairs railing to see all this), took up positions beneath the chandelier in the Blue Room. The Cabinet retreated to the Red Room, and the President and First Lady began greeting the representatives of the nations of the world on behalf of the United States.

Dad loved this aspect of his presidency. He thought the pomp and ceremony encouraged respect as well as friendship for the office and the American nation. Gradually, Mother came to feel the same way.

After shaking hands with the President and First Lady, the diplomats were escorted into the Red Room to meet the Cabinet. Then everyone went to the State Dining Room, where coffee, tea, sandwiches, and cake were served, and the Marine Band played dance music until midnight.

It was exhausting to shake hands with 1,000 people and get up the next day and perhaps shake hands with another 300 at a tea. Sometimes there were two teas in a single day. Toward the close of the social season Mother wrote to me: "These two weeks are really going to be a handshaking two weeks—conservative estimate forty-one hundred—I'll be plenty glad when February 19th arrives!" When someone asked her how she did it, she laughed and said: "I have a strong tennis arm."

The truth was somewhat more painful. Mother wrote me two letters about the February 1947 reception for Lord Alexander, the governor general of Canada, and his wife. "They arrive at four for tea, then dinner & the lengthy reception. Help! (or leave off the "p" and add an "l")." The next day she wrote to tell me how much she liked the handsome British couple. She added almost casually: "The reception of course was horrible—1341—& my arm is a wreck this A.M."

During the fall of 1946, Mother rang down the curtain on another White House activity that had attracted a lot of attention from the press: her Spanish class. In the fall of 1945, a friend had persuaded her that it might be good for inter-American relations—and also good publicity for the Trumans—if the First Lady invited a group of Cabi-

net wives and prominent Washingtonians to study the language with
her in the White House. Study groups were an old Independence
tradition, and Mother said yes. Soon she was meeting each week in
the White House library with Mr. Ramon Ramos, a very dignified,
earnest professor of Spanish, and a dozen ladies, including Graham
Black, Supreme Court Justice Hugo Black's wife, Margaret Patterson, wife of Robert Patterson, Dad's Secretary of the Army, and
Mamie Eisenhower.

I had more than enough studying to do at George Washington
University, so I stayed away from this sideshow. But Dad and I got a
lot of laughs from listening to Mother's complaints about some of
the members of the class, who apparently thought it was a strictly
social occasion and never looked at a book from one week to the
next. Mother studied hard and acquired a working knowledge of
Spanish.

For the climax of their matriculation, Mother turned the White
House kitchen over to Mr. Ramos, and she and several others joined
him to cook a Spanish lunch. I have no recollection of the menu, but
I will never forget the odors that were still wafting through the
executive mansion when I walked in that afternoon. Dad said the
place smelled like a garlic factory. We teased "Señora" Truman about
it for days.

During these same months, Mother really took charge of the
White House. Under her first ladyship, she was determined that the
place would be clean. She did not go so far as to don white gloves
and inspect for dust, navy and marine style. But she was constantly
eyeing end tables and windowsills and pointing out to Mr. Crim, the
head usher, that his large staff was less than perfect in the dustcloth
department. She also took an interest in the grounds. When people
all over the country sent her iris bulbs, because a friend in Independence had said she liked them, she issued special instructions to the
gardener to plant them in a single bed behind the executive offices in
the west wing.

One battle Bess fought largely in vain was with her maid, Julia,
who was proud of her efficiency. The moment Mother took off a
dress, Julia would pounce on it and put it away on the third floor.
One of the less charming aspects of life in the White House was the
complete absence of closets, which meant you could keep only a few
dresses within reach—a very frustrating experience when you were
trying to decide what to wear. Mother repeatedly told Julia not to

take anything upstairs until she got a specific order. Julia never seemed to get the message.

It is somewhat mind boggling to go through Mother's papers and see the incredible mish-mash of problems with which she dealt. Here's a typical month in the fall of 1946:

She had to issue a statement denying a Walter Winchell story that I had spent the summer in New York having an operation on my nose.

Saks Fifth Avenue started sending her free nylons. She told them to stop it.

A soldier appeared at the gate with a gift for me, a pearl pin. The guards found out he was AWOL and using an assumed name. The Secret Service wanted to know what to do with the pin. Mother told them to send the pin back to the store and refund the money to the soldier, who was in enough trouble already.

A theatrical friend of a New York friend applied for a Reconstruction Finance Corporation (RFC) loan and asked her to put in a good word for him. She asked RFC examiners to check him out, and they reported that he was a deadbeat, had been blacklisted by a half dozen government agencies and was being sued by his own lawyer for an unpaid fee. He did not get a good word from the First Lady.

On one aspect of her first ladyship Bess remained adamant. No press conferences. She entertained the women reporters at teas and even went to their luncheons. But it was off the record all the way. If they wanted any information, the questions had to be submitted in writing. There are about two dozen of these forlorn questionnaires in Bess's papers, with her answers written beside the questions. If the reporters had any sense, they would have given up in 1945. Here is how she answered the first question of a relatively short list, then.

"On what date were the President and Mrs. Truman married? Was it a church wedding, if so where is the church located and what is its name? Who performed the ceremony and is he still living? Who attended the bride and who served as best man? How were the bride and groom dressed? How many guests were present? Was there a large or small reception afterwards? Where did the couple go on their honeymoon?"

Bess's answer consisted of one line: "June 28, 1919."

She was surprisingly candid about some things, even though her answers remained terse. When someone asked her in 1946: "If it had been left to your own free choice, would you have gone into the White House in the first place?" she replied: "Most definitely would *not* have." Asked if she found being First Lady enjoyable, she answered: "There are enjoyable spots . . . but they are in the minority."

"Do you think there ever will be a woman President of the United States?"

"No."

"Would you want Margaret ever to be a First Lady?"

"No."

"If you had a son would you try to bring him up to be President?"

"No."

"Has living in the White House changed any of your views on politics and people?"

"No comment."

As time passed, that last answer got to be her favorite on these lists. In 1947, *Newsweek* magazine became so exasperated, they printed an entire set of Bess's replies, as read by Reathel Odum, under the head, "Behind Mrs. Truman's Social Curtain: No Comment."

Having married a newspaperman, I can sympathize somewhat with the press's vexation. But the American public did not seem to be bothered in the least by Bess's taciturnity. In fact, they rather liked it. Harry Truman, who was no slouch at judging the reaction of the man and woman in the street, was of this opinion. In the fall of 1947, he sent me clippings of the stories that the desperate reporters had constructed out of non-answers to another questionnaire.

The New York Times, for instance, tried to find political significance in the statement that Bess "wouldn't miss a Democratic Convention if she could help it." This reduced Dad and me to helpless laughter. In this letter, Dad wrote: "It looks as if your mamma has gone 'Potomac,' as all people do who stay in the White House long enough. When you write to her you might ask her what caused this outburst.

"I'm glad she did it," he added. "It will make a hit everywhere."

Along with politics and diplomatic receptions, Mother had another worry on her mind during these closing months of 1946 and the beginning of 1947: me.

I had graduated from George Washington University in June 1946 and forthwith announced that I intended to pursue a career as a professional singer. Mother was not pleased, and Grandmother Wallace, who had quite a lot to say on the subject, was appalled. In her opinion, a lady could not possibly have anything to do with show business, even the classical music branch of it, and remain a lady.

Mother persuaded me to go home with her to Independence, consult with my voice teacher, Mrs. Strickler, and think it over for the summer. I can see now that she hoped I would change my mind. Mary Paxton Keeley's son had gotten married by this time and presented her with a grandchild that fall. Bess wanted me to do the same thing.

She said as much to Dad in an August letter, hoping to solicit his support. "Of course I'd like to be a grandpa," he replied. "Except for having to call you gramma it would be very nice. But if the child wants to sing, let her try it. She has a lovely voice but I hope the prima donnas . . . do not spoil her. Think maybe she is past the spoiling stage by now, anyway."

Perhaps you can see why I tend to favor my father, just a little, in my writing about the Trumans. Dad supported my ambition whole-heartedly, even though he knew that it would complicate his presidency, and the presidency would complicate my career. To give Mother her due, she refrained from throwing her weight around in any dictatorial way. But she continued to lobby against me behind the scenes.

As I began spending more and more time in New York taking voice lessons, Bess complained to the President, especially when he too deserted her in the White House for a brief vacation in Key West. Dad did his best to soothe her, but he did not change his mind. "I am sorry about Margie's not getting back for any of the W.H. functions," he wrote. "Looks as if we've lost her for good and it's a wrench—but we'll have to stand it I guess. Glad the teas turned out to be not so bad as usual."

When I took an apartment in New York and began my long career as a resident of that city, Dad wrote rather mournfully to his mother and sister about my departure. But he still did not change his mind.

Margaret went to New York yesterday and it leaves a blank place here. But I guess the parting time has to come to everybody and if she wants to be a warbler and has the talent and will to do the hard work necessary to accomplish her purpose, I don't suppose I should kick.

Most everyone who has heard her sing seems to think she has the voice. All she needs is training and practice.

Gradually, Mother accepted Dad's point of view. Later in the year, she received a letter from her old friend, Arry Calhoun. She had moved to Vancouver, but distance did not alter Mother's fondness for her. "I was so delighted to hear from you!" she wrote. She inquired about the weather in the Northwest and expressed a hope that her son, Peter, whom she had adopted after the death of her baby, and her sister, Kathleen, would move out there to join her. "There's nothing quite like one's family," Mother wrote, with an almost audible sigh. "Heavens! How I miss mine!" Then she reported on me. "Marg is busy with her music and so deeply interested in it that *nothing* else matters. I am thankful, tho, that she has an excuse to skip this grind."

As I began the hard work that every singer confronts to reach and maintain professional quality, I received a letter from Dad that I still treasure.

It takes work, work and more work to get satisfactory results as your pop can testify. Don't go off the deep end on contracts until you know for sure what you are getting—and what *you* have to offer.

I am only interested in your welfare and happy future and I stand ready to do anything to contribute to that end. But remember that good name and honor are worth more than all the gold and jewels ever mined. Remember what old Shakespeare said, "Who steals my purse steals trash, but who filches my good name takes that which enriches not himself and makes me poor indeed." A good name and good advice is all your dad can give you.

Early in 1947, I got a tremendous break when the conductor of the Detroit Symphony Orchestra, Karl Kreuger, invited me to make my debut with his musicians over a nationwide radio hookup. In spite of a sore throat that kept me in bed for the previous four days, I performed well enough to win praise from an encouraging number of critics. Mother telephoned me from the White House and Dad from Key West, where he was taking a brief vacation. Bess was considerably cooler than Dad in her remarks, but she told me that an avalanche of flowers and telegrams were pouring into the White House and the number of telephone calls had forced them to shut down the switchboard.

I received $1,500 for that performance, and on the second or third day after my return to Washington I asked Mother to go shopping with me. I knew exactly what I wanted to celebrate my success: a lovely mink scarf. The saleslady beamed as I casually told her to charge it to Mrs. Harry S. Truman. "Oh no you don't," Mrs. Truman said.

"What?" I said dazedly.

"You bought it, you pay for it. You're making your own money now."

She was absolutely right, of course. But she also enjoyed reminding me that if I was going to be a career woman instead of a housewife and mother, I had better learn how to cope with my expensive tastes.

When I began a concert tour in August 1947, Bess added that to her list of responsibilities. In letter after letter, she reminded me of the basic rules she and Dad had laid down. I was to take no freebies from anyone. When I went into the South, she fretted over the possibility that Vietta Garr, who was traveling with me, might be barred from some hotel and it would get into the newspapers. She consulted with various people and reported that they assured her no hotel in the South would do such a thing, as long as it was clear that Vietta was my maid. I was also regularly sent stamps and told to use them, "if even on postcards." Other letters ended with "Send that wire!"

To my surprise, along with all these orders Mother mingled some pretty expert press agentry. I launched that first concert tour in Pittsburgh. Mother organized an expedition of prominent friends, including Perle Mesta, to support me. Mother reported that Perle had been "all steamed up" about going to Los Angeles to see me, but she had persuaded her to join the Pittsburgh junket.

After that concert, Mother wrote me a note that I still cherish. "You did a darn good job last night, Margie & I was mighty proud of you. We flew after all & had a perfect trip! (This from me!)"

While trying to run me, Bess was also running the White House. She scrutinized every bill that came into the personal side of the operation and often added them up again to make sure the staff knew their arithmetic. Running the White House is a little like running a hotel, with the added complication of having your own personal expenses tangled up in the business budget. She and Dad went to extreme lengths to make sure that Drew Pearson and his ilk did not find anything to snipe at in this area. They even paid their own dry cleaning bills, although the White House had a resident valet.

I like to joke about Mother's penchant for penny pinching. But when the Trumans added up income and outgo for the first year in the White House, it became apparent that they needed every cent she could save. They had exactly $4,200 left from the President's supposedly munificent salary of $50,000 a year.

As we have seen, Bess's first impulse was to tell the world it was none of its business how she dressed. But she soon had to face the fact that the First Lady's clothes were under intense scrutiny all the time. She decided to place her couturial confidence in a darkhaired,

Greek-born designer named Agasta. I believe Evalyn Walsh McLean steered her in this direction, and it turned out to be good advice. Agasta had taste and tact. She never talked to the press, beyond supplying them with descriptions of new dresses, as Mother introduced them.

While the First Lady was launching a social season that remained unmatched for splendor and dignity (in her memoirs, Edith Helm called it "the most spectacular of my long life"), the Truman presidency was in deep trouble. In the 1946 elections, the Republicans won control of both houses of Congress and declared war on the Democrats. Simultaneously, the Russians, seeing a divided government and a U.S. Army and Navy that had been demobilized into impotence, became more aggressive and arrogant. They backed a guerrilla army in Greece and threatened Turkey. The British, traditional stabilizers of the balance of power in Europe, were bankrupt, and the French and the Italians were not in much better shape. On the other side of the world, the Communists were smashing up Chiang Kai-shek's corrupt regime in China and threatening the free half of Korea.

When the British abruptly informed the United States that they could no longer support the Greek government in its war with the Communist guerrillas, Dad was faced with the first great foreign policy challenge of his administration. To bolster his political support in this crisis, Dad replaced Secretary of State Jimmy Byrnes with General George C. Marshall, the man who as Army Chief of Staff had been the architect of America's victory in World War II. This change came as a shock to Mr. Byrnes, who thought he had won a victory when the President fired Henry Wallace.

A doctrinaire conservative like Mr. Byrnes was not the man Dad needed to help him rally the majority of the country to meet the Communist challenge. He wanted a man like General Marshall, who was above politics. Proof of the wisdom of Dad's choice was the response of the Republican-controlled Senate. They unanimously ratified the General's appointment the same day it was submitted.

Dad's admiration of General Marshall was unqualified. The day he came to the White House to accept his new assignment, Dad noted on his desk diary: "The more I see and talk to him, the more certain I am he's the great one of the age. I am surely lucky to have his friendship and support."

I am quite certain that Mother was the first person to hear about this decision to give General Marshall the second most important job

in the administration. I am equally certain it won her enthusiastic
backing. This was a good example of how the Truman partnership
worked in the White House. More often than not, in those evening
discussions, Mother listened as Dad talked out alternatives. She was
particularly good at cautioning him against people like Jimmy
Byrnes, who were mainly interested in enlarging their personal reputations at the President's expense. She was equally good at spotting
people whose first loyalty was to the country and the President. For
her, as well as Dad, George Marshall was the prototype of this sort of
man. Mother was equally fond of his wife, a woman of marvelous
charm and grace.

Dad particularly valued Mother's opinion regarding the political
impact of his decisions on the American voter. Most of the time she
was a cautionary voice, warning him against impulsive decisions.
Only rarely did she suggest a man for a job, or recommend a change
in a policy.

If she expressed an opinion with which Dad disagreed, that was
the end of it. He had the final say. Dad's appointments secretary, Matt
Connelly, who saw more evidence of Mother's influence on Dad than
anyone else, considered this the most important aspect of the Truman
partnership. "She never nagged him," Matt said. "Once he made a
decision, whether or not she agreed with it, she accepted it."

With General Marshall on his team, Dad tackled the Greek crisis.
Working day and night (on the heels of an exhausting effort to prepare a budget and legislative program to submit to the hostile Congress) Harry Truman put together a historic departure in American
foreign policy. On March 12, Dad went before a joint session of
Congress and asked them to approve $400 million in military aid for
Greece and Turkey. It was the first time any president had ever proposed such aid when the nation was not at war.

Even more important to the history of our century was Dad's
declaration of support for nations struggling to resist Communist
conquest. Without mentioning the Soviet Union by name, he
equated it with the totalitarian regimes of Germany and Japan. "I
believe that it must be the policy of the United States to support free
peoples who are resisting attempted subjugation by armed minorities
or by outside pressures," he said. With those momentous words, the
President was declaring to the world—and to Joseph Stalin in particular—that the era of doubletalk was over. Henceforth, the United
States regarded Soviet Russia as an enemy of freedom.

The day after Dad delivered that now famous speech, Mother

insisted that he take a vacation. He headed for Key West, and his letters from there show how important Mother's intervention was. "I had no idea I was so tired," he wrote. "I have been asleep most of the time [since he arrived]. . . . Even drove to the beach instead of walking as I did before." He added that "Steelman [John Steelman, Assistant to the President] and Clifford [Clark Clifford, White House counsel] were as nearly all in as I was so it is a good arrangement all around."

Dad wrote me an emotional letter from Key West. It is an interesting comment on his eighteen-month struggle to reach an understanding with Moscow for the sake of world peace.

We had a very pleasant flight from Washington. Your old dad slept for 750 or 800 miles—three hours—and we were making from 250 to 300 miles an hour. No one not even me (your mother would say) knew how . . . worn to a frazzle the chief executive had become. The terrible decision I had to make had been over my head for about six weeks. Although I knew at Potsdam that there is no difference in totalitarian or police states, call them what you will, Nazi, Fascist, Communist or Argentine Republics. . . .

Your pop had to tell the world just that in polite language.

The submarine base at Key West was becoming a favorite presidential refuge, but Dad had yet to persuade Mother to join him. She saw it as an all-male setup (which it was) and thought Dad would have a better time horsing around with Charlie Ross and Admiral Leahy, playing poker and drinking a little bourbon beyond the range of her critical eye. But he wanted her near him more and more as the presidency gathered momentum, and he went to work in his usual shrewd fashion to tempt her southward. He described a fishing trip that he and Admiral Leahy had taken, praised the sunshine, and assured her that she and her mother would enjoy it.

The President's confidence in Bess's support continued to grow, even though, according to the pollsters, his popularity with the voters was sinking so fast it would take one of the submarines from Key West to locate it. At the end of June in 1947, when Bess took her mother home to 219 North Delaware, he wrote her a teasing letter that recalled all the shows they had seen together, in particular, *The Girl from Utah*, with its hit song, "They'll Never Believe Me." You'd just said you'd take a chance on me," he wrote. "Wasn't it a terrible chance? Never did I think I'd get you into all the trouble you're in now. Well you didn't have to take the chance, did you?"

Chapter Twenty-two

Less than two months after he wrote that letter to Bess, a major event occurred in Harry Truman's life that had nothing to do with politics. His mother died at the age of ninety-four. He had been prepared for it ever since another fall had left Mamma Truman bedridden. In the spring of 1947, while he was pushing the Greek-Turkish aid bill through Congress, she had come so close to death, Dad flew to Missouri to be at her side. He signed the historic aid bill in his Muehlebach Hotel office on May 22.

Two days later, Mamma Truman amazed the doctors by awakening and demanding a slice of watermelon. For the next two months, she seemed to be recovering. Dad went back to work in the Great White Jail, as he called the White House. He wrote Mother a wry account of a typical day in the summer of 1947.

Had . . . a hell of a day. Had a long meeting with the secretaries at nine o'clock. Admiral Leahy 9:45 to 10:10, Steelman and Jacob S. Potofsky at 10:15. Potofsky is Sidney Hillman's successor and he wanted to reassure me that the [CIO] Political Action Committee is 100 percent for me. Adolf Berle, Jr. came in yesterday to assure me that the New York Liberal Party is 100 percent for me. "Ain't that funny." Neither of 'em is for anybody but themselves and their own special interests.

Had to listen to Burt Wheeler [Senator Burton K. Wheeler of Montana] for one whole hour tell me all about South America. He went down there on a special mission ($10,000 fee and expenses) but he knows all about Brazil, Uruguay, Argentina and Chile. Another funny one. Senators and ex-Senators go to S.A., Germany, Japan, China, spend two or three days and know all about the countries and know all the answers. Guess I'm dumb.

The foreign minister of Peru came in and gave me a beautiful silver tray. . . . Then I had to receive forty-two Democratic national committeemen and women from Texas, Oklahoma, Arkansas, Louisiana, Mississippi, Tennessee, Kentucky and West Virginia.

Had a good time with them and told them a lot, as they did me.

Then to top off the morning had to listen to Mrs. Ogden Reid [owner of the New York *Herald Tribune*] for twenty minutes. She didn't take a long breath!

On July 26, he was in a very Missouri-ish mood.

This is turnip day and Nellie Noland's birthday. I sent her a telegram—did not refer to turnip day. My old baldheaded uncle, Harrison Young, told me that July 26 was the day to sow turnips—sow them "wet or dry, twenty-sixth of July." In 1901 he went to the seed and hardware store in Belton and stated to the proprietor, Old Man Mosely, a North Carolinian, that he wanted six bushels of turnips seed—enough to sow the whole county to turnips. Mosely asked him what he expected to do with so much seed. My old uncle told him that it was his understanding that turnips are 90 percent water. Nineteen hundred one was the terribly dry year. Therefore if the whole farm were planted to turnips maybe the drought would be broken.

You and I graduated that year and I spent quite some time on the farm, then Tasker Taylor [a classmate] was drowned in the Mo. River just above the Independence pumping station and I became a timekeeper for L. J. Smith's railroad construction outfit. That experience was very useful to me when those R.R. hearings were going on.

You see age is creeping up on me. Mamma is ninety-four and a half because she never lived in the past. I'll never be ninety-four and a half but I'm not going to live in yesterday either.

Dr. Graham went out today [to see Mamma Truman] and is to call me tonight. . . .

Dad barely finished that letter when he got a phone call from his sister Mary. Mamma Truman had contracted pneumonia and was sinking fast. Dad rushed to his plane. About an hour after they took off, he was dozing in his cabin when his mother's face suddenly appeared before him with amazing clarity. A few minutes later, Dr. Wallace Graham, the White House physician, told Dad they had just received word that Mamma Truman was dead. "I knew she was gone when I saw her in that dream," Dad said. "She was saying goodbye to me."

Two days after her funeral, Dad was back in the White House, still grief stricken. He wrote me the following letter.

Someday you'll be an orphan just as your dad is now. I am going up to Shangri-la today and will meet your ma at Silver Spring on Monday as I return to town. Wish you were coming back with her. This place is a tomb without you and your mother.

I have been looking over the thousands of letters, cards & telegrams about your old grandmother. They come from every state and every country and are very kind. Have heard from the Pope, King George, Chiang Kai-shek, the Queen of Holland and every President in the Western Hemisphere.

But the ones I appreciate most come from home. Heard from men and women your mother and I went to school with—some I hadn't heard from in forty years. Got one from the colored man who always waits on me at the Kansas City Club and one signed Fields [White House head butler] . . . one signed by all the sergeants who guard my plane. I like them more than all the topnotchers. . . .

Mamma Truman's death removed from Dad's life the other woman to whom he had turned again and again for the emotional support he needed to maintain his balance in the presidency.

If anything confirms the truth of my analysis of Harry Truman's motives in 1944, when Eddie McKim brought Mamma Truman into Dad's presidential thoughts, it is the incredible number of letters he began writing to his mother from the moment he entered the White House. As a senator, he had written to her no more often than a dutiful, busy son might be expected to correspond. In the White House his letters multiplied incredibly; often he wrote every day—with the same candor and wealth of detail he put into his letters to Bess.

Now Martha Ellen Truman was gone and that meant Harry Truman's need for Bess's support intensified. I am referring here to emotional support, not to any advice he might get from her on the blizzard of problems he faced. His daughter, yours truly the biographer, was out of the picture, crisscrossing the continent on concert tours. I am not sure if Bess was aware of this deepened need. She was not given to analyzing anyone, including herself, psychologically. But I think she sensed it on an intuitive level.

The best piece of evidence was her willingness to join him and me on a diplomatic mission to Brazil in September 1947. Persuading Mother was a feat in itself, because the trip involved flying across thousands of miles of sea and jungle. Even a flight to Missouri was torture to her. Dad made the decision almost on the spur of the moment, another obstacle. Mother usually did not like to be taken by surprise.

Twenty nations had been meeting in Rio de Janeiro to discuss inter-American security. They startled everyone, including themselves, by coming up with a treaty that banned aggression in the Western

Hemisphere. Brazil was also celebrating the 125th anniversary of its independence. President Truman decided to go down there, sign the treaty personally, and help the Brazilians celebrate. Bess succumbed, I think, for a special reason.

The trip was a sentimental journey for Mr. and Mrs. Truman. A number of times in his early letters, Dad had mentioned his desire to take Mother—or send her—on a tour of South America. Every woman has, I think, a romantic place she has longed to visit. For Mother it was the Latin half of the New World. Harry Truman knew this, and I think it played no small part in his decision to go to Brazil.

It also made very good political sense, I should add. It was part of a program Dad had launched earlier in the year to build solidarity between the United States and the countries of our hemisphere. Already he had visited Mexico and Canada with tremendous success.

In a long letter to her mother from Rio de Janeiro, Bess made no attempt to conceal her nervousness about flying. "The heavy clouds & fog lifted from the city just before we came in yesterday. . . . When we circled the bay (it's perfectly enormous) we were flying with one wing down towards the water & it looked as if we were going right into it, which I didn't enjoy."

She also disliked the ride from our embassy to the site of the conference, the Hotel Quitandinha in the resort city of Petropolis, in the mountains about thirty-eight miles north of Rio. The only approach to the site was up a steep, curving two-lane road, with a sheer drop of 1,500 feet only inches from our tires and not a guard rail in sight. In spite of a heavy rain, Bess told her mother that we "went at a *very* lively gait and took the hairpin turns at a terrible speed." I don't remember being that scared, but it was not the most enjoyable car ride I have had.

Bess also found fault with her daughter's antics in Rio. One night I went partying with several members of the staff. No one, including me, seems to have remembered to tell the President and First Lady where we were going. When we got back at 2 A.M. they were both pacing the floor. Mother gave me hell right on the spot, and Dad gave the staff more of the same the next morning.

What Bess loved most about Rio were the gardens. "The flowers and shrubs are out of this world," she told her mother, from whom she had inherited her love of growing things. "The gardens in front of the embassy are gorgeous. The hibiscus are all double & a brilliant red. There are a lot of other flowers and flowering shrubs that are like nothing I've ever seen before."

Rio was marvelous. The Brazilians could not have been more hospitable and enthusiastic. But for the Trumans, the high point of the trip was our voyage back aboard the USS *Missouri*. For twelve days we were more or less insulated from nasty columnists, international crises, critical congressmen. Best of all, we had to shed all pretensions to being VIP's when the ship crossed the equator. That was when King Neptune came aboard to initiate all pollywogs [first-time crossers] into his domain.

The more ridiculous the costume in which a pollywog greets the king, the better. The goal is to amuse him and make the initiation less rigorous. Mother donned a sport shirt and a baker's hat. It is a sight I will never forget. I did not look much better in a raincoat, boots, and sou'wester hat, all three sizes too big for me.

After greeting his majesty (actually a chief petty officer wearing dungarees and a cockeyed cardboard crown), we retired for the night to await our punishment. The next morning the "No. 1 pollywog," the President of the United States, was the first to approach Davy's throne and beg for mercy. He got off by promising to sign autographs for Davy and his pirate escorts and to supply them with Corona Corona cigars for the rest of the voyage.

Mother seemed to be in trouble for a while. Davy accused her of sowing "typical feminine disregard of our royal whim" by having "so cozened and comforted our No. 1 pollywog and otherwise made home so delightful for him that you have delayed for many years this long-sought audience with Harry S. Truman." However, the No. 1 shellback aboard, Admiral Leahy (he had crossed the equator aboard the battleship *Oregon* in 1898), interceded for her, and Davy decided to grant his first amnesty in several centuries.

The rest of us were not so lucky. I had to bow down six times before his majesty and lead six ensigns in singing "Anchors Aweigh." Charlie Ross and the other members of the presidential party took even worse punishment. They got clamped to an operating table and had some royal medicine—a mixture of alum, mustard, quinine, and epsom salts—poured down their throats. Then they got ducked in the royal tank and ran a gauntlet of electrically charged pitchforks. I began to dislike the rough stuff, but Mother, having dealt with an unruly mob of Delaware Street males, loved every minute of it. She laughed hardest when the reporters got the business.

There was a new sense of solidarity—and not a trace of self-pity—

in Dad's letters to Mother that fall. She returned to Missouri for a few weeks to close the house for the winter and bring her mother to Washington. During this period, Harry Truman pushed through the Republican Congress one of the great foreign policy initiatives of our time, the Marshall Plan.

Earlier in 1947, the President had responded with both his heart and his head to the description Undersecretary of State Will Clayton had brought back from a tour of Europe. The center of western civilization was close to collapse, harried by food shortages, industrial stagnation, and Communist threats from without and within its national borders. The $12 billion Harry Truman eventually persuaded Congress to appropriate transformed Western Europeans from a people without hope to a strong, prosperous community again.

Bess played a part in this struggle, which was fought both in the press and among the public as well as in Congress. Rather than present the spectacle of VIP's feasting while Europe was starving, she canceled all the state dinners for the 1947 social season. To prove she was not shirking her job, however, she continued the receptions, which involved the really herculean handshaking. The receptions did not require any serious outlay of food—and incidentally, no liquor was served at them. This was not Bess's idea. It was a White House tradition.

Hindsight makes it sound easy, but the letters President Truman and Bess exchanged reveal how tough it was to get the Marshall Plan through Congress. He rehearsed with Bess many of the arguments he used to rally support for the program. "To feed France and Italy this year [1948] will cost 580 million, the Marshall Plan 16.5 billion. But you know in October and November 1945 I cancelled 63 billion in appropriations—55 billion at one crack. Our war cost that year was set at 105 billion. The 16.5 billion is for a five year period and is for *peace*."

A Russian war, which he saw as a very strong possibility, "would cost us $400 billion and untold lives, mostly civilian. So I must do what I can. I shouldn't write you this stuff but you should know what I've been facing."

What tormented Dad was the attitude of the Republican and southern conservative "squirrelheads" (his term), who were living in 1890. They were more interested in overriding President Truman's veto of their giveaway tax bill than in the crisis of western civilization.

Not all the Republicans were squirrelheads, of course. The key to reaching the thoughtful moderates was Arthur Vandenberg, the earnest, idealistic senator from Michigan who had become a good friend of Harry Truman during their years together in the Senate. Dad worked tirelessly to convert Senator Vandenberg into an internationalist and succeeded magnificently. Bess played a part in this campaign, too, doing everything in her power to charm the Senator's wife. In late September, Dad wrote to her: "Sen. Vandenberg was highly pleased at the flowers we sent his wife in the Detroit Hospital."

Not to be discounted in the subtleties of the legislative process is Bess's influence with other senator's wives. Early in 1947, she wrote to me: "The Senate women's luncheon today was something! The nicest one they have ever had, they said."

The President shared with Bess the climax of his struggle with Congress—the meeting with the Democratic and Republican leaders in the Cabinet Room on September 29. He listed each of them by name, including Vandenberg. The list filled half of one page of the letter. Most of them are forgotten now, but Bess had met all of them and had a good grasp of their personalities. First Robert Lovett, the Undersecretary of State, and then Secretary of State Marshall spoke and answered questions. "After everyone had had his say, I stated the case categorically and told them what we faced and what in my opinion we had to do," Dad wrote. "There was no objection!"

Bess was pessimistic about her man's chances, as usual. She thought the Republican and southern negativists would override the tax veto and sink the Marshall Plan too. This is an interesting glimpse of how "support" worked in the Truman partnership. It did not mean that Bess was always a cheering section. As Dad wrote in an earlier letter, "I'm happier when I can see you—even when you give me hell." Basic to the partnership was the principle that Bess would express her own opinions. Even if they disagreed, the important thing was that she was there, caring.

There were ample grounds for pessimism on the eve of the Marshall Plan vote. Bess remembered what had happened when Congress ran amok against President Roosevelt in 1937. "You are right about what I'm facing," Dad wrote. "But I've got to meet it with all I have. It may not be enough but if the Almighty didn't make my brain container as big as it should be, I'll have to use what he gave me. Congress will get its share of the responsibility but

I can't and won't shirk mine."

As he prepared a radio speech to the nation, Dad filled in Bess on another day in the White House.

I've had the usual day. The British ambassador brought in Admiral Tenney, who was with Roosevelt in the Red Sea when he met Ibn Saud. He said F.D.R. was in a heck of a fix for a smoke. And he couldn't smoke or drink in the presence of the old Arab King. He said that when the luncheon was served Ibn and F.D.R. each had to go down to the "dining saloon" (as he called it) in an elevator. The King of Arabia went first. When F.D.R. went down he stopped the elevator halfway and smoked three cigarettes so he could stand the lunch. . . .

Had Myron Taylor in too. Looks as if he and I may get the morals of the world on our side. We are talking to the Archbishop of Canterbury, the bishop at the head of the Lutheran Church, the Metropolitan of the Greek Church at Istanbul, and the Pope. I may send him to see the top Buddhist and the Grand Lama of Tibet. If I can mobilize the people who believe in a moral world against the Bolshevik materialists, who believe as Henry Wallace does—"that the end justifies the means"—we may win this fight.

Treaties, agreements, or a moral code mean nothing to Communists. So we've got to organize the people who do believe in honor and the Golden Rule to win the world back to peace and Christianity.

Ain't it hell!

Dad's radio speech did a marvelous job of rallying popular support for the Marshall Plan. "We're putting it over," he wrote exultantly to Mother. He dismissed as minor worries the overriding of his tax veto and political firestorms such as the wrath of the nation's Catholics, who were mad at him for declaring Tuesday instead of Friday a meatless day to free up food for the starving Europeans. The Catholics did not like getting stuck with two meatless days. It was one of those vote-getting details that slipped by the President and his staff, because they were concentrating on trying to save western civilization.

Something else was visible in these late 1947 letters to Bess: a growing presidential confidence. Others saw it too. One of the closest and most astute observers was Charlie Ross.

In the summer of 1947, Charlie's two-year leave from his job at the St. Louis *Post-Dispatch* was up. Instead of going back to the paper, he resigned and enlisted for the duration of the Truman tenure. This was doubly remarkable because Charlie was troubled by agonizing bouts of arthritis. Worse, he already suffered two mild heart attacks from working those eighteen-hour White House days. He concealed these danger signals from Dad and Mother—and perhaps from himself. He was equally debonair about a warning his doctor gave him early in 1948, that he had only four more years to live.

On Christmas Day 1947, Charlie wrote Dad a memorable letter. He said that the past two-and-one-half years had been "the most rewarding years of my life." He praised the "good team" that Dad had assembled for some of this feeling. "But the greatest inspiration, Mr. President, has been . . . you as President, you as a human being . . . . My admiration for you, and my deep affection, have grown steadily since the day you honored me with your trust."

I know Dad showed this letter to Mother. It made her doubly proud of having urged Dad to hire Charlie and eternally grateful to Mary Paxton Keeley for cheering her on. As this letter demonstrated, Charlie had become much more than a press secretary. He was a counselor, a friend. Only those who are close to a president understand how much he needs this kind of support.

Unfortunately, Charlie Ross's view of Harry Truman was not shared by a great many people, as 1948 dawned. Almost everyone assumed that Dad would not run for reelection. Seldom has a president sunk so low in the public opinion polls. According to their statistics, only 36 percent of the population approved of the way Harry Truman was doing his job.

As late as September 24, 1947, Dad himself, seemed to share this low opinion. On that day he wrote to Bess: "I'd be much better off if I were out or licked and I suspect you and Margie would be much more pleased." But the support Bess gave him throughout the struggle for the Marshall Plan—and winning that fight—changed his attitude dramatically.

I suspect that Dad also may have been thinking about one of the last conversations he had had with Mamma Truman, a month or two before she died. She asked him if Senator Robert Taft was going to be nominated for president by the Republicans in 1948. "He might be," Dad said.

He knew that among all the Republicans she disliked (and she definitely disliked all of them) Senator Taft was the most detested. "Harry, are you going to run?" she asked.

"I don't know, Mamma," Dad replied.

"Don't you think it's about time you made up your mind?" she asked.

Bess demonstrated what she was thinking by deciding to invite the Wallace family to join us for Christmas in the White House, instead of going home. She thought it might be the next to last Christmas of the Truman presidency, and she wanted her family to enjoy the White House without a smog of defeat dampening everyone's spirits. Fred and Chris and their two children, Uncle George and Aunt May, and Uncle Frank and Aunt Natalie joined us for a very pleasant holiday.

Early in 1948, Bess wrote to Nellie Noland, Ethel's sister, that "it just didn't seem right, not to go home for the holidays, but after all the family arrived it didn't seem to make any difference." It was another glimpse of the intensity of her feelings for the Wallace family. No matter where they were geographically, when they were together Mother felt at home.

It was partly to make Mother feel more at home in the White House that Dad got involved in a pitched battle with Congress and the press in these first months of 1948. One of the chief pleasures of 219 North Delaware Street were its porches, particularly the back porches, where the family whiled away more than one summer afternoon or evening, secure from prying eyes. With the Truman partnership running smoothly again, Dad hoped Mother would spend more of her summers in Washington. He decided the White House ought to have a back porch and soon found the perfect place for it— on the second floor, behind the six columns of the south portico.

You would have thought he had just announced he was going to replace the White House with a lean-to or a split-level bungalow, to hear the howls from Congress and the press. Representative Frederick A. Muhlenberg, a Pennsylvania Republican who claimed he was the only architect in Congress, declared the porch was "illegal" as well as aesthetically wrong. *The Washington Post* accused Dad of "meddling" with a building that did not belong to him. The Fine Arts Commission, composed exclusively of what Dad called "high-hats," intoned that the porch would "permanently change the appearance of the south facade."

Dad ignored them and hired William Adams Delano, a former chairman of the Fine Arts Commission, to design the porch. Mr. Delano approved the idea heartily, which silenced the Fine Arts Commission. He agreed with Dad's contention that the porch was a major improvement that was needed to complete the White House's design, as well as to give the presidential family a place to relax outdoors in warm weather without 20,000 people staring at them.

As Dad explained it, the porch "broke the skinny perpendicular lines" of those portico columns. It also eliminated the need for seven ugly awnings that jutted between the columns during the summer to keep the sun out of the Blue Room on the first floor.

All these arguments made very good sense, and every presidential family since the Truman days has used—and praised—the porch. But no one, as far as I know, has connected its creation to 219 North Delaware Street.

Meanwhile, serious politics and incessant first ladying remained the order of the day. The major battle on the presidential front was persuading the Republican Congress to vote for the North Atlantic Treaty Organization. By this time the cold war had begun in earnest. Russia, as Dad wrote in a letter to Bess, "has at last shown her hand, and it contains the cards [Secretary of State] Marshall and I thought it would." Few sensible Americans could think otherwise, after the Communist coup that seized Czechoslovakia at the end of February 1948.

This turning point in Soviet-American relations put President Truman under terrific strain. Bess again became alarmed at his exhaustion and insisted on another vacation at Key West. He went down there at the end of February 1948. The international situation did not improve and he began to think we might be at war with Russia in thirty days. He told me this in a long, hair-raising letter on March 3. Whenever war threatened, Dad thought of its impact on my generation of Americans, who would have to fight it. He felt a need to explain to me how hard he had tried to avoid it.

In this letter, he went all the way back to his Senate career and his achievements there, which led to the vice-presidential nomination. Then he turned to the years of his presidency.

Well the catastrophe we all dreaded came on April 12 at 4:35 P.M. At 7:09 I was the President. . . . Then I had to start in reading memorandums, briefs, and volumes of correspondence on the World situation. Too bad I hadn't been on the Foreign Affairs Committee or that F.D.R. hadn't informed me on the situation. I had to find out about the Atlantic Charter, which by the way does not exist on paper, the Casablanca meeting, the Montreal meeting, Teheran meeting, "Yalta" . . . and other things too numerous to mention. . . .
        Then came Potsdam. . . . I felt that agreements made in the war to keep Russia fighting should be kept and I kept them to the letter. Perhaps they should not have been adhered to so quickly because later I found the only

way to make Russia keep agreements. I did not know that then. Perhaps if we had been slower moving back [our troops] we could have forced the Russians, Poles, Bulgars, Yugos etc to behave. But all of us wanted Russia in the Japanese War. Had we known what the Atomic Bomb would do we'd never have wanted the Bear in the picture. You must remember no tests had been made until several days after I arrived in Berlin.

Adm. Leahy told me that he was an explosives expert and Roosevelt had just thrown $2,600,000,000 away for nothing. He was wrong. But his guess was as good as any. Byrnes thought it might work but he wasn't sure. He thought if it did we would win the Japanese War without much more losses but we still needed the Russians. . . . We entered into agreements for the Government of Germany—not one of which has Russia kept. We made agreements on China, Korea and other places, none of which has Russia kept. So that now we are faced with exactly the same situation with which Britain + France were faced in 1938/9 with Hitler. A totalitarian state is no different whether you call it Nazi, Fascist, Communist or Franco Spain.

Things look black. We've offered control and disarmament through the U.N. giving up our one most powerful weapon for the world to control. The Soviets won't agree. They're upsetting things in Korea, in China, in Persia (Iran) and in the Near East.

A decision will have to be made. I am going to make it. . . . I just wanted you to know your dad as President asked for no territory, no reparations, no slave laborers—only Peace in the World. We may have to fight for it. The oligarchy in Russia is no different from the Czars, Louis XIV, Napoleon, Charles I and Cromwell. It is a Frankenstein dictatorship worse than any of the others, Hitler included.

I hope it will end in peace.

In his letters to Mother while on this vacation, Dad concentrated on domestic matters. She was well briefed on the international situation, thanks to her nightly conferences with the number one expert on it, the President of the United States. In this letter he discussed his struggle to reach the American people to counter the misrepresentation of his efforts for peace by left-wing Democrats and right-wing Republicans.

The weather here is ideal. It is hell to have to go back to slavery and the lickings that I'll have to face from now on. But it must be done.

The meeting with Gov. Cox [newspaper publisher James A. Cox] the other day is bearing fruit. I sent Clifford [Clark Clifford, White House counsel] to Miami yesterday to meet with Cox and his five managing editors. He has a paper in Miami, one in Atlanta, one in Dayton and two in Springfield Ohio. Clark said that the Governor was enthusiastic over his meeting with me and that he is working out a plan to support the Democratic program as set out by me as President. So that time is not wasted. Whenever I can meet these people and tell them personally what I'm trying to do they always come in to camp, because I'm only trying to do what's best for the country and to obtain a just peace in the world. It's very discouraging however when your best efforts are misrepresented and distorted by deliberate lies—and by people who surprise by their maliciousness. . . .

I sent Margie a fat historical letter for her future use.

Dad returned from Key West to give another historic speech before Congress, calling for a renewal of the draft and swift passage of the money for the Marshall Plan. He urged Congress to support the treaty of alliance recently signed by the nations of Western Europe— the first step to NATO—and condemned the Soviet Union for having "destroyed the independence and democratic character of a whole series of nations in Eastern and Central Europe." He bluntly accused them of planning to export the same brand of tyranny to the rest of Europe.

It seems strange, now, with our old friend hindsight smiling beside us, that Americans could not recognize Harry Truman as the man who was rallying the free world at a crucial turning point in history. But the very people who were supposed to care about that sort of thing, the Democratic Party's liberals, the supposed heirs of that destroyer of isolationism, Franklin D. Roosevelt, were a lot more worried about losing the election to the Republicans. Personifying this desertion of the President were FDR's sons, Elliott and Franklin D. Roosevelt Jr., who issued statements urging the Democrats to draft General Eisenhower.

For Mother those first six months of 1948 were not all politics. I had sort of returned to the fold and was having severe doubts about my singing career. My first concert tour had been a financial success, but I had begun to question the kind of coaching I was getting and the direction in which I was being steered by my advisers. While I mulled, Mother (with Dad's collaboration) lured me back into the presidential orbit. Mother tempted me with invitations that few twenty-four-year-olds could resist, such as a chance to go to the Mardi Gras in New Orleans and, incidentally, to christen a Mississippi River tugboat named after Dad.

We traveled to the Queen City of the South by train. I marveled at the way Mother was so agreeable about getting off at every city on

our route to greet reporters and photographers and delegations of
women who filled our arms with flowers. Atlanta, Montgomery,
Mobile, Biloxi, we smiled through them all. It only dawned on me
as we got to New Orleans that my supposedly nonpolitical Mother
was *campaigning*. And Harry Truman had not yet even announced he
was going to run for a second term!

That announcement came a few months later, in a speech Dad
made to the Young Democrats Dinner at the Mayflower Hotel. With
Mother and me sitting in the audience, Dad condemned the liberal
"calamity howlers" who were wailing that Truman could not win. "I
want to say to you that for the next four years there will be a Democrat in the White House and you are looking at him."

Mother was pessimistic about his chances. Not once throughout
the spring or summer of 1948, or even in the fall when the campaign
was picking up steam, did I hear her express any confidence in Harry
Truman's reelection. When I or anyone else among the tiny band of
true believers told Dad he was going to win in spite of the polls or the
newspapers or the empty campaign chest, Mother remained silent.

India Edwards, the Democratic National Committeewoman, had
breakfast with Dad and Mother in the fall. India had remained
staunchly behind the Truman candidacy, ignoring the panicky liberals. "India," Dad said in his teasing way, "sometimes I think there are
only two people in the whole United States who really believe I am
going to be elected. But the Boss here is not one of them."

That negative opinion did not stop Bess from rooting fiercely for
the candidate—and working long hours on his behalf. That spring of
1948 was the most exhausting time Bess spent in the White House. A
glance at her schedule would daunt an Olympic decathlon winner.
Take April 13, for instance. That day four separate groups of women
came to the White House, and Bess literally shook hands from morning until night.

Early in May, one of the White House women reporters noted
Bess's awesome pace. "After shaking hands with 1,800 guests Tuesday
afternoon, Mrs. Truman began another two weeks of luncheons,
teas, receptions," she wrote. There was the picnic for the Senate
Ladies' Luncheon Club and a reception for the members of the
American Law Institute and a garden party for veterans in Washington hospitals and a luncheon given by the B'nai B'rith and a reception for the National League of American Pen Women. The topper
was a reception on May 4 for 3,000 government women.

On May 12, Mother walked into my bedroom with an almost berserk smile on her face. "I can't believe it," she said. "Tomorrow there's absolutely nothing on my calendar. Let's celebrate."

We went to lunch with Mrs. Davis, our neighbor at 4701 Connecticut Avenue in 1945. We had a marvelous gab fest, of which not a single word was political. "Now what would you like to do?" I asked.

"Go for a ride in the convertible," Bess said. The Secret Service men were aghast at the idea of the First Lady and First Daughter in an open car, as Mother knew they would be. But they learned to keep their alarums to themselves most of the time. So we cruised around Washington in the May sunshine, with three or four agents gnawing their fingernails in a car behind us. "Go slow so I can window-shop," Mother said. The driver obeyed, and we had a wonderful time.

While Bess toiled on the social front, President Truman was not exactly idle on the political front. In Germany, the Russians were becoming more and more nasty about permitting the western Allies access to the city of Berlin. A blockade was in the making and with it the threat of war.

In Washington, the Eightieth Congress was heading for adjournment, having contemptuously refused to pass a single piece of legislation Harry Truman had submitted to them. The liberals were still trying to draft Eisenhower, and Henry Wallace had announced that he was going to run for president as the candidate of the Progressive Party. The southern Democrats were in virtual revolt because the President had ordered the end of racial segregation in the armed forces.

What to do? There was only one alternative, as Harry Truman saw it. He had to take his case to the people. He decided to do it before the Democratic National Convention, to silence the calamity howlers by showing them there was broad popular support for his record as president. He told Bess that he wanted her and me to come with him on a "nonpartisan" trip across the country to inspect such government properties as the Grand Coulee Dam and to deliver a commencement address at the University of California.

There was not a word of protest from Bess, in spite of the fact that Grandmother Wallace was seriously ill. Her heart was beginning to fail, and that caused severe swelling in her legs, which forced her to stay in bed. In other years, such an illness would have prompted Bess to cancel every social and political obligation in sight. Instead, she took Grandmother home to Independence and persuaded me to join them there. A week later, on June 6, 1948, Mother and I boarded the seventeen-car presidential train in Omaha.

By that time Dad had made a few stops in Ohio and Indiana, where his remarks about the Eightieth Congress and their betrayal of the farmer and the workingman were not exactly nonpartisan. In Omaha it was more of the same, and he laid it on with ever more scorching language as we rolled through Wyoming and Idaho and Montana into Washington. There, Dad's old Senate friend, Governor Mon Wallgren, made a crucial contribution to the Truman campaign style. He began introducing Mother and me at every stop. People seemed to like it, even though we did nothing but smile and wave.

Next, Senator Robert Taft, the dour leader of the Senate Republicans, made another contribution to Trumanology. In a speech in Philadelphia he accused Harry Truman of "blackguarding Congress at every whistle station in the West."

J. Howard McGrath, the chairman of the Democratic National Committee, promptly telegraphed the mayors of thirty-five cities and towns that we had visited, asking them how they liked being called whistle-stops. Dad, with the same instinct that prompted the Americans of 1776 to make that condescending British tune "Yankee Doodle" into a song of defiance, began talking about his whistle-stop campaign.

In Seattle and Los Angeles, which are somewhat above whistle-stop status, we Truman loyalists got a look at the depth of the President's support. The sidewalks were jammed with cheering people as we rode through these cities. The Los Angeles crowd was well over a million. Dad gave rousing speeches in both places. That warm-up tour, which many people have forgotten, convinced most of the White House staff that Harry Truman could win in November, no matter what the polls said.

The success of this first campaign trip is reflected in the sunny letter Dad wrote Mother on their twenty-ninth wedding anniversary.

Twenty-nine years! It seems like twenty-nine days.

Detroit, Port Huron, a farm sale, the Blackstone Hotel, a shirt store, County Judge, a defeat, Margie, Automobile Club membership drive, Presiding Judge, Senator, V.P., now!

You still are on the pedestal where I placed you that day in Sunday school in 1890. What an old fool I am.

Touched as she undoubtedly was by this letter, Mother remained a doubter about Dad's chances for reelection. This opinion did not imply any criticism of his performance as president. It was just her pessimism at work. She kept her opinion to herself and, as we have seen, worked her head off to help him win.

The same do or die spirit was not shared by large sections of the Democratic Party. Both parties had chosen Philadelphia for their nominating conventions. The Republicans were meeting first. So dispirited was the Democratic National Committee, they humbly asked the GOP if they would leave up their flags and bunting so the Democrats could save the cost of putting up fresh decorations. Apparently they were hoarding their cash for the 1952 campaign.

The Republicans convened in Philadelphia on June 21, 1948, and they could not have been more arrogant. The nominated Thomas E. Dewey for president and Earl Warren for vice president and talked as if they were already in the White House. Clare Booth Luce said President Truman was "a gone goose," and threw in a comment on Bess that drove Dad up the wall. She called her an "ersatz First Lady."

In the White House, we were momentarily distracted from these political slings and arrows by an awful personal tragedy. One of my frequent escorts during the first three White House years had been a tall, handsome ex-naval officer named Bobby Stewart. I was half in love with him and so was my friend Drucie Snyder, Secretary of the Treasury Snyder's daughter. Bobby dated her as often as he dated me. We had met Bobby and his parents, Louise and Earl Stewart, through the Snyders.

As brilliant as he was good-looking, Bobby had been raised in Paris and spoke fluent French and a half dozen other languages. His father was an international businessman, his mother was a tiny red-haired woman from Indiana with a fey sense of humor. Bobby was her only son and the center of her universe. On June 17, Bobby was flying from Denver to New York for Louise's birthday. The airliner hit a transformer outside the Pittsburgh airport and crashed, killing everyone on board.

Drucie and I were devastated. Mother was almost as upset. To use an old-fashioned phrase, her heart went out to Louise Stewart. With everything Dad had on his mind, she prevailed on him to join us for the funeral ceremony at Arlington National Cemetery. It was one of the hottest days in the history of Washington, D.C. We sat in the little chapel and listened to Louise sob. There was nothing left of Bobby but his arm, which was in a small coffin on the altar.

Ten days later, on June 27, 1948, Dad sent the bereaved parents a long letter. "I was very fond of Bobby," he wrote. "I think he had a great future. It is my hope that you will make Bobby's spirit realize that future. I believe you can do it." He suggested that each year they pick out a boy and a girl in Anderson, Indiana, Louise's hometown, and Columbia, Missouri, Earl Stewart's hometown, and give them enough money to get them through high school. "In a four year course you would be supporting sixteen young men and young women for a fundamental education—much more important to the young people than college. You would only take those who could not afford the cost of going to high school. . . .

"You'd make Bobby immortal! You'd have the greatest life interest in the world looking after these young people—and I'm sure God Almighty would be pleased."

This is from a man who was only ten days away from going to Philadelphia to confront a hostile, divided Democratic Convention. He was struggling to hold the party together, raise money for the campaign, and to keep the Russians out of Berlin. Although Harry Truman wrote this letter, I am absolutely certain that its real author was Bess. Throughout these politically frantic weeks, she sent flowers, wrote letters, and paid visits to Louise Stewart, trying to help her deal with her grief.

Months later, on a voyage to France, Louise Stewart wrote to Bess: "I appreciate with all my heart your many many wonderful kindnesses to me. I guess that it is really what keeps me going most of the time. I keep trying to pick up the pieces of my life but often it seems quite hopeless. But neither you or Bobby expect me to fall down on my face and so I'll keep trying, but without you I don't think that I'd make it. . . ."

Shortly after Dad wrote that letter to the Stewarts, Mother and I rushed to Independence. Grandmother Wallace was gravely ill. From the White House, Dad wrote Mother a dramatic letter on the eve of the convention. The situation was one enormous, confusing stew. The southerners and the liberals were at each other's throats. Everyone in the world was giving the President advice.

I've been trying to write you ever since arrival here but just now succeeded in getting it done. I've had only one walk, that yesterday morning for twenty minutes and no swim at all.

Went over the platform again at 4:00 P.M., came back to the [White]

House at seven, had a big dinner and went to bed at eight-thirty. Never been as tired and groggy in my life. . . .

Yesterday was most hectic. Matt [Connelly] kept running in people to talk to me—people I didn't want to see. These birds around me have all turned politicians and precinct captains—and they know nothing about it.

Finished the outline for the platform and sent it to Philly . . . and had Fred Vinson to dinner. He stayed until 11:30 P.M. talking about everything.

I still don't know what our program is. Biffle [Leslie Biffle, Secretary of the Senate] called and said he had a suite for you and Margie at the Drake. Evidently they expect you to come to the convention Tuesday or Wednesday. I don't know which. I'm supposed to go there Wednesday or Thursday. Maybe I can tell you what we are supposed to do Sunday on the phone. I don't know now. It's worse than Chicago if that's possible. I wish I'd stayed on the farm and never gone to war in the first place!

He could write that last line to Bess now because he knew that she was on his side, in spite of the pain his confrontations with history had caused her.

Chapter Twenty-three

Bess and I joined Dad in the White House a few days before the convention began on July 12, 1948. For the first three days we watched the proceedings on television, an historic first for both the President and the American people. (Dad instantly foresaw what it meant for the President: "No privacy anywhere," he wrote in his diary.) The convention was not very cheerful viewing. The liberals introduced a civil rights plank that won after a floor fight, and most of the southerners walked out to nominate their own candidate, Governor Strom Thurmond of South Carolina.

I have always liked the reason Mr. Thurmond gave for bolting the Democratic Party in 1948. A reporter pointed out to him that he had not objected when Franklin D. Roosevelt had run on a platform replete with the same promises of justice and equal opportunity for America's black citizens.

"But Truman really means it," Thurmond said.

Rumors swirled around various alternate candidates, from Eisenhower to Claude Pepper to Alben Barkley. Dad remained perfectly calm and in close touch with what was really happening. On the evening of July 14, we went up to Philadelphia by train and watched the end of the wrangling in the almost airless Convention Hall. It took most of the night for them to get through nominating Harry Truman for president and Alben Barkley for vice president. Not until 2 A.M. did Dad make his acceptance speech to the exhausted delegates.

He gave a speech that shocked those bedraggled Democrats awake, as if they had all been wired to a dynamo—which, metaphorically, they were. "Senator Barkley and I will win this election and make those Republicans like it—don't you forget that!" he began. "We will do that because they are wrong and we are right."

He recalled what the Democratic Party had done for the farmer and the workingman in the past sixteen years. It had given them social security, rural electrification, crop price supports, unemployment insurance. If the farmers and labor "don't do their duty by the Democratic Party they are the most ungrateful people in the world!" He castigated the Eightieth Congress for all the things that had not been done to control inflation, clear slums, fund better schools and social welfare programs. Then he unleashed a lightning bolt.

On the 26th Day of July, which out in Missouri we call Turnip Day, I am going to call Congress back and ask them to pass laws to halt rising prices, to meet the housing crisis—which they are saying they are for, in their platform.

At the same time I shall ask them to act upon other vitally needed measures. . . .

Now, my friends, if there is any reality behind that Republican platform, we ought to get some action from a short session of the Eightieth Congress. They can do this job in fifteen days, if they want to do it. They will still have time to go out and run for office. . . .

Pandemonium was the only word to describe the Convention Hall. For two solid minutes, those previously dispirited Democrats stood up on their chairs and roared their enthusiasm for Harry S. Truman. Beside me, Mother was chuckling delightedly. She was one of the few people in Philadelphia who knew all about Turnip Day. A year before, you will recall, Dad had written her a letter on July 26, noting that it was Turnip Day—and Nellie Noland's birthday.

Mother and I went home to Missouri after the convention to be with Grandmother Wallace, who had had another sinking spell. Mother proceeded to con me into painting the kitchen and pantry. She told me I would enjoy it. She loved to paint and redecorate that old house as much as her mother did. I enjoyed it too for about three days. But with Mother as foreman, it turned into a lifetime job. One coat, two coats, were not enough. I was still painting in mid-August.

Meanwhile, the President was grappling with a major crisis in Europe. After months of threat and bluster, the Russians had clamped a total blockade on Berlin. Dad responded with a massive airlift that kept the city alive without resort to shooting our way through on the ground. The situation remained very tense, and the Secretary of the Army did not help matters by abruptly calling General Lucius Clay, the American commander in Germany, home for consultations. Dad wrote Mother that Clay's return had stirred up a "terrific how-dy-do for no good reason. Marshall [Secretary of State]

and I had decided it was not necessary for him to come and so told
Forrestal [Secretary of Defense]—but you know how smart that Defense setup thinks it is."

Next, Secretary Forrestal intensified the "how-dy-do" by suggesting to the President that he turn over our atomic bomb arsenal to the
army to use when they saw fit. "Wouldn't that be a nice peace gesture?" Dad wryly asked Mother.

He was happy to report that in spite of appearances to the contrary,
"it looks like the Russkies are going to come in without a fight." If
this happened and the situation in the Middle East also calmed down.
"Things will be in such shape in foreign affairs that we can go to
work in earnest on that bunch of 'Hypercrits' known as Republicans.

"They sure are in a stew and mad as wet hens. If I can make them
madder, maybe they'll do the job the old gods used to put on the
Greeks and Romans."

Those last two sentences reveal the secret reason for the Turnip
Day session, a strategy that Dad had obviously shared with Mother.
By this time, she was enjoying the campaign. Deep in her woman's
heart, Mother loved a good fight. She kept this combative side of
herself carefully concealed, but it was the secret of her success as a
tennis and basketball player in her youth.

Her enthusiasm for the contest with Congress was so strong, she
sent Dad a telegram of congratulations (which she persuaded me to
sign with her) on the message he sent to the Turnip Day session when
they gathered in muggy Washington, D.C., on July 26. I can see now
that Bess was doing everything she could to keep her man's morale
high.

Dad responded with a letter to me, which he knew Mother would
also see.

I was highly pleased to get . . . the telegram from you and your mother
about the message to Congress.

You seem to have been slaving away at your paint job and your garden. I
am hoping to see an excellent result in each instance. . . .

I am somewhat exhausted myself getting ready for this terrible Congress.
They are in the most turmoil any Congress I can remember ever has been.
Some of them want to quit right away, some of them want to give the
Dixiecrats a chance to filibuster and the Majority are very anxious to put the
Pres. in the hole if they can manage it.

It will take a few days for the message to sink in completely.

In the meantime I shall take it easy and let 'em sweat.

On September 11, from the *Williamsburg*, Dad told Mother how the first part of the campaign was shaping up. "Farm speech at Des Moines on Sept. 18, conservation at Denver on the 20th, reclamation at Salt Lake City on the 21st. . . . Then San Francisco, L.A. San Diego, Arizona, Texas, Oklahoma, Ky. West Va and Washington D.C. Seems like a nice little trip—what?"

Before we launched that expedition, there was a trip to Detroit to speak to an immense Labor Day rally. Mother did not go with us. She went out to Denver to act as honorary godmother at the christening of Fred Wallace's third child, Charlotte Margaret. She had to get special permission from the Archbishop of Denver to participate in the ceremony. (Chris Wallace was a Catholic and Freddy had become a convert.) It was one more illustration of her intense involvement in her youngest brother's life.

I acted as hostess on the train to Detroit and got a preview of what the "nice little trip" was going to be like. We were up at 6:15 A.M., and Dad made six speeches, including the major address to 200,000 roaring workers in Detroit. He joked with Mother about it in a letter a few days later, admitting that "six speeches on Monday was rather strenuous." He added that he had told the reporters that this was "only a sample of what they'd get on the western trip."

That sums up better than several dozen paragraphs from me the pace of the Truman whistle-stop campaign of 1948. Mother joined us in Des Moines, and we rumbled across the American continent with the candidate speaking from 6 A.M. in the morning until midnight on some days. The routine at each stop soon became as polished as a vaudeville act. First Dad emerged on the observation platform of the last car and got an ovation. The local politicians would greet him and he would give a brief speech. Then he introduced Mother as "the Boss" and me as "the one who bosses the Boss."

Sometime during the first week, I noticed that Mother was not exactly enthused by this introduction. I sensed that she did not like the suggestion that she let me push her around, the possible implication that I was a spoiled brat, which reflected on her standing as an American mother. Seeking to head off an explosion, I approached Dad and said, very confidentially: "You know, I don't think Mother really likes you calling me her boss."

Dad thought about it for a second, obviously calculating risks and advantages. "It gets a good laugh," he said.

I remained the Boss's boss.

The high point of that first postconvention swing was our visit to the home of former Vice President John Nance Garner in the little town of Uvalde, Texas. We arrived at 5 A.M. on Sunday, October 26. That did not bother Dad, of course. He thought that was the hour when every right thinking, right living American should get up. The rest of us were practically comatose.

Fortunately the citizens of Uvalde kept the same farmers' hours. Some 4,000 of them whooped and howled into the rising sun at the depot, with the seventy-nine-year-old Mr. Garner leading the cheers. They presented Dad with an angora goat wearing a gold blanket with red lettering which read: "Dewey's Goat." Dad loved it. After posing for pictures with the frisky creature, Dad announced: "I'm going to clip it and make a rug. Then I'm going to let it graze on the White House lawn for the next four years."

We then sat down to the most awesome breakfast I have ever seen or tried to eat. There was white-wing dove and mourning dove, bacon, ham, fried chicken, scrambled eggs, hot biscuits, Uvalde honey, peach preserves, and gallons of coffee. As we finished this feast, Dad gave Cactus Jack a small black satchel. He said it contained "medicine, only to be used in case of snakebites." It was the same high quality Kentucky bourbon the Vice President used to invite Senator Truman to share when he visited Mr. Garner's office in his Senate days.

Outside his house, Mr. Garner described Dad as an "old and very good friend." Those words guaranteed Harry Truman the votes of the numerous Texas conservatives, who regarded Mr. Garner with almost reverential affection. After all, he had walked out on Franklin D. Roosevelt rather than support him for a third term. Dad responded by calling Cactus Jack "Mr. President." That was what he used to call him in the Senate. Whereupon Mother astonished everyone by breaking her rule of silence and making her only speech of the campaign. "Good morning," she said, "and thank you for this wonderful greeting."

We got back to Washington from that first trip with (according to Dad's count) 140 stops and 147 speeches behind us. Edith Helm, the White House social secretary, informed Mrs. Truman that the capital's hostesses and diplomats and social climbers were in a dither because she had not yet announced a schedule of formal dinners and receptions. Mother let them dither. She issued a statement that the President was too busy campaigning to discuss the subject with him.

There was another reason for this delay, which Mother wisely declined to mention. The White House was in danger of collapsing. She and Dad had been worried about it for more than a year. Their alarm began when Dad noticed how the floor in his upstairs oval office shook when the color guard stamped across it to bring the colors downstairs to begin an official reception. He ordered an inspection that reported various ceilings, including the one in the State Dining Room, were staying up only from force of habit. Nothing but a few rusty nails were supporting them.

For most of 1948, we lived with a forest of steel pipes in our bedrooms and sitting rooms. They were supposed to hold up the ceilings, but they could do nothing about the rot that was destroying the old timber. In the summer of 1948, one leg of my piano broke through the floor. Next the engineers reported that Dad's bathroom was in danger of falling into the Red Room, and they were worried about the stability of his bedroom, too. They moved him into Lincoln's bedroom.

Can you imagine what the press would have done with this story during the 1948 campaign? The whole mess would have been blamed on Harry Truman. The White House would have become a metaphor for his collapsing administration. Mother's decision to say nothing about it and take the heat for the lack of a formal social season was one of her major, hitherto unknown contributions to Dad's fight to become president in his own right.

This did not mean the First Lady was escaping her handshaking chores. We were barely off the train on October 16 when Mother gave a tea for 150 members of the Democratic National Committee. I particularly remember the night Dad gave a radio speech denouncing the Eightieth Congress's antilabor bill, the Taft Hartley Act, which they had passed over his veto. Mother had been standing up all afternoon, shaking hands with hundreds of members of the Colonial Dames of America. As we started downstairs to watch him speak, I thought she looked terribly tired and suggested we use the elevator.

We could not get the thing started. The elevator, in keeping with the decrepit condition of the rest of the White House, would only go down if you took the button off, stuck a pencil in the hole and gave it a twist. That night I had to give it about a dozen twists to get it going. If Mother had not been standing beside me I would have used some very unladylike language. She barely noticed my agitation. Her mind was on the speech that Dad was about to give. By this time, all of her, heart and soul, body and mind, was in the fight.

A few days later, we rumbled out of Washington for the final whistle-stop campaign. The number of people who came down to see us off was not encouraging. As far as Washington, D.C. was concerned, Harry Truman was still a loser. Hadn't fifty leading journalists predicted in *Newsweek* magazine that he was going to get beaten so badly, the Democratic Party might disappear? Mother glowered at the tiny band of mostly White House staffers who were waving goodbye. It was not a presidential sendoff. "Evalyn Walsh McLean tells me that all everybody talks about is who's going to be in Dewey's cabinet," she said.

Once more the candidate proceeded to wear out everyone but himself and the people who came to hear him. In the Midwest, even in New England—where Harvard sophisticates supposedly scorned Farmer Truman—the crowds kept getting bigger and more enthusiastic. The pollsters and pundits paid no attention to this phenomenon. Their charts and numbers still kept telling them it was a Republican year.

Somewhere in the vicinity of Lima, Ohio, Mother told the candidate that if he called her the Boss once more, she might get off the train. That was her way of killing off the Boss's boss part of the act. Dad surrendered. By that time he was getting tired of it too.

On the train, Mother spent most of her time with Dad. She let the staff take care of greeting the numerous politicians who got on and off at various stops as we crossed state lines. She felt it was more important to keep her eye on the President, to make sure he did not go over the edge into total exhaustion. She also functioned as a quiet cheering section and subtle critic, telling him how she thought the latest speech had gone over and suggesting small ways to improve the routine.

Often she played mother to other members of the staff, who were working unto exhaustion just like the President. As we approached San Francisco, assistant White House counsel George Elsey came into the car with a speech that Dad was supposed to make in about two hours. He had not yet had time to go over it. We were having dinner, and George was very apologetic about interrupting us. But he was also more than a little frantic. "Mr. President, you've really got to read this as soon as possible, in case you want any changes—" he began.

"George," Mother said. "You look frazzled. Have you had any dinner?"

George shook his head.

"Eat this," Mother said, pushing her dessert, a piece of apple pie, across the table to him.

George ate apple pie for his dinner while Dad read the speech.

One of the nicest developments of the campaign from Mother's point of view was Mrs. Roosevelt's emergence as a Truman backer. Although Dad had appointed her to the U.S. delegation to the UN, where she became chairman of the Commission on Human Rights, she had been conspicuously silent throughout the draft-Eisenhower campaign launched by her sons. But when she saw and heard Dad's fighting campaign, she changed her mind and made a six-minute pro-Truman speech by radio from Paris.

Eleanor Roosevelt also tried to persuade her sons to return to the Democratic Party. However, to her considerable exasperation, they declined. Mother had nothing to do with Mrs. Roosevelt's change of mind. But she felt her endorsement was an implicit approval of her first ladyship, even though it was so different from Mrs. Roosevelt's approach to the job.

St. Louis was the climax of our whistle-stop career. Dad let his staff toil over a speech that was, in many respects, a masterpiece. But by this time, he had acquired so much confidence in his ability to speak extemporaneously from a set of notes that he threw it aside and went after the Republicans and their bland candidate the way he once tackled unruly hogs in his mother's barnyard.

Of all the fake campaigns, this one is the tops so far as the Republican candidate for President is concerned. He has been following me up and down this country making speeches about home, mother, unity and efficiency. . . . He won't talk about the issues, but he did let his foot slip when he endorsed the Eightieth Congress.

I have been all over these United States from one end to another, and when I started out the song was—well, you can't win, the Democrats can't win. Ninety percent of the press is against us, but that didn't discourage me one little bit. You know, I had four campaigns here in the great state of Missouri, and I never had a metropolitan paper for me the whole time. And I licked them every time!

People are waking up to the fact that this is their government and that they can control their government if they get out and vote on election day. That is all they need to do. . . . People are waking up, that the tide is beginning to roll, and I am here to tell you that if you do your duty as citizens of the greatest Republic the sun has ever shone on, we will have a government that will be for your interests, that will be for peace in the world, and for the welfare of all the people, and not just a few.

A reporter for *The Washington Post* said that if Harry Truman won by a whisker, he would give the credit to his performance that night in St. Louis.

Our hegira ended at 7:25 P.M., October 31, 1948, when our train clanked into the Missouri Pacific Railroad depot in Independence. "It's grand to be home," Dad told the crowd that welcomed us. It was a sentiment that Mother (and I) heartily endorsed. We had traveled 31,700 miles, and the candidate had made 356 speeches to a rough total of 15 million people. At 219 North Delaware Street, Mother did exactly what any woman would do after spending the previous two weeks riding the rails. She made sure she had an appointment at her hairdresser's the next morning for a wash and set.

The next evening, Bess demonstrated how much she wanted Harry Truman to win this election. She agreed to allow twenty reporters and at least as many technicians to invade 219 North Delaware while Dad made a radio address to the nation from the living room. She even let a photographer take a picture of him, as he again appealed to the American people to take charge of their own government and to ignore what the pollsters and the press were telling them.

The next day, after we all voted at 10 A.M., Dad went into his usual election day routine. He calmly announced that he was sure that he was going to win, and if he was wrong, it was too late to worry about it. Whereupon he disappeared. Mother and I were left to cope with the reporters, who grew really frantic that evening when Harry Truman leaped into the lead by a million votes and stayed there, far ahead of Republican Dewey, Progressive Wallace, and the Dixiecrat candidate, Strom Thurmond. By this time, Dad was sound asleep in a hotel in Excelsior Springs, about forty miles from Independence.

In the house, I, the true believer from the start of the campaign, was taking charge of things. I refused to let Mother or Grandmother turn on the radio, where that dedicated Truman hater, H. V. Kaltenborn, kept on saying that Dewey would pull ahead eventually. I spent most of my time on the phone to the Washington headquarters of the Democratic National Committee, where staffers such as Bill Boyle (soon to become chairman) were getting the count direct from precincts and districts in cities and states all over the country. I whooped out the latest good news while my doubting elders sat there, not quite able to believe it.

As the Truman lead became insurmountable, the reporters assaulted the house with a fervor unseen since D-Day. They established a beachhead on the porch, and Mother sent me out to deal with them. After five or ten minutes of sparring—I was getting pretty good at this sort of thing—I finally convinced them that Dad was not in the house.

Mother finally decided to imitate the candidate by going to bed. By this time, it was well past midnight and she was very tired. But as she said goodnight, a wicked smile crept across her face. "I wonder if Clare Booth Luce will think I'm real, now," she said.

What memories must have crowded her mind, as she waited for sleep, all the other elections, but above all the one in 1940, where Harry Truman's faith in himself and his destiny had carried him to victory. Tonight was the ultimate justification of that faith. I wonder if Mother grieved, just a little, for the times when her pessimism had made it difficult for her to share that faith. But the emotion was swiftly replaced by the pride, the pleasure, of winning this supreme triumph.

Mother was up early the next morning. She had her usual light breakfast and began examining the house, agreeing with Grandmother that the place needed a good cleaning. Suddenly this housewifely conversation was interrupted by a tremendous racket. Dewey had conceded defeat at 10:14 A.M. A few minutes later, every whistle and car horn in Independence started blowing, and they were soon joined by the air raid sirens. For a moment, Mother thought time had somehow unraveled, that she had gone back forty years and it was November 11, 1918, Armistice Day. But this time, Harry Truman was not just one of about 2 million victors being saluted. All that noise was for him and no one else.

Fogged out from lack of sleep, I was uptown when the uproar exploded. I wandered into a store and said: "What's all that noise about?" Fortunately the storekeeper was an old family friend. After answering my question, he suggested I go home and get some sleep. I should have taken his advice, but I didn't.

Refreshed from a good night's sleep, Dad was at the Muehlebach Hotel in Kansas City, where his staff had spent the night. He had been awakened in his Excelsior Springs hideaway at 4 A.M. by his excited Secret Service man, Jim Rowley, who could no longer resist telling him the good news. They turned on the radio and listened to H. V. Kaltenborn still predicting Truman's defeat, although he was 2 million votes ahead. The two of them laughed uproariously. Dad put on a natty blue suit, had a leisurely breakfast and drove to Kansas City at 6 A.M. He was the freshest man in a room full of glassy-eyed reporters and politicians when Dewey conceded.

Back in Independence, after the whistles and horns stopped blowing, the local politicians realized that they did not have even a shred of a plan to throw a victory party for their native son. They had gone along with the rest of the country's presumption of a Truman defeat. After some frantic telephone calls to 219 North Delaware Street and the Muehlebach Hotel, they announced that Dad and Mother and I would greet well-wishers that night in the Courthouse Square.

The well-wishers turned out to be a wild-eyed mob of 40,000 from all parts of Jackson County. Talk about disorganization! You've heard about those New York City traffic jams called gridlock. This was peoplelock. No one could move. Men climbed onto the roofs of cars, perched in trees. Parents hoisted children on their shoulders. The streets running into the square were packed solid with cheering Democrats. The local police were swamped. The Secret Service was in a panic. But Dad did not mind the pandemonium in the least. "Protocol goes out the window when I am in Independence," he said. Then he grew serious. "I thank you very much indeed for this celebration, which is not for me. It is for the whole country. It is for the whole world."

Mother and I stood beside him, smiling. For her, this explosion of admiration and affection from her friends and neighbors was tremendously satisfying.

The next morning, we headed back to Washington on our campaign train. I crawled into a berth and got the first real sleep I had encountered in forty-eight hours. So I have to rely on other eyewitnesses for what happened en route. Dad meant what he had told the celebrators in Independence. But humility did not preclude a little private crowing, especially over the red-faced pollsters and journalists. Mother was ahead of him in this department. She chortled when she heard that Drew Pearson had filed a column for the day after the election, analyzing "the closely knit group around Tom Dewey who will take over the White House eighty-six days from now." At St. Louis, someone brought onto the train a copy of the Chicago *Tribune*, with the headline, DEWEY DEFEATS TRUMAN. Bess thrust it into Harry Truman's hands and he held it up for a famous picture.

In Washington, D.C., a stupendous crowd met the train at Union

Station. It is a miracle that some people were not crushed to death. Mother looked out the window at the wildly smiling faces and frantically waving hands and turned to me. "Remember how many came down to see us off last month?" she said.

Victory was not going to make an optimist of her.

But she enjoyed every minute of that celebration in her adopted hometown. The Washington, D.C. police band played ruffles and flourishes and "Hail to the Chief," the presidential song, as we were escorted through the crowd to a seven-passenger open touring car. We rode through the streets with Dad and Vice President Barkley sitting on top of the back seat. Over 800,000 cheering people jammed the sidewalks while bands, official and impromptu, seemed to be playing "I'm Just Wild About Harry" on every corner.

I suddenly remembered something my tennis champion mother had said when Dad was nominated for vice president in Chicago. "It's nice to win," I yelled, above the din.

"You bet it is," Bess Wallace Truman said.

Chapter Twenty-four

Mother was still enjoying the victory the next morning, when Mr West, the assistant usher with whom she worked on the menus for official dinners, came into her office and congratulated her. She picked up a copy of a recent issue of *Time* with Dewey on the cover. "It looks like you're going to have to put up with us for another four years," she said.

But most of those four years, it soon became apparent, would not be spent at the White House. The engineers and architects who had been inspecting the mansion told Dad that the building was literally in danger of falling down on top of us. There was only one solution—we would have to move to Blair House, and the White House would have to be completely renovated.

Fortunately, we did not have to flee across the street like refugees. The victorious President had inveigled Mother and me into joining him and his crew at Key West for a well-earned vacation. We would move out of the Great White Jail, when we returned.

That Key West vacation was not only well-earned, it was badly needed. Bess was as exhausted as Dad and came down with an alarming cold and sore throat that all but prostrated her during our last two days in the White House. Dad was so upset, he could not sleep and kept appearing at her door at 3 and 4 A.M. to make sure she took her medicine.

A combination of sunshine and elation soon had the Trumans restored to what Dad liked to call "fighting trim." We had a good time at Key West on that first visit. Everybody was in a mood to clown, do impromptu jigs and laugh their heads off at almost anything. There is a wonderful picture of Mother in near convulsions over a wacky pre-inaugural costume parade staged by the White House staffers and correspondents.

That gives me a chance, here, to say something about Mother's laugh. It was a unique sound, which spilled out of the center of her body. Hearty would be an old-fashioned way of describing it. In this book I have inevitably spent a lot of time describing the serious side of Mother's life. But I want to go on record here about how much she loved a joke, and how often she laughed at the pomposity and pretentiousness and downright silliness that afflicts the human race.

Mother and I slept on the presidential yacht, *Williamsburg*, at Key West. We let the males inhabit the spartan quarters ashore and play poker and practical jokes on each other and drink whiskey to their wicked (as they liked to imagine themselves) hearts' content. As a dividend to this first visit for the two of us, Mother and I took a cruise to Cuba aboard the *Williamsburg*. Mother particularly enjoyed this look at another part of South America. We saw the Morro Castle, shopped on the Prado, and had champagne with Señora Prio, Cuba's First Lady, at the Presidential Palace. At no time during the visit did Mother use the Spanish she had studied during the first years at the White House. Fearing that a mistake would get into the newspapers, she made no attempt to let the Cubans know she had a good grasp of their language.

On the way home from Havana, we ran into the tail end of a hurricane, which made for a mighty rough voyage. Fortunately, I am immune to sea sickness and so was Mother. I guess I inherited it from her. Dad, on the other hand, was never happy at sea, although he did, by sheer willpower, master airsickness. A few days later, Mother had the President out on the still choppy ocean, on the stern of a fishing boat. She tartly reminded Dad that he had extravagantly praised the fishing at Key West and had yet to take her out for a troll. She took fiendish pleasure in inflicting this on him. She knew Harry Truman hated to fish. But on this and all subsequent visits to Key West, a fishing expedition became a fixture of the vacation.

We did not realize just how important this vacation was to Mother's health until we got back to Washington. Early in December, we journeyed to Norfolk, Virginia, to present a massive silver service to the battleship *Missouri* on behalf of our native state, which had paid for it. In the midst of the ceremony, which included a twenty-one-gun salute fired practically into our eardrums, Mother developed a severe nosebleed. Doctor Graham took her behind the scenes and tried to stop it by applying pressure, but that did not work. He finally had to cauterize the veins in her nose. Back in Washington, he immediately took Mother's blood pressure and discovered it was 190—alarmingly high. It was grim evidence of the strain she had been under during the campaign—and the previous three and one half years in the White House. Dr. Graham put her on medication and banned salt from her diet.

Meanwhile, we moved out of the White House into Blair House and took over its next-door twin, Lee House, in the bargain. Mother announced that the formal social season was canceled, and the secret of the collapsing White House was finally released to the press.

Now the big question was what to do about the tottering mansion. Should it be ripped down to the foundations and replaced by an entirely new building? Dad consulted Mother on this decision and found she emphatically agreed with his instinct that no matter how thoroughly the old building might have to be gutted, some of it should be preserved. Mother felt that there should be continuity as well as change in this symbol of the presidency. She pushed hard to keep at least the outer walls. The engineers scraped off the white plaster and found sturdy brick underneath it. They decided the walls could be saved.

It took several months to reach this decision. During the last month of 1948 and the first weeks of 1949, Bess was far more preoccupied by two other problems. Her mother again became seriously ill early in December. Grandmother was eighty-six at this point and Mother was so alarmed, she summoned Fred Wallace from Denver. His presence seemed to inspire Madge Gates Wallace to rally, and by the time we went home to Independence for Christmas, she was almost well again.

A few weeks later, Bess wrote to Mary Paxton Keeley, who was so fond of Grandmother: "We were afraid for a day or two [Mother] was not going to make it. But we got her back here [to Washington] by air and she seemed no worse for the trip. And she can have every attention here and be under my eye too. She has to be coerced into doing a lot of things."

The inauguration was not so easily solved. Mother had to buy an entire wardrobe for the various functions, and so did I. As usual, she insisted a Wallace family Christmas had first priority and did not get down to the business of choosing some of her dresses until we went back to Washington. To complicate matters, Agasta, her Washington couturier, seldom made evening dresses, so Mother chose Madame Pola of New York to create two of these. That required dashes to Gotham for fittings. Between these expeditions and moving into

Blair House, Agasta grew somewhat frantic. On January 12, 1949, with the inauguration only eight days away, she was still shopping for the right material!

That day, Agasta found a "lovely piece of raw silk" (she wrote) "that is very new." She was right about the silk. It was a fascinating mixture of iridescent black and gray. From it she made the two-piece gray-and-black outfit Mother wore to the inauguration ceremony. It had a straight skirt and a peplum jacket with which Mother wore a hat of moonstone straw cloth, trimmed with a single mauve-pink rose embedded in black tulle.

Agasta also created a very pretty short blue moire faille dinner dress, with the fullness gathered into folds at the side of the skirt and held with an enormous navy blue rose. Mother wore this dress to the dinner for Dad and Vice President Barkley. For her inaugural reception—with the White House closed, the reception was held at the National Gallery of Art—Madame Pola created a gown of pearl gray satin with silver lamé and a silver thread design in the shape of a feather. It was cut on princess lines, floor length, with a little train. The deep V-neck was outlined with cutouts of the feather motif. It often has been displayed at the Smithsonian.

I was fond of that dress, but I adored Mother's ball gown. It was made of black panne velvet cut on slender lines, the skirt draped to one side. It had a deep circular collar heavily encrusted with hand-drawn white Alençon lace. The collar fell gracefully over her shoulders, forming a lovely oval neckline. I have already used the word regal to describe Mother when she wore an evening dress. In that gown, the word had to be spelled with a capital "R."

The inauguration was a continuation of the victory celebration, as far as Mother was concerned. For the entire week, she did not give me a single order or cautionary warning, even though I practically ignored sleeping and eating. She bubbled with good humor and, as tireless as Dad, played hostess to droves of Wallace and Truman relatives and every real and imaginary VIP in Missouri. One thing that she particularly enjoyed was the tons of money the inaugural committee had to spend on the parade, the ball, the whole works. The Republican Congress, certain that Dewey was going to be elected, had voted $80,000 to guarantee a real bash. For a penny pincher like Mother, this was ecstasy indeed.

Another thing that pleased Mother was Dad's decision to make it the first integrated inauguration in our nation's history. Hotels and

restaurants were bluntly informed that if they attempted to bar anyone because of the color of his skin they would find themselves in
court about ten seconds later. It was the perfect answer to the insults
Congressman Adam Clayton Powell had flung at Bess in 1945.

At the same time, Mother's realism did not permit her to ignore
the serious side of the inaugural. As Dad raised his hand to take that
solemn oath on the steps of the Capitol, I glanced at Mother and saw
tears on her face. They were a mixture of joy and sadness. She still
rejoiced in Dad's victory, but she knew that the next four years were
not going to be easy.

As we settled into life at Blair-Lee House, Mother made the pleasant discovery that in the Turnip Day special session, Congress, again
presuming the next president would be Republican, had voted to
raise his salary from $50,000 to $100,000, and given him a $50,000
expense account. This eased some of the pressure on the Truman
budget. No longer did Mother have to worry about that thin $4,200
margin of error before the precipice of debt.

At the end of January, I went off to New York to resume my
singing career. Grandmother Wallace, who thought I had fallen out
of love with this idea, was very upset. She wept and said all sorts of
awful things about her granddaughter appearing on the stage.
Mother did not say a word against my decision—and behind the
scenes she did her best to calm her mother. In fact, as a show of
support, Mother parted with Reathel Odum, who by this time had
become an invaluable First Lady's aide. Reathel came to New York
with me as a companion—not a chaperone. I made it clear that I had
had enough minding to last me a lifetime. In New York, I began
studying under a new voice coach.

In Washington, Bess tackled the formidable problems of being
First Lady in Blair-Lee House. She decided to move some of the
choicer pieces of furniture from the executive mansion to give the
new quarters a White House flavor. She also had several doors cut
between the two buildings, which converted them into one house,
more or less.

The real problem was entertaining the Washington social horde,
which grew more numerous with every passing day. The maximum
number Blair House could handle for dinner was 18, for teas, 250.
This meant diplomatic dinners and receptions and all the other functions I listed on page 294 had to be done three and four times, instead
of just twice. When a foreign premier or president or king visited,

Bess decided they would give a state dinner at the nearby Carlton Hotel, using the White House staff and White House traditions of table decorations, and, of course, diplomatic protocol.

On the presidential side of things, in his inaugural address Dad had startled the world with his announcement of his Point Four program to share our scientific knowledge with underdeveloped countries. To sustain this outreach and continue his policy of peace through strength among the free nations, he chose a new Secretary of State, Dean Acheson. (Secretary Marshall had announced his intention to retire before the election.) Mother was delighted with this choice— and I am sure that her advice played a part in it. She felt this suave, intellectual New Englander understood Harry Truman, and she admired his grasp of foreign affairs. She also liked his charming, vivacious wife, Alice.

Secretary Acheson performed magnificently in his first major assignment, the creation of the NATO alliance, in spite of the fulminations of Senator Taft and other isolationist Republicans. On the domestic front, Dad launched his Fair Deal program—which was aimed at giving all the citizens of the republic, small businessmen and farmers, blacks as well as whites, a just share of our postwar prosperity.

I won't go so far as to say that Mother coined the term "Fair Deal," but it was an idea she emphatically approved. No one was more anxious than she to see Harry Truman emerge from FDR's shadow. She bristled at the idea that the Truman administration was a continuation of the New Deal.

Dad summed up the Fair Deal's philosophy in a letter to a prominent businessman early in 1949. "I think small business, the small farmer, the small corporation are the backbone of any free society and when there are too many people on relief and too few people at the top who control the wealth of the country then we must look out."

This was an opinion that Bess Wallace Truman shared. It had a personal dimension for her, because in 1947 the Waggoner-Gates Mill, a small corporation by the standards of American big business, had ceased producing Queen of the Pantry Flour, after sixty-four years. The Waggoners, who were majority stockholders, had decided to sell the business, because it was no longer very profitable. Frank Wallace, who had devoted twenty years of his life to trying to keep it afloat, was "sick about it," Grandmother Wallace told her daughter.

After much wrangling with the Waggoners, the company staggered
on as a local mill, producing flour for bakeries and restaurants and
other large buyers. It finally shut down for good in 1953.

In his '48 victory, Dad had carried Democratic majorities into both
houses of Congress. But he soon discovered that this did not mean
smooth sailing for his legislative program. Southerners, after treach-
erously deserting the party in the election, were eager to call themselves Democrats and use their seniority to grab key committee
chairmanships. They promptly went into business as obstructionists
and political saboteurs in alliance with Truman-hating Republicans
such as Robert Taft.

Nevertheless, 1949 was the happiest, most peaceful year of the
Truman presidency. The '48 victory gave Mother and Dad a feeling
that they could finally catch their breaths and take the time to enjoy
themselves a little. For Mother this took the form of inviting more
personal friends to Blair House for lunch or dinner, or, if they were
from out of town, for a weekend visit. I may be flattering myself, but
I think she was a little lonely without me around.

One day Mother sat down with Edith Helm and announced in a
solemn voice that she wanted to arrange a luncheon in honor of a
member of the White House staff. Under no circumstances was any
mention of it to be made to the press. Mrs. Helm dutifully got out
her appointment book and asked who the guest of honor was going
to be. She presumed it was Charlie Ross or someone of his lofty rank
in the circle around the President.

Mother's eyes twinkled. "You."

After thirty years of sending out invitations for other people, Mrs.
Helm was more than a little thrilled by this idea. She and Mother
worked out the guest list together, inviting mutual friends such as
Perle Mesta; Mrs. James Thomson; the daughter of Missouri's 1912
presidential candidate, Speaker of the House Champ Clark; and Mrs.
D. Buchanan Merryman, aunt of the Duchess of Windsor. Mother
discovered from a conference with the Blair House housekeeper that
Mrs. Helm particularly liked an exquisite set of blue-and-gold
Lowestoft china and this was used for the table. The White House
florist made a lovely blue-and-gold centerpiece to match the china.

The luncheon was a triumph of hospitality—and privacy. The
reporters never heard a word about it. That was the best part of it, as
far as Mother was concerned.

Another of 1949's highlights, for Mother, was a visit by Winston

Churchill and his wife. Mother gave an official dinner for them in the dining room of Lee House. I did not have to be lured to Washington for this fete. I came like a speeding bullet. It was a very cheerful evening. The great Englishman showered compliments on President Truman for the Marshall Plan and the NATO alliance. Mother glowed. Although she was chary of her praise, she loved to hear other people say nice things about Dad. It was especially nice to hear them from a man of Winston Churchill's stature.

At that dinner, Mother tried to add a touch of 219 North Delaware by directing the housekeeper to serve one of Vietta Garr's best dishes, stuffed cucumbers, with the fish course. The cook apparently decided he did not have to consult with Vietta on the recipe, and the result was an inedible disaster. I will never forget the expression on Mother's face when she tried to cut one of those things. They were still raw. That cook was soon on his way to some greasy spoon, where he belonged.

No one said a word about this culinary misfortune, of course, and afterward Mr. Churchill gave Mother a beautifully bound copy of his little book on painting. She asked him to inscribe it. He sat there for about fifteen minutes, brooding over that task, and finally just wrote: "For Mrs. Harry S. Truman from Winston S. Churchill." I remember being disappointed when I nosily peered over Mother's shoulder and read this inscription. I had been expecting him to come up with some brilliant bit of Churchillian rhetoric. He may have pondered such an alternative and decided this simple statement was a better match to Mother's personality. I now think he was right.

While I was struggling to find my way in show business, the First Lady gave her blessing to a pioneering theatrical experiment—shipping an American production of Shakespeare abroad for the entertainment of supposedly snobbish Europeans. The man who managed this feat with a lot of support and encouragement from Mother was a former Independence English teacher, Blevins Davis, who had gone to New York in the 1930s and became a successful Broadway producer.

In 1946, Blevins married the widow of railroad baron James Norman Hill. When she died in 1948, he inherited $9 million. In 1949, Denmark invited the United States to send a company to perform *Hamlet* in Elsinore Castle, where the story began, and Blevins put his money and theatrical experience at the disposal of the United States. Mother smoothed his path to State Department approval and the production, starring Clarence Derwent, Walter Abel, and an un-known actor named Ernest Borgnine, was a tremendous hit.

This was the beginning of a whole series of theatrical companies that Blevins took abroad in the next few years. The climax of these artistic expeditions was his production of *Porgy and Bess*, which toured Europe from London to Moscow to almost continuous ap-plause. Blevins's pioneering, which put a severe dent in his fortune, eventually led to the creation in the mid-fifties of a State Department division that routinely sends artistic companies abroad. Few people know that Bess Wallace Truman was the godmother of this good idea.

Another of Mother's invisible contributions to the country was less spectacular but far more important. When Harry Truman be-came president, the budget for the National Institutes of Health was about $2 million. This was hardly surprising. The days of all-out war on cancer and other killer diseases were still in the distant future. Most of America's money was being invested in the shooting war to defend the country and the world against the fascist threat.

During the '48 campaign, Mother had met and liked Florence Mahoney, a lively woman who was married to a relative of James A. Cox. He was the newspaper publisher whom Dad had met in Florida in 1947 and persuaded to back his policies. Mrs. Mahoney had be-come interested in the politics of the nation's health through her friendship with Mary Lasker, the philanthropist widow of a public relations executive who had contributed millions to medical re-search. Mrs. Mahoney suggested to Mother that the National In-stitutes of Health could become the center of a massive effort to conquer major diseases such as cancer. Mother found this a fascinat-ing idea and went to work on making it a reality.

For the next four years at budget time, Mother urged Dad to increase the NIH funding. The result of her quiet advocacy is visible in the dollars and cents record. By the time Harry Truman left the presidency in 1952, the NIH was getting $46 million from the federal government, a twenty-fold increase. It obviously helps to have the First Lady for a lobbyist.

Florence Mahoney told me that for three decades she has yearned to tell this story, but she abided by Mother's unwavering refusal to give her permission. With a shrewdness that goes back to her first interview after Dad was nominated for vice president, Mother never wanted anyone but Dad to get credit for the achievements of his administration. She never forgot the way the newspapers had tried to make Harry Truman look like a Pendergast yes-man, then a cheap imitation of Franklin Roosevelt. She never wanted anyone to be able to say that Harry Truman got his ideas from his wife.

During these first happy months of the second term, I spent most of my time in New York, practicing hard. I was getting pretty independent, and Mother acknowledged this in small ways. When my friend Jane Watson, daughter of IBM's president, became engaged to Jack Irwin and asked me to be a bridesmaid, Mother agreed to give a small dinner and dancing party at Blair House for them in May. She sent me the menu she had worked out and asked for my approval. This almost convinced me, at the age of twenty-four, that I was an adult at last.

Mother came up to New York for the wedding, which was at Brick Presbyterian Church. Lawrence Tibbett, the Metropolitan Opera's first American-born star, who sang at the ceremony, greeted her in the vestibule. "I just saw Margaret. She's in the wings," he said.

Mother was somewhat startled by this casual transformation of a church into a theater. "If I told that to your Grandmother," she said, as we discussed the wedding the next morning, "she'd go into shock." Mother's eyes twinkled. I realized that she thought it was funny.

That year, Harry Truman wrote Bess another memorable anniversary letter. She had gone home to Independence early in June to supervise the continuing repairs on the house.

Thirty years ago I hoped to make you a happy wife and a happy mother. Did I? I don't know. All I can say [is] I've tried. There is no one in the world anyway who can look down on you or your daughter. That means much to me, but I've never cared for social position or rank for myself except to see that those dear to me were not made to suffer for my shortcomings. . . . I'm very sure that if you'd been able to see into the future . . . you'd have very definitely turned your back on what was coming.

Business failure, with extra responsibility coming [he's referring to my birth], political defeat at the same time. Almost starvation in Washington those first ten years and then hell and repeat from 1944 to date. But I wouldn't change it and I hope you wouldn't. . . . Remember the Blackstone, Port Huron, Detroit Statler, the trip home? Maybe in 1953 we will be able to take that trip over again.

Dad was really ebullient that year. He even had the nerve to revive a custom he had dropped somewhere around 1913, calling Mother "Miss Lizzie," when he wanted to make her mad. The man just liked to live dangerously! That June, when Mother went home, he wrote to Ethel Noland: "Hope you've seen Miss Lizzie by this time." He speculated about what would have happened to him if "Miss Lizzie" had "gone off" with one of her early beaus. "Harry . . . probably would have been either a prominent farmer in Jackson County or a Major General in the regular army and not have been half so much trouble and worry to his 'sisters and his cousins and his aunts.' "

During these first sunny months of the new term, Bess was also cheered by her mother's surprising return to good health. After seeming to be in an inexorable decline, Grandmother Wallace's Christmas rally continued, and by the time she went back to Independence in June, Dr. Wallace Graham, the White House physician, told Dad she was in better health than at any time in the previous two years.

Among the presidential political family, however, a tragic situation developed with Secretary of Defense James Forrestal. He was the last holdover from FDR's cabinet but he had given unstinting loyalty to Harry Truman. He had been savagely battered in two big political brawls, the unification of the armed services into the Department of Defense and the recognition of Israel. He had backed the President in the teeth of the quarreling generals and admirals in the first one but had made no secret of his disagreement with Dad's decision to recognize Israel. It was an honest difference of opinion, but Drew Pearson and his ilk declined to admit such a possibility. They smeared Mr. Forrestal at every opportunity.

A sensitive, emotional man, he simply broke down under the beating. He became more and more mentally disturbed and Dad finally had to ask him to resign. He entered Bethesda Naval Hospital for treatment for severe depression. Bess was deeply affected by this political agony—it stirred her deepest sympathies. On Easter Saturday, she sent Mr. Forrestal a bouquet of roses. He wrote her a touching reply.

"My dear Mrs. Truman: The flowers you sent are beautiful and have helped brighten a bleak day. I am moved that you should trouble to send me a token but it's typical of your thoughtfulness. A Happy Easter to you and the President and Miss Truman. You all deserve it."

He signed it: "Faithfully." A few days later, his faith, whether in himself or his country, ran out. He leaped to his death from his hospital room.

Mother was terribly shaken. Dad was enraged. He considered

Drew Pearson the murderer of James Forrestal and said so. Some people thought this was an extreme statement. Perhaps it was, in a literal sense of the word. But in the emotional context of his marriage, as I have explained it in this book, it is easy to see why Dad's anger was intensified by his knowledge of the impact of Mr. Forrestal's suicide on Mother.

That summer in Independence, Mother went on a diet to reduce her weight as well as to control her high blood pressure. Serious dieting while on Washington's merry-go-round of official lunches and dinners was very difficult. She cut down drastically on her calories and rigorously banned all salt and salted meats from her menus. The result was impressive. Her blood pressure came down and she lost twenty pounds. Later in the year she sat for one of her best photographs, in the living room of 219 North Delaware. Here was proof positive of her change of heart about being First Lady—she let a photographer inside her sanctuary, not to win an election but just to take her picture.

Back in Washington at the end of the summer, Bess found herself and our house in the political headlines. A favorite congressional tactic when a president is riding high is an investigation that smears innuendos all over his administration. A classic of this brand of capital throatcutting was launched in August, when Senator Clyde R. Hoey of North Carolina began an investigation of so-called five-percenters in the Truman White House. It would be a waste of time even to try to summarize this tangle of allegation and rumor about favors done and presents given in return for them. But Mother was amazed to discover that she had been one of the recipients of a deep freeze, given by one of the favor seekers back in 1945.

After four years of living at a White House pace, that date seemed almost prehistoric. But the statement was true, as far as it went. In 1945, Mother had remarked while talking on the phone to General Harry Vaughan, Dad's military aide, that neighbors were sending her gifts of food that had overflowed the old icebox. One of the favor seekers was in General Vaughan's office and overheard the conversation. He offered to get Mother a deep freeze and, for good measure, sent one to each of a half dozen other members of the administration.

Mother sent a thank you note to the man who shipped the freezer—and thought no more about it until a few weeks later, when the smell of rotting food filled the kitchen. The freezer was a lemon. She had the Secret Service cart it away to the dump and went out and bought her own freezer. Throughout the mudslinging session about these gifts, Mother never said a word to a reporter or anyone else. It was not her style to respond to smears. This whole disgraceful episode, which ended without a single member of the administration even being accused of breaking a law, only confirmed her opinion of the press.

Mother was far more concerned about the terrible beating Dad's military aide, General Harry Vaughan, took in this affair. She totally backed Dad's refusal to accept his resignation, which he offered because he thought he had become a liability to the President. "Harry," Dad said, "we came in here together and we're going out of here together. Those so-and-so's are trying to get me, through you." Mother was very fond of Margaret Vaughan, the General's wife. She was also fond of him.

Mother's rather straitlaced public image gave rise to a lot of rumors that she disapproved of General Vaughan and Fred Canfil and other rowdy characters whose company Dad enjoyed in his off-duty hours. Nothing could be further from the truth—as long as they kept their antics out of the newspapers. She recognized that these men gave Dad some badly needed relaxation. I sometimes suspect that she wished her mother had not made her so much a lady that she did not feel free to join them. As I have said earlier in this chapter, she liked a hearty laugh as much as Harry Truman.

General Vaughan and Mother had some amusing correspondence in which he sensed, I think, this conflict. He addressed her as "My Dear Lady" and wrote in the most elaborate style, as if he were a courtier addressing a queen. He was the only member of the President's inner circle who had the nerve to tease mother. She let him get away with it because he also told her a lot of funny stories. This was his forte in the Oval Office and more often than not Dad would say: "Tell that one to Bess."

One of Mother's favorites concerned a faithful member of the Methodist church who missed three services in a row. The minister called on him to ask why. "Parson," the man said. "My clothes are so shabby I'm ashamed to go."

"We'll take care of that," the minister said. He collected a complete new outfit for him from charitable parishioners and delivered it forthwith. The next Sunday the old boy still did not show. A little peeved, the minister paid him a visit. He found him sitting on the front porch all dressed up. "What's the matter, Joe?" he asked. "I expected to see you at the services today."

"Well I'll tell you, Parson," Joe said. "When I got dressed up in these new clothes I looked so prosperous that I went to the Episcopal church."

While General Vaughan writhed and Dad angrily defended him, Mother worked incredibly hard at Blair House, with its triple and quadruple entertaining requirements. A random two-week sample of her schedule in 1949 shows no less than thirteen major engagements, ranging from a Congressional Club breakfast to a musical luncheon given by the Democratic Women's National Council to a handshaking marathon with a group of Home Demonstration Agents from Vermont. She opened the National Flower Mart on the Pilgrim Steps of Washington Cathedral and received the Society of Sponsors of the U.S. Navy. "So went the busy days," wrote Edith Helm in her memoir of her White House years, which blissfully ignored the brutal politics that swirled around her polite social world.

Mother did not have that privilege. She had to smile her way through these wearying chores and sit down with the exasperated President in his study that night and discuss what could—and could not—be done.

One of the things they discussed surprisingly early in this second term was whether Harry Truman would run for president again. The Republican Eightieth Congress had rammed through the Twenty-second Amendment in 1947, barring a president from serving more than two terms. The wording of the measure exempted the incumbent president from the prohibition, so Dad was eligible to run in 1952.

Mother made it very clear that she was totally opposed to the idea. That led to the problem of finding a successor who would and could carry on the Democratic Party's policies abroad and at home. This was, in Dad's mind, an absolutely vital task. Looking over the potential candidates, he did not find many promising names. Some lacked stature, others experience in national and international affairs. Only one man seemed to combine both: Fred Vinson, whom he had first appointed Secretary of the Treasury, then Chief Justice of the Supreme Court. Mr. Vinson had been a popular congressman, a very successful executive in the Roosevelt and Truman administrations and a chief justice who was often praised for the smooth operation of the highest court. This experience in the three branches of government made him, in Dad's opinion, uniquely qualified to be president.

As early as March 1949, on a visit to Key West, Dad wrote to Mother that "the Big Judge," as he called Mr. Vinson, was coming to see him. "I have to talk to him on some very important things, which affect the future of the nation." He urged Mother and me to join them. "You'll have a wonderful weekend and I'll be able to tell you what I have in mind as a result of my talk with Vinson."

Mother decided she preferred a weekend with me in Manhattan. So Dad talked with Mr. Vinson without her. The discussion was maddeningly inconclusive. Mr. Vinson was like the girl in the song. He would not say yes, but he would not say no. He was very happy on the Supreme Court and obviously reluctant to leave it. But he insisted he was ready to do whatever Harry Truman thought he should do for the good of the country.

As the year 1949 ended, the sunny political skies began to darken in ways far more serious than the attempt to smear General Vaughan. In September, U.S. intelligence discovered that Soviet Russia had exploded an atomic bomb, breaking America's nuclear monopoly. Next came the dismaying news that much of the breakthrough had been achieved by stealing atomic secrets with the help of various espionage rings in Great Britain and the United States. The media already had echoed with allegations about Communist influences in the government, thanks to a much-publicized confrontation between a former State Department official, Alger Hiss, and a former Communist, Whittaker Chambers, before a hearing of the House Committee on Un-American Activities. When Mr. Hiss denied knowing Mr. Chambers and insisted he had never given him secret State Department documents, he was indicted for perjury.

In China, Chiang Kai-shek's Nationalist regime collapsed under a final Communist onslaught, and he fled to Taiwan with the remnants of his army and government. This too produced fodder for the anti-Communist witch-hunters, who tried to pin the "loss of China" on the Truman administration. Dad responded to all these challenges. After weeks of thought and analysis, he released the news of the Russian bomb in a way that minimized a panicky response. After more study of intelligence reports and the best scientific advice, he decided that the Russians were capable of building a hydrogen bomb and ordered the United States to begin construction of that terrifying weapon. Dean Acheson released a white paper that made it clear Chiang Kai-shek, not the United States, had lost China.

But politicians—and reporters—are not satisfied by a calm statement of the facts once they scent the possibility of creating a sensation. Early in February 1950, the greatest sensation monger of the era, Senator Joe McCarthy of Wisconsin, stepped onstage with a speech in Wheeling, West Virginia, accusing Dean Acheson of harboring 205 Communists in the State Department. Dad contemptuously dismissed the telegram the Senator sent to him demanding action.

But McCarthy was soon joined by a host of unsavory allies, such as Senator Kenneth Wherry of Nebraska. They concentrated most of their venom on Dean Acheson for losing China and declaring that he would still consider Alger Hiss a friend, even after he had been convicted of lying under oath about being a Communist. But they also flung accusations at John Snyder, who had succeeded Fred Vinson as Secretary of the Treasury, and at any other department where dissatisfied bureaucrats or out-and-out nuts told them that Communists were employed.

Although Dad did not give the public a hint that he took the witchhunters seriously, their assaults and the enormous responsibility involved in the decisions on atomic weapons took a heavy toll of his nerves and energy. McCarthy and his allies were undermining the keystone of his presidency, a bipartisan foreign policy. In a letter to his cousin, Ralph Truman, Dad wrote that he was in the midst of "the most terrible struggle any president ever had." In mid-March 1950, headaches began to torment him for the first time in years.

Alarmed, Mother urged a retreat to Key West to regain his strength and equilibrium. As usual on such matters, he took her advice. But the worries did not go away in the Florida sunshine. From there he wrote her one of the most anguished letters of his presidency.

After reporting the good news that his head had stopped hurting, he turned to the political situation. "You see everybody shoots at me, if not directly, then at some of the staff closest to me. I'd much rather they'd pound me directly. The general trend of the pieces is that I'm a very small man in a very large place and when some one I trust joins the critical side—well it hurts. I'm much older and very tired and I need support as no man ever did."

Earlier in the letter, he mentioned that Chief Justice Fred Vinson had paid him another visit. "The Chief Justice is one man in high place who still believes in me, trusts me and supports me. . . . What has made me so jittery—they started on Snyder and have almost broken him, then Vaughan, whose mental condition is very bad. Now they are after the top brain man in the Cabinet [Dean Acheson]. The whole foreign policy is at stake just as we are on the road to a possible solution. . . . I'm telling you so you may understand how badly I need *your* help and support now."

On this visit, Dad again discussed with Chief Justice Vinson whether he would become his successor. He wanted to begin laying the groundwork for making him a viable candidate. He reminded Mother of Mr. Vinson's loyalty during the '48 campaign, when he asked him to go to Moscow to see if he could make a breakthrough for peace with Stalin. "He didn't want to go," Dad recalled, in this letter. "But he said, 'I'm your man to do what you want me to do for the welfare of the country.' How many Congressmen, Senators, even Cabinet Officers would have said that?"

The linkage in this hitherto unpublished letter between a conference with Mr. Vinson and the hint in the opening lines that Mother had joined "the critical side" convinces me that they were still debating the question of Dad running in 1952. With Mr. Vinson still on the fence, Mother was urging Dad to find another candidate. He was still hoping the Chief Justice would make up his mind.

A few days later, the Key West sunshine had restored Dad's optimism and energy. He wrote Mother another letter, noting that Styles Bridges of New Hampshire, a hitherto respectable Republican conservative, had joined the McCarthyite red-baiters. He had decided to answer these demagogues with another whistle-stop tour that would tell people the truth. "We'll take them to town as we did before," he promised her.

Back in Washington, President Truman apparently settled the question of running again and ended the tension it was causing between him and his wife. A month before he launched his counteroffensive against McCarthy, he sat down at his desk and wrote one of those memorandums to himself that are the closest he came to keeping a diary. It is not only a significant document in the history of the Truman marriage and their political partnership. It contains some of Dad's profoundest thoughts on the presidency.

I am not a candidate for nomination by the Democratic Convention.

My first election to public office took place in November 1922. I served two years in the armed forces in World War I, ten years in the Senate, two months and 20 days as Vice President and President of the Senate. I have been in public service well over thirty years, having been President of the United States almost two complete terms.

Washington, Jefferson, Monroe, Madison, Andrew Jackson and Woodrow Wilson as well as Calvin Coolidge stood by the precedent of two terms.

Only Grant, Theodore Roosevelt and F.D.R. made the attempt to break that precedent. F.D.R. succeeded.

In my opinion eight years as President is enough and sometimes too much for any man to serve in that capacity.

There is a lure in power. It can get into a man's blood just as gambling and lust for money have been known to do.

This is a Republic. The greatest in the history of the world. I want this country to continue as a Republic. Cincinnatus and Washington pointed the way. When Rome forgot Cincinnatus its downfall began. When we forget the examples of such men as Washington, Jefferson and Andrew Jackson, all of whom could have had a continuation in the office, then will we start down the road to dictatorship and ruin. I know I could be elected again and continue to break the old precedent as it was broken by F.D.R. It should not be done. That precedent should continue—not by a Constitutional amendment but by custom based on the honor of the man in the office.

Therefore to reestablish that custom, although by a quibble I could say I've only had one term, I am not a candidate and will not accept the nomination for another term.

I am sure Dad showed this magnificent statement to Mother and I am equally sure that she glowed as she read it. That settles it, she thought. She could look forward to the next two years in the White House with something very close to tranquillity. She could anticipate a future in which she and her husband would finally have some time together to enjoy themselves as private citizens.

The alert reader may have noted that I wrote that the statement "apparently" settled the question. History, Bess's old foe, was about to unsettle it—and a lot of other things.

Chapter Twenty-five

The McCarthy-bashing whistle-stop tour was a happy expedition. Dad celebrated his sixty-sixth birthday on the train. Here's a glimpse of that day from my diary.

Monday, May 8, 1950. They gave Dad a huge cake at Ottumwa. He's had 13 or 14 cakes today. We got off in the pouring rain at Lincoln, Nebr. I got soaked but it was warm anyway. The crowds have been tremendous even in the rain. They have smiling faces and are very enthusiastic.

Although Dad made over fifty speeches in ten days, there was none of the tension, the frantic pace of the '48 campaign train. Mother had a smile on her face most of the time. But she did not consider Joe McCarthy a laughing matter, and she heartily approved the way Dad went after him. So did the people who cheered and clapped.

I won't blame it on the birthday cakes, but something in the food or water got to me and Mother toward the end of this expedition. We returned to the White House and took to our respective beds for several days. I recovered first and Mother threw me into the social breach, ordering me to play hostess for a luncheon she was giving in honor of Perle Mesta, whom Dad had just appointed ambassador to Luxembourg. I fled back to New York after this chore, convinced that I had the better deal, even if I never got another break in show business.

The TV impresario Ed Sullivan took me to lunch at Sardi's and invited me to appear on his "Toast of the Town" in the fall. It would be my national TV debut. Mother was impressed. She remarked in her wry way that I might actually turn out to be able to make a living after all.

Grandmother Wallace and Vietta Garr flew to Independence for the summer. Mother took the train out to get things settled at 219 North Delaware. Whenever she could manage it, Mother preferred to travel on the ground. Flying was torture to her. Grandmother Wallace did not seem to mind it, and the shorter trip meant less strain on her fragile health.

Dad pursued Mother with cheerful letters. He reported that he had had a physical examination and Dr. Graham pronounced him in good shape. "[I] hope to stay that way for at least another two years, six months and twenty days. Then the millennium."

He was still pursuing his plan to retire at the end of the term. He went on to describe a ceremony in the Cabinet Room, in which he presented Vice President Barkley with a gold medal from Congress for his many years of public service. Significantly, Chief Justice Vinson was there and he made a "nice little speech" about how thoroughly the Veep deserved the honor. The Chief Justice was an old friend of Barkley and a fellow Kentuckian—but it was also a chance to make him feel part of the Truman administration.

Most of Dad's and Mother's thoughts were on American politics that spring. The midterm elections were coming up in November, and they did not want to lose control of Congress. That was the only reason Dad decided to accept a degree from the University of Missouri—to gain a platform to help Democratic candidates in the state. Mother remarked in her acerbic way that the university had only taken six years to get around to honoring Missouri's first president. Dad agreed that she was "right" about them "in every particular." But he had "other fish to fry"—in particular the Republican senator who was up for reelection, Forest O'Donnell.

The political skies seemed to be brightening. After his trip to Missouri for the degree, Dad told Mother he had read all the New York, Baltimore, and Washington newspapers that had accumulated in his absence and there was "not a mean remark in them." He was even more amazed by cordial editorials in the St. Louis *Post-Dispatch* and *Globe Democrat*. "I am sure I'm slipping," he joked.

He was proud of his speeches in Columbia and in St. Louis. "They made a complete resume of the foreign policy of the United States. No one can misunderstand it or garble it. . . . It has taken five years to get to this point. *I am hoping two more will wind it up*" (italics mine).

Notice the reservation in those last words. I am sure Mother noticed it. Dad was convinced he was fighting for peace in the world and there was still a part of his mind where he was ready to risk his health and his partner's wrath, if necessary. "It's an awful responsibility," he wrote. "That's what I was thinking when I looked down on those two thousand young people . . . on Friday."

In this upbeat frame of mind, Dad flew to Independence on June 24 to celebrate his thirty-first wedding anniversary. It was, in keeping with Mother's wishes, to be the quietest of quiet visits, if possible. The White House issued a statement all but admonishing the public to leave the President and his family alone. This reduced the number of spectators outside 219 North Delaware to a mere 100 when he arrived.

Later in the day, Freddy and Chris and their children joined the rest of the Wallaces and the Trumans for another family reunion (I had arrived on the 19th). After dinner we sat out on the back porch, which Mother had had widened and screened-in earlier that year, chatting about everything and nothing in particular. About 10 P.M., we decided it was chilly and retreated to the library. We were barely settled there when Dad received a call from Washington.

He returned with a grim look on his face. "That was Dean Acheson. The Communists have invaded South Korea."

"Oh Harry," Mother said. She seemed to sense, instantly, what it meant.

"I'm going to stay here tonight. It may not be as serious as it sounds. Tomorrow I want everyone to pretend it's business as usual."

I don't think Dad got much sleep that night. Nor did Mother. She could see the havoc this Communist foray would create in American politics, with Senator McCarthy yammering in the wings. Nevertheless, the next day we were all good soldiers. We went to Trinity Church and chatted with neighbors as if it was just another sleepy summer Sunday in Independence. Dad drove out to the family farm in Grandview (he had repurchased part of it during his first term) to see about putting a new roof on the house. All of this play acting was motivated by Dad's desire to prevent the news from Korea from creating a panic.

At 11:45 A.M., as we were about to sit down to an early family dinner, the phone rang again. I can remember the pain on Mother's face as Dad went to answer it. This time, Dean Acheson said there was no doubt that it was an all-out invasion of South Korea. Seven tank-led divisions of the North Korean Army were smashing south in a bid to conquer the whole country. Dad returned to the dining room, sat down and, with that amazing calm that he could muster in a crisis, began eating dinner. In a matter of fact voice, he told us the bad news and said he was going to return to Washington immediately.

So much for Mother's hope for a quiet anniversary. It was gone—

and so were the sunny political skies of 1949. So was the President's peace of mind. So was that promise to retire in 1952. Everything was up in the air, whirling around almost as horrendously as the world on April 12, 1945, when Franklin D. Roosevelt died.

As the news spread throughout Independence (and the rest of the country, of course), people leaped into their cars and headed for North Delaware Street to see if they could get some clue to what was happening from the President's conduct. Soon there were twenty-five cars a minute crawling past our house, thickening the humid air with their exhaust fumes. Mother and I drove to the airport with Dad and watched him take off. He was so impatient, he ordered the pilot aloft without the navigator. He appeared at the last second, racing beside the taxiing plane in a car, and leaped out and crawled into the cockpit on a rope ladder. This did nothing to assuage Mother's usual anxiety about Dad while he was airborne.

Knowing this, Dad somehow found time to write her a letter the next day from Blair House. "We had a grand trip after we were in the air," he reported. He also told her that the conference with his cabinet officers and advisers in Blair House on the night of June 25th had been "a most successful one." He thought there was a chance "that things may work out without the necessity of mobilization." Then he admitted (as usual, to her alone) the impact of the crisis on him. "[I] haven't been so badly upset since Greece and Turkey fell into our lap. Let's hope for the best." He ended the letter with: "Lots and lots of love and many happy returns for the thirty-first year of your ordeal with me. It's been *all* pleasure for me."

Korea annihilated most of the summer and fall of 1950 from Mother's point of view. It was constantly on Dad's mind. She had little to contribute to this morass of troop commitments, strategic worries in Europe, the Middle East, the question of rearming the country, and keeping a lid on inflation. Although she was very worried about her mother, who was having another sinking spell, she spent most of the summer with Dad, sharing his anguish as the North Korean Army defeated the first poorly prepared American troops rushed from Japan and drove them into a defensive perimeter around the port of Pusan.

One worry that Bess could and did share was the President's relationship with General Douglas MacArthur, the commander of the United Nations forces in Korea. Dad had never been fond of him. They were almost totally opposite personalities—one indulging in flamboyant self promotion, the other abhorring it; one given to elaborate rhetoric, the other to blunt truths; one the quintessential professional soldier, the other the prototype of the citizen soldier.

Dad was well aware that the General had political ambitions and was in constant communication with right-wing Republicans in Congress. That only intensified his irritation when MacArthur began acting as if he had his own foreign policy during the awful summer of 1950. First he made an unauthorized trip to Formosa to confer with Chiang Kai-shek, supposedly to see if we could use Chiang's aging soldiers in Korea. Since one of the prime worries on Dad's mind was the possibility of Communist China entering the Korean conflict, this was not only idiotic, it was flagrantly dangerous. Dad sent W. Averell Harriman to Japan to explain our policy to the General.

At the end of August, MacArthur sent a statement to the annual convention of the Veterans of Foreign Wars, in which he condemned as defeatists and appeasers anyone who did not agree with his embrace of Chiang. Dad told his Secretary of Defense, Louis Johnson, to order MacArthur to withdraw the statement. Instead, Johnson said it was just "one man's opinion." Neither he nor anyone else in the Defense Department had the nerve to differ with MacArthur. Furious, Dad sent the General a personal order and the statement was withdrawn. That was the end of Louis Johnson as Secretary of Defense. He was shortly replaced by General Marshall.

Nevertheless, Dad gave his approval for General MacArthur's daring plan to land two divisions at Inchon, far behind the enemy's lines, to trap and destroy the North Korean Army. The operation was a brilliant success, and the Communists soon ceased to exist as an organized force. Remnants fled across the border into North Korea, and Harry Truman was faced with another fateful decision. Should they be pursued? Everyone from *The New York Times* to the United Nations Security Council to the U.S. Congress said yes. It looked like a perfect chance to obliterate North Korea and unify the country.

Dad gave MacArthur permission to cross the border—but hedged it with warnings and provisos about the danger of a Communist Chinese intervention. To underscore this concern, he flew to Wake Island to confer with "God's right hand man," as he called the General in a letter he wrote to Nellie Noland while airborne. The meeting was cordial, and MacArthur assured the President that he was confident the Red Chinese would not intervene. He also apologized for his statements about Formosa.

Mother was hard at work first ladying throughout these weeks of political-military turmoil. On top of her usual schedule, she launched a series of afternoon parties for soldiers wounded in Korea that did wonders for the morale of these young men. Only 100 could be invited at a time, because of the size of Blair House. But Mother solved that problem by multiplying the number of the parties. Most of the time, she prevailed on Dad to join her in greeting the guests, many of whom were badly crippled. Early on, Dad noticed that only soft drinks and coffee were being served. He suggested adding beer, which proved very popular.

Somewhat to the consternation of the staff, Mother gave these very special guests the run of Blair House, letting them play the piano, sit on the priceless antique furniture, and drink from the valuable china. She invited my numerous Washington friends to help her play hostess.

Whenever I was in town for a visit, I volunteered for duty—without a word of complaint, so help me. It was agonizing for all of us to think that American young men were bleeding and dying again in a foreign war. We all shared Mother's desire to show them how much we appreciated their sacrifices. None of us dreamt, as we smiled and chatted through these affairs, that the President and First Lady would soon be menaced by gunfire.

I was not available for such worthwhile chores very often. Most of my life was spent packing and unpacking suitcases during those trying days. I was a purple pin on the map my booking agent maintained to keep track of his singers, violinists, and pianists as they crisscrossed the country. My career was doing very nicely, I thought, and apparently so did the audiences and critics, who continued to be very kind to me, by and large.

On November 1, 1950, I was in Portland, Maine, preparing for a concert that night. Dad spent an unnerving morning in the executive wing of the White House (that part of the mansion was still functioning) getting ominous reports of a Chinese Communist presence in North Korea. He returned to Blair House for lunch with Mother and Grandmother Wallace, then took a nap—a custom he had adopted to help him handle the sixteen-hour presidential day. Mother chatted with Grandmother Wallace in her bedroom, which she seldom left. She was eighty-eight and growing more and more feeble.

At 2:50 P.M., Mother and Dad were scheduled to go to Arlington

National Cemetery to dedicate a statue to Field Marshall Sir John Dill, a British member of the Combined Chiefs of Staff during World War II. It was a gesture aimed at underscoring our solidarity with allies who had contributed soldiers to the United Nations Army in Korea.

It was a warm day and most of the windows and the front door of Blair House were open. Only a lightly latched screen door stood between intruders and the interior of the building. Of course, the idea of intruders never entered anyone's head. Pedestrians were allowed to stroll along the sidewalk only a few feet from the door. There were guards on duty in sentry boxes on the east and west ends of the yellow brick and stucco building. But no one, including the President and First Lady, had the slightest sense of danger from this proximity to the public.

At a few minutes after 2 P.M., Mother left Grandmother Wallace and entered her second-floor bedroom to begin dressing for the trip to Arlington. Suddenly an incredible series of blasts erupted from the street below her windows. In two minutes, there were no less than twenty-seven staccato explosions. Mother rushed to the window and looked down on a shocking sight.

One of the guards, Leslie Coffelt, was writhing on the ground in a death agony. Another guard was lying in the gutter clutching a shattered leg. Two other men in shabby civilian clothes were lying on the sidewalk, bleeding profusely. There was blood everywhere.

Mother fled into Dad's bedroom crying: "Harry—someone's shooting our policeman!"

Dad dashed to the window and stuck out his head to get a good look at the carnage. "Get back, get back," the surviving guards and Secret Service men on the street implored him. They did not know what was going to happen next. Dad retreated to the door of his room and peered out. A husky Secret Service man was crouched at the head of the stairs with a submachine gun pointing at the front door.

Dad did not mention that to Mother. He calmed her down and told her to go back and finish dressing. He would find out what had happened and tell her on the way to Arlington. He soon learned that he and Mother had come alarmingly close to being killed. Two Puerto Rican nationalist fanatics, Oscar Collazo and Victor Torresola, had noticed Blair House's easy access from the street and tried to shoot their way into the building. They failed largely because

Collazo's gun had jammed when he pulled the trigger, giving the guard he was trying to murder time to draw his own gun and return his fire.

Torresola had gunned down guards Coffelt and Joseph E. Downs in the west booth. But the mortally wounded Coffelt put a bullet through Torresola's brain as he raced toward the door. Collazo was stopped on the steps by a hail of bullets from other policemen and Secret Service agents and toppled to the sidewalk with three bullets in him; unfortunately none were fatal wounds.

Mother was terribly shaken by this senseless act of violence. It seemed to confirm all the intimations of disaster she had sensed when Dad became president. She was particularly anxious to make sure her mother did not hear about it. She issued orders to Vietta Garr, who was still with us as Grandmother's companion, to say nothing to her and passed similar commands to the Blair House staff.

With her iron self-control, Mother was able to join Dad and drive to the ceremony in Arlington as if nothing had happened. There, as Dad airily dismissed their brush with death with the comment, "Presidents have to expect such things," Mother thought of me in Portland. She rushed back to Blair House and telephoned me at my hotel. She knew I had spent the afternoon in seclusion, as most singers do before a concert. Thereafter, however, Mother's usually strong sense of reality deserted her.

"I just want you to know everyone's all right," she said.

"Why shouldn't everyone be all right?" I asked. "Is there anything wrong with Dad?"

"He's fine. He's perfectly fine," Mother said. "I'll talk to you later tonight, after your performance."

It was an indication of how shaken Mother was that she did not seem to realize that people read newspapers and listened to the radio in Portland, and it was virtually impossible for me to get from the hotel to the concert hall without someone telling me what had happened. Reathel Odum, Mother's ex-secretary, who was traveling with me, conferred with my manager, and they jointly decided to tell me what had happened. They did not want a local reporter to undo me with a question seconds before I went on stage. Once I was reassured that Dad was all right, I relaxed and sang without the slightest nervousness.

For Mother, the assassination attempt cast a shadow of anxiety over the remaining months of Dad's presidency. No longer could she

justify her occasional defiance of the Secret Service, lest Dad be
encouraged to do the same thing. Having survived about 50,000 high
explosive shells in World War I, he was totally fatalistic about the
danger. He discussed this attitude and other aspects of the assassination attempt in a letter to his cousin, Ethel Noland.

I'm really a prisoner now. I'm like the "600" and the cannon, only mine
are guards and they are trying to keep me out of the "mouth of hell."
Everybody is much more worried and jittery than I am. I've always thought
that if I could get my hands on a would-be assassin he'd never try it again.
But I guess that's impossible. The grand guards who were hurt in the
attempt on me didn't have a fair chance. The one who was killed was just
cold bloodedly murdered before he could do anything. But his assassin did
not live but a couple of minutes—one of the S.S. men put a bullet in one ear
and it came out the other. . . . I was the only calm one in the house. You see
I've been shot at by experts and unless your name's on the bullet you needn't
be afraid—and that of course you can't find out, so why worry.

For a professional worrier like Mother, this was no reassurance.
She dismissed Dad's complaints when the Secret Service decreed a
temporary ban on his morning walks and insisted on taking him
from Blair House to the White House in a heavily guarded car, which
picked him up in the back alley. She had to depart and return in the
same furtive fashion, which she disliked as much as he did.

The assassination attempt may have had something to do with her
decision not to go home with him on November 5 for a two-and-a-
half-day visit to dedicate a Liberty Bell replica, given to Independence by the people of Annecy-le-Vieux, France. A small army of
Secret Service men and Kansas City police followed Dad everywhere—even when he had dinner with Frank and Natalie Wallace.
Mother decided in advance that she could not stand it and stayed in
Washington.

There, Blair House became a mansion under siege. After November 1, 1950, pedestrians were no longer permitted to walk past it. The
number of guards was increased. Even the streetcar platform was
removed from the avenue in front of the house to make sure that a
would-be assassin could not mingle with a crowd of people waiting
there. All these precautions only reminded Mother of that day of
carnage and terror.

There were numerous other threats on Dad's life, which he did not
mention to Mother or me. Early in 1951, he explained to his cousin,
Ralph Truman, why he could not attend the reunion of the Thirty-

fifth Division. Stressing that it was "completely confidential," Dad wrote: "The Secret Service have received more than the usual number of threats to rub me out at the reunion. You know I never worry about those things. . . . But some good fellow who has three or four kids may be killed—to keep me from that fate."

Almost all these threats were stirred by the hate-filled diatribes of Joe McCarthy and his Republican friends. The mentally unbalanced found it a perfect focus for their paranoia to believe that the President and his Secretary of State were Communist agents.

Unfortunately, a dismaying number of voters were influenced by McCarthy's linkage of Communist aggression in Korea with his baseless charges of subversion at home. General MacArthur did not help matters when, on the eve of the elections, he demanded permission to bomb the bridges over the Yalu River to stop the Communist Chinese from crossing them. Once more the General did not seem to be able to grasp that this would give them the pretext to intervene in massive force. By maneuvering the President into issuing a refusal, the General made Harry Truman look weak and indecisive—and convinced most of Dad's staff that MacArthur was working with the Republicans.

The November elections were an unnerving blow to Dad's hope of leaving behind him in 1952 a bipartisan foreign policy that would guarantee a peaceful world. Although the Democrats did not lose control of Congress, the top leadership in the House and Senate was defeated. Scott Lucas, the Senate Majority Leader, lost in Illinois, Francis M. Myers, the Democratic whip, lost in Pennsylvania. That enabled the Republicans to crow that the voters had repudiated not just these men, but the President.

Even more painful was the success of the professional red-baiters. Richard Nixon won a Senate seat in California by claiming that his opponent, Helen Gahagan Douglas, was "pink right down to her underwear." Everett Dirksen defeated Scott Lucas by talking about "young men coming back in wooden boxes," killed by Communists. Senator Millard Tydings was crushed in Maryland by a barrage of innuendos and outright lies, such as a faked picture of him with Communist leader Earl Browder. Joe McCarthy had vowed to get Tydings and Lucas, and his success was certain to intimidate Democrats in both houses and encourage Republicans to imitate the "unmitigated liar," as Dad called him.

Seldom in their thirty-one years of marriage had Bess seen Harry

Truman so downhearted. He blamed himself for not keeping the pressure on McCarthy. As usual, he had put the national interest, coping with the Korean War, ahead of politics. Now that conflict was spiraling out of control, after seeming to be on the brink of victory only a few weeks earlier. More and more reports of Red Chinese intervention flowed into the Pentagon and over to the White House. Then the reports suddenly ceased. The Chinese disappeared.

In Korea, General MacArthur decided the Chinese were bluffing. He ordered a "final offensive," which would bring the soldiers "home by Christmas." Ignoring cautionary warnings from the Joint Chiefs of Staff, he sent his soldiers north to the Yalu River border between North Korea and Red China. On November 28, 300,000 Chinese troops struck the United Nations Army with overwhelming force and sent it reeling into chaotic retreat. Suddenly, Dad was faced with the possibility of a military and political catastrophe of terrifying proportions.

On top of this nightmare came a terrible media snafu. At a press conference on November 30, instead of concentrating on Harry Truman's historic declaration that the United States would *not* abandon Korea in the face of this Chinese sneak attack, the reporters seized on his answer to a question about the possible use of the atom bomb and distorted it into a frenzy of headlines that Dad was about to use nuclear weapons to end the war.

As always, when the press twisted Dad's words and intentions, Mother was very upset. Another person very close to the President was even more upset: Charlie Ross. As press secretary, he felt responsible for avoiding such upheavals. Usually, Charlie sensed trouble from the way reporters were pushing a line of questioning and asked the President to restate and clarify his replies at the end of a press conference. This story got away from Charlie for a very good reason. He and everyone else on the White House staff were operating in a daze of exhaustion. Ever since the Chinese attack, the lights in the west wing never went out, and sleep was snatched on couches and jammed-together chairs.

I was far away from this turmoil, purple pinning it from concert hall to concert hall on a tour that had begun on October 1, when the news from Korea had been sensationally good. The tour was scheduled to end with a concert in Constitution Hall on December 5, 1950. Dad spent most of the day conferring with British Prime Minister Clement Attlee, who had rushed to Washington for a conference when he read the misleading headlines about the atomic bomb. Dad was in the process of turning this impolitic visit into a very useful discussion of how to deal with the Chinese in Korea.

At the end of the afternoon, Dad gave Charlie Ross a summary of his talk with Mr. Attlee for release to the press. Charlie planned to brief the reporters, have dinner, and join Dad and Mother at Constitution Hall for my concert. Dad left for Blair House and Charlie handled the briefing in his usual smooth style. The TV reporters asked him if he would repeat himself for their cameras and he wearily agreed. As they set up their equipment on his desk, Charlie joked with his secretary about his TV style. Suddenly he slumped in his chair. Dr. Graham, the White House doctor, was frantically summoned, but by the time he got there, Charlie was dead. His tired, damaged heart had failed.

Dr. Graham called Dad. He walked into Mother's bedroom with tears streaming down his face and said: "Charlie Ross just dropped dead at his desk." Mother wept too. She was not a crying type ordinarily. But there were so many memories storming through her mind and heart. She remembered that blithe and brilliant editor of *The Gleam*, in 1901. She saw him strolling down Delaware Street, holding Mary Paxton's hand. She did not know, then, the unique pain the news would stir in Mary's heart. (That night, Mary later told her, she awoke hearing Charlie calling her name.) Mother also thought of the pain it would cause Charlie's wife, Florence, and his two sons.

The Trumans' tears were brief. Sheer necessity required self-control. Mother raised the most urgent question. Should they tell me? She decided on the same approach she had taken to the attempted assassination. She persuaded Dad that it would be better to wait until after the concert.

Here, again, I think Mother's instinct to protect me, as she had tried all her life to protect and support her brothers and everyone else whom she cared about, led her to make a mistake. It would have been better to have told me that Charlie had died. I might have decided to make a statement about him before I sang. I could have announced that I was dedicating this performance to his memory. I might have changed my repertoire for the evening.

Instead, by presidential order, I was surrounded by a wall of Secret Service agents and aides who kept the press at bay and me in ignorance. Mother and Dad and their guest, Prime Minister Attlee, went to Constitution Hall and enjoyed my performance. So, as far as I could tell, did the rest of the audience, if their generous applause proved anything. Afterward, Dad was effusive, even for him. He hugged me and said he had never heard me sing better. I can see now that watching me perform was his only happy moment in a devastating week.

The next morning Dad was up at dawn, as usual. He opened *The Washington Post* and read a horrendous review of my performance by their critic, Paul Hume. Without saying a word to me or Mother, who would have stopped him, he dashed off a note to Mr. Hume that told him in very Trumanesque language what he thought of him. Among other picturesque suggestions, he said Mr. Hume sounded like "an eight ulcer man on a four ulcer job with all four ulcers working." Dad had one of the White House servants mail it for him, thus circumventing his staff, who also tried to persuade him to think over such letters before he sent them.

Mr. Hume promptly released the letter to the press, and the hullabaloo temporarily knocked the Korean War off the front pages. Mother was very upset. She always hated to see Dad blow up in public. But this time, knowing all the circumstances, she could not bring herself to reprimand him.

Dad never regretted that letter. He insisted that he had a right to be two persons—the President of the United States and Harry S. Truman, father of Margaret, husband of Bess Wallace. "It was Harry Truman, the human being who wrote that letter," he said.

A memorandum he wrote a few days later gives an even better picture of his state of mind.

Margie held a concert here in D.C. on Dec. 5th. It was a good one. She was well accompanied by a young pianist name of Allison, whose father is a Baptist preacher in Augusta, Georgia. Young Allison played two pieces after the intermission, one of which was the great A Flat Chopin Waltz Opus 42. He did it as well as it could be done and I've heard Paderewski, Moritz Rosenthal and Joseph Lhevinne play it.

A frustrated critic on *The Washington Post* wrote a lousy review. The only thing, General Marshall said, he didn't criticize was the varnish on the piano. He put my "baby" as low as he could and he made the young accompanist look like a dub.

It upset me, and I wrote him what I thought of him. I told him he is lower than Pegler and that was intended to be an insult worse than a reflection on his ancestry. I would never reflect on a man's mother because mothers are not to be attacked although mine has [been].

Well I've had a grand time this day. I've been accused of putting my "baby" who is the "apple of my eye" in a bad position. I don't think that is so. She doesn't either, thank the Almighty.

In addition to personal matters I've had conference after conference on the jittery situation facing the country. Attlee, Formosa, Communist China, Chiang Kai-shek, Japan, Germany, France, India, etc. I've worked for peace for five years and six months and it looks like World War III is here.

I hope not—but we must meet whatever comes—and we will.

A few weeks later, Dad wrote another interesting letter about my singing career. It gives the reader a glimpse of how much thought he and Mother had given to being parents in the White House.

My dear Miss Heggie:

I have just read your story in the *Woman's Home Companion*—"What Makes Margaret Sing?"

It is lovely. Thank you from my heart. The vast majority of our people can never understand what a terrible handicap it is to a lovely girl to have her father the President of the United States.

Stuffed shirt critics and vicious political opponents of mine sometimes try to take it out on Margie. It's her dad they are after and Margie understands. You have come more nearly stating the situation in its true light than anyone who has made the attempt.

I hope sometimes you'll make a study of the families of the Presidents. It is most interesting. Martha Washington and her children and what happened to them. Abigail Adams, Dolly Madison, the wife of Andrew Jackson and how she was hounded to her grave. Mrs. Lincoln, the most mistreated of all the White House First Ladies except Mrs. Cleveland, the first Mrs. Woodrow Wilson and the Wilson daughters, Alice Roosevelt Longworth, Mrs. Coolidge and Herbert Hoover's sons. Of course we are too close to Franklin Roosevelt and his daughter and sons to evaluate what the White House did to them.

You've made a contribution to history that will help some Ph.D. in the future to evaluate all these families I've mentioned.

Hope you'll regard this communication as one from a fond father and keep it confidential. Only my "mad" letters are published!

I had left Washington the day the Hume letter was mailed and was in Nashville, Tennessee, when the uproar exploded. Mother did not know what I thought of it all. She approached me warily on the telephone, as if I was a ticking bomb. "What are you going to do?" Mother asked.

"There's only one thing to do," I said. "Hold a press conference." By this time I had developed a fair amount of expertise and some pretty good rapport with reporters. When they showed up in force later that day, I handled them, if I may brag a little, pretty coolly. They asked me what I thought of the letter. "I'm glad chivalry isn't dead," I replied.

They asked me if the letter would hurt my career. "Not at all," I said. "It will sell tickets."

Mother, who still considered a press conference on a par with a visit to a cage full of cobras, was impressed. She called me the next day and congratulated me. "I'm going to stop worrying about you," she said.

I think she did, for about a week, anyway.

Chapter Twenty-six

A very tired, embattled president now faced a hostile Congress and a bitter, frustrating war. As 1951 began, Bess was deeply concerned about Harry Truman's health. That made her even more concerned about the issue that she thought they had resolved in early 1950: whether he would run for another term.

Multiplying this agony of the Truman partnership was the sense of having a tremendous triumph snatched away by the unpredictability of men and events. It was hard to believe in the first months of 1951 that in October 1950 Americans had been celebrating the destruction of the North Korean Army and hailing President Truman as a wizard. In this book I have described hindsight as the historian and biographer's friend. But when politicians play the hindsight game, ugly feelings emerge. It is so easy to second-guess a president when things go wrong. Everyone from Joseph P. Kennedy to Herbert Hoover urged us to cut and run in Korea. Instead, Harry Truman declared we would fight the Chinese to a standstill and then negotiate.

That is exactly what the UN Army did under the inspiring leadership of a new general, Matthew B. Ridgway. It was not easy. General Ridgway and his Commander in Chief faced the most difficult military task any American general and his president have confronted in the history of the United States. The General had to convince a shaken army full of drafted soldiers, who wondered what they were doing in Korea in the first place, that they could defeat an enemy who vastly outnumbered them. Ridgway did it by appealing to their honor, their pride in themselves as American soldiers.

While this agonizing turnaround took place in Korea, Dad had to fight off a savage Republican onslaught in Congress against the dispatch of American troops to Europe to bolster NATO. The isolationists whom he thought he had helped Franklin Roosevelt defeat in

1944 were back in business with a vengeance. Dad finessed them by appointing an acclaimed advocate of international cooperation, General Dwight D. Eisenhower, to head NATO. The General appeared before the Senate Foreign Relations Committee and stoutly supported the President's policy.

Simultaneously, Dad grappled with the vastly unpopular issue of price controls and higher taxes to prevent inflation. As that specter receded, he had to referee a brawl between the Treasury Department and the Federal Reserve Board about the nation's monetary policy. Simultaneously, Senator J. William Fulbright of Arkansas launched an investigation into the Reconstruction Finance Corporation, which spread smear and innuendo over several members of the White House staff. As usual, there were no indictments, no proof of wrongdoing. Another ambitious senator, Estes Kefauver, made headlines with an investigation of the links between local politicians and organized crime. Once more the big loser was the Democratic Party, to which neither senator seemed to realize he belonged.

The toll of these cumulative strains on the sixty-seven-year-old president was scary. Bess pressed him to vacation in Key West and he took her advice, but the stays were brief and the rest did not restore him to his old "fighting trim." That made Mother all the more anxious to get an answer from Chief Justice Fred Vinson about his willingness to run as Dad's successor. Poppa Vin had kept Dad waiting a full two years by now, protesting that he would do whatever the President asked him for the good of the country but never quite committing himself as a candidate.

April, which T. S. Eliot called the cruelest month, lived up to its reputation by producing the biggest crisis yet. General MacArthur was still the Supreme Commander in the Far East. (General Ridgway commanded the army on the Korean battlefield.) In Tokyo, MacArthur was privately infuriated that his predictions of imminent disaster and calls for forty or fifty atomic bombs on China had been proven fatuous by the UN force's stand against the Chinese. When General Ridgway went over to the offensive and chewed up thirty or forty Chinese divisions while fighting his way back to the thirty-eighth parallel dividing North and South Korea, MacArthur's pique only grew nastier. Adding to his sulk was the General's presidential ambitions. If anyone was going to get credit for winning peace with honor in Korea, his name had to be MacArthur. He began trying to sabotage Dad's plan to negotiate with the Chinese.

With the help of State Department experts on the Far East, Dad spent long hours drafting a proposal that would let the Chinese withdraw from Korea with a minimum loss of face. He sent MacArthur copies of various drafts of this proposal, so he would know exactly what was going on. On March 24, 1951, on the eve of the announcement of the President's offer, MacArthur issued his own statement—an arrogant ultimatum calling on the Red Chinese to get out of Korea or risk the invasion and destruction in China itself. The threat was patently nonsensical. We did not have an army big enough to invade China if we scraped together every man in uniform from Europe and the United States. It also ignored an explicit order from the President to refrain from all policy statements.

Later, Dad recalled his fury at this act of insubordination.

I couldn't send a message to the Chinese after that. He prevented a cease-fire proposition right there. I was ready to kick him into the North China Sea at that time. I was never so put out in my life. It's the lousiest trick a commander-in-chief can have done to him by an underling. MacArthur thought he was proconsul for the government of the United States and could do anything he damn pleased.

The moment Dad heard about this statement, he decided that General MacArthur had to be fired. He knew it would cause an uproar, and he did not want to endanger appropriations for the Marshall Plan and NATO then before Congress. Biding his time, he ordered General Omar Bradley, chairman of the Joint Chiefs of Staff, to remind MacArthur of the presidential order against policy statements.

MacArthur ignored this warning. When Joseph Martin, the Republican Minority Leader in the House, sent him a copy of a speech he had just made, attacking the Truman foreign policy, MacArthur responded with warm words of praise. Once more he revived the idea of using Chiang Kai-shek's aging army on Formosa. "Your view with respect to the utilization of the Chinese forces on Formosa is in conflict with neither logic nor . . . tradition," he wrote. He went on to imply that the diplomats and politicians in power did not understand the necessity of totally defeating communism in Asia.

On April 5, Martin rose in the House of Representatives to heap more abuse on the President's policy—and quoted from MacArthur's letter. Dad decided it was time to act. He called in four top advisers—General George C. Marshall, who had returned to the administration as Secretary of Defense; Dean Acheson, Secretary of State; W. Averell Harriman, who was serving as Secretary of Commerce but who had wide experience in foreign affairs; and General Omar Bradley, Chairman of the Joint Chiefs of Staff.

On his calendar, Dad jotted the results of this meeting.

I call in Gen. Marshall, Dean Acheson, Averell Harriman and General Bradley and they come to the conclusion that our Big General in the Far East must be recalled. I don't express any opinion or make known my decision.

There was one adviser in this crisis who already knew the President's decision. The MacArthur conflict was exactly the sort of problem Dad discussed with Mother. From her comments later, I am certain that the President had wholehearted backing from his political partner for this decision. If there was one thing Bess Truman valued, it was loyalty, and one thing she despised, it was disloyalty. General MacArthur had proven himself disloyal to a president who had supported him in spite of his horrendous mistakes in judgment that brought us to the brink of disaster in Korea.

Dad ordered Secretary of the Army Frank Pace to go to Tokyo and inform the General of his dismissal in private, stressing the regret that everyone felt at being forced to make the decision. Dad did not want to wound or humiliate General MacArthur. Although he disliked his flamboyant, egocentric style, he recognized and valued MacArthur's contributions to the army and the nation in two world wars. Before Mr. Pace, who was on an inspection tour of Korea, could obey this order, a reporter from the Chicago *Tribune* called the Pentagon and asked if "an important resignation" was brewing in Tokyo. The call was relayed to General Bradley at the White House. General Bradley warned Dad that news of the firing had apparently been leaked and MacArthur might be planning to resign first and try to humiliate the President with a public denunciation.

"He's going to be fired," Dad said. But the only choice, now, seemed to be a cable to the General and a public announcement in Washington. Dad ordered his advisers and staff to discuss the pros and cons of this decision. While they debated in the Cabinet Room, Dad returned to Blair House to have dinner with Mother. We can be sure that he discussed his continuing reluctance to hurt MacArthur's feelings with his partner—and I am pretty certain what she told him. The hard side of Bess Wallace Truman's personality was unquestionably in charge on the subject of Douglas MacArthur. She heartily agreed with Assistant Press Secretary Roger Tubby, who was arguing in the Cabinet Room that there was no reason to spare MacArthur's feelings when he had behaved in such an "unethical, insolent, insubordinate way" toward the President.

At 10 P.M., Dad's top advisers trooped into Blair House to inform him that a majority favored an immediate dispatch of the dismissal orders to Tokyo. Still Dad hesitated, although he authorized the White House press office to begin mimeographing his presidential orders firing MacArthur and appointing General Ridgway in his place. When it came to wounding the feelings of anyone, even a dangerous political antagonist, the tenderhearted side of Harry Truman's personality held him back. He was still hoping to contact Secretary of the Army Pace, who remained out of reach in Korea.

Then came word from the White House press office that the Mutual Broadcasting System was getting ready to carry a big story from Tokyo. Dad made the final decision. The mimeograph machines started working overtime to print dozens of background documents, and calls went out to all the reporters and photographers assigned to the White House. At 1 A.M., Dad went before the newsmen to announce Douglas MacArthur's dismissal.

With deep regret, I have concluded that the General of the Army Douglas MacArthur is unable to give his wholehearted support to the policies of the United States government and of the United Nations in matters pertaining to his official duties. In view of the specific responsibilities imposed upon me by the Constitution of the United States and the added responsibility which has been entrusted to me by the United Nations, I have decided that I must make a change of command in the Far East. I have, therefore, relieved General MacArthur of his commands and have designated Lt. General Matthew B. Ridgway as his successor.

The next day, Dad jotted on his desk calendar a seemingly offhand comment.

Quite an explosion. Was expected but I had to act.
Telegrams and letters of abuse by the dozens.

This is the Truman understatement to end them all. The national uproar was stupendous. All the pent-up frustration with the limited war Dad was fighting in Korea, the ugly suspicions of treason in high places stirred by Senator McCarthy and his followers, came to a boil over MacArthur's dismissal. Dad was hanged in effigy, denounced by city councils and state legislatures. One-hundred-and-twenty-five-thousand outraged telegrams poured into the White House in the next two days. Threats on Dad's life multiplied tenfold.

In Congress, one of McCarthy's imitators, Senator William E. Jenner of Indiana, declared that the country was "in the hands of a secret inner coterie which is directed by agents of the Soviet Union." He called for President Truman's immediate impeachment. The Chicago *Tribune* concurred. The paper called Dad "unfit, morally and mentally, for his high office." Congressman Richard Nixon declared: "The happiest group in the country will be the communists and their stooges."

This incredible outpouring of vilification took a heavy toll on Bess's nerves. It revived the fear that had troubled her at the beginning of the first term—that Dad would become as hated by approximately half the American people as Franklin D. Roosevelt had been. During the worst of the MacArthur frenzy, it looked as if all the people had turned against their president. He was even booed when he and Mother went to the opening day of the baseball season.

Calmly, with magnificent poise, Dad responded to this frenzy with reason. He never lost faith in Thomas Jefferson's dictum, "the people will come right in the end." But to come right, the people must be given the facts. Dad went on television and talked honestly, plainly, to his fellow Americans. "I have thought long and hard about this question of extending the war in Asia. I have discussed it many times with the ablest military advisers in the country. I believe with all my heart that the course we are following is the best one."

With all this abuse burdening her mind, Bess had to continue smiling through her usual round of receptions and official dinners and teas. Early in the spring, her mother's health went into another downward slide. Grandmother's mind began to wander; she became very forgetful and would wake up Bess in the middle of the night to ask her anxious questions about Fred and other members of the family. By the time Bess took her back to Independence for the summer, the First Lady was almost as exhausted as the President.

Dad assumed the uncharacteristic role of family worrier after talking to her on the telephone one night early in June. "Your voice sounded as if you were very tired last night," he wrote. "Please get some rest. That's what you are home for. . . . Please take care of yourself. I don't think you fully understand that I can face the world and all its troubles if you and Margie are all right. I don't think I can do it if you are not."

Meanwhile, General MacArthur as a boiling political issue was slowly evaporating. A special Senate committee headed by Richard Russell of Georgia launched a careful investigation of his dismissal. One after another, the top military men in the nation, from General Marshall and General Bradley to General Hoyt Vandenberg, the chief of the Air Force, supported the President's decision and confirmed that General MacArthur had been insubordinate. They also took some rather large pieces out of the General's military reputation. General Lawton Collins said that MacArthur had violated almost every basic rule of military strategy in his "home by Christmas" drive to the Yalu River in November 1950.

When General MacArthur testified before the committee, it soon became clear that he was unable to prove his claim that he had a policy and President Truman had no policy. He admitted that the United States would be insane to invade Manchuria and begin a war with China's 400 million people. The senators—and the American public—gradually realized that MacArthur's cry, "there is no substitute for victory," was a hollow slogan.

On June 25, 1951, a year to the day after the Korean War began, Dad wrote Mother an anniversary letter that reflected this major change in public opinion.

I'm leaving for Tennessee shortly to speak at the dedication of an air research center, named for General Arnold. I'm going to tear the Russians and the Republicans apart—call a spade just what it is and tell Malik [Jacob Malik, Russian ambassador to the UN] if Russia wants peace, peace is available and has been since 1945. This is the anniversary of the flight from Independence a year ago that has been quite a day in history. All the papers except the sabotage sheets gave me the best of it yesterday.

This week contains another very important—most important—anniversary. Thursday will be thirty-two years. What a thirty-two years! I've never been anything but happy for that anniversary. Maybe I haven't given you all you're entitled to, but I've done my best, and I'm still in love with the prettiest girl in the world.

Hope all are well. We'll talk to Margie in Rome next Sunday.

As you might gather from that last line, at this point I was adding to the Trumans' worries. I was whirling around Europe on a six-week tour with my friend Annette Davis Wright and my secretary (and friend) Reathel Odum. It had started off as a vacation, with me proudly announcing I could and would pay my own and Reathel's way. But I had forgotten that my name was Margaret Truman. The President and First Lady explained to me that politicians on both sides of the iron curtain would be asking their advisers and intelligence people what the visit meant. There was also the problem of security. Only two Secret Service men could be spared to go with me. That was not enough to protect us if we stayed in hotels and guest houses. By the time all the details were worked out, we were booked into nothing but embassies and legations.

I still managed to have a wonderful time, dining with such lofty figures as Winston Churchill and the King and Queen of England, spending twenty minutes in a private audience with Pope Pius XII, and doing my best in many interviews to play goodwill ambassador in England, France, Holland, Luxembourg, and Italy.

What was the First Lady of the United States doing while her daughter was making like a princess on parade? A letter that caught up to me in London brought me down to earth. The First Lady was painting the back stairway and steps at 219 North Delaware Street. "There'll probably be some of it [painting] left for you to do in July!" she warned me. "Mr. Gregg [the carpenter] is making a cabinet for the pantry & that will require *several* coats."

She filled me in on other details of life in the Gates-Wallace manse. "Grandmother is taking all of us to the Plantation [a local restaurant] tomorrow to dinner. She surely has come to life since she has been home—but [she is] back at her old tricks. Waked me up twice before 7:30 this morning wanting me to call to make the reservations. [She] thought it was already Sunday. You can easily imagine how *happy* I was!

"May [Wallace] is having the [Bridge] Club Tuesday and I guess that will start the parties. All this is pretty humdrum compared to the glamorous things you will be doing."

Next came the inevitable reminder to write. She wanted to hear all about whom we had met, what we had seen at each stop. She particularly hoped that Reathel, who had worked so hard for me and her, would "enjoy every minute" of the trip. Then a final "Mother" touch. "Don't forget flowers to the Queen . . . along with a note."

I can see now that painting the old house was exactly the sort of relaxation Mother needed after the harrowing six months she had just spent in Washington. I was also stirred to see how much sheer pleasure she took in thinking about me having a good time. I guess you have to become a parent yourself before you can understand how love makes this phenomenon possible.

Bess spent the summer of 1951 in Independence fretting over her mother. She urged Mary Paxton Keeley to pay a visit. "Mother would love to see you if you get there on a good day. Today is a bad one—doesn't remember one thing for five minutes even. Told Vietta I haven't been in to see her today and I have been in there not less than ten times."

Dad paid her a brief visit in July and spent the rest of the time worrying about the war in Korea, which dragged on although the Communists had implicitly admitted they could not win by agreeing to begin peace negotiations late in June. He could not ask Mother to leave Grandmother Wallace, but he could not resist going back to his old tactic of letting her know what she was missing.

Early in September, he sent her a marvelously detailed report of a baseball game he attended to celebrate the fiftieth anniversary of the American League. Chief Justice Vinson was along and "knew all the old players and all the new ones." The owner of the Washington Senators, Clark Griffith, sat next to Dad and told him "what the various players on the Washington team should have done and didn't do." Dad had absolutely no interest in baseball, but he knew that Mother was going crazy, reading this. She would have loved every minute of it. Dad ended the torture by remarking: "Old Clark said Washington lost because you were not present. I agreed with him."

A few days later, Mother persuaded Dad to take a five-day vacation in Independence on his way back from San Francisco, where he opened a conference that led to the signing of a treaty of peace with Japan. It was the best rest he got all year. Most of the time he just lazed around the house and backyard or strolled over to chat with the Nolands and other neighbors.

When Bess returned to Washington with her mother later in the month, she immediately reopened the question of Chief Justice Vinson and his candidacy. The longer it slid along, the more she feared that Dad might be persuaded by the party politicians or his staff to run for another term. This time Dad really pressed the Chief Justice. After another three months of hemming and hawing, he said no. He did not think he could handle the strain of four years in the White House. He also feared he would embroil the Supreme Court in politics if he became a candidate.

Mother was even more disappointed than Dad, if that was possible. The Big Judge's refusal threw everything back to June 25, 1950. Harry Truman was not the sort of man to walk out on his deep sense of responsibility for achieving a peaceful world. How much ground she had for worry is visible in a letter Dad wrote to Dwight Eisenhower in mid-December 1951.

> The columnists, the slick magazines and all the political people who like to speculate are saying many things about what is to happen in 1952.
>
> As I told you in 1948 and at our luncheon in 1951 [when Dad appointed him NATO commander], do what you think best for the country. My own position is in the balance. If I do what I want to do I'll go back to Missouri and *maybe* run for the Senate. If you decide to finish the European job (and I don't know who else can) I must keep the isolationists out of the White House. I wish you would let me know what you intend to do. It will be between us and no one else.

Ike replied in a handwritten note on January 1, 1952, disclaiming any political ambitions. "The possibility that I will ever be drawn into political activities is so remote as to be negligible," he wrote. Unfortunately, this only increased the possibility of Dad running for another term. At this point, he and everyone else presumed that Ike was a Democrat and the Republican candidate would be Robert Taft. The thought of him in the White House was behind that sentence in the letter to Ike about keeping the isolationists out. Memories of Mamma Truman's detestation of this sour-faced Republican added fuel to Dad's determination.

Back in the White House after a Christmas visit home, Dad's diary jottings and letters reveal his divided state of mind—of which Bess was all too aware. "What a New Year's Day!" he wrote on January 1. "1952 is here and so am I—gloomy as can be. But we must look to the program of world peace, and keep on looking. . . . I wish I was seventeen instead of sixty-seven."

On January 3, with that amazing ability to look objectively at himself, he wrote an essay on his health and strict diet, which he disliked. It began with a fatherly, if highly opinionated, comment on my appearance, as he assessed it over the Christmas holidays.

> Margie looked very well except she's too thin. These damned diets the women go for are all wrong. More people die of dieting these days than of eating too much.
>
> My good doctor is all the time trying to cut my weight down. Of course he's right and I should weigh 170 pounds. Now I weigh 175. What's five pounds between my doctor and me?
>
> When I went into World War, I weighed 145 pounds. After two years service I weighed 155. While I was in the Senate I was ten pounds heavier—165.

When I moved into the White House I went up to 185. I've now hit an average of 175. I walk two miles most every morning at a hundred and twenty eight steps a minute. I eat no bread but one piece of toast at breakfast, no butter, no sugar, no sweets. Usually have fruit, one egg, a strip of bacon and half a glass of skimmed milk for breakfast; liver & bacon or sweet breads or ham or fish and spinach and another nonfattening vegetable for lunch with fruit for dessert. For dinner I have a fruit cup, steak, a couple of nonfattening vegetables and an ice, orange, pineapple or raspberry for dinner. So—I maintain my waist line and can wear suits bought in 1935!

This meditation suggests a president who was in fighting trim. But Mother knew better. She saw the slow erosion of Dad's vitality as he began his eighth year in the White House. It took him longer to recover from his bouts of exhaustion. As he approached his 68th birthday he found it harder and harder to keep working a sixteen-hour day.

With all these worries on their minds, Dad and Mother still found time to remember ordinary people who had crossed their paths and came to them now in need of help. Here is Dad's reaction to a problem Mother brought to his attention. The memorandum was addressed to White House aide Don Dawson, a savvy lawyer who usually dealt with much weightier problems.

Mrs. Ricketts was the manager of 4701 [Connecticut Avenue] when we lived there. She has become invalided and needs a place to stay.

She is an Eastern Star, who has kept up her dues. She wants to go to the Eastern Star Home, which is the only place she can go. Make them take her. She's one of the 153,000,000 who have no pull except the President. She has the right to go to the home.

If this damned District of Columbia had old age homes where a paid old age retirement could be arranged the "boss" & I could take care of the situation. But there is none. So only the Eastern Star home is left. If the good old lady was not eligible, I wouldn't raise hell about it. But *they* are cheating her. Stop it.

Mrs. Ricketts got into the home.

Meanwhile, the question of running again in 1952 was still rumbling around Dad's mind. It crept into a letter he wrote and decided not to send to *The New Yorker* magazine.

I've been reading your Jan. 5 Talk of the Town—and you've been taken in by one of Missouri's lovable old fakirs, Cyril Clemens—at one time there was a t before the s! He claims to be a seventh—it may be a seventeenth—cousin of Hannibal's (Missouri not Carthage) well known humorist, Mark.

He has carried on a copious, one way letter writing for his I.M.T.S. [International Mark Twain Society] for years & years. How I wish my lamented friend and press secretary, Charlie Ross, had lived to see you taken in!

He is the International Mark Twain Society and he merely puts people into it without a "by-your-leave" or any other formula. You'll get in now and no doubt be the recipient of nutty letters like the enclosed—which is my latest.

I don't know him, never saw him and don't want to. But of all the things to happen—the *New Yorker* to be hooked. . . . Mark, himself, was a kind of charlatan and fakir—but all natives of Missouri love him—he was the lying columnist of his day. We have lots of 'em now but no Sam Clemenses.

This is a personal & confidential communication. You may publish it when I retire—which may be some time yet.

Dad wrote that last sentence the day after General Eisenhower announced that he might be responsive to a draft for the presidency—less than a week after writing the letter I have just quoted, denying all political ambitions. At the same time, Senator Henry Cabot Lodge revealed that the General was a Republican who had voted for Dewey in 1948. The Eisenhower for President organization promptly opened offices in half the states in the country. If Ike did not know this campaign was about to begin, he had to be the most naive man alive. If he knew it, his letter to Dad comes awfully close to a lie.

This only added urgency to Dad's search for a Democratic candidate. His number one choice was Adlai Stevenson, the popular governor of Illinois. In his four years as chief executive of that pivotal state, he had built a distinguished record. He was a moderate, acceptable to the party's conservatives and liberals. Dad invited Mr. Stevenson to Blair House for a talk on January 22, 1952. Personally, they hit it off well. The governor listened to Dad's sermon on the importance of keeping the presidency in Democratic hands and said he was deeply impressed by the offer and awed by the responsibility.

Dad thought this was an acceptance. Several days later, he discovered Mr. Stevenson thought he had said no. Listening to reports of this confusion—and noting Dad's growing irritation with the Eisenhower candidacy, Mother became more and more alarmed. She could see the whole scenario heading straight to a renomination in July. One night she sat down with Dad in his study and told him that she could not survive another four years in the presidency. She did not think he could do it either—but she was speaking for herself, first.

That warning shook Dad to the depths of his soul. A few weeks later, he convened a meeting of his top aides, to which he invited Chief Justice Vinson and a few other close friends. One by one, he asked them whether he should run again. Each said no. With a candor that he always encouraged from his friends and his staff, they told him they were worried about his growing exhaustion. If he ran and won, which they were certain he could do, he would be seventy-three by the time he left office.

Perhaps Dad was hoping that Poppa Vin might be moved by this dramatic scene to change his mind. If so, it did not work. The Chief Justice only concurred with the rest of the room, that Harry Truman should not run again.

This informal poll did not mean the issue was decided, by any means. Like all presidents, Dad often ignored or overruled the advice of his cabinet and staff. He really believed that sign on his desk, "The buck stops here." Only he could decide, finally, what was best for the nation.

A few days later, Matt Connelly, his appointments secretary, heard his decision—and why. Matt had just come from a party given by Les Biffle, the secretary of the Senate, one of the men who had talked Dad into becoming vice president in 1944. Mr. Biffle still saw himself as a president maker. He and everyone else at the party denounced Adlai Stevenson's reluctance to run and dismissed him as a candidate. They all said Harry Truman was their only hope, the only man who could beat General Eisenhower.

Back at the White House, Matt found Dad still in his office, working late as usual. Matt told him what they were saying at the Biffle party. Dad listened, growing more and more upset. "Matt," he asked, "Do you think the old man will have to run again?"

Matt's normally cheerful Irish-American face grew somber. With Charlie Ross gone, he was closer to the Trumans than any other member of the staff. He pointed to a portrait of Bess on the wall to the left. "Would you do that to her?" he asked.

Dad looked at the portrait, and at the photograph of Mother on his desk, the one he had carried through France in World War I. Slowly, sadly, he nodded. "You know if anything happened to her, what would happen to me?"

Matt nodded. He knew.

"All right," Dad said. "That settles it."

In mid-March, Dad went to Key West for another vacation. Mother did not go with him. She had a very important job to do— supervising the final preparations for the reopening of the renovated White House. She had kept in close touch with the Fine Arts Commission that redecorated the downstairs rooms. In her files are reports on their progress four- or five-inches thick. Upstairs, she worked with decorators from B. Altman's on our private quarters.

Late in March, Bess gave the women reporters a tour of the house. She was rewarded for her courtesy with some tough questions on the topic that was absorbing everyone in Washington. "Would you like to spend four more years here?" one of the reporters asked.

"You're not going to get a yes or no out of me on that one," Bess said.

"Could you stand it if you had to?"

"I stood it for seven years," Bess said.

Mother was very good at keeping secrets.

Dad returned from Key West looking much more like his old self. Mother greeted him at the airport with the news that the White House was ready for his inspection. Naturally, the former builder of county courthouses and hospitals wanted to see it immediately. They were greeted at the front door by the staff. Mr. Crim, the head usher, gave Dad a gold key. Mother was amused to discover it opened nothing.

The President followed the First Lady through the gleaming East Room, Green Room, Blue Room, Red Room, and State Dining Room and pronounced them all magnificent. Mother went off to preside at a Salvation Army dinner, and Dad continued his inspection for most of the evening. One might wonder if regaining this now really palatial mansion might have given Harry Truman second thoughts about his decision. But raising that question would only prove you did not know Harry Truman very well.

On March 29, every Democratic VIP in the country crammed into the Washington Armory for the Jefferson-Jackson Day dinner. Dad was the principal speaker. On the dais, he sat next to Alice Acheson, the Secretary of State's wife. On the way to the dinner, Alice had asked her husband if he thought the President might say something about running again in his speech. "Not at all," replied Mr. Acheson in his most autocratic tone, one of the many reasons why he was a superb Secretary of State. Mrs. Acheson, properly subdued, dropped the subject.

After dessert, Dad took out the binder containing his speech. He opened it to the last page and showed it to Mrs. Acheson. The final paragraph read: "I shall not be a candidate for reelection. I have served my country long, and I think efficiently and honestly. I shall not accept a renomination. I do not feel that it is my duty to spend another four years in the White House."

"You, Bess and I are the only ones here who know that," Dad said.

Mrs. Acheson wondered if he ought to reconsider one last time. She asked Dad if she could tell the Secretary of State, who might want to try to talk him out of it. Dad shook his head. His mind was made up and not even the eloquence of the most brilliant man in his cabinet could change it now.

Dad gave a magnificent speech that night. He summed up the achievements of the Democratic Party at home and abroad. It was a great record. Under his leadership, the United States had restored the strength of the free world and met the challenge of Communist aggression. He scorched the Republican isolationists and red-baiters who were undermining our bipartisan foreign policy and summed up the Democratic Party's record of service to the farmer, the worker, and world peace.

Finally, he paused. "Whoever the Democrats nominate for President this year, he will have that record to run upon," he said. Then he read his statement, announcing his decision not to seek another term. General Vaughan had his eye on Mother while the words spread shock and dismay through the assembled Democrats. "She looked," the General said, "the way you do when you draw four aces."

The reporters rushed to Governor Stevenson's table to ask him if he was a candidate. They should have talked to Bess Wallace Truman. For the first and only time during her eight years as First Lady, she might have given them an interview. I can almost see the head on the story:

BESS TRUMAN SAYS SHE
IS THE HAPPIEST WOMAN
IN WASHINGTON, D.C.

Chapter Twenty-seven

Back in the restored White House, Bess found herself working harder than ever. Several major state visits, which had been put off so that the foreign guests could enjoy the $5 million worth of splendor that the Trumans had created for future presidents, now became realities.

First to arrive was Queen Juliana of the Netherlands and her husband, Prince Bernhard. Mother was especially eager to greet the royal couple, who had been most hospitable to me on my tour of Europe in 1951. When I got home, I had strongly recommended inviting them. I suspected they and the Trumans would hit it off well, and I was right. Mother and the Queen became instant friends. They were both down-to-earth, no-nonsense women. In fact, the Queen gave Congress the kind of address that Bess would have given them, if she had ever been granted the opportunity.

Dad was proud of his ability to talk to people like a Dutch uncle. Queen Juliana gave the isolationists and red-baiters the business, like a Dutch aunt. She told Congress that the United States was the leader of the free world whether they liked it or not, and it was up to them to face that responsibility.

Mother sat in the gallery, beaming.

The next important guest to arrive—not on a state visit basis, of course—was Eleanor Roosevelt. She came to Washington to report to Dad on a trip she had just made to the Middle East. The Trumans took her on a tour of the White House. She especially liked the way Mother had redecorated the battered old sun porch on the third floor. With a new tile floor and rattan furniture, it was a great place to relax, and it had a marvelous view of the city. Best of all, it was practically invisible from the street.

Mrs. Roosevelt was also full of admiration for another item Mother had added to the family rooms: closets. No longer could the maids drive the First Lady crazy by putting her clothes away on the third floor before she could decide whether she wanted to wear them again.

Official state dinners and luncheons now marched in a virtual procession through the State Dining Room. A diplomatic reception produced 1,500 hands to shake. To make it even more wearing, the new White House air-conditioning system failed.

Dad, meanwhile, was up to his neck in another crisis, the steel strike of 1952. Although our young men were still dying in Korea, the patriots in the executive offices of the mills were unable to put their country ahead of a quick buck. The result was a shutdown that threatened to create dangerous shortages of ammunition and weapons. Dad was outraged and ordered the federal government to seize the mills.

Before taking this step, he had conferred with Chief Justice Fred Vinson, who had assured him that the move was legal and the Supreme Court would support him. When the case went to the court, the Big Judge turned out to be unable to persuade the rest of the Justices to agree with him. Dad was humiliated, and thenceforth I began to take a very dim view of the Vinsons. I thought both Mother and Dad were too susceptible to their flattery. I never succeeded in changing their minds about them.

The net effect of this national spasm was another outpouring of vitriol against Dad. He was called a Caesar, a Hitler, a Mussolini, a power-mad bully. Worse, from Mother's point of view, the steel crisis, which included press conferences, a TV address to the nation, and endless meetings with advisers and lawyers from the Justice Department, produced the scariest bout of presidential exhaustion yet. Dad actually fell asleep in a chair while resting at Blair House, an unprecedented event. He put off signing important papers because he was too "shaky." For Mother, this reaction only confirmed the wisdom of her opposition to another four years in the White House. After seven and a half years of crises, Dad was close to burnout.

Instead of urging a retreat to Key West, Mother decided to issue an edict: no more night work. After dinner, the President of the United States would *not* go back to his office. Dad obeyed the order, most of the time.

When he managed to forget the harassments of the Oval Office, Dad resumed one of his favorites pastimes—teasing "Miss Lizzie." It was always a sign that things were going well between him and

Mother. One of his better moments came on Good Friday, when Mother and I went to morning services at the Washington Cathedral. We returned to find Dad waiting to have lunch with us. Mother went on at some length about the beauty of the ritual at the Cathedral, the excellent music. "And what are you two good Episcopalians going to have for lunch on Good Friday?" Dad asked.

At that moment, almost as if he had stage managed it, lunch was served: hamburger. I laughed and Mother looked sheepish. She had approved the menu, earlier in the week, without giving much thought to it.

P.S. We ate it.

Around this time, another trip to church produced some amusing dialogue—and some serious thoughts about religion in one of Dad's diary jottings. His opinions on this subject had not changed very much from the days when he wrote his first letters to Bess Wallace.

Jefferson's birthday. Bess & I walk across Lafayette Square to St. John's Church for 8 o'clock service. Mr. Searles, one of the White House ushers, tells Mrs. T. she's done a good deed—taking a Baptist to an Episcopal service! I've gone with her time and again to her service—and she has gone with me to the 1st Baptist Church.

I've never been of the opinion that Almighty God cares for the building or the form that a believer approaches the Maker of Heaven and Earth. "When two or three are gathered together" or when one asks for help from God he'll get it just as surely as will panoplied occupants of any pulpit. Forms and ceremonies impress a lot of people, but I've never thought that The Almighty could be impressed by anything but the heart and soul of the individual. That's why I'm a Baptist, whose church authority starts from the bottom—not the top. So much for churches.

Early in June, Mother had a White House reception that meant more to her than any of the state dinners or diplomatic fol-de-rol. She invited 1,450 wounded veterans to the new White House. She marshaled a contingent of VIP's, including the President, the cabinet members and their wives, Mrs. Woodrow Wilson, and a squad of generals and admirals to shake hands with them. Dad went back to work in a very determined mood, as he told Ethel Noland in a letter. "I spent the rest of the day discussing ways and means to keep the country and the world off the skids as a result of the awful [Supreme] court decision. But we'll make it."

Shortly thereafter your biographer took off for another tour of Europe, this time with my best friend, Drucie Snyder Horton (Treasury Secretary John Snyder's daughter). Drucie was married and the mother of a daughter, but I persuaded her to leave both husband and child for six weeks of high living. I don't think Mother quite approved. No power on earth could tear her away from me during the early years of my existence. But she resigned herself to the deplorable habits of the younger generation and let us go without any particularly devastating comments.

Mother came up to New York to see us off. We had tea at the Carlyle Hotel the day before we sailed. Drucie and I were in the highest imaginable spirits. We swigged our tea as if it was champagne. "Marg! Drucie!" Mother exclaimed, appalled at the way we were picking up our teacups. "Surely your mother, Drucie, taught you how a lady drinks tea. I know I've tried to teach this one," she said, gesturing to me.

"Try to pick up that cup with one finger," I said.

Mother tried—and failed. The cup weighed at least a pound. I think this was the day she gave up trying to make a lady out of me (and Drucie, whom she frequently treated as a second daughter). It was bad enough that I never listened to her anymore. Even technology was against her.

Not long after I arrived in Europe, Mother requested me to refute a recurring rumor that she was the daughter of one Robert Wallace, who was still living in Ireland. I was on my way to Ireland, and she ordered me to "settle [it] once and for all" at a press conference in Dublin. Her father's name, she told me, was "David Willock Wallace and he was born in Independence, Missouri." She was "sick and tired" of the way the story kept popping up.

It saddened me that Mother felt she had to tell me my grandfather's name. It is an indication of how seldom he was mentioned at 219 North Delaware Street. Now that I understand how Mother coped with this burden, I can see this calm, almost offhand message as another example of her courage. In Ireland, I did as I was told, and David Willock Wallace's real story remained where it belonged during Mother's lifetime—buried.

In London, I got an amusing letter from Mother, again demonstrating her marvelous ability to get even with Dad. Remember the Key West fishing expeditions? Writing on July 4, she serenely informed me that "Fred Vinson and Dad and I are going to the baseball game this afternoon. Double-header! I haven't seen one in years. 'Mamma' Vinson said she wouldn't sit on a hard seat that long."

How do you like that for sweet revenge? For teasing her about missing a baseball game the previous summer, she planned to make the
President of the United States sit through two games, knowing that
he would prefer to be almost anywhere else.

Unfortunately, it rained early in the second game. The First Couple stuck it out for an hour and finally went back to the White House.
Undaunted, Mother demanded and got a presidential escort to a
night game on July 5.

These were straws in the wind, you might say, except that there is
precious little wind in humid Washington during the summer, when
Congress is seldom in session. Along with dutifully continuing her
First Lady chores, Mother quietly began working into her schedule a
lot of things that she wanted to do. Old Independence friends, such
as Helen Souter and Arry Ellen Mayer Calhoun, were invited for
weekends of reminiscence and gossip.

Dad also decided to enjoy himself a little in the closing months of
his presidency. You will recall that he turned down with great regret
an invitation to attend a reunion of the Thirty-fifth Division shortly
after the assassination attempt in 1950. In June 1952, he accepted
another invitation and flew to Springfield, Missouri, for a delightful
celebration—which brought him and a future president of the
United States together. Here is the story in Dad's own words.

Drove into Springfield in an open car with Vivian & Mary [his brother
and sister] in the back seat. It was like 1948. There were at least 100 thousand
people on the streets yelling as usual "Hello Harry," "There he is" and "We
want you again." But, I am sorry to write, "They can't have me again."

At the Colonial Hotel the streets were jammed in every direction with
enthusiastic fans.

Had dinner with the family in a room next door to my suite. . . . Soon as
dinner was over we went to the Shrine Mosque where a wonderful entertainment was given by the 35th Division Committee. The winners of the
Square Dance contest danced for us. . . . Then Ronald Reagan and his wife
Nancy Davis with Gene Nelson, Virginia Gibson and Mrs. Grover
Cleveland Alexander came over from the premiere of "The Winning Team,"
and gave us a half hour of grand entertainment.

I would not want to have been within earshot if someone with a
crystal ball had told Dad he was applauding a future Republican
president. In those days, Ronald Reagan was a Democrat.

Later in July, Dad and Mother flew to Chicago for the Democratic
Convention. It is interesting how many conflicting emotions Mother
had when that city was mentioned. It was the first stop on her

honeymoon and the place where, in 1944, her presidential tribulations began. Now she could think, with some justification, that
things had come full circle, as she attended a Chicago convention
that did not nominate Harry Truman for anything. Instead she
watched Dad as he performed like the master politician that he was,
maneuvering his influence around the convention to win the nomination for Adlai Stevenson.

When Dad arrived in Chicago, the convention had recessed. Senator Estes Kefauver, whom Dad preferred to call "Cowfever," had
some 360 votes, and Governor Stevenson had about 330. The rest of
the votes were being held by favorite sons. Without Dad's intervention, there was a good chance that Kefauver, a man with no loyalty to
anyone but himself, would have gotten the nomination. Dad ordered
Averell Harriman of New York and Joseph Dever, the governor of
Massachusetts to release their delegations. They obeyed and Mr.
Stevenson was promptly nominated. That was the beginning, not
the end, of the Trumans' tribulations.

Dad never really warmed to Adlai Stevenson, although he tried
very hard to like and understand him. Mother liked him. She almost
always liked born gentlemen, men with courtly manners and
debonair wit. But she agreed with the politician she had married that
Mr. Stevenson behaved deplorably as a presidential candidate.

By playing Hamlet until the last moment, he forfeited the opportunity to build him up as the Democratic Party's wholehearted
choice. In the campaign that followed his nomination, he betrayed a
lack of judgment that dismayed Mother and infuriated Dad. Bess
wanted to see her man get the credit that was coming to him for his
eight grueling years in the White House. Instead, Adlai Stevenson
decided he had to run *against* Harry Truman's record. He was intimidated by Republican outcries about the mess in Washington, McCarthy's red-baiting, and the protracted struggle in Korea, which we
were winning on our terms.

Several times Dad became so infuriated, he wrote letters to Mr.
Stevenson that would have blown him and the Democratic Party
apart if he had mailed them. Here are the explosive opening lines of
one he dashed off in early August of 1952.

Dear Governor:
    I have come to the conclusion that you are embarrassed by having the
President of the United States in your corner in this campaign.
    Therefore I shall remain silent and stay in Washington until Nov. 4.

Dad then recounted the story of Mr. Stevenson's coyness about the nomination and the way Dad had rescued him from rejection in Chicago. He then described what Mr. Stevenson had done to the Democratic Party thereafter.

Then you proceeded to break up the Democratic National Committee, which I had spent years in organizing, you call in the former mayor of Louisville [Wilson Wyatt] as your personal chairman and fired [Frank] McKinney, the best chairman of the National Committee in my recollection.

Since the convention you have treated the President as a liability. . . . I have tried to make it plain to you that I want you elected—in fact I want you to win this time more than I wanted to win in 1948.

But I can't stand snub after snub by you and Mr. Wyatt.

On August 16, 1952, Governor Stevenson allowed himself to get mousetrapped by one of the oldest dodges in the newspaper business. The Oregon *Journal* asked him if he could "clean up the mess in Washington." Mr. Stevenson fell for it, replying solemnly that he had cleaned up a big mess in Illinois and thought he could clean up Washington. At the White House, an exploding president again reached for his pen.

Dear Governor:

Your letter to Oregon is a surprising document. It makes the campaign rather ridiculous. It seems to me that the Presidential Nominee and his running-mate are trying to beat the Democratic President instead of the Republicans and the General of the Army who heads their ticket.

There is no mess in Washington. . . . The Dixiecrats and the Taft Republicans along with Nixon, Knowland, Harry Byrd and the seniority chairman of the Key Committees of the House and Senate make the only mess in the national scene.

I was not in the White House when these letters were written, but I know Mother—and his own common sense—stopped Dad from mailing them. By and large, Bess believed it was better to suffer fools and foolishness in silence than run the risk of making yourself sound foolish by attacking them.

Mother also regretted the antagonism that developed between Dad and the Republican Party's candidate, Dwight Eisenhower, during the campaign. Ike's military skin was very thin, and when Dad went after him for duplicity and his virtually nonexistent political experience, the General took it very personally. Mother liked Ike and was even fonder of his wife, Mamie, whom she had gotten to know fairly well during the year of the White House Spanish class.

Bess stayed out of the 1952 campaign. Dad went whistle-stopping with me for family. Mother's ostensible reason was Grandmother Wallace's health. After celebrating her ninetieth birthday on August 4, she became very feeble and almost completely bedridden. But I think Mother's withdrawal said something about the campaign, too. She felt Harry Truman had had enough political combat to last two lifetimes. She would have preferred to see him make a dignified withdrawal from the presidency.

Dad was too much a fighter, too much a Democrat to the marrow of his bones, to accept this idea. He was also too deeply involved in the ongoing momentum of the presidency. For instance, he might have turned the campaign around if he had agreed in October to the Communist demand to forcibly repatriate the 132,000 Chinese and Korean prisoners in UN hands. Dad refused. "We will not buy an armistice by turning over human beings to slaughter or slavery," he said. The Communists replied by launching a series of attacks on the UN Army that inflicted heavy casualties, and cost the Democrats millions of votes.

Dad took the catastrophic Democratic defeat of 1952 very personally, at first. No one seemed to appreciate the principles for which he had tried to stand. "For seven years the country had faced the Soviet threat—in Iran, in Greece and Turkey, in Berlin, and in Korea and Indochina—and faced it successfully. Yet one demagogic statement made the people forget!" he all but cried out in one of his diary notes. He was referring to Ike's declaration that he would "go to Korea" and end the war with some unspecified (and, as it turned out, nonexistent) wizardry.

To the crestfallen President, the people seemed to have repudiated the party to which he had given his heartfelt allegiance all his life. Having semi-withdrawn from the battle, Mother was able to take a calmer, longer view. She reminded Dad that the Democratic Party had been trounced in the past. It did not mean the end of the world or the ruin of a president's reputation. She recalled Woodrow Wilson's exit from the presidency after World War I, broken in health and spirit. Harry Truman was a long way from either fate.

Gradually—it took about two months—Dad began to see the defeat differently. He realized that the war and the character-assassination tactics of McCarthy and his imitators, whom Ike never repudi-

ated, had stampeded many voters. Even more decisive was the power
of Ike's World War II reputation. Nothing else explained the 6-mil-
lion-vote Republican majority. "The country from an economic
standpoint was never in better condition," Dad wrote in one of his
diary jottings. "There are 63,000,000 employed . . . and only 1.4
million out of work. More farmers own farms . . . than ever before
in this or any other country. Wages for all workers are at an all time
high. Business profits are at record rates. Yet propaganda, character
assassination and glamour overshadowed these hard facts."

He was looking history in its ambiguous, treacherous face now.
Bess had helped him do that. During these same months, she drew
him slowly back into the personal dimension of their lives. She also
reached out to him from a need of her own. About three weeks after
the election, Grandmother Wallace had a stroke. There was no longer
any doubt that she was dying. Mother scarcely left her bedside,
except for a cabinet dinner on the night of December 4, at which
Adlai Stevenson was the guest of honor. Day by day, Grandmother
grew weaker. Then came pneumonia. She slipped into a coma and
died quietly at a little past noon on December 5, 1952.

For forty-nine years Mother had struggled to surround Madge
Gates Wallace with a healing love. At times it had been a burden that
would have destroyed a woman who lacked Bess Wallace Truman's
inner strength. Now, at last, she could feel she had triumphed over
the blow that fate had struck in 1903. Although Grandmother never
had been able to resume a normal life, her daughter's devotion had
enabled her to live with dignity and grace. In spite of her limitations,
she remained an essentially loving and lovable woman.

Dad sat with Mother as Madge Gates Wallace died. Then he took
charge and summoned the White House usher, J. B. West, Mother's
best friend on the staff. He made arrangements for us to take Grandmother Wallace to Independence. The next day, in one of his diary
jottings, Dad showed that he had long since forgiven his mother-in-
law for her early hostility to his courtship of Bess Wallace.

Yesterday at 12:30 my mother-in-law passed away. She was a grand lady.
When I hear these mother-in-law jokes I don't laugh. They are not funny to
me, because I've had a good one. So has my brother. My mother was a good
mother-in-law to Vivian's and my wife. It gives me a pain in the neck to
read the awful jokes that the so-called humorists crack about mother-in-
laws.

Today we go to Missouri to bury her. Four years ago, 1946, I was on the same errand for my mother. [Dad was off by a year; it was 1947.] The sabotage press . . . made it appear that I was wasting public money to be decent to my mother. May God forgive them. I can't and won't.

The same lice will do the same publicity job when I take Mrs. Wallace, Bess and Margaret home to bury the mother-in-law.

To hell with them. When history is written they will be the sons of bitches—not I.

In accordance with Grandmother's wishes, her funeral was simple. To avoid the inevitable hordes of curiosity seekers, Mother decided to have the service at 219 North Delaware. Madge Gates Wallace was buried in the Gates family plot—not with her husband, who lay in the Wallace family plot. In death as in life, the tragedy that ended their marriage and marked their children continued to sunder them.

Mary Paxton Keeley came to the funeral to say farewell to her substitute mother. Not once but three times in the next few months, Bess mentioned in her letters how much this meant to her. "I don't know when I have been so touched, that you came all the way up from Columbia for Mother's services," she wrote in one of her last letters from the White House. "And you know what it would have meant to her."

Grandmother's death drew dozens of letters of sympathy from Mother's Washington and Independence friends. Many of the latter recalled happy times on Delaware Street. For Mother the death must have accentuated the sense of things coming to a close. But it also removed a burden that she had borne without complaining to anyone for five decades.

For the first time in her life, Bess was not obligated to live at 219 North Delaware Street. To Dad's amazement, she proposed that they take an apartment in Washington, D.C. and live there most of the time. I think she may have been motivated in part by her opposition to his idea of returning to Missouri and running for the Senate. She did not want to see him go back into politics under any circumstances. But she was also influenced by her genuine fondness for life in the nation's capital, where she had acquired so many lively friends.

How serious Mother was about this is visible in a letter she received from Arry Calhoun, telling her how much she enjoyed her farewell visit in the White House. "When you really get settled in your Washington apartment, do let me hear from you and have your address," Arry wrote. "I do hope you find one you like and a good servant to go with it."

If the Democrats had won the election, I think Mother might have
persuaded Dad to try this idea. But the hostility and downright
meanness with which the Republicans greeted Dad's attempt to make
an orderly turnover of the government made him very dubious.
Already, triumphant right-wing senators and congressmen were
talking about hearings that would put half the Truman administration in jail for treason or corruption or both. Harry Truman decided
it would be very bad for his mental health and his blood pressure to
live in a Washington, D.C. run by Republicans. It would be far better
for his dignity and his peace of mind if he went home to Independence.

In contrast to the bristling communications between the President
and president-elect, Bess invited Mamie Eisenhower for a tour of the
White House on December 1. They had a very pleasant visit, and
Mrs. Eisenhower wrote Mother a note the day after she returned to
New York, thanking her for her "graciousness." She added a sweet
comment on Grandmother Wallace. "I know your heart must be
heavy with sorrow."

It was a time of farewells. The newspaperwomen held a luncheon
for Mother and demonstrated that they held no grudges for all those
"no comments." On the contrary, her steadfast determination to be
herself had obviously won their hearts. At the luncheon one of the
members read a long poem in praise of her—so far as I know the
only First Lady so honored. The opening stanzas declared that for
them, Bess Truman would always be "far more than a figure in
history."

> We will think of you, rather, as a friend,
> Whose kindnesses never seemed to end
> The appreciative little longhand note
> For something nice that somebody wrote,
> Or the flowers when somebody was sad or ill,
> With a card that is surely treasured still.
>
> And your wonderful way with a White House guest,
> Who might be nervous at such a test,
> And who probably never even knew
> That the feeling of ease was due to you—
> To your tact and kindness and savoir-faire
> Which made hard things easy when you were there.

Apropos of that thoughtfulness, Mother called in Mr. West as we
began packing and asked him if I could take the furniture in my

White House suite with me, if she replaced it. "I don't see why not," Mr. West said. He and I and the First Lady drove to a local department store and bought an identical set on the spot. What's more, Mother paid for it! That really impressed me.

Another more serious example of her thoughtfulness is a letter Mother wrote to the head of the Secret Service, praising William Shields, the agent who had had the difficult task of guarding her. "He has been unfailingly efficient and courteous and untiring," Mother wrote. "No one could have done a better job." This was true Christian charity, considering how much Mother abhorred the whole idea of anyone watching her.

In these final weeks, Dad had the last laugh on Mother and me about the White House ghosts. We still tended to pooh pooh the whole idea. No one had knocked on our doors in the middle of the night. I will let Dad's diary tell the rest of the story.

. . . I went to bed and read a hair-raiser in Adventure. Just as I arrived at a bloody incident, the Madam bursts into my bedroom through the hall door and shouted, "Did you hear that awful noise?"

I hadn't and said so—not a popular statement. So I put on my bathrobe and made an investigation.

What do you think I found after looking all around? Why that Margie's bridge table had fallen from in front of the fireplace in her bedroom and knocked over the fireguard! [I used the bridge table to keep out the winter wind.]

It must have made a grand ghost sound where Margie and her mamma were sitting in Mrs. T.'s sitting room!

It sure did. Mother and I were scared silly.

So we arrived at that farewell day, January 20, 1953. President-elect Eisenhower managed to be unpleasant right up to the last minute, refusing the traditional pre-inaugural lunch at the White House and at first insisting that Dad should pick him up at the Hotel Statler instead of paying the outgoing president the final courtesy of picking him up at the executive mansion. When Ike finally yielded on that point, he proceeded to hit a new low in pettiness by refusing to get out of the car to greet Dad on the White House steps.

All this unpleasantness only made Mother realize that Dad was right, they would be miserable living in Washington, D.C. with this sort of president in the White House.

If the Republicans had hoped to end the Truman presidency on the sourest possible note, they failed. There were still a lot of people in

Washington who remembered the good and the great days of the past eight years. They swarmed into Union Station to give the Trumans the most amazing send-off any outgoing presidential couple ever got from the jaded, jaundiced reporters and politicians of the District of Columbia.

You could have sworn that they had overheard Bess Truman's acid comments about the forlorn little band who saw the Trumans off on the final whistle-stop tour in the fall of 1948 and were determined to erase that bitter memory. You could almost think, if you were in a very positive frame of mind, that they were trying to prove that Washingtonians could, once every century or so, see beyond winning and losing elections to such human values as integrity and courage and kindness.

Never mind my sarcasm. Dad loved the send-off—and Mother loved it even more. It was the tribute she felt Dad deserved, the one that seemed to have eluded him in the bitterness and frustration of the losing campaign.

The trip home almost turned into a whistle-stop tour. In town after town through West Virginia, Ohio, Indiana, and Illinois, delegations of Democrats came down to the train to pay homage to the Trumans. As a result, the train was an hour late when they pulled into the familiar Missouri Pacific depot at Independence at 8:30 on the night of January 21, 1953. There they got the warmest tribute yet. The Kansas City American Legion Band was blasting out "The Missouri Waltz" and a crowd of at least 10,000 people roared welcome home. Dad's voice was choked with emotion as he thanked them. Another 1,500 people waited in the streets around 219 North Delaware Street to repeat the welcome in a more neighborly accent. "This is the climax," Dad said.

A week later, as they settled into being private citizens again, Dad wrote a letter to one of his old Washington friends, revealing how Mother felt about this triumphant homeward journey. "Bess and I were talking of our thirty years experience in elective office, our trials and tribulations, our ups and downs and she remarked that our send-off from Washington and our reception at home and along the way made it all worthwhile."

Chapter Twenty-eight

One of the first things Mother had said she planned to do when she returned home was take down the iron fence that the Secret Service had put up around 219 North Delaware Street. The Trumans were not in residence very long before she saw that this was not a good idea. At least 5,000 people a week walked or drove past the house. The fence was the main protection from souvenir hunters, who would have stolen every flower in the gardens and pried every clapboard off the first floor.

The Secret Service had said goodbye to Mr. and Mrs. Truman in Union Station in Washington, D.C. At that time, the United States did not give much thought to the welfare of its ex-presidents. The town of Independence contributed a lone policeman, but he could not be on duty all day and all night.

There was someone peering at Mother and Dad every time they came out the front door. Sometimes they did more than peer. While I was home for a visit, a man stood at the gate looking and acting very strange. The local policeman was nowhere to be seen. I came out on the porch and yelled, "Go away." When he did not depart, Mother called the police. They took him into custody and found out he was an escaped mental patient carrying a loaded .45 pistol.

Dad did not let this incident deter him from strolling around his home town. One of his diary notes from the spring of 1953 gives a good picture of him "at large."

This morning at 7 A.M. I took off for my morning walk. I'd just had the Dodge car washed a day or two ago and it looked as if it had never been used.

The weather man had said it would rain so I decided to put the washed car in the garage and use the black car which was already spotted and dusty. My sister-in-law, watching me make the change, which required some maneuvering due to the location of several cars in the drive way, wanted to know if I might be practicing for a job in a parking station!

I went on down Van Horn Road (some call it Truman Road now) and took a look at the work progressing on the widening for a two way traffic line through the county seat. A shovel (automatic) and a drag line were working as well as some laboring men digging in the old fashioned way. The boss or the contractor was looking on and I asked him if he didn't need a good strawboss. He took a look at me and then watched the work a while and took another look and broke out in a broad smile and said "Oh yes! You *are* out of a job aren't you."

A day or two ago I was walking down Farmer Street about 7:30 A.M. when a nice old lady and a gentleman standing in a door way that opens directly on the sidewalk asked me if I would please cross the street as they wanted to talk to me. I crossed over and the nice grey haired lady said to the man "You tell him, I'm shaking so I can hardly talk." The old man told me that his wife wanted me to write my name in their granddaughter's note book. The granddaughter lived in Detroit and was very sure that anybody in Independence [could] get me to do whatever was wanted. I'd never seen the old people before but I signed the granddaughter's autograph book.

A day or two before that I was walking up the hill at Union and Maple and was stopped by a bunch of boys and girls for the purpose of having a picture made with a young man named Adams who was running for President of the Student Council. I wonder how he came out. That stunt may have beaten him.

With no pension from his grateful (that's sarcasm) country, Dad might have been justified in taking one of the hundreds of lucrative job offers that were showered on him during these first months of retirement. But he steadfastly maintained that he was not going to sell the prestige of the presidency to anybody, no matter how high the bids went. If he made any money, he would do it by the sweat of his brow and brain, writing his memoirs. Mother, ever practical, decided this meant they had better economize and that henceforth the ex-president would cut the grass at 219 North Delaware Street.

Dad just smiled and said he would get around to it as soon as possible. The grass continued to grow. Mother began wondering aloud what the neighbors thought of the lawn. If the grass got any higher, it would look as if Harry Truman had gone back to farming and was raising a wheat crop in the front yard. (You can see where I got my sarcastic streak.) Mother seemed to have forgotten she was dealing with a man who had outwitted Stalin and Churchill and de Gaulle not to mention Franklin Roosevelt and Jimmy Byrnes when they tried to order him around.

One Sunday morning, as Mother was getting ready for church,

she heard the brisk rattle of a lawn mower beneath her window. She looked out and saw the ex-president cutting the grass and cheerfully greeting neighbors who were on their way to church. It was pretty obvious to the whole town that its most famous citizen was skipping divine services that morning.

From a religious point of view, this did not bother Mother in the least. But she believed in keeping up appearances—especially in Independence. "What do you think you're doing?" she asked her Sunday grasscutter.

"What you asked me to do," Dad said, with a fiendishly innocent smile.

The next day, Mother hired a man to mow the lawn.

The biggest problem the former first couple encountered in their first year of retirement was the mail. A literal avalanche of letters, some 70,000, arrived in their first two weeks in Missouri. It was obviously impossible to deal with this problem at home, and Dad set up an office in Kansas City and hired a staff to get things organized. Meanwhile, Bess had some organizing of her own to do. On January 27, a tractor trailer and an army truck deposited my grand piano and all my White House furniture, plus boxes full of mementos, gifts from heads of state, her official papers, making an obstacle course out of the interior of 219 North Delaware. Almost the same day, Mother had a carpenter at work inside the house, making the attic airtight so she could store some of these things up there. She also had storage closets built for her White House wardrobe, which was much too extensive for Independence.

Dad was soon commuting to Kansas City every day, like a regular workingman. Retirement was simply not in his vocabulary. Aside from that, he had some very real work to do. He needed to organize his papers to write his memoirs, whereby to skewer a few Republicans and leave a record for historians to ponder. He was also anxious to get to work on deciding where and how to build the Harry S. Truman Library to store the 3.5 million official documents from his administration.

That left Mother at home staring at unpacked crates and more furniture than she knew what to do with. "I don't think we'll ever get straightened out in this house," she told Mary Paxton Keeley early in February. To complicate matters, the arthritis in her hands suddenly worsened. In a March letter to Mary Paxton Keeley, she admitted: "[I] am somewhat handicapped in doing things with my hands."

Fortunately, Vietta Garr was on hand to do the cooking—Mother never did acquire any enthusiasm for that line of work. She promptly rejoined the Bridge Club, of course, but that only met once a week. That left her alone a lot of the time in 219 North Delaware. It was an eerie experience. For the first time in the fifty years she had spent in that house, her mother was no longer there. It was this mixture of loneliness and boredom that turned my stay-at-home mother into a world-class traveler.

She took Dad by complete surprise with the announcement that she thought it would be a good idea to accept oilman Ed Pauley's invitation to vacation on his estate on Coconut Island in Hawaii. She maneuvered me into joining them for this trip. "I hate leaving the house looking as it does," she told Mary Paxton Keeley, as a gesture of appeasement to her housewife's conscience. In other eras, that would have been a prelude to not leaving it. But this time she left it without a qualm, as far as I could see.

It was one of the best vacations we ever had. We started off in a style that we never achieved before (or since). Averell Harriman loaned us his private railroad car. It had everything from a chef to a woodburning fireplace. To keep the flying to a minimum—or maybe to stretch out the vacation—Mother insisted on going by ship from California. Hawaii was at its lushest. We drove to Honolulu through the Pali Pass with Mother exclaiming at the beauty of the tropical flowers. We all oohed and aahed at the spectacular view from the Pali Lookout. Mostly we lazed on the beach, and Mother did a little fishing with her partner, who kept feeling sorry for the fish, as usual. Mother went right on hauling them in, also as usual.

Dad kept a diary for part of the trip, which included an expedition to the "Big Island" of Hawaii. Notice his fascination with the new facts he was learning. At the age of sixty-nine, he still found the world a fascinating place.

After we had been on [Coconut] island a few days I sent word to Admiral Radford [Commander in Chief of the Pacific] that [I] would like to visit the Island of Hawaii and see the great volcano Mauna Loa. The Admiral sent me a C-47 in charge of two fine Navy Commanders and we were airborne at 7 A.M. It is a 200 mile flight from Oahu to Hawaii. The weather was perfect. I had a good view of Molokai the leper island and at an elevation of 11,200 feet saw the Island of Maui with its 10,500 foot extinct volcano. The Navy men told me that we had the first clear day in two years at that time of day. The weather was perfect when we arrived in Hawaii. We flew over the saddle between Mauna Kea and Mauna Loa. These volcanoes are snow capped and rise to heights above the sea level of 13,800 and 13,700 feet respectively. The sea at a distance of 3 miles out is 18,000 feet deep so that from base to top these volcanoes are more than 32,000 feet high!

We landed at Hilo [capital of Hawaii] at about 10:30 and they gave us the usual all out reception. We drove around the city and then to the Interior Dept's building in Volcano Park where Dr. Macdonald [director of the Hawaiian Volcano Observatory] showed some pictures of the eruptions of Mauna Loa in 1949 and 1950. . . . He told me that more than 600 million cubic yards of lava had overflown the side of the volcano and gone down to the ocean in a molten river. Thousands of fish were killed and a great many new varieties from the depths came to the surface. . . .

When we arrived at the air field [for the trip back] it was raining and I mean it was pouring down. A couple of native ladies thanked me for the rain. They said that Peli the Goddess of the Great Volcano was weeping because I was leaving! But they surely needed the rain. They said that Peli was happy when I came and gave us clear weather and sorry when I left, hence the rain.

On the flight back . . . we took off in the terrific rain and in ten minutes were in sunshine. We saw a school of whales below us off Maui. The navy men said that meant good luck. Well we landed safely in time for dinner.

With his usual confidence in his indestructibility, Dad was unbothered by that harrowing takeoff. Mother was terrified but she did not show it. She had decided that if the Trumans were going to keep traveling, she had to overcome her fear of flying. With some help from her remarkable will power, she soon had it licked. That trip to Hawaii was only the beginning of the Trumans' trips, almost all by air.

In the summer of 1953, they went to Washington by car. The motive was nostalgia, not fear of flying. "Isn't it great to be on our own again, doing as we please as we did in the old Senate days?" Mother said as they rolled along.

They stopped for lunch in Hannibal, Missouri, and were promptly recognized by a couple of former county judges. Every waitress and all the customers in the restaurant had to shake hands and get autographs. In Decatur, Illinois they asked a gas station attendant for directions to a good motel. He recognized them and notified the chief of police and everyone else in town. They were soon being guarded by two detectives and four policemen, with whom, out of politeness, they had to have supper.

In Pennsylvania, a state trooper pulled them over, not because they were speeding, but because he wanted to shake hands. The news-papers promptly reported Harry Truman had gotten a ticket. Telling all this to a friend from Arizona who had invited them for a visit, Dad mournfully concluded he and Mother could not go anywhere as just plain folks "until the glamour wears off."

Speaking of cars, since Mother would not let him or anyone else, including her daughter, drive her Chrysler, Dad bought himself a two-tone-green Dodge coupe. One day he tried to negotiate the very narrow back gate of the house and scraped all the chrome off it. Mother was triumphant. That proved her contention that he was not qualified to drive her car.

About two weeks later, Dad got a call at the office. It was Mother, sounding glum. "I missed the turn at that darn gate and scraped all the chrome off my Chrysler," she said. I would never have let her forget it. But Dad just dropped the subject.

The Trumans had a wonderful time in Washington that summer, getting the lowdown on President Ike's headaches with Senator McCarthy and other political problems, foreign and domestic. But they came away still convinced that they could not spend as much time in the capital as they would have preferred. A few years later, in an interview in *This Week*, Mother said that ideally, she would have liked to spend six months in Washington and six months in Independence each year.

But it was not an ideal world. Before the first year of their retirement was over, Dad was forced to go on the radio to defend himself against slanderous statements by Richard Nixon and other Republicans about Communists in his administration. The last straw was a subpoena from the House Un-American Activities Committee, which Dad scornfully rejected, citing a half dozen other presidents who had done likewise when Congress tried to breach the separation of powers between the branches of the government.

Mother was less than pleased by this return to the political wars. She did her best to play peacemaker. In October 1953, Ike came to Kansas City to make a speech. Mother suggested it might be nice if Dad telephoned him and said he wanted to welcome the President to Jackson County. The call was not returned and an even deeper chill descended on the Eisenhower-Truman relationship. In May 1954, when Mother and Dad paid another visit to Washington, Dad announced he was not going to ask for an appointment to see the President because of the previous snub.

As the outgoing president meets the incoming one in 1952, that smile on Mother's face is genuine. Dad looks like his jaw might crack under the strain. (*AP*)

A rare picture of Dad escorting Mother and Eleanor Roosevelt in 1954, at a dinner where they both received "Daughter of the Year" plaques. (Don't ask me why.) Over the years Mother and Mrs. Roosevelt became good if not close friends. (*Courtesy of the Truman Family*)

The traveling Trumans posed for this picture after lunch with the Churchills at Chartwell in 1956. On the far left is Lady Soames. Her husband, Sir Christopher Soames, is on the far right. Next to him is Max Beaverbrook, the publisher. Sarah Churchill is standing next to Mother. (*Courtesy of the Truman Family*)

Signora Truman and her husband sampled the splendors of Venice on this leg of their 1956 European tour. The crowds that surrounded them reminded Dad of 1948. Mother gave the newspapermen her usual reply: "No comment." (*UPI*)

I am invisible, but definitely in this picture. Mother and Dad allowed me to be the first TV reporter to interview them at home—for "Person to Person" in 1954. Ed Murrow had asked me to do the show because he was going to London. (*Kansas City Star*)

Beaming Grandpa and Grandma Truman prepare to take on babysitting for the first (and last) time. My husband Clifton and I are departing for Europe on the S.S. *United States* in 1960. Sons Clifton and William look pretty dubious about the whole idea. (*Courtesy of the Truman Family*)

In 1962, Jack and Jackie Kennedy invited the Trumans and the Daniels (you can barely see us in the back row) for a weekend at the White House. We had a wonderful time. Mother was enthusiastic about Jackie's redecoration of the White House. (*Courtesy of the Truman Family*)

Chief Justice Earl Warren chats with Dad and Mother and President Lyndon Johnson at the White House on a 1966 visit. (*Courtesy of the Truman Family*)

(*Left*) I've always liked this picture of the other woman in Dad's life, Mamma Truman. Behind her on the mantel are pictures of her children—Dad, his sister Mary and his brother Vivian. (*Right*) I took this picture of Grandmother Wallace in her room at Blair House in 1949. She died in the White House late in 1952, at the age of ninety. (*Courtesy of the Truman Family*)

The Trumans at home in Independence during the later years. Notice those books piled all around them. Dad read three or four biographies and histories at a time. Mother preferred murder mysteries. (*Courtesy of the Truman Family*)

At Dad's funeral, Lieutenant General Patrick F. Cassidy presents Mother and me with the flag that had covered his coffin. In the background are my husband, Clifton Daniel, my four sons, and my aunt, May Wallace. (*Kansas City Star*)

Three First Ladies, one present and two past, came to Mother's funeral. Here they are in the front pew, left to right: Nancy Reagan, Rosalynn Carter, and Betty Ford. Knowing that Mother wanted a very simple service, with no fanfare, I at first refused to let this picture be taken. My husband persuaded me that it was a historical moment that should be recorded. (*Courtesy of the Truman Family*)

Dad and Mother lie side by side in the courtyard of the Truman Library. On her stone is engraved, at Dad's order: "First Lady, the United States of America, April 12, 1945–January 20, 1953." (*Chuck Hotler—McGrew Colorgraphics*)

Politics temporarily vanished in June 1954. While attending an outdoor performance of *Call Me Madam*, which Mother wanted to see because it was about her old friend Perle Mesta, Dad became violently ill. The chest pains and nausea could have meant a heart attack, and Mother rushed him back to Delaware Street, where Dr. Wallace Graham, who had left the White House to practice medicine in Kansas City, diagnosed a more familiar ailment, a cranky gallblad-der. Tests revealed it was infected, and Dr. Graham decided to re-move it.

For a while, Mother spent most of the day and half the night in the hospital. The seventy-year-old patient recovered from the surgery nicely, but a bad reaction to some antibiotics made him a very sick man again. When he came home, Bess revealed the full extent of her worries by installing an air conditioner in the downstairs bedroom where Dad convalesced. Not only did it blow a big hole in her budget, she had to convince the convalescent to let her turn it on. Dad always maintained that he liked his air pure, and he did not care whether it was hot or cold.

What got Dad back on his feet faster than the air conditioner was the offer by the city of Independence of a large chunk of Slover Park, only a few blocks from 219 North Delaware Street, as a site for his library. He accepted a startup check from the Independence Chamber of Commerce on the back porch on July 22, 1954, while Bess smiled proudly in the background.

Mother had pushed quietly but firmly for an Independence site from the moment they came home, although attractive offers had come from the University of Missouri and others. Her sister-in-law's father, Colonel William S. Southern, had supported the idea enthusi-astically in the *Examiner*. I suspect Mother had passed the word to him, subtly or openly, as she did when trying to fight off the vice presidential nomination in 1944.

A year later, on Dad's seventy-first birthday, Mother was host to 150 VIP's at the ground-breaking ceremony. To an old White House pro, 150 visitors were hardly more than a warmup in the handshak-ing department, but Mother also undertook to feed this small horde a first-class Missouri country dinner—at 219 North Delaware Street. It was a sight I thought I would never see if Mother lived to be 1,000— there she stood at the door of her sanctuary, greeting each guest as he or she entered the vestibule. Dad was the next greeter inside the foyer, and I played traffic cop in the hallway, steering everyone into the dining room, where country ham, smoked turkey, and hot biscuits awaited them.

The dinner, which was cooked in our home kitchen by Vietta Garr and a few temporary assistants, was served buffet style, and the guests ate at tables in the yard. For a final touch, the dessert was a birthday cake in the shape of the yet to be built library. The highest-priced public relations wizard in the country could not have done a better job of kicking off the campaign to raise the $1,750,000 needed for the building.

That day demonstrated how completely Bess Wallace had become Harry Truman's political partner. History was on both their minds in 1955. Dad published the first volume of his memoirs, *Year of Decisions*. In the preface, he paid tribute to Mother's share in the history he was writing, as well as in the preparation of the book. "I owe a great debt of gratitude to Mrs. Truman, on whose counsel and judgment I frequently called." I can assure you that Mother read every word of every draft of that book.

Around Christmastime that year, Dad walked into the living room and found Mother sitting before the fireplace, in which a brisk blaze was crackling. All around her were piles of letters. As she finished one, she tossed it into the fire. "Bess," Dad said. "What are you doing?"

"Burning our letters," she said.

"Bess," Dad said. "Think of history."

"I have," Mother said, and tossed another letter on the fire.

We now know that she spared most of Dad's letters. Instead, with that determination to stay in the background that was the essence of her role in their partnership, she burned almost all of her letters to Dad.

I wish I could tell you there was no more pain involved in the political side of the Truman partnership. But the following year, when the Democrats convened in that fateful city, Chicago, there were a few final pangs. After the 1952 disaster, Dad had had a reconciliation of sorts with Adlai Stevenson. But it was neither profound nor lasting. Dad tried to prod Mr. Stevenson into assuming the leadership of the Democratic Party but he did little or nothing to create a meaningful opposition to the Republicans. In 1955, Dad urged him to announce he was a candidate for the nomination, but Mr. Stevenson preferred to play Hamlet again.

More than a little angry, Dad turned to Averell Harriman as his candidate. He had been elected governor of New York and was doing a good job. He was thoroughly qualified in the foreign policy field, having been a top troubleshooter for FDR and Dad in dealing with Moscow. At the convention, however, it soon became apparent that Mr. Stevenson's friends had control of the party machinery and Mr. Harriman did not have a chance. Dad proceeded to show his stubborn side. He decided to call a press conference and announce that he was backing his man, anyway.

Mother was very upset. She sought out Tom Evans, the owner of KMOC in Kansas City, one of the two friends who had been on the inside of the nomination for vice president in 1944. When Dad announced he was not going to run again in 1952, Tom had sent him a telegram warmly approving the decision. Mother later said it was "the nicest wire she had ever received." Tom understood how she felt about Dad, and she had no hesitation about speaking frankly to him. "Tom," she said. "Can't you do something to stop Harry? He's making a fool of himself."

Tom was shocked to see tears on Mother's face. It was the only time he had ever seen her weep.

For me, that is one of the most painful scenes in this book. But I am afraid Mother was right. In spite of telling himself and others that it was a mistake to try to exercise political power too long, Dad's passionate involvement in the Democratic Party made it difficult for him to take his own advice. The 1956 Chicago Convention taught him that lesson, the hard way. With the help of Tom Evans, Mother persuaded him to withdraw his support of Averell Harriman and endorse Mr. Stevenson. Alas, President Eisenhower trounced our Democratic Hamlet again, leaving Dad totally frustrated.

In between these political spasms, Mother found herself managing a wedding—at last. In the closing months of his presidency, Dad had remarked that the only thing he now wanted out of life was a grandson. When reporters asked me if I planned to do anything about that, I froze them, and Mr. President, by replying that the chief executive must have been short on things to talk about that day. I am convinced that Mother put him up to that reminder that I was still single. Mary Paxton Keeley had not one but two grandchildren whom she brought to Independence for several visits. There was also a steady stream of "kodaks," as Mother called them, in Mary's letters.

To give her credit, Mother did her best to stay out of my love life. To give me credit, I tried even harder to keep her out, knowing her penchant for taking charge of things. On a Christmas visit in 1955, I received a number of telegrams and a couple of bouquets from an editor at *The New York Times* named Clifton Daniel. I had met him several months earlier but neglected to give him our unlisted Independence telephone number. Being an ingenious newspaperman, he decided to communicate with me via Western Union and the local florist.

"Who is this?" Mother asked.

"A man I met," I replied, and that was pretty much all she heard until I called her in January 1956 to tell her that Clifton and I were engaged, and I wanted to be married in Independence on April 21. Mother and Dad promptly came to New York to meet Clifton and were charmed by him in about ten minutes. We had no difficulty swearing them to secrecy about our engagement until March 15, when Mother and Dad would announce it in Independence.

Everything seemed settled on that front until I received a call on or about March 10. The famous bridge club was meeting on March 12, and Mother said that they would never forgive her if she did not tell them. I told her it was a good thing she was no longer in the White House, with all sorts of state secrets in her head, if that was the best she could do with my secret. I was only teasing, of course, and agreed to let her move the announcement up three days and go to the bridge club free to tell all.

On other fronts things did not go so smoothly. Mother drew up a guest list for me, half of whom I rejected. I did not want swarms of politicians at my wedding, and I also wanted to eliminate several friends who had acquired the unfortunate habit of using my name to get publicity for themselves. One in particular went back to my Gunston Hall days, and Mother was genuinely shocked that I would not invite her and her mother. It was a clash between a lady of the previous generation and a woman who felt sincerity was more important than propriety.

Several times the wires between Independence and New York grew more than a little overheated. In the end, I won most of the battles, but Mother could claim a few victories too. One of hers was somewhat pyrrhic, although she never knew it. Because Clifton was a Baptist and we were being married in an Episcopal church, the rector in Independence announced that regulations required Mr. Daniel to take an hour's instruction in his wife's faith. I exploded and threatened to get married in City Hall. Mother said she was tempted to tell me to make it New York's City Hall.

In a fury I called Dr. Kinsolving, rector of St. James Church in New York and an old friend. He suggested Clifton and I pay him a visit. I agreed with some trepidation. When we were settled in his study, Dr. Kinsolving leaned back in his chair and asked Clifton what he thought of the Yankee's chances that year. For the next hour, they proceeded to talk baseball. I learned enough lingo to become a sportscaster, if worse ever came to worst. Finally, Dr. Kinsolving glanced at his watch and said: "Well, now you can tell your man in Independence that you have spent a very educational hour with a learned Episcopalian cleric."

I never told Mother what we really talked about.

The wedding went beautifully. We kept the guest list small enough to have the reception at 219 North Delaware Street, not too dissimilar from Mother's reception in 1919—except for the army of photographers and reporters outside the iron fence. They never let me forget my name was Margaret Truman, even though I was doing my best to change it.

Clifton and I were scarcely back from our honeymoon when the ex-president wafted Mother off on a sort of second honeymoon of their own. A year before, Dad had written confidentially to me, "Your mother is moaning that she sits at home so much but I'll remedy that!" In mid-May 1956, they took off for six marvelous weeks in Europe with Stanley Woodward, chief of protocol while they were in the White House, and his delightful wife. They had a good time, in spite of coping with swarms of newsmen and mobs of curious citizens. "The jam at the Paris, Rome and Naples stations was like Washington in 1948 after the election," Dad wrote to Tom Evans.

There was only one bad moment on the trip, as far as Mother was concerned. That came at Chartwell, Winston Churchill's estate, in the midst of an otherwise happy visit with the former prime minister and his family. Mr. Churchill told Dad that nothing could make him happier than seeing Harry Truman become president of the United States again. The great Englishman seemed to think that Dad could make a comeback, as the prime minister did after being ousted in 1945. Mother said nothing, and Dad quietly told him "there was no chance of that."

To which Mother no doubt said a silent "Amen."

The next important item on Mother's agenda was that grandchild. Since Clifton and I had decided to have a family, we did our best to cooperate. By early June 1957, I was in my ninth month, and the tension at 219 North Delaware was worse than it had ever been in the White House. Every time the telephone rang, Mother broke speed records for seventy-two-year-old ex-athletes to get to it. One morning the telephone rang at 7 A.M. This had to be it, Mother thought, practically tearing the phone out of the wall.

It was Harry Rosenthal, the local AP reporter, asking Dad's opinion on some political development in Washington. The poor man got most of his skin taken off by Dad later in the day, when he held a press conference on the now-forgotten crisis.

My doctor finally decided to end the suspense by performing a cesarean. This only redoubled the tension in Missouri. To guarantee a fast start, Mother asked her hairdresser, Doris Miller, to come to the house on the night of the operation to give her a permanent. Clifton Truman Daniel finally came into this world just after midnight on June 5. Mother and Dad were on a train to New York the next morning. Dad wanted to fly, but Mother insisted on playing it safe. She was not going to let a plane crash ruin her long-delayed (in her opinion) encounter with her first grandchild.

Now I can appreciate some of the feelings that flowed through Mother's heart as she held Kif (a name he no longer tolerates) in her arms. The odd way life has of denying our early wishes and then granting them later, in its own good time. Mother had wanted a son. Now she had a grandson, which was in some ways more satisfying. Mother's delight in this blessed event was entirely private, of course. She had nothing to say to the reporters.

The ex-president, now Grandfather Truman, had so much to say, one could easily have gotten the idea that he was the father. On the way out of the hospital after their first visit, he held an impromptu press conference while my husband went searching for a taxi. There was a marvelous picture in the New York *Daily News* of Clifton standing on the outskirts of the crowd of reporters, trying to tell Dad that the taxi was waiting. I have always been glad I married a newspaperman who understood the ways of the press (and of ex-presidents).

Proof, if any was needed, that Dad was practically gaga was the misinformation he gave the reporters about the child. He announced that the baby had a full head of red hair. This from the man who always talked about getting the facts straight! Dad saw what he wanted to see—that Truman blood had won its biological war with Daniel blood. Red hair runs in the Truman family. Unfortunately, the baby's hair, which was indeed very full, was jet black.

When I came home with the baby, I thought Mother might be ready with a set of guidelines and instructions. But she scarcely offered me a word of advice. She said she had been out of the "baby business" too long to know what the experts were advising nowadays. Instead she filled the mails with descriptions of the child for the benefit of Mary Paxton Keeley and others.

There was a new serenity in the Truman partnership as they approached their thirty-eighth anniversary on June 28, 1957. I think I can claim some of the credit for it, as the mother of Clifton Truman Daniel. Also, Dad had finished his memoirs, and his library was about to be dedicated. Time was already changing a lot of people's opinion of Harry Truman's place in history. The Eisenhower administration floundered into a second term with the Democrats in control of both houses of Congress. The Truman era began to look better and better to everyone.

On June 28, 1957, Dad wrote Mother the best anniversary letter of them all.

June 28, 1920 One happy year.
June 28, 1921 Going very well.
June 28, 1922 Broke and In a bad way.
June 28, 1923 Eastern Judge. Eating.
June 28, 1924 Daughter 4 mo. old.
June 28, 1925 Out of a job.
June 28, 1926 Still out of a job.
June 28, 1927 Presiding Judge—eating again.
June 28, 1928 All going well. Piano. Al Smith.
June 28, 1929 Panic, in October.
June 28, 1930 Depression. Still going.
June 28, 1931 Six year old daughter.
June 28, 1932 Roads finished.
June 28, 1933 Employment Director.
June 28, 1934 Buildings finished. Ran for Senate.
June 28, 1935 U.S. Senator. Gunston.
June 28, 1936 Resolutions [Committee] Philadelphia [Convention].
         Roosevelt reelection.
June 28, 1937 Grand time in Washington.
June 28, 1938 Very happy time. Margie 14.
June 28, 1939 Named legislation.
June 28, 1940 Senate fight coming.
June 28, 1941 Special Senate Committee. Margie wants to sing.
June 28, 1942 Also a happy time.
June 28, 1943 Lots of work.

June 28, 1920   One happy year.

June 28, 1921   Going very well.

June 28, 1922   Broke and in a bad way.

June 28, 1923   Eastern Judge. Eating

June 28, 1924   Daughter 4 mo. old.

June 28, 1925   Out of a job.

June 28, 1926   Still out of a job.

June 28, 1927   Presiding Judge - eating again

June 28, 1928   All going well Piano. Al Smith.

June 28, 1929   Panic in October.

June 28, 1930   Depression. Still going.

June 28, 1931   Six year old daughter

June 28, 1932   Roads finished

June 28, 1933   Employment Director.

June 28, 1934   Buildings finished. Ran for the Senate

June 28, 1935   U.S. Senator Junior

June 28, 1936   Resolutions Philadelphia. Roosevelt reelected.

Harry Truman wrote Bess Truman many wedding anniversary letters. This one, celebrating the 38th year of their marriage, was her favorite. She kept it on her desk and after his death reread it almost every day. *(Courtesy of the Truman Family)*

HARRY S. TRUMAN
FEDERAL RESERVE BANK BUILDING
KANSAS CITY 6, MISSOURI

June 28, 1937 Grand time in Washington.

June 28, 1938 Very happy time. Margie 14.

June 28, 1939 Named legislation.

June 28, 1940 Senate fight coming.

June 28, 1941 Special Senate Committee
Margie wants to sing.

June 28, 1942 Also a happy time

June 28, 1943 Lots of work.

June 28, 1944 Talk of V.P. Bad business

June 28, 1945 V.P. & President. War End

June 28, 1946 Margie graduate & singer
80th Congress.

June 28, 1947 Marshall Plan + Greece + Turkey

June 28, 1948 A terrible campaign. A grand time 28th Anna Happy day.

June 28, 1949 President again. Another happy day.

June 28, 1950 Korea — a terrible time.

June 28, 1951 Key West — a very happy day.

June 28, 1952 All happy. Finish Jan 20, 1953

June 28, 1953 Back home. Lots of Roses.

June 28, 1954 A happy 35th

HARRY S. TRUMAN
FEDERAL RESERVE BANK BUILDING
KANSAS CITY 6, MISSOURI

June 28, 1955 All cut up but still happy.

June 28, 1956 A great day — more election

June 28, 1957 Well here we are again
as Harry Jones would say.

Only 37 to go for the
diamond jubilee!

H.S.T.

Here are some
ones + some fills.
If it is not enough
for a proper show
there will be more
comming.

Your no account
partner, who loves you
more than ever!

June 28, 1944 Talk of V.P. Bad business.

June 28, 1945 V.P. & President. War End.

June 28, 1946 Margie graduate—80th Congress.

June 28, 1947 Marshall Plan & Greece & Turkey. A grand time 28th
              Anniversary.

June 28, 1948 A terrible campaign. Happy day.

June 28, 1949 President again. Another happy day.

June 28, 1950 Korea—a terrible time.

June 28, 1951 Key West—a very happy day.

June 28, 1952 All happy. Finish Jan. 20, 1953.

June 28, 1953 Back home. Lots of Roses.

June 28, 1954 A happy 35th.

June 28, 1955 All cut up but still happy.

June 28, 1956 A great day. More elation.

June 28, 1957 Well here we are again, as Harry Jobes [an old friend]
              would say.

Only 37 to go for the diamond jubilee!

H.S.T.

Here are some ones & some fives. If it is not enough for a proper
show there will be more coming.

Your no account partner, who loves you more than ever!

Chapter Twenty-nine

Growing old has its sorrows as well as its joys. Mother encountered one of her saddest moments not long after Dad wrote her that anniversary letter. In the fall of 1957, her brother Fred suffered a heart attack in Denver. She rushed to his bedside and was with him when he died a few days later at the age of fifty-seven. Fred's life had been a sad struggle against alcohol. He had tried to be a decent husband and father in spite of it. Mother had tried to give him some of her strength and found that life did not work that way. So she did the next best thing: She never stopped loving him and his family.

Before I wrote those words, I spent most of a day reading hundreds of pages of letters from Fred's wife, Christine, to Mother. They never mention Fred's drinking. The theme is gratitude to Mother for an endless stream of presents to Christine and Fred and the children, for visits and letters and calls that gave the family the feeling that Bess Wallace Truman was always there, reaching out to them with her love.

Like his father, Fred died penniless. Mother and Dad had to pay to ship his body back to Independence for burial. Thereafter they sent Christine and her children a monthly check. This may not impress those who recall that *Life* magazine paid Dad $600,000 for his memoirs. But after he paid 67½ percent in taxes and finished paying the staff he had to hire to organize his papers and help him with the research, and incidentally handle the thousands of letters that kept arriving, he had exactly $37,000 left when the second volume was published in 1955. What rescued the Trumans from a lot of financial anxiety was the old bugaboo that kept them from marrying for the better part of ten years—the Truman farm.

Early in Dad's presidency, a group of Jackson County friends had bought the farm, intending to preserve it as an historic site. In 1946, when Dad saw that his income as president was roughly equal to his outgo, he decided to purchase it from them. In part it was an attempt to console his mother, who felt the loss of it keenly, although she never said a word of reproach or complaint about it. In the mid-fifties, Dad sold most of the 600 acres to a real estate developer for a shopping center. He retained an acre or so around the house for history's sake. The deal ended all financial worries for his brother Vivian and sister Mary, as well.

This affluence did not mean Mother stopped pinching pennies. She still scrutinized every bill that came into the house and frequently caught the adding machines off by a few dollars. But she now felt free to continue to indulge her favorite hobby—sending roses to friends on anniversaries and on other happy occasions, such as the day someone sailed to Europe. There are several letters from Louise Stewart, who was still struggling to cope with the loss of her son Bobby, thanking her for this testimony to their continuing friendship.

After another happy trip to Europe in 1958, Dad's political worry machine started heating up again, as he got thinking about who was going to be the Democratic candidate in 1960. Mother was more interested in her grandson, if her letters to Mary Paxton Keeley are any indication. She reported on his weight and height—nineteen pounds and twenty-eight inches long—and one tooth. "Marg says he eats everything in sight," she wrote, and then, like the veteran older sister that she was, added: "She doesn't half know what that means!" (I didn't.)

Sometime in 1958, Mother discovered a lump in her left breast. For reasons that remain baffling, she did nothing about it. Although it grew bigger and bigger, she continued to ignore it. She seems to have decided she was going to die and only wanted to live long enough to enjoy two major events of 1959, the Democratic Party's salute to Dad's seventy-fifth birthday on May 8 in New York and the birth of her second grandchild, scheduled for a few weeks after that date.

By this time the tumor had become so large, Mother was stuffing handkerchiefs into the right side of the bodices of her dresses to keep people from noticing it. She did her utmost to get out of the trip to New York for the birthday jamboree. But Dad was adamant about her coming along. He wanted her to get her share of the credit for the partnership.

To keep out of the public eye as much as possible on their departure from Independence, she sent Dad ahead to the station, telling him she had some last minute repacking to do. Her brother George drove her to the station, and she sat in the car a block away while Dad talked with reporters and cut a birthday cake that local admirers had prepared for him. Only as the diesel whistled around the bend did she tell George to take her that last block, accept an orchid from the local well-wishers, and get on the train.

While they were dressing in the hotel room in New York, Dad noticed the tumor. He was tremendously alarmed and told me about it. At first the combined arguments of the two of us could not budge Mother. "I want to see my grandson born," she said, perfectly calm while we whirled around her in a near frenzy.

We finally prevailed, and when she returned to Independence, she went almost directly to Research Hospital for surgery. The tumor was by this time the size of a grapefruit. It was not cancerous. But it had invaded the lymph nodes of both arms, and Dr. Graham decided to do a mastectomy and to remove all of the lymph nodes as well. True to her tradition of telling the press nothing, Mother ordered us to issue a statement omitting any mention of a mastectomy.

Dad was in a terrible state of anxiety, worrying about Mother and me simultaneously. I relieved him of 50 percent of his worries by giving birth to William Wallace Daniel on May 19, 1959, the day after Mother's operation.

It took Mother a long time to recover from her operation and from the inevitable psychological pain every woman feels after losing a breast. Dad's letter to my husband, written almost two months after the surgery, gives us a glimpse of him as her combination nurse and guardian.

Dear Clif:

You do not know how very much I appreciated your letter of June 29th with the clipping about the meeting at the Astor Hotel where Margaret accepted the Page One Award [from the New York Newspaper Guild] for me. If the mirror should break I can always read the citation standing on my head.

I am very happy that Master Clifton Truman Daniel is learning about the birds and the bees. A fellow can't start too young, in my opinion.

I am happy that you like your new country place. If I can just get Grandma to behave herself and follow the doctor's instructions, maybe we can get there to see you before you move back to New York. Her progress is slow, but she is getting along as well as can be expected, after that terrific shock.

P.S. Tell Margie to make the kids—and their daddy—behave just as I *once* did with her and her mother!

That fall, Mother and Dad came to New York to pronounce their approval of William Wallace Daniel, even though nature had contrived to make this bearer of the Wallace name look much more like a pure Truman. The Daniels, of course, never even got into the equation in the opinion of Grandma and Grandpa Truman. Mary Paxton Keeley was no better than her oldest friend. She was always sending Bess pictures of her grandchildren and asking Mother if she agreed that they were Paxtons. Invariably, Mother said yes. The feminists who claim marriage obliterates a woman's identity would have some trouble fitting these two ladies into their theory.

Meanwhile, another spasm of politics was heading Bess's way. Dad had journeyed to Washington early in 1959 to confer with other Democratic chieftains on the party's nominee for 1960. Mother had declined to go with him. Part of the reason was the tumor in her breast, but her refusal was also a not so subtle negative vote against his participation. For a year, Dad had been pushing Senator Stuart Symington of Missouri as the Democratic nominee. He even went so far as to say that he would not mind being appointed senator in his place if he won the election. Mother made him retract that one, fast.

From Washington Dad wrote her an emotional letter—the last—at least the last that has survived—of the 1,600 letters he wrote to Bess Wallace Truman. It sums up how highly he valued her as a political partner—while providing a fascinating glimpse of the Democrats' disarray as they approached the 1960 election.

You'll never know how badly you are missed. Yesterday evening I went out to the Acheson's for dinner. The Woodwards and Florence Mahoney were there. I had a chance to talk to Dean before the others came, and Dean, Stanley and I had a session after dinner.

As you know, we are up against it for a winning candidate in 1960. After much discussion we came to the conclusion that, at the present time, Stuart Symington is the best bet.

Dean said, and it's true, that we have a dozen good second-place men but no real honest to goodness first-place men. I've had a session with some of the new Senators and expect, today, to have lunch with Hart of Michigan, Hartke of Indiana, Jennings Randolph [of West Virginia] and Alaska's two.

Sam Rayburn says he's anxious to see me. I've talked to Lyndon Johnson but things are nowhere near settlement for a proper course. Maybe they never will be and then God help the country.

I've almost become a pessimist! Again, I wish, with everything I've got, that you were here.

We are facing the most serious situation since 1859.

Hope all's well with you. I've had two walks yesterday and this morning all by myself. How good that is!

All the love in the world.

Bess's reply to this call to arms was: horsefeathers. She refused to get excited about the Democratic Party and told Dad he was crazy if he went to another convention at the age of seventy-six. Let the next generation fight it out among themselves—that was her attitude.

He took her advice about not going to the convention in Los Angeles, but he remained intensely interested in what was happening there. The front-runner for the nomination, Senator John F. Kennedy of Massachusetts, had come to Independence in the spring of 1960 seeking Dad's endorsement.

He did not get it. Dad could not overcome his visceral dislike of Joe Kennedy, Jack's father. He could not forget Mr. Kennedy's isolationist past. He had been opposed to fighting Hitler in World War II and had issued a panicky call for a retreat from Korea, when the Chinese intervened.

Dad did not think Jack Kennedy was ready to be President of the United States. He also feared that Kennedy's nomination would lead the Democrats into the same disaster that befell them when they nominated Al Smith in 1928. He thought there were still too many Protestants in the Democratic Party who could not accept a Catholic president.

When Lyndon Johnson asked him if he should accept Kennedy's offer to run for vice president on his ticket, Dad advised him to say no. Mr. Johnson accepted the offer anyway and worked hard to change Dad's mind about JFK. An unsent letter Dad wrote to Dean Acheson in late August 1960 shows that the Trumans' enthusiasm for the nominee remained tepid.

I have been as blue as indigo since the California meeting in L.A. It was a travesty on National Conventions. Ed Pauley organized it and then Kennedy's pa kicked him out! Ed didn't consult me!

The Convention should have helped immensely if it had been in Chicago, St. Louis or Philadelphia. But it wasn't held at any of those places. You and I are stuck with the necessity of taking the worst of two evils or none at all. So—I'm taking the *immature* Democrat as the best of the two. Nixon is impossible. So there we are. . . .

I'm afraid that this immature boy who was responsible for picking out five great Senators [Dad is referring to JFK's book, *Profiles in Courage*] may not know anymore about the Presidency that he will occupy than he did about the great Senators. Only one, Henry Clay, belonged in the list. I sent him a list of a dozen or so but it wasn't used. So, what the hell, you and I will take it and not like it but hope for the future.

Before the 1960 campaign was over, Dad was making speeches for the Democratic ticket. As it turned out, John F. Kennedy needed Harry Truman's help, Lyndon Johnson's help, and help from a lot of other Democrats to win. But win he did, even it it was by a whisker manufactured by Boss Daley of Chicago. For Dad and Mother it was one of the most satisfying presidential victories in memory, because the man who went down to defeat was their least favorite Republican, Richard Nixon.

One aspect of this changing of the guard pleased Mother almost as much as the election of a Democratic president. "Who do you think called the other day?" she asked me in one of our telephone get-togethers.

"Khrushchev?" I suggested, unseriously.

"No. Ike."

It seems that ex-President Eisenhower wanted some advice on setting up his library and was wondering if ex-President Truman was ready to negotiate a truce. Mother urged Dad to say yes and when Ike came to Kansas City to help rededicate the World War I Liberty Memorial on Armistice Day, 1961, he visited Dad in his office at the library and the two of them jointly agreed to bury their political hatchets. It was a good thing they did, because only a week later Sam Rayburn died and they sat side by side in the front pew for the service.

Bess remained far more interested in her grandchildren. Her letters to Mary Paxton Keeley filled her in on their development and when she last saw them, whether in New York, or Bermuda, or Florida. Politics were never mentioned. But there were a lot of comparisons of their mutual woes with arthritis. Both had developed this disease. Both lived up to Mary's motto that the only way to meet trouble was to take it standing. Mary kept on working, turning out books about Missouri and more historical dramas. None reached Broadway but several had successful Missouri productions. She also turned part-time painter, creating an historical mural for Calvary Episcopal Church in Columbia. Bess cheered this new creativity. She called the mural "the most interesting thing you have ever done."

Each Christmas, Bess and Mary continued their sixty-year tradition of exchanging Christmas presents. Mary usually gave Mother books, but sometimes—another tradition of their youth—she gave her something she had made herself. A handmade dish towel inspired one of Mother's liveliest lines. She said she could not think of a better present, because these days, it was hard to find a dish towel "you can't throw a dog through." That made me wonder what in the world they were really up to in those supposedly sedate 1890s.

Another custom Bess and Mary began in their old age was sending each other flowers. They did it at all times of the year, but most of the gifts were in the winter, when their spirits needed lifting. "I found your amaryllis here when I got home," Bess wrote when she returned from Key West in 1960. "It's been years since we had one. Mother was always interested in them. I can hardly wait for it to bloom." A few years before, Bess sent Mary a rose in December. She remarked that it was not much of a present because she would have to wait until spring for it to bloom. But it was a very special flower, named for Mrs. George Marshall, "one of the most delightful persons I have ever known."

Both women needed this kind of spiritual sustenance. Mary's son Pax became a department store executive and moved to a distant state. She was lonely in Columbia, even though she was feted and fussed over as the oldest living graduate of the University of Missouri's School of Journalism. Mother tried to be philosophic about my becoming a confirmed New Yorker, but she missed me and yearned to see her grandchildren more often. "It's too bad we have to be so far from our only children," she wrote to Mary. "But maybe it's better for them!" That was one strong-willed mother talking frankly to another one, if I have ever seen it.

In the early sixties, death cut a swath through both the Paxtons and the Wallaces. Several of Mary's Independence relatives died. But Mother had far heavier blows. Frank Wallace had been ailing for some time with a combination of ills. His health had never been robust. Bess tried hard to keep up his morale. She took him for rides in the car and was always sending him goodies Vietta baked. Suddenly, in the spring of 1960, it was Natalie Wallace who was ill. She underwent surgery for cancer and died three weeks later. Frank simply could not handle the loss. He died ten weeks after her, on August 13, 1960.

In the spring of 1963, Mother's younger brother, George, died a slow, painful death from lung cancer. From Mother's point of view, 1963 was not a good year. In January, Dad started complaining about strange pains in his abdomen. Bess insisted on a checkup and the doctors discovered an intestinal hernia. It was a serious operation for a man of seventy-nine, and he took a long time to recover.

In November 1963, came a political shock of awful proportions, President Kennedy's assassination. Having come so close to that fate himself, Dad was terribly shaken by it. For the first time in his life he was unable to face reporters, who naturally wanted his reaction to the tragedy. He took to his bed and let Mother handle the questions.

For Mother and Dad the assassination was especially painful because they had grown genuinely fond of the young president and his wife. The Kennedys had invited the Trumans (and Clifton and me) to the White House for a weekend in 1962, and we had had a wonderful time. Jack made a witty speech about how the Kennedy administration should really be called the third Truman administration because he had so may ex-Trumanites on his staff. Mother was very enthusiastic about Jackie's redecoration of the White House. But it was more than this relatively brief friendship that made the assassination so painful for Mother and Dad. Those who have lived in the White House are united by a special bond that all but defies explanation to outsiders.

Jack Kennedy's tragic death brought the Secret Service back into the Trumans' lives. Suddenly jittery about the safety of ex-presidents, Congress appropriated money for lifetime protection. Mother reacted as if they had just told her she was going to have to spend four more years in the White House. Conveniently forgetting the several nuts who had appeared on our doorstep with loaded guns, she insisted that she and Dad did not need protection in Independence. Clifton and I protested in vain. She refused to allow the Secret Service men on the property. The next thing we knew, Dad was reading the bill and found a clause in it permitting the ex-president to refuse the protection.

Things were at an impasse when the telephone rang one night. "Bess," said a familiar Texas voice, "this is Lyndon." With the infinite number of things on his mind, the President found the time to call and cajole Mother into letting the Secret Service return. I will always be grateful to him for that act of thoughtfulness. Mother had to admit she too was impressed. She finally agreed to let the Secret Service guard Dad during the day, while he was working in the library, and traveling to and from 219 North Delaware. But she still would not let them into the house, or even onto the property.

Then came an incident that made Mother realize the Secret Service could be very useful. On October 13, 1964, in the middle of his eightieth year, Dad slipped and fell in the bathroom on the second floor. He struck the edge of the tub, fracturing two ribs. The fall also broke his eyeglasses, which cut his eyebrow and forehead. A maid found him and called the police and an ambulance. If Mother had allowed the Secret Service to install "panic transmitters"—small beepers the size of cigarette packs—in the house, much time could have been saved.

The period of that fall and Dad's slow recuperation from it was another difficult time. In 1965, when Mary Paxton had a show of her paintings and photographs in Columbia, Mother mournfully wrote that they could not come. "We can't drive that far anymore." In March 1967, when she and Dad flew to Key West to spend two weeks with the Daniel tribe, she remarked that it was the first time they had left Independence in more than two years. "It's the longest I have stayed home since 1934," Mother said. It was very clear that she did not like being so housebound. For all her intense loyalty to 219 North Delaware Street, part of her heart had been transplanted to Washington, D.C, and points north, east, south, and west. If she had her way, she would have spent at least half her time traveling.

I kept her interested during these years by giving birth to two more sons, Harrison Gates Daniel and Thomas Washington Daniel. Mother frankly was baffled by my predilection for a large family. When I told her Thomas was on the way, she remarked, "Well, you're not a Catholic, so I can only conclude you're careless."

That was one of my last encounters with Mother's hard side. She doted on all four boys when they visited her. She let them call her "Gammy" without a murmur of protest and did not seem to care what they did to her precious house as they careened through it. She beamed while they fought mock battles in the living room, making twice as much noise as I ever dared to make at my most obstreperous. Gammy could also be depended on for a steady supply of Vietta's brownies at all hours of the day, with a cautionary "Don't tell your mother."

Politics remained very much a part of the Truman's lives, along with grandparenting. During Lyndon Johnson's presidency, he visited Dad and Mother in Independence six times. Mother was particularly pleased by his tribute to Dad when he signed the Medicare Bill at the Truman Library in 1965. The President said it was the culmination of a twenty-year effort to guarantee every American decent health care that Harry Truman had begun in 1945.

Later, Mr. Johnson came seeking Dad's support for his policies in Vietnam. Dad gave him a very general statement, which praised the patriotism of the men fighting there far more than the policy of the President who had sent them. He did not agree with the way Mr. Johnson was fighting the war, and he became more and more disillusioned with his presidential leadership.

Although Dad and Mother remained fond of Mr. Johnson personally, they were both disappointed with his decision not to seek another term in 1968, which gave the war protesters a chance to crow that they had driven him out of office. They thought he should have taken his case to the people and let them decide, as Dad had done in 1948.

The election of Richard Nixon was another shock. Even more surprising was a cautious query from Washington asking if the Trumans would tolerate a visit from the new president in early 1969. That special bond which links the residents of the White House prevailed over old animosities, and the Trumans' answer was yes. The Nixons called and stayed twenty minutes. The two men discussed foreign policy, while Mother showed Pat Nixon through the house. They then adjourned to the Truman Library, where Mr. Nixon gave Dad the Steinway piano that had been on the second floor of the White House when we arrived in 1945.

Mr. Nixon was impressed by Dad's insights into the problems the country was facing at home and abroad. "He's up on everything," he said, as he left. The same was true of Mother. When I wrote that she was more interested in her grandchildren, I was referring to emotional intensity. She too remained in very close touch with the country's travails in Vietnam and the unrest at home. Like Dad, she read three or four newspapers a day.

In the spring of 1972, not long after Mr. Nixon had mined Haiphong Harbor to force the North Vietnamese to agree to a peace treaty, Mother asked a visitor what he thought of it. The visitor said he thought it was a good idea. Mother nodded emphatically. "If he'd been president," she said, gesturing to Dad on the other side of the room, "we'd have it done it six years ago."

During these years, Dad's health slowly deteriorated. He began having attacks of vertigo which forced him to give up his morning walks. Arthritis in the hips and knees made it difficult for him to negotiate the stairs. On November 22, 1972, Bess wrote to Mary

Paxton Keeley to thank her for another gift of amaryllis. "Harry is not at all well," she remarked at the close of the letter. "I have excellent help with him but I still have many things to do."

On December 5, doctors decided to bring Dad to Research Hospital to see if they could clear up some alarming congestion in his lungs. He rallied remarkably at first, but his eighty-eight-year-old heart could not stand the strain. Episodes of "cardiac instability," as the doctors called it, brought him near death several times. Mother spent almost all her time at the hospital, and I spent a lot of my time on planes between New York and Kansas City.

In mid-December, as Mother sat with Dad, a familiar voice called "Bess—Bess—" from the doorway of the room.

It was Mary Paxton Keeley. At the age of eighty-seven she had come all the way from Columbia to be with Mother at this saddest hour of her life. She had used her reporter's savvy and moxie to get past the Secret Service. "Your visit to the hospital did me a lot of good," Mother wrote, some weeks later. Then, underlining every word, she added: "I'm glad you talked the Secret Service man into letting you by." Her private war with the Secret Service never ended.

As December drew to a close, I became as worried about Mother as I was about Dad. She was rapidly reaching the point of total exhaustion. As usual, she did not take my advice when I urged her to go home for at least one night and get some real sleep. She even spent Christmas eve at the hospital. Finally, on Christmas night, I persuaded her to come home with me. Dad had slipped into a coma and there was nothing we could do to help him.

At 7:52 the next morning, Dr. Graham called to tell us Dad had died. For a long time I felt terribly guilty about persuading Mother to come home. She wanted to be with him even though he was no longer conscious. But it seemed, like many decisions made under stress, the right one at the time.

Mother and I were touched by the enormous outpouring of grief and affection from all parts of the nation. Lyndon Johnson and his wife, Ladybird, and President Nixon and Mrs. Nixon came to the house to offer Mother their sympathy. Radio and television stations devoted hours to Dad's achievements, and newspapers seemed to have nothing else in them. But it was the response of the average Americans that Mother found most affecting. A deluge of telegrams and telephone calls poured into the Truman Library. Most touching to Mother were the thousands of Missourians who stood in line for as long as six hours to pay their respects to Dad when his body was brought to the library on December 27.

The army had planned an elaborate five-day state funeral for Harry S. Truman. It called for bringing Dad's body to Washington to lie in state in the rotunda of the Capitol and then returning him to Missouri for burial. Clifton and I decided this would be a terrible ordeal for Mother. It also conflicted with her wishes. "Keep it simple, simple," Mother told us.

As our representative at a conference with the army, Clifton worked out a two-day ceremony, which would take place entirely in Independence. This enabled his fellow Missourians to express their affection for Dad, while Mother was able to remain in seclusion for a day and regain a little strength.

Mother helped me prepare the guest list for the funeral service on December 28. The list was limited to 250—the capacity of the Truman Library's auditorium. Along with famous friends such as Hubert Humphrey and Clark Clifford, there were old Independence friends and people who had worked for the Trumans—the painter, the gardener, the maid, Dad's barber.

Typical of Mother's attitude was her response to a family friend who was traveling with his four children when our invitation reached him. He asked the army to reserve rooms for the children at the Muehlebach Hotel, adding that he understood that they could not come to the service. "Of course they can," Mother said and allotted them four seats.

Mother and I were good soldiers. We remained dry-eyed during the service in the auditorium. Only when we went into the library courtyard for the burial and Battery D of the 129th Field Artillery, Dad's old outfit, fired a twenty-one-gun salute with six howitzers did I notice tears glistening in Mother's eyes.

Those booming guns were reminding Bess of the first time Harry Truman had responded to history's challenge. She was hearing him tell her, in a moment of presidential anguish: "I wish I never went to war in the first place!" She was remembering other tears, shed in the living room or on the porch of 219 North Delaware in that first wartime summer while a distressed soldier whispered how sorry he was to cause her pain. She was remembering that same soldier, wearing a cocky grin, bounding up the steps of that old house in 1919 to give her an exultant kiss. She was remembering so many things that I could never share in my daughter's grief.

Finally, the guns stopped firing. The army band stopped playing. The commanding general removed the flag from Dad's casket and carefully folded it and presented it to Mother. She handed it to me. A soldier stepped forward and laid a blanket of red carnations, Dad's favorite flower, on the casket. It was Bess Wallace's last gift to Harry S. Truman.

Chapter Thirty

My first concern, after we had recovered from the early stages of grief, was where Mother should live. I suggested moving to New York, where she could have a small apartment near me and Clifton and enjoy her grandchildren to her heart's content. She vetoed the idea. Now that she was free to go anywhere she chose, she decided to stay at 219 North Delaware Street. The house had become more than a refuge to her now. It was a kind of shrine to her life with Dad and with her mother and brothers. They were all around her there in memory and she did not want to leave them.

On her desk in her upstairs bedroom, Mother placed that anniversary letter Dad had written her in 1957, summarizing thirty-eight years of their marriage. She often sat down and read it before coming downstairs in the morning. Although she missed him acutely, she reached out to other friends who needed comforting. Chief among these was Mary Paxton Keeley, who had suffered a horrendous blow several months before Dad died. Her only son, Pax, had developed a kidney disorder exactly like the one that had killed his father. He became very angry with his mother for never telling him how his father had died. In her eagerness to think of him only as a Paxton, Mary had practically blotted Edmund Keeley out of her memory.

Pax had both kidneys removed and was put on a dialysis machine to await a kidney implant when a donor made one available. Alas, he developed complications and died before they could find one. "My tear glands have dried up," Mary told Bess. "I could not even cry when Pax died. [She had done so much weeping already.] I wanted to when they blew taps."

They set each other examples of womanly courage in these lonely years. Mary told Bess she blessed her father "for making me fearless." In a lively discussion of women's lib, Mary remembered how all the boys wanted to be firemen when they were growing up. Now women were taking tests to be firemen. One had just flunked because she could not lift a 100-pound bag. Mary thought this sort of feminism was pretty silly and wondered if they would try out for longshoreman next. "I was born liberated," she wrote.

Mary got ahead of Bess again in the grandchildren sweepstakes by being able to report a great grandchild, a son by her granddaughter Linda. Describing him at four months, she remarked that it was "the ideal age of man because they don't even look as though they want to say NO, their favorite word later." I can see Mother nodding emphatic agreement. What a dim view of males older sisters (Or is it liberated women?) acquire!

I was particularly pleased by a long discussion they had of my biography of Dad. Mary called it a "remarkable achievement." I realize she is somewhat prejudiced, being my godmother, but she is also a very tough critic. She shredded several other books written on the Trumans in her letters to Mother. Mary said she was particularly touched by my tribute to Charlie Ross. By this time, Mary had sent Mother a book of her own autobiographical reminiscences, in which she revealed her broken engagement to Charlie. Mother was fascinated, naturally. "I can't get over not even suspecting that you and Charlie were engaged," she wrote. "You had a raft of suitors about that time and I suppose that threw me off."

Mother enjoyed Mary's books about the old days in Independence. The two of them chuckled over Frank Wallace's adventures with his dog U-Know and their quarrels with the Southern family, who complained about the noise the Paxton and Wallace tribes made on summer nights. Bess remembered with delight the way Mary's father had told off "Sneaky Bill" Southern when he tried to impose a nine o'clock curfew on the neighborhood so he and his wife could get some sleep.

In the same letter, Mother commented on how stirred she was by a biographical sketch of Mary's mother, which Mary wrote for the contemporary Mary Paxton study club. "It brought back many things I haven't thought of for a great many years," she said, in what I think is a guarded reference to her father.

She may have thought about the painful memories of the past. But she was not prepared to talk about them. Around the time Mother turned ninety, my friend Mary Shaw Branton ("Shawsie") was working on a history of the Swope murders for a study club to which she belonged. She realized that she had a marvelous living witness to the grisly events in Mother. Shawsie called me and asked if she could interview her. "You better ask her," I said.

Shawsie arrived at 219 North Delaware Street armed with a tape recorder and a long list of questions. Mother greeted her warmly. She was another of my friends whom she regarded almost as a daughter. Shawsie explained the purpose of her visit. She assured Mother that anything she said would be confidential. She would not be quoted publicly, or even semiprivately within the confines of the study club.

Mother slowly but very firmly shook her head. "You might as well put that away," she said, gesturing to the tape recorder. "I will not say one word to you or anyone else on that subject."

She served Shawsie tea and chatted for a half hour about her grand-children, Shawsie's children, and other homey topics. But the Swopes remained in that world of silence to which Mother consigned the painful part of the past.

Yet she remained acutely sensitive and sympathetic to old friends who were struggling with present problems. She felt very badly when she learned that Mary Paxton Keeley had spent Christmas 1973 alone. "It would have been a grim day for me if I had not been able to go to Margaret's," she wrote. She told Mary how much she enjoyed her letters and apologized for not answering them one for one. Her arthritis made her writing "practically illegible."

For Mother and me, the telephone became more important than the mails, for several reasons. One was her deteriorated handwriting and the other was my bad record as a correspondent. We chatted long distance three or four times a week. She let me worry about her and generally ignored my various pleas. I argued and argued with her to air-condition the house and escape those awful Missouri summers. "Do you know how much that would cost?" she said. I grew almost as blue in the face trying to persuade her to abandon the upstairs bedroom and sleep downstairs in her mother's old room. After about two years of refusals, she capitulated on that one.

Although her arthritis grew steadily worse, forcing her from a cane to a walker and finally to a wheelchair, Mother did not retreat from life—or from politics. She surprised me completely by getting into the political endorsement game on her own. The 1972 campaign, when the press had trashed the Democrats' vice presidential nominee, Senator Tom Eagleton of Missouri, because he had had psychiatric treatment for depression, had aroused Mother's ire. Although she was very worried about Dad's health at that time, she wrote Senator Eagleton a letter expressing her sympathy and continued faith in him as a man and a politician. When the Senator came up for reelection in 1974, she let him know through Shawsie Branton that she wanted to help him.

Senator Eagleton called on Mother and they had a very lively conversation about the Democratic Party. She confided to him her low opinion of George McGovern, the Democratic nominee in 1972, because he had allowed left wingers to capture the party. "It's not the Democratic Party I knew," she said.

A few months after this visit, Senator Eagleton asked Mother to become honorary chairman of his campaign. After some discussion with me, she agreed. The Senator won a very satisfying victory.

Two years later, in 1976, Mother tried to do the same thing for Stuart Symington's son, Jim, when he decided to run for the Senate, after several successful terms as a congressman. He wrote to Mother asking if she would agree to be the honorary chairman of his campaign. Not only did she say yes, she wrote him a letter (unfortunately lost) which dissected the flaws of his prospective opponents in language so vivid he was flabbergasted. Here was one ninety-one-year-old lady who was not out of touch!

The Symington-Truman team would undoubtedly have won that election if the Supreme Court, in one of its more dubious decisions, had not struck down the law limiting campaign donations and expenditures. Running against a tycoon who spent $2.6 million on television ads, Jim got swamped. It was a sad example of new but definitely not better politics pushing out the old style.

Later in 1976, Mother got a win with another endorsement. From her hospital room at Research Medical Center (where she was receiving treatment for her arthritis), she issued a statement backing State Senator Ike Skelton in his race for the Fourth Congressional District seat, which included Jackson County. Through her lawyer, Rufus Burrus, Mother declared that she had known Ike and his mother and father and other members of his family for years and was planning to get an absentee ballot so she could vote for him. In the primary, Mr. Skelton had not run well in Jackson County. With this kind of support from the countys' oldest politico, he won handily.

Mother enjoyed these forays into politics. She particularly liked her collaboration with Tom Eagleton because her honorary cochairman was Stan Musial, one of baseball's all-time greats. When Senator

Eagleton visited her on the eve of the campaign, they spent as much time discussing baseball as politics. "She knew every player in the Kansas City Royals starting lineup and had very strong opinions of the plusses and minuses of each one," the Senator told me, bafflement in his voice. He did not realize he was dealing with an ex-third baseman.

Harry Vaughan, who continued to live near Washington, D.C., kept Mother up on the latest doings in that turbulent town. One of his best letters concerned Mr. Nixon's dilemmas during Watergate.

"My dear Lady," he began, as usual. "As you may have gathered from the press, Mr. Nixon is a very worried man. He is not sleeping very well.

"One night he had a dream that he was talking to George Washington.

"Nixon: 'Mr. President, I am in a bit of trouble. What would you advise me to do?'

"Geo: 'Tell the truth.'

"Nixon: 'I'm afraid it's too late for that. I'll have to think of something else.'

"The next night he had a similar interview with Harry Truman.

"Nixon: 'Mr. President I'm in a lot of trouble. What should I do?'

"HST: 'Tell 'em to go to hell.'

"Nixon: 'I have tried that but it does no good.'

"The third night he was confronted by Abe Lincoln.

"Nixon: 'Mr. President, I'm in grave difficulties. What would you advise?'

"Abe: 'Take a night off and go to the theater.' "

Considering the smears that were flung at Dad's administration about the "mess in Washington," it was pretty consoling for Mother to see Richard Nixon, one of the chief accusers, create the biggest presidential mess in history. But her pleasure was sharply tempered by her awareness of the damage that Watergate and a berserk Congress have done to the presidency. Even under Lyndon Johnson's tenure, Dad often had said to her, "I'm glad I'm not our grandchildren." She shuddered to think of what he would say about the maze of restrictions and oversight committees with which Congress has virtually crippled the President's executive powers.

Nevertheless, Mother enjoyed the amazing upsurge of enthusiasm for Dad in the wake of Watergate. She chuckled when she saw Republican Gerald Ford described as Harry Truman's "No. 1 fan" and was delighted when the Truman Library told her how often they got calls from the Ford White House asking for information on Dad. When President Ford came to Independence to dedicate a statue to Dad in 1976, he and his wife Betty had a very pleasant visit with Mother. She liked Betty Ford's forthright style as First Lady, even though it differed from hers.

As for her own popularity, Mother remained resolutely indifferent. Told that she had been listed in the Gallup Poll among the top twenty most admired women in America, her response was: "I don't know why." That brought all possibilities of an interview to a dead stop.

Mother's opinion of the White House's tenants did not improve very much when we finally elected a Democrat president in 1976. Jimmy Carter was Harry Truman's opposite in so many ways, it was hard even to think of him in the same political party. Mother was a little hurt (and I, my father's daughter, steamed) by the way the Carters ignored her except for a few perfunctory birthday messages for their first three and a half years in the White House.

Only when Mr. Carter found himself lagging in the polls as he began his run for reelection against Ronald Reagan did he and his wife suddenly discover Bess Truman and start writing her unctuous letters. For a final touch of pure gall, Mr. Carter decided to kick off his campaign in Independence, in an attempt to identify himself with Harry Truman's come-from-behind style. He visited Mother but he did not get anything that remotely suggested an endorsement. All he was able to say when he left the house was "Mrs. Truman asked me to point out that she has a heart full of love for the people of this country."

Mother demonstrated the sincerity of this statement in her own unique way. She became deeply interested in a proposition that John Snyder, Dad's Secretary of the Treasury, brought to Independence in 1978. He and other former members of the administration wanted to create a memorial to Dad. But they knew he disliked having a street or a building named after him. So they came up with the idea of creating a Truman Scholarship Program that would educate young men and women for government service.

Mother gave the idea instant approval. It echoed, on a far more ambitious scale, the suggestion Dad had sent to Louise and Earl Stewart when their son was killed. Bess Wallace had yearned to go to college just as much as Harry Truman, so it was, really, a perfect memorial for both of them. Mr. Snyder, Clark Clifford, and others went to work on Congress, and before another year had passed, the legislators had voted $30 million to set up the fund. Mr. Snyder functioned as the first chairman and kept Mother well informed about the progress of the program. She read a sampling of the applications each year and loved to hear about the enthusiasm and gratitude of the winners.

As her arthritis worsened, Mother's world slowly contracted. She could no longer travel and could only leave the house in a wheelchair. We found a satisfactory housekeeper for her, a practical nurse named Valerie La Mere, who took her to the library and for an occasional shopping expedition. On these outings, Mother disliked being treated like a sacred relic or venerable personage. She always insisted on getting in line at the library and checking out her books like everyone else.

One day she discovered she did not have her card. The librarian grandly said it did not matter. "Yes it does," Mother snapped. "I'm no different from anyone else. If I don't have a card, I can't take out these books." The librarian finally persuaded her to let him check them out on his card.

If you ask ordinary citizens of Independence what they remember about Mother, they will invariably cite her thoughtfulness. When her hairdresser Doris Miller's mother became ill, Mother called every day to ask for her. "If anyone was in trouble or sick, she wanted to do something for them," Doris says. When Doris's married daughter had a baby shower, Mother came with a gift. The older Mother grew, the more democratic with a small "d" she became.

Mother also retained a very strong sense of who she was, from a historical point of view. In the late seventies, a Fourth of July parade approached the house. Mother was sitting on the porch in her wheelchair. As the flag went past, Mother slowly, painfully rose to her feet. She knew what that flag meant to Dad. It meant the same thing to her.

Most of the time, Mother cherished her memories. She read and reread Dad's thirty-eighth anniversary letter. She corresponded with Christine Wallace about the happy days of the past (and firmly avoided all mention of the unhappy days.) "There are so many good times and fun things to remember," Christine wrote, in one of her nicest letters. She recalled the bull sessions she and I and Freddy used to have with Mother during the 1930s on the night we arrived home from Washington. She remembered (and I did too, with tears in my eyes) Mother sitting on the step up to her bedroom talking about FDR and Eleanor and Huey Long and Cactus Jack Garner. She joked about the backyard croquet games, my back yard shows with the Henhouse Hicks, the fun of peeking at Christmas gifts after midnight church, the silly rhymes and gifts at Christmas dinner.

Chris asked Mother if she remembered the Christmas tree Freddy sent that looked like an oil derrick in its crate and left a black smudge on the living room ceiling. She reminded her of the kibitizing that went on every year when we decorated the tree. She even remembered my risking Grandmother's wrath by eating cream cheese and olive sandwiches on the living room sofa. "It's fun to think back and a bit sad but a nice sadness," Chris concluded. "We are lucky to have all those good memories." I think she was trying to tell Mother that without her, there would not have been such good memories.

When Mother was not reminiscing, she read books—amazing numbers of them. They included biographies and popular novels. But more and more as she grew older, she turned to mysteries. I was already a devotee and hoping to become the writer of a few. Soon we were shipping each other tales of murder and mayhem by the box. We both loved intricate plots and interesting backgrounds.

When I decided to set my stories in Washington, D.C., she could not have been more pleased. By the time my first novel, *Murder in the White House*, came out, her eyes had failed so badly, she could not read it herself. But she had one of her nurses read it to her. I did not expect—or get—extravagant praise. She just said it was a "good job."

One of the happiest things about Mother's last years was the presence of her sister-in-law, May Wallace, who lived only a few dozen feet away in her house on Van Horne Street. She visited Mother frequently and was a cheerful, attentive link to the past. On Mother's ninety-sixth birthday, in 1981, May was the spirit behind a festive party.

Then, in all too quick succession came those hazards of extreme old age, a fall and a stroke, which left Mother unable to communicate with those around her. She slowly slipped away over the next twelve months, in spite of frequent trips to the hospital for treatment. My one consolation—and I think Mother's, too—was that death came to her at home in her first-floor bedroom, in the house she had loved so long and so well.

Simplicity was the keynote of Mother's funeral, even more than Dad's. Only 150 people were invited to the small Episcopal church where she and Dad were married. The mourners included her few living Independence friends and many of the maids and nurses who had cared for her. But history could not be excluded from this personal world. I invited the First Lady, Nancy Reagan, and a former First Lady of whom Mother was fond, Betty Ford. A third, Rosalynn Carter, arrived, uninvited. The photographers begged me for permission to take their picture, as they sat together in the front pew.

I said no, at first. I had issued an edict banning all photographers from the service. I knew it was what Mother would have wanted. But my husband, ever a good newspaperman, persuaded me to let them take the picture, for history's sake.

Mother was buried beside Dad in the courtyard of the library. The only flowers were a blanket of orange-yellow talisman roses, her favorites. On her tombstone, according to Dad's order, has been cut her name, date of birth and death—and one final line: "First Lady, the United States of America, April 12, 1945—January 20, 1953."

In a way, that says it all. But I could not help thinking of two last things. One was a comment Dad made to Mother during a visit to the library a few years before he died. He took her into the courtyard and pointed to the gravesite. "We're going to be buried out here," he said. "I like the idea because I may just want to get up some day and stroll into my office. And I can hear you saying, "Harry—you oughtn't!""

The final thought is the last line of the last letter Mary Paxton Keeley wrote to Mother before age silenced their ninety years of loving friendship. "No one could take your place in my life."

So many others could pay that same tribute to the sustaining power of Bess Wallace Truman's love. Harry Truman. Madge Gates Wallace and her three sons and their wives. Friends as diverse as Arry Calhoun and Louise Stewart. Last, but by no means (I hope) least—Margaret Truman Daniel.

INDEX